About the edito

'Jìmí Adé~~sina~~ ~~is~~ ~~Professor~~ ~~of~~ Sociology at ~~Rhodes~~
previously taught and studied at the ~~University~~
University of Warwick. He is a member of the Ex

Yao Graham is coordinator of the Third World Network-Africa, a pan-African
research and advocacy organisation based in Ghana.

Adebayo Olukoshi is Executive Secretary of CODESRIA. He has formerly served as
Director of Research at the Nigerian Institute of Institutional Affairs.

About this Series

The books in this new series are an initiative by CODESRIA, the Council for the Development of Social Science Research in Africa, to encourage African scholarship relevant to the multiple intellectual, policy and practical problems and opportunities confronting the African continent in the 21st century.

Publishers

CODESRIA in association with Zed Books

Titles in the Series

African Intellectuals: Rethinking Politics, Language, Gender and Development
EDITED BY Thandika Mkandawire (2005)

Africa and Development Challenges in the New Millennium: The NEPAD Debate
EDITED BY J. O. Adésínà, A. Olukoshi and Yao Graham (2005)

Urban Africa: Changing Contours of Survival in the City
EDITED BY A. M. Simone and A. Abouhani (2005)

Liberal Democracy and Its Critics in Africa:
Political Dysfunction and the Struggle for Social Progress
EDITED BY Tukumbi Lumumba-Kasongo (2005)

Negotiating Modernity: Africa's Ambivalent Experience
EDITED BY Elísio Salvado Macamo (2005)

Insiders and Outsiders: Citizenship and Xenophobia in
Contemporary Southern Africa
Francis B. Nyamnjoh (2006)

African Anthropologies: History, Critique and Practice
EDITED BY Mwenda Ntarangwi, David Mills and Mustafa Babiker (2006)

Intellectuals, Youths and African Development: Pretension and Resistance in African Politics
EDITED BY Bjorn Beckman and Gbemisola Remi Adeoti (2006)

About the Publishers – CODESRIA

The Council for the Development of Social Science Research in Africa (CODESRIA) is an independent organisation whose principal objectives are facilitating research, promoting research-based publishing and creating multiple forums geared towards the exchange of views and information among African researchers. It challenges the fragmentation of research through the creation of thematic research networks that cut across linguistic and regional boundaries.

CODESRIA publishes a quarterly journal, *Africa Development*, the longest-standing Africa-based social science journal; *Afrika Zamani*, a journal of history; *African Sociological Review*; *African Journal of International Affairs* (*AJIA*); *Africa Review of Books* and *Identity, Culture and Politics: An Afro-Asian Dialogue*. It co-publishes the *Journal of Higher Education in Africa* and *Africa Media Review*. Research results and other activities of the institution are disseminated through 'Working Papers', 'Monograph Series', 'CODESRIA Book Series', and the *CODESRIA Bulletin*.

Africa and Development Challenges in the New Millennium

The NEPAD Debate

Edited by

'J. O. Adésínà, Yao Graham and A. Olukoshi

CODESRIA
DAKAR

in association with

Zed Books
LONDON & NEW YORK

and

UNISA Press
PRETORIA

Africa and Development Challenges in the New Millennium was first published in 2006 by
Zed Books Ltd, 7 Cynthia Street, London N1 9JF, UK
and Room 400, 175 Fifth Avenue, New York, NY 10010, USA
www.zedbooks.co.uk

and in South Africa by UNISA Press
PO Box 392, Pretoria RSA 0003

in association with

CODESRIA,
Avenue Cheikh Anta Diop,
X Canal IV, BP3304 Dakar, 18524 Senegal.
www.CODESRIA.org

Designed and typeset by Long House, Cumbria UK
Cover design Andrew Corbett
Printed and bound in Malta by Gutenberg Press Ltd

Distributed exclusively in the United States by Palgrave Macmillan,
a division of St Martin's Press, LLC, 175 Fifth Avenue,
New York 10010, USA.

CODESRIA would like to express its gratitude to the Swedish International Development
Cooperation Agency (SIDA/SAREC), the International Development Research Centre (IDRC),
Ford Foundation, MacArthur Foundation, Carnegie Corporation, the Norwegian Ministry of
Foreign Affairs, the Danish Agency for International Development (DANIDA), the French
Ministry of Cooperation, the United Nations Development Programme (UNDP), the
Netherlands Ministry of Foreign Affairs, Rockefeller Foundation, FINIDA, NORAD, CIDA,
IIEP/ADEA, OECD, IFS, OXFAM America, UN/UNICEF and the Government of Senegal for
supporting its research, training and publication programmes.

ISBN: CODESRIA 2-86978-146-6
ISBN: Zed Books edition 1 84277 594 4   (cased)
1 84277 595 2   (limp)
ISBN: Zed Books edition 978 1 84277 594 3   (cased)
978 1 84277 595 0   (limp)

Contents

Tables, Figures and Box

Tables

Figures

Box

Contributors

'Jìmí O. Adésínà is professor of sociology at Rhodes University in South Africa. He was educated at the University of Ibadan, Nigeria and gained a doctorate at the University of Warwick in the United Kingdom. He is the president of the South African Sociological Association, a member of the Executive Committee of CODESRIA, and secretary-general of the African Sociological Association. He has written extensively in the fields of labour, development studies and social theory. His works include *Labour in the Explanation of an African Crisis* (1994).

Kwasi Anyemedu was senior lecturer in the Department of Economics, University of Ghana for many years. He also served as managing director of the now defunct State Gold Mining Corporation (SGMC). He undertook a one year sabbatical to help the Ghana Trades Union Congress (GTUC) strengthen its Research Department. For some time before his death in 2003 he worked as a research associate with the Accra-based research and advocacy organisation, Third World Network Africa.

Tayeb Chenntouf holds a PhD in History from the Paris Institute of Political Studies, and is a Professor of Modern and Contemporary History at University of Oran (Algeria), and Deputy Chair of the Association of African Historians. He has also served as visiting Professor at Nice University, senior researcher at the CNRS in Paris, member of the Higher Council for Education, and member of CODESRIA Executive Committee. He organised the Third Congress on Maghreb History and Civilisation (1986) and the symposium on the State in Maghreb (1998). He has authored several books including *Le monde contemporain*, *l'Algérie Politique* (1830–1954), *Le Maghreb au présent*, *Etudes d'histoire algérienne* (18è-19è siècles). He is currently writing a book on contemporary Maghreb.

Dot Keet is Zimbabwean by birth, Southern African in engagement and commitment. She is a senior research associate at the Alternative Information and Development Centre in Cape Town. She is a seasoned researcher and has taught African and international political economy in various countries in Southern Africa, most recently at the Centre for Southern African Studies at the University of the Western Cape.

Throughout these years, she was also engaged in liberation struggles and post-liberation reconstruction and development, especially in Angola and Mozambique, and most recently in South Africa.

Eddy Maloka is the chief executive officer of the Africa Institute of South Africa (AISA) and president of the Association of African Political Science (AAPS). Previously, he was adviser to the former premiers of Mpumalanga and Gauteng. He worked between 1992 and 1995 as a Mellon Research Fellow at Cape Town University. His research on political and developmental issues in Africa includes the history of the liberation struggle in South Africa. He writes a weekly column for the *Sowetan* newspaper. Among his published works are *Basotho and the Mines: a Social History of Labour Migrancy in Lesotho and South Africa, c. 1890–1940* (2004); *The South African Communist Party in Exile 1963–1990* (2003); *Africa in the New Millennium* (2003); and *Problematising the African Renaissance* (2000).

Sam Moyo is the executive director of the African Institute for Agrarian Studies (AIAS) in Harare, Zimbabwe. He has more than 25 years of research experience on rural development issues, especially land and natural resources management, civil society organisations as well as capacity building and institutional development. He has been involved in several major publications, including *The Land Question in Zimbabwe* (1995) and *Land Reform under Structural Adjustment in Zimbabwe* (2000).

Zo Randriamaro is a gender and human rights activist from Madagascar. She is a sociologist by training and has served as an expert on gender, economic and trade issues for major international development organisations, including United Nations agencies and USAID. She has worked extensively as a researcher and produced several publications on gender and economic justice issues in Africa. Formerly manager of the Gender and Economic Reforms in Africa (GERA) regional programme, she recently joined the board of directors of the Women's Environment and Development Organisation (WEDO).

Alexander Sekou Sangare is currently visiting professor at the Department of Economics of the University of Turin, Italy. He was at various times assistant professor at the University of Cocody-Abidjan, Côte d'Ivoire, research fellow at DELTA (now PSE)-CNRS-Ecole Normale Supérieure, Paris, France, and Bodø Graduate School of Business, Norway, and visiting scholar at the Research Department of the International Monetary Fund (IMF), Washington, DC, USA. He was educated at the universities of Yaoundé, Abidjan (undergraduate), Nice-Sophia Antipolis, Paris IX-Dauphine, Aix - Marseille III (graduate and doctorate), Ghent, Erasmus-Rotterdam (European Erasmus exchange programme), Cologne and Bonn (post-doctorate). His research interests include international, financial and industrial economics, and he has published widely in these fields.

Ian Taylor is senior lecturer at the School of International Relations, University of St Andrews; Professor Extraordinary at the University of Stellenbosch, South Africa; and visiting lecturer to the Faculty of Development Studies, Mbarara University of Science and Technology, Uganda. He received his MPhil from the University of Hong Kong and a DPhil from the University of Stellenbosch, South Africa. His recent publications include NEPAD: *Towards Africa's Development or Another False Start?* (2005) and *Stuck in Middle GEAR: South Africa's Post-Apartheid Foreign Relations* (2001). He co-edited *Africa in International Politics: External Involvement on the Continent* (2004) and *Regionalism and Uneven Development in Southern Africa: the Case of the Maputo Development Corridor* (2003).

Chibuike U. Uche is currently a senior lecturer in Banking and Finance at the University of Nigeria, Enugu Campus. He holds a doctorate degree in accounting and finance from the London School of Economics and Political Science. His dissertation, 'Banking Developments in Pre-Independence Nigeria: a Study in Regulation, Control and Politics', was awarded the International Economic History Association Prize for best doctoral dissertation completed between 1997 and 2000.

Y. Z. Ya'u is a researcher and civil society activist, and an electrical engineer by training. He taught for many years at Bayero University, Kano. He is the executive director, Centre for Information Technology and Development (CITAD), Kano, Nigeria. He has published widely in the areas of youth, mass media and information and communication technologies (ICTs). He has co-authored or co-edited several books, including *The Years of Darkness: Academic Freedom in Nigeria: 1993–1998* (1998), *ASUU under the Leadership of Jega* (2004) and *Great Nigerian Students: Radical Nationalism and Movement Politics* (2005). He is currently working on a book to be entitled 'ICTs and Democratisation in Nigeria: Prospects, Problems and Future Directions'.

Abbreviations

AAF-SAP African Alternative Framework to Structural Adjustment Programmes
AMREF African Medical and Research Foundation
APPER Africa's Priority Programme for Economic Recovery
AUF Agence Universitaire de la Francophonie
CARE Cooperation for Assistance and Relief Everywhere
CDAW Colonial Development and Welfare Act
CICIBA Le Centre International des Civilisations Bantu
CODESRIA Council for the Development of Social Science Research in Africa
COSATU Congress of South African Trade Unions
CRO Commonwealth Relations Office
CSSDCA Conference on Security, Stability, Development and Cooperation in Africa
CSSRC Colonial Social Science Research Council
EAISR East African Institute of Social Research

FDI Foreign Direct Investment
FHI Family Health International
HSIU Haile Selassie I University
IAI International African Institute
ICAES International Congress of Anthropological and Ethnological Sciences
IDRC International Development Research Centre
IFAN Institut Français d'Afrique Noire
IMF International Monetary Fund
IRD Institut de Recherche pour le Développement
IUCN International Union for Conservation of Nature and Natural Resources
KEMRI Kenya Medical Research Institute
NAI New African Initiative
NEPAD New Partnership for Africa's Development
NORAD Norwegian Agency for Development Cooperation
ORSTOM Organisation Recherche Scientifique et Technique Outre Mer
OSSREA Organisation for Social Science Research in Eastern and Southern Africa

PAAA Pan African Anthropology
Association
PAR participatory action research
PLA participatory learning and
action
PPA participatory poverty assessment
PRA participatory rural appraisal
PRGF Poverty Reduction and
Growth Facility
PRSP poverty reduction strategy
paper
RAI Royal Anthropological Institute
RLI Rhodes Livingstone Institute
RRA rapid rural appraisal
SIDA Swedish International
Development Agency
UNAIDS Joint United Nations
Programme on HIV/AIDS
UN-NADAF United Nations New

Agenda for the Development of
Africa in the 1990s
UN-PAAERD United Nations
Programme of Action for Africa's
Economic Recovery and
Development
USAID United States Agency for
International Development
UZ University of Zimbabwe
WAISR West African Institute for
Social Research
WHO World Health Organisation
WWF World Wildlife Fund
ZIDS Zimbabwe Institute of
Development Studies
ZIMWESI Zimbabwe Programme on
Women's Studies, Extension,
Sociology and Irrigation

Preface

The papers in this volume were first presented at a conference jointly organised by Third World Network-Africa (TWN-Africa) and the Council for the Development of Social Research in Africa (CODESRIA) in Accra, Ghana in April 2002 under the theme Africa's Development Challenges in the Millennium.

The contemporaneous launch of the New Partnership for Africa's Development (NEPAD) and the African Union (AU) in 2002 generated within African society a level of interest and debate not experienced for many years about the role of pan-African institutions in responding to the challenge of development. NEPAD has been installed as the 'economic programme of the AU', and its formulation and launch in particular generated considerable controversy and debate for two related reasons – the manner in which the policy developed and its contents.

The stranglehold that the Washington Consensus established over economic policy in Africa from the 1980s was a defeat for a possible pan-African response to the economic crisis, no matter what the limitations of the 1980 Lagos Plan of Action (LPA) were. In place of an approach that gave some centrality to pan-African collective responses, African governments entered into subordinate bilateral relations with the International Monetary Fund (IMF), the World Bank and supporting bilateral lending agencies. At one level, therefore, the transformation of the OAU into the AU and the initiation of a pan-African economic strategy in 2001 in the form of the OMEGA Plan of Senegalese President Abdoulaye Wade, and the Millennium Action Plan (MAP) of South Africa's Thabo Mbeki could be seen as the acknowledgement by African leaders that the continent's economic crisis could not be resolved only on the basis of programmes conceived solely around the nation-state.

The manner in which the OMEGA Plan and the MAP evolved in the New African Initiative (NAI) before discussions with the G8 firmed it into NEPAD fed into domestic frustrations about the continuation of autocratic economic policy making despite the political liberalisation of the 1990s. The popular protests and upheavals that contributed to the democratic advances were not simply against autocracy and repression but in many cases were also verdicts on the destructive and traumatic impact of Structural Adjustment Programmes (SAPs) across the continent. That advance of democracy did not only light up the gloom cast by authoritarian politics in the majority of African countries but also relieved the pain of neo-liberal economic reforms. It is now clear, however, that political liberalisation has merely produced the paradox of political liberalisation co-existing with the continuation of profoundly undemocratic economic policy making in most countries; the World Bank, IMF and allied bilateral lending agencies retain the last word even as the newly opened up media and elected representatives of the people in legislatures across Africa engaged in lively debates. Africa's people have gained a voice on but not control over economic policy. This was the backdrop to the launch of NEPAD.

The failures of NEPAD united both supporters and critics of its policy orientation. The energies that presidents Thabo Mbeki, Olusegun Obasanjo, Abdoulaye Wade and Abdel Aziz Bouteflika invested in discussions and negotiations with G8 officials to hammer out a mutually acceptable NEPAD contrasted sharply with the exclusion of broad sectors of African society and institutions. Not only the usual critics in civil society or business but, more significantly, national legislatures – which would be expected to provide the legitimating link between executive and people – were treated just as shabbily as the people who elected them. The defence that elected heads of state and government have both the power and the responsibility to take initiatives on behalf of their peoples completely missed the point of the criticisms. African people expected that a pan-African economic initiative would depart from the Washington Consensus in both the manner of its making and in its substance.

The democratic deficit in the making of NEPAD and the accompanying heavy sell of its merits were not accidental. NEPAD was and remains a controversial policy in its essentials, many of which are discussed in the papers in this volume. If domestic SAPs in Africa tore up the post-colonial nationalist compact, NEPAD gutted the long-held belief that a pan-African economic strategy should promote less not more dependence on foreign capital. Though NEPAD's new regionalism is not wholly without tensions and contradictions, as an economic strategy it seeks coherence with what had unfolded in Africa's domestic economies in the preceding two decades. Through the links that have been formally established with G8 policy, through frameworks such as the 2002 G8 Africa Action Plan adopted in Kananaskis in 2002, and agreements at subsequent G8 Summits between the African leaders driving NEPAD, the strategy has also become a vehicle for the long-sought coherence in economic policy making at all levels between African institutions and the G7 and the institutions under its control especially the Bretton Woods institutions.

Nearly 100 African activists and scholars took part in the April 2002 TWN-Africa–CODESRIA meeting in Accra. It used the procedural and substantive controversies around NEPAD as a take-off point for a wider discussion about Africa's development challenges, in both contemporary and historical perspectives. The four-day event, including the resolution adopted at the end, was an important intervention of popular expression in the run-up to the Kananaskis G8 Summit at which NEPAD formally received the G8 imprimatur. The Accra meeting was important not only in the immediately obvious sense of the positions it took in the debates about NEPAD. An additional significance which is easily overlooked was the fact that an activist organisation, TWN-Africa, cooperated with a scholarly research grouping, CODESRIA, to organise the event: the result was a useful mix of both scholars and activists at the conference. The struggle for political democratisation in Africa had seen activists and scholars across the continent march in united ranks and shared danger, a trend that has continued in the struggle against neo-liberal economic policies where scholars and activists have both been at the frontline of protest movements.

All the participants in the Accra conference recognised the importance of continuing the kind of collaboration that it represented and the challenges to be overcome if the collaboration is to be successful. TWN-Africa, CODESRIA and participants offer these papers as a contribution to the strengthening of relations between advocacy organisations and research institutions so that together we can continue to produce the union of analysis and activism required to help fulfil the desires that led many Africa people to raise their voices against how NEPAD was made and the strategic pillars of the policies it contains.

Adebayo Olukoshi
Executive Secretary
CODESRIA

Yao Graham
Coordinator
Third World Network-Africa

Introduction

'Jìmí O. Adésínà

In April 2002, the Council for the Development of Social Science Research in Africa (CODESRIA) and the Third World Network-Africa (TWN-Africa) jointly organised a major international conference in Accra, Ghana, on the key developmental challenges facing Africa at the dawn of the new millennium. The conference was held against the background of two separate but related processes, the one derived from the long-standing institutional engagement by CODESRIA and TWN-Africa with the problematic of development in Africa, the other arising from the mobilisation of new energies, symbolised by the quest for a new partnership for Africa's development, to ensure that the new millennium brings new hopes that Africa might be able to secure its development as a continent in a world characterised by accelerating inequalities. Taking both processes into account meant the Accra conference was structured with the dual objective of taking stock of the continent's past experience and proceeding from there to develop an agenda for the future that might help to overcome the pitfalls of yesteryear while promoting innovative approaches for tomorrow. The pitfalls of the past were acknowledged by the conference planning team as being multi-faceted in nature, and including a range of concerns that have been at the heart of the historical and contemporary blockages to Africa's ability to turn the tide of underdevelopment and dependence. Within the African scholarly community, these pitfalls were already well known, as they have been extensively debated by succeeding generations of researchers and activists. The hope was, therefore, that the conference stock-taking would entail a creative revisiting of past and existing challenges to the transformation of livelihood on the continent with a view to breaking new grounds for research and policy. To this end, CODESRIA and TWN-Africa, in combining their institutional strengths, also sought to make the conference a framework for an experimental joint discussion between African academics and the growing community of civil society intellectuals on a scale that does not frequently happen in Africa.

Africa's development has been central to CODESRIA's intellectual mandate and *raison d'être* since its inception in 1973. The Council has evolved into the leading pan-African scholarly platform for thinking through the development challenges facing Africa using the conceptual frames and methodologies of the social sciences and the humanities. As the Council grew and its membership and focus widened, development issues have remained a pivotal and sustained element of its agenda, irrespective of the shifts in focus that have occurred in the scholarly and policy debates; so has the *methodological interdisciplinarity* that is central to development studies. The Council's flagship journal, *Africa Development*, reflects this abiding concern. In linking scholarship and issues of the economic, social and political well-being of Africa and its peoples, the Council continues to serve as a pan-African platform for nurturing a type of scholarship that is socially grounded. Since 1973, the Council has consistently been at the forefront of a scholarly agenda that is Africa-focused and Africa-driven – prodding, protesting, challenging, critiquing, and providing theoretical and policy alternatives. At the dawn of the twenty-first century, the long-standing problems of development confronting the African continent and dating back several centuries still remained critical issues of concern. The case for a special conference to re-examine these challenges was, however, further strengthened by the fact that as the twentieth century closed, not only did the development problems facing Africa become even more compelling, the margins that previously existed for independent development paths also seemed to have become significantly narrowed under the constraints of a new imperialism.[1] The 2002 conference was, therefore, the start of a new initiative within the Council to confront this vicious nexus and launch its new Rethinking African Development initiative involving both the development of a new research programme area and the renewal of a critical engagement with African policymakers. The primary objective of the new CODESRIA initiative is to take the African development debate beyond the impasse in which it has seemed to be entrapped, and to produce viable alternatives to the dominant orthodoxy that has mal-adjusted economies and contributed to the weakening of states. Thus, while this book carries *The NEPAD Debate* as its sub-title, the concern of the collection is much wider and the issues covered represent only the first step in a long-term engagement within CODESRIA with the intellectual and policy challenges of development alternatives in Africa.

Over the years, TWN-Africa, for its part, has combined reflective intellectual efforts with direct, front-line activism in response to the new imperial project as it is manifested in Africa through the economic and social policy prescriptions of the Bretton Woods institutions, the trade liberalisation agenda of the World Trade Organisation (WTO), and the activities of transnational corporations. From its headquarters in Accra, Ghana, TWN-Africa has sought to build popular consciousness around the key development challenges facing the peoples of Africa; it has also invested energies in building a consciousness in policy communities across the continent of the limitations of unidirectional economic liberalisation. The pan-African network of activists it has nurtured over the years to engage in civil society work and policy advocacy is generally recognised as comprising people who are well-schooled in the promotion of social engagement without the postmodern mindset that divorces the local from the global. Trade regimes and trade negotiations have been particularly central to the works of TWN-Africa in recent years. In the post-Uruguay Round period, not only have the new trade regimes become prejudicial to Africa's development prospects, but the renewed tendency to switch between multilateral, bilateral and unilateral trade regimes demonstrates the efforts of major industrial countries to secure trade terms that are advantageous to them and their transnational corporations. The negative implications of these trade regimes for a coherent African agenda have and will continue to inspire the work of TWN-Africa; they also provided an objective basis for the decision by CODESRIA and the Network to bring together scholars, intellectuals and activists to reflect on Africa's development challenges.

However, there was a more immediate concern in the convening of the 2002 conference, relating to the second aspect of the two related processes mentioned earlier. In July 2001, the Organisation of African Unity's Assembly of Heads of State adopted the New Africa Initiative (NAI) as their broad blueprint for re-launching efforts at securing the development of the continent. In many ways, the NAI was meant to signal a new determination by the leaders to invest the necessary effort to ensure that the promise of the twenty-first century does not pass the continent by. In October 2001, an updated version of the NAI, the New Partnership for Africa's Development (NEPAD), was released after a meeting in Abuja, Nigeria. The NEPAD document excited a considerable amount of international interest and was immediately the subject of many consultations around the world. It was therefore clear that the CODESRIA-TWN conference on the development challenges facing Africa could not be complete unless participants were able to reflect on the NEPAD initiative. This was all the more so as one of the strong marketing points for NEPAD centred on the claim that it was a wholly African initiative, a point which was contested by critics, but which nevertheless resonated in an international development community that was already preoccupied with issues of ownership in the development process. The NEPAD document and the debates that were crystallising around it were discussed during various sessions of the Accra conference. But as is evident from the structuring of this collection, the NEPAD debate was not treated by participants in the conference in isolation from the broader development challenges but, rather, as one element, and, at the time, the latest one, in the range of possible options available to the continent. In other words, the engagement with NEPAD at the conference was undertaken within the wider, long-term development concerns of the two organisations – CODESRIA and TWN-Africa – that convened the meeting. These concerns, as is evident in this volume, are not driven by a single ideological or discursive framework or by a single perception of neo-liberal globalisation. Opinions on both sides of the development and NEPAD debates are reflected in this volume – indeed, one of the chapters in the book was produced in reaction to some of the views expressed at the Accra conference that reflected the angry responses of African civil society organisations to the NEPAD document. Optimism, concerns, and scepticism are reflected in this volume in equal measure, in a way that provides the reader with a rich texture of diverse opinion on contemporary development in Africa, with a central assurance in each chapter of the commitment to the continent that their authors share with one another and with the wider African development community.

The perception that several pathways lead to the same market may be inappropriate when dealing with development challenges. There are appropriate and inappropriate policy options; discourses rooted in different paradigms may produce significantly divergent results; competing diagnoses and prognoses will yield hugely different consequences for different fractions of society. Nevertheless, we proceed, in this book, from the position that the people with whom we engage in sometimes acrimonious dialogue are not necessarily of a fundamentally different ilk. The critical concern is to emphasise what is already known: ideas matter; finding appropriate policies for particular cases is extremely important. When the victims of policies are far removed from the drafting and execution of these ideas, those who exercise the responsibility of developing policies must show considerable caution – and humility. The problem, as always in matters of ideas and policies, is that they reflect specific social locations, visions, and growth paths. A chosen path reflects a commitment to one set of options among the variety of alternatives and trade-offs available, and the choice made has consequences that are beneficial for some and grave for others. Good intentions are never enough! Furthermore, commitment to a particular policy bundle will reflect specific ideas about the role of agency and the types of responses that are considered appropriate to the different kinds of constraints that are encountered. Thus, the argument that has become commonplace in discussions on African development alternatives that 'imperialism [or transnational capital] is too powerful ...' and that, as a result, realistically all we can hope to do is find accommodation within it commits those who propound it to a particular policy path; it is a choice with specific consequences. The NEPAD framework is one such choice. However, this book rests on the premise that addressing the matters raised by policy choices, and the global configuration of class or social agency that they signify, cannot be fully undertaken within a disembodied scholarship or an atavistic disengagement. Neither the organisations that convened the Accra conference nor the authors whose contributions have been included in this collection feel that we have the luxury of cynicism or the comfort of pessimism. This book should, therefore, also be seen as part of a wider project of social commitment and engaged scholarship.

The discussion in the remaining part of this Introduction is divided into two main sections. The first provides an overview of the various contributions that make up this volume and seeks to tie the arguments in the different chapters together. The second section engages with trends in the development discourse since the 2002 conference, doing so by focusing on three high-profile reports issued by Kofi Annan, Jeffrey Sachs and Tony Blair. Particular attention is paid to the tension between trade and development in the three reports, as well as their perspectives on aid and the African debt. In overviewing the three reports, an attempt will be made to assess the extent to which they reinforce or vitiate some of the arguments made in this collection. In 2002, the demand for debt cancellation was dismissed out of hand by some as a 'loony' demand made by people with no understanding of economics, or who failed to grasp the 'moral hazard' of such debt 'write-off'. Today, however, the real moral hazard would seem to be how this earlier position espoused by the international financial institutions and most donors could be squared with the about-turn represented by the agreement reached in Paris on 21 November 2004 to write off 80 per cent of the 'debt' owed by Saddam Hussein's Iraq to the leading industrial countries and to Saudi Arabia and Kuwait.[2]

Africa's development in the age of neo-liberal globalisation

This book is divided into three parts. Part 1 is concerned with an assessment of the NEPAD document from the two broad perspectives that predominate in the debate within Africa on the initiative: the first highly critical of the basic neo-liberal foundations of NEPAD, and the second more sympathetic to the initiative primarily because it is seen as an autonomous, Africa-initiated and Africa-owned blueprint. Part 2 is concerned with the main sectoral challenges in Africa's quest for sustained development. This part uses the NEPAD document as the discursive premise but going on to advance specific policy priorities and, in some cases, alternatives for addressing Africa's development concerns. Part 3 addresses the challenge of financing Africa's development. As indicated earlier, there is no single discursive framework, ideological commitment, or posture towards NEPAD or the development question running through these chapters, or the entire book for that matter. The concern is to reflect the best and most articulate of the different shades of opinions expressed at the Accra conference, doing so in a way that also projects the diversity of perspectives in the African development debate and as an input into the much-needed effort at re-thinking development. No such re-thinking can be successful if some arguments are ignored; conversely, the airing of all competing points of view might be a *sine qua non* for the development of a minimum consensus around key areas for priority action.

Debating NEPAD: conceptual issues in development paradigm
The concerns in the chapters in Part 1 of this collection are partly meta-analytical and partly generic. In Chapter 1, Adésínà is concerned with unearthing the development paradigm that underlies the NEPAD document, its discourse and policy trajectory. He argues that NEPAD's discursive framework and development paradigm derive from the 'post-Washington Consensus' context – not in the sense in which Joseph Stiglitz used the concept to seek to go beyond neo-liberalism but in the sense of its deployment in James Wolfensohn's Comprehensive Development Framework (CDF). The latter is a reformulation of neo-liberal orthodoxy with added attention to political and social 'conditionalities'. A transactional approach to social policy and politics, focused on facilitating market transactional regimes, defines the attempt at reworking orthodox neo-liberalism through the CDF. Adésínà notes that NEPAD's reading of Africa's post-colonial history derives from the 1981 Berg Report – much of it inspired by the Public Choice Theory. Contrary to the marketing of NEPAD as a 'poverty reducing' development framework, Adésínà argues that both in its discourse and policy choices, NEPAD provides no discernable anti-poverty strategy – unless it is assumed that 'trickle down' economics is poverty reducing. Furthermore, NEPAD rehashes the same policy instruments that have deepened Africa's structural crisis during more than 25 years of International Monetary Fund (IMF)/World Bank structural adjustment. Its narrative conflates the ideological claims of the leading commissars of neo-liberalism with the reality of capitalism. There is little awareness that there are competing models of capitalism, and that the neo-liberal version of the market that is presented as the only one that is truly available is little more than an abstraction and corresponds to no known reality in world economic history. In

embracing the neo-liberal model of the market, therefore, the NEPAD document signalled a regressive shift in Africa's troubled engagement with adjustment programming: the authors of the document wittingly or unwittingly took responsibility for the destructive policy instruments that had been unsuccessfully applied by the Bretton Woods institutions and which even many in the African policy community frequently contested for their inappropriateness. In taking responsibility for the policy instruments of the international financial institutions, the authors of the NEPAD document also seemed to acquiesce to the demand that Africans should take responsibility for the neo-liberal project in Africa in the name of a false notion of local policy ownership. Adésínà's contribution foregrounds the argument that NEPAD reflects the antinomies of South Africa's engagement with the rest of the continent; the birth of the initiative also represents a fundamental shift in African politics – the repudiation of the social compact that marked the nationalist project in Africa by a new corps of African political and business leaders (Olukoshi 2002, Adesina 2004b).

Ian Taylor's chapter explores the extent to which the forces driving NEPAD represent part of an 'emerging transnational élite'. According to him, rather than being a new social project, NEPAD encapsulates an emerging compact between the different fractions of the emerging transnational élite – North and South. The sympathetic hearing that NEPAD has received from the Northern fractions of this transnational élite is 'precisely because the message they are communicating eases responsibility for growing world inequality and African immiseration for any particular policies that cause such processes and, rather, pins the blame on the amorphous phenomena known as "globalisation"'. NEPAD's subtext, Taylor argues, is that 'it is the ways in which globalisation acts on Africa, and not the very contents of it, that are the sources of Africa's woes'. To that Taylor might have added the frequently rehashed view, popular in the international financial institutions, that consists of blaming endogenous agents and 'poor' domestic policies for Africa's 'failure to develop'. This view appears to be built into the NEPAD framework too. Yet, at the heart of the NEPAD project are several contradictions between stated goals and the means for achieving them. To cite one example: NEPAD argues for unrestricted commitment to global free trade, on the one hand, and seeks a fairer, more equitable global regime that delivers development for Africa, on the other; it concedes that the policy instruments that define the current neo-liberal globalisation have failed to benefit Africa but proceeds to argue for more of the same. The solution to Africa's 'marginality' is for the continent to become more firmly 'locked into globalisation'.

If most of the analysis in this collection is critical of the discourse and prognoses that underscore the NEPAD document, Maloka's chapter offers a radically different approach. The chapter is a response to the various critiques of NEPAD that have developed, both at the Accra conference and elsewhere. His arguments cover four broad areas. First is the attempt to classify the critics of the initiative; second is a six-point summary of the criticisms that have been made; third is an articulation of what he considers the motivation of the critics – which he suggests is mostly locational. The fourth is a response to both the critics and the different points of criticism. The response developed by Maloka also offers an alternative genealogy of and rationale for NEPAD and what he believes is pragmatically feasible given the range of options available to Africa. Maloka's focus is, therefore, also an attempt to build a bridge between NEPAD and its critics, and to bring the latter on board.

Maloka identified two broad clusters of NEPAD critics: the non-African and the African. The former is exemplified, he argues, by North-based scholars like Patrick Chabal who argue that NEPAD is likely to founder on the rock of the 'neopatrimonialism' and 'failed states' that constitute the essential defining feature and character of African polities and political practice. The African critics include intellectuals and activists, civic organisations and unions. Their grouse is defined by such issues as lack of consultation in the crafting of the NEPAD document, the conceptual and ideological underpinnings of NEPAD, etcetera. The South African component of the African critique of NEPAD, Maloka argues, is primarily driven by domestic disputes with the government and the African National Congress (ANC) over the Growth Employment and Redistribution (GEAR) macro-economic programme. For the critics of NEPAD in the rest of the continent, their disagreement with NEPAD is a continuation of the struggles they have been waging against the structural adjustment programmes of the IMF and the World Bank. Maloka also argues that some of the African critics of NEPAD, including prominent figures like Adebayo Adedeji, are simply uncomfortable with the fact that the repository of intellectual resources for development thinking and programming on the continent is moving away from the United Nations Economic Commission for Africa (UNECA) and in the direction of the African Union. To the claim that the crafting of the NEPAD document lacked any popular base because its design was not the product of a broad-based consultation, Maloka responds that it is the business of leaders to lead, and that is exactly what they did in taking the lead to launch the NEPAD initiative.[3]

Sectoral challenges
Part 2 of this collection focuses on sectoral issues and opens with Sam Moyo's chapter which examines the efficacy of NEPAD's agriculture strategy. Moyo's main focus is on agrarian transformation. As he argues,

NEPAD's approach is based on the liberalisation of markets and limited state intervention. The framework's 'lack of an explicit commitment to promoting equity in general and within the agricultural sector in particular is not only surprising but is also indicative of its "trickle-down"' mooring, which is immensely naïve about how actual agricultural policy works even in the OECD countries. It is a strategy that calls for internal reforms 'as a route to improved agricultural development with little concern expressed for the improved regulation of the transnational agrarian market system' or the global 'multilateral governance system which affects agriculture'. For a 'development' framework that acknowledges that Africa engages with the global economy as a producer of primary produce, and calls for a shift from this, there is no coherent industrial strategy. Indeed, the NEPAD document does not contain any 'vision for land and agrarian reform linked to an industrial development strategy that could cumulatively lead to development'. This, as we will argue further below, is crucial to understanding the futility of a global engagement strategy that puts 'market access' at its core. This is also an issue to which Dot Keet's chapter in this volume speaks at length. Moyo reminds us that 'the NEPAD agricultural strategy is entangled in an institutional framework ... that has ... overseen the demise of African agriculture'. As Randriamaro also argues, neither does it afford us any means for addressing rural poverty and its gender dimensions. The alternative framework that Moyo offers requires an 'integrated development strategy' driven by five core elements: 'land reform, integrated trans-sectoral rural production ... rural infrastructure development, institutional reform, and regional integration'. In many ways, the Lagos Plan of Action (LPA) of 1980 may have to be our starting point.

Sekou Sangare's concern is with mapping out a credible industrial policy for African countries. The dependence on primary commodities and the excessive outward orientation of production processes and structures are two characteristics of African economies that explain their vulnerability to external shocks. The problems both of economies of scale and inter-sectoral (horizontal) linkages, he argues, make adjustment to the shocks even more difficult. The impact of IMF/World Bank stabilisation and liberalisation programmes has been to damage the strong growth in the manufacturing sector that countries like Côte d'Ivoire and Kenya experienced in the 1960s and 1970s. What Sangare offers is a diagnosis similar in tone and focus to the LPA. Sangare also examines the nature of investments made and factors informing the choice of investment destination, as well as the relationship between investment decisions and flows, growth, and several social and economic indices. He highlights the kinds of investments that are important for producing a framework for industrial development in Africa. Sangare also reviews the results of research on three types of investment: 'specific investment', 'bearable investment', and public investment. He argues that findings which show that firms can create as well as destroy value deserve attention. The structural problems in many of the economies and the 'high risk associated with the business environment' are likely to attract the wrong types of investment: short-term, speculative, and uninterested in sectors requiring long-term commitment. Yet the latter is precisely what is required. Sangare highlights the importance of public investment in a guided market, strategic state planning, and extensive public sector investment in human resource development, research and development (R&D), and infrastructure, as well as policies targeted at industrial development. In crafting a new industrial policy, Sangare argues not for the reinvention of import-substituting industrialisation, but 'industrialisation of complimentarity' involving endogenous inter-sectoral linkages in the context of a 'horizontal integration of African countries'. This is not the infrastructural integration that NEPAD suggests – which is more concerned with facilitating trade and lowering the cost of 'doing business in Africa' – but an industrial development agenda in a framework similar to the LPA.

This brings us to trade policy and the trade regimes issues in the NEPAD document, the focus of Dot Keet's chapter. She examines the trade and trade-related proposals in the NEPAD document, its understanding of Africa's location within the global trade regime, and the relationship between infrastructure development and economic growth. She argues that the linkages are more complex than NEPAD acknowledges. 'Setting up sophisticated structures in advance of and to stimulate ... economic process, without the necessary systems and appropriate infrastructure to maintain and service them, and without the economic agents and activities to fully utilise or effectively employ them, could simply create more vast "white elephant" projects.' Further, the bigger and more complex the project the more the 'adverse pressure on Africa's external balance of payment and its external indebtedness'. Public–private partnership, so central to NEPAD, is not necessarily the solution to the dilemma – a position which brings us back to developmental issues that ought to inform policy as opposed to the ambition, targeted primarily at foreign investors, of simply reducing the cost of 'doing business' in Africa. Keet argues that NEPAD's a priori focus on foreign aid and capital is a radical departure from the attention the African Alternative Framework to Structural Adjustment Programmes (AAF-SAP) and proposals for the African Economic Community (AEC) sought rightly to focus on the critically important objective of mobilising domestic resources. The AEC also had built-in 'compensatory and redistribution mechanisms ... for more balanced development, equity and stability' within the economic communities. It provides for 'industrial specialisation in order to enhance the complementarities of African economies, and expand the intra-community trade base [with] due account being taken for national and regional resource endowments'. NEPAD provides for no such integrated industrial development approach. The place accorded to the Regional Economic Communities (RECs) in the NEPAD strategy differs completely in meaning and effectiveness from the one envisaged in the AEC; the NEPAD approach is essentially a preoccupation with *trade without development!*

A trade-driven approach, Keet notes, reflects South Africa's strategic economic interest and the advantage that its transnational corporations and state-owned enterprises hold *vis-à-vis* the rest of sub-Saharan Africa. Keet demonstrates how South Africa's negotiating position at the WTO has often been at odds with the one canvassed by the Africa Group. She also shows how the NEPAD document (whose core is in turn derived from the MAP document) relentlessly puts forward South Africa's position at the WTO as the Africa-wide position in spite of the fact that it is a position that the Africa Group has consistently rejected. The regional trade liberalisation agenda that NEPAD puts forward will 'without other deliberate, countervailing programmes and corrective measures' work to the advantage of the bigger economies like South Africa, and its trans national corporations currently fanning out across the continent. Where the Africa Group has been pushing for a fundamental review of the Uruguay Round-related agreements like TRIPs, NEPAD puts forward South Africa's (and the industrial countries') position, which reduced the Group's complaints to technical issues in compliance. As Keet demonstrates, the NEPAD document is concerned with securing an endorsement of the Singapore Issues[4] – again something that South Africa has been pushing but which the Africa Group has consistently rejected.

Y. Z. Ya'u's chapter focuses on information and communication technology (ICT) issues in African development and the promise of bridging the digital divide that has been set out as an objective of policy. He surveys the range of indicators often employed to determine the location of a region or country on the world digital map. While African countries generally register quite low on these indicators, he points to the spatial skew within these countries. Three cities in Nigeria, for example, account for 60 per cent of fixed telephone lines in the country; 85 per cent of Liberia's lines are in its capital, Monrovia. Ya'u examines various efforts at 'bridging the digital divide' – from the telecentres funded by the International Development Research Centre (IDRC) to UNECA's African Information Society Initiative (AISI). Since Ya'u's paper was originally written, new data available indicate that Africa's teledensity has changed significantly but this doesn't change the fundamental points he makes in the chapter. Indeed, NEPAD's teledensity target has been achieved two years ahead of target but to very little positive effect from a developmental point of view: it was private-sector driven without a wider social or economic objective and strategy underpinning it, and was achieved through pre-paid mobile phone (GSM) penetration, hardly the development-aiding teledensity of choice. Indeed, rather than being a cause for instant celebration, it may be detrimental to investment in the backbone infrastructure needed for the achievement of high-speed bandwidth and connectivity. The issue, therefore, is not teledensity per se but what manner of teledensity. As Ya'u argues, ICT should be seen not so much as a signifier of modernity but as a tool for leveraging development. The dissonance in African ICT policymaking is amply captured by the fact that 'while ministers responsible for economic planning were meeting with the ECA in May 1996' to consider the AISI, the ministers responsible for telecommunication were meeting in Abuja, Nigeria, to consider a different document on telecommunication policy! Ya'u argues that the digital challenge is more than just playing a catch-up game of numbers. The linkages between technological diffusion and production speak to issues of endogeneity in research and development – a developmental focus raised by several authors in this book and which is relevant to the ICT sector too. An ICT sector driven by a consumerist approach is likely to be oblivious of the long-term effects on national economies of domination by a handful of transnational corporations, on the one hand, and the negative balance-of-payment effects of the consumer culture itself, on the other. Both concerns were central to the fiscal crisis of the 1970s, and the structural problems in Africa's unreformed post-colonial economies.

Tayeb Chenntouf's chapter focuses on the educational and scientific policies articulated in the NEPAD document. He notes the significant gains recorded in the educational sector during the first two decades of African independence, and the sharp decline that was subsequently registered in the period from the 1980s onwards, often as an outcome of the stabilisation and adjustment policies deployed by governments under the directives of the Bretton Woods institutions. The reversals that occurred in the educational sector were taking place at the time when the world was experience the 'third technological revolution', a revolution that emphasizes knowledge over and above physical endowments. Taking up a theme similar to Sangare's, Chenntouf reiterates the centrality of public spending for the advancement of the educational sector. He urges that such public spending as may be undertaken should be channelled in a manner that seeks to ensure that the educational sector has a positive impact on long-term endogenous growth. Public expenditure on education should also be geared towards contributing to the creation of an environment 'favourable [for] technological innovation'. The critical issue, to return to a recurring theme in this collection, is developmental and about inter-sectoral linkages; it is an issue that calls for coordination and planning in ways that transcend the market-based logic of NEPAD.

Chenntouf identifies eight priority areas for the educational, cultural and scientific sectors of African countries. Among these, he underscores the need to move urgently in making the orthography of African languages available, a suggestion that takes us back to Ya'u's concern about endogenously driven ICT.

Financing Africa's development

Part 3 of this collection addresses the financing of Africa's development. Randriamaro's chapter serves as a bridge between the broad interrogations of NEPAD's 'development' discourse that have been undertaken and the specific intellectual and policy concerns about financing development. She focuses on the gender dynamics of the development process and the livelihood issues facing poor women that NEPAD failed to address or appreciate. She argues that the discussion of domestic resource mobilisation and private capital flows in the NEPAD document is trapped in a neo-liberal framework. The policy instruments proposed for the realisation of NEPAD's objectives also fail to appreciate the degree to which the neo-liberal framework undermined the livelihood of most African women over a period spanning two decades or more. Randriamaro's chapter also combines her critique of NEPAD with an assessment of other 'initiatives' like UNECA's Compact for African Recovery. She observes that both NEPAD and the UNECA Compact share the same orientation. Randriamaro calls for 'a new partnership for women's economic empowerment' and the advancement of the interests of the poor based on gender sensitivity and locally rooted analyses of the challenges facing Africa.

Uche's chapter examines the experience of the ECOWAS Fund for Cooperation, Compensation and Development as an example of the effort to develop local institutions for development financing. His verdict is straightforward: the history of the ECOWAS Fund has not been a successful one. Uche identifies some of the factors responsible for the comatose state of the Fund. These include a lack of political will on the part of the member states, ill luck (including loss of the Fund's resources invested in some failed banks such as the Bank of Credit and Commerce International), and an excessive optimism in the anticipated synergy which member states were expected to build among themselves. Uche argues that initiatives such as the ECOWAS Fund 'are unlikely to yield any meaningful results ... because the problems that have helped entrench underdevelopment in the region have also helped to prevent such institutions from achieving their objectives'. The challenge, however, is not to abandon such initiatives altogether; the arguments in most of the other chapters in this book show the importance of such compensatory and financing mechanisms for Africa's regional development strategy. In

a context and a historical moment characterised by the fiscal disem-
bowelling of the African state, the micro-management of African
economies by external agencies, the intensifying donor-dependence of
many African countries, and severe balance-of-payment instability
experienced across the continent, a critical point of departure is also to
put the issue of the reform of the international structures of power back
on the agenda. But so too is the importance of a fundamental change in
the nature of the state–citizens nexus in many of the countries of Africa,
and the strengthening of member states' commitment to their own
institutions. For, even in the context of enormous external constraints,
governance is about the act of the possible: in policy and especially
leadership matters.

Anyemedu examines the problems associated with the financing of
Africa's development through aid flows and the antinomies of such a
'development' strategy. In spite of the declaratory statements in the
NEPAD document calling on Africans to take responsibility for their own
development, the heavy focus on aid in the document, and the strategic
place that foreign development assistance occupies in the approach laid
out for the realisation of set objectives exposes the dependent mindset
that informed the document's framing. Anyemedu doubts that the
amount of aid that NEPAD anticipates can be realised; but even if it can,
he is concerned about the increased vulnerability to policy conditionalities, and the aid dependence that such aid flows portend. The policy
atrophy that the aid relationship with the 'donor' community produces is
a major element of the current crisis of state capacity and state–society
nexus, especially over the past two decades. Given that the NEPAD
document claims to be an African initiative, the amnesia its authors
display regarding Africa's experience with aid dependency and policy
conditionality is a revealing aspect of the entire NEPAD strategy. Also
intriguing is the latent assumption that aid can be treated as grants.
Anyemedu reminds us that a loan qualifies for aid if it 'includes a grant
element of more than 25 per cent'; the remaining 75 per cent goes to
swell the debt burden of the recipient country! Africa's experience of
technical aid expenditure, for instance, shows that it does 'not always
directly benefit the recipient economy.' In spite of the promise by the
United States and other donor countries to untie aid, recipients' expenditure of US aid is statutorily linked to the employment of the services of
US companies. A 'bold initiative' on Africa's development should strive
to transcend the 'aid-for-development' mantra if it is truly to mark a
radical departure from previous experience.

In addition to aid, Anyemedu also examines private capital flows and
domestic savings as sources of development financing. Much of the
inflow in the 1980s and the 1990s went into the extractive industry (a
typical enclave economic activity), mergers and acquisition, and

privatised state enterprises rather than into greenfield investments. He queries the assumption that private capital is inherently developmental and, in so doing, challenges the thinking that informed the claim in the NEPAD document that what Africa needs for its development is to attract more private capital inflow, reduce the 'risks' to investors (who are invariably foreign), curtail the cost of doing business, and address problems of 'governance'. Anyemedu also observes that in spite of increased liberalisation, Africa did receive a higher flow of foreign direct investments (FDI) and the investments that materialised mostly flowed into countries that can hardly be accused of 'good governance'. He outlines specific steps that could be taken in helping to deliver on the declaratory statements and sentiments expressed in the NEPAD document.

Reflections on NEPAD and the aftermath

Some of the key developments that have occurred since the 2002 CODESRIA/TWN-Africa conference have confirmed the saliency of several of the issues raised in this book, including some of the criticisms made of the mainstream discourse on development. However, there were also a number of developments which call for further reflections, some of which we will address in this section. Several of these developments are captured in a number of high-profile reports compiled since 2002 and in fact mostly issued during the course of 2005. Interestingly, these reports continue to proclaim concerns for Africa within the same development discourse that shaped the design of the NEPAD initiative. Three of the most interesting of the reports are the Sachs Report (Investing in Development, 2005), the [Kofi] Annan Report (In Larger Freedom, 2005), and the Blair Commission Report (Commission for Africa's Our Common Interest, 2005). The reports share a discourse that combines remarkable enthusiasm for doing everything with an equally remarkable reluctance seriously to interrogate the current global economic architecture and the inequities it embodies. In the process, the development discourse is replaced by or subordinated to a trade and aid discourse. In this fundamental sense, the three reports share a common purpose with NEPAD both in terms of what they affirm and with regard to the issues on which they are silent.

In spite of the different emphases in the three reports on the priorities that need to be pursued, they are united by the collective amnesia they share about Africa's unhappy experience over the last two-and-half decades of International Monetary Fund (IMF)/World Bank structural adjustment. At the level of policy, the reports suggest that the responsibility of African countries is to do more of the same things they were told to do by the Bretton Woods institutions: deepen economic reform (that is, market liberalisation and privatisation) and improve 'governance'. Both the Sachs Report and the Annan Report require poor countries to 'recommit themselves to … putting in place the policies and investments to drive private-sector led growth and maximize domestic resources to fund national development strategies' (Annan 2005, p. 55). Added to these are the complementary issues of 'strengthening governance [and] combating corruption' (Annan 2005, p. 55) – a theme central to the Blair Commission Report.[5] The Commission for Africa showed at length how Africa has been negatively impacted by the debt burden, the agricultural subsidy policies of the West, and the trade practices of major OECD countries. Yet it argued that the common thread running through Africa's development difficulties 'is the weakness of governance and the absence of effective states' (2005, p. 24).

The three reports endorse the idea of 'a more development-oriented trade system' but do so by calling for less 'trade-distorting subsidy' and for fewer non-tariff trade barriers within the existing global trade regimes; they also argue for more debt relief, and increased aid as the solution to Africa's 'resource-gap'. As Hardstaff (2005, p. 1) has noted in particular reference to the Sachs Report, these reports 'simply bypass the past 20 years of failed IMF/WB structural adjustment programme as if it never happened' or 'donor' responsibility for what has become an endemic development crisis in many of the African countries. The effect is to impose a blanket silence on the key issues that continue to undermine the development prospects of the countries of Africa. For instance, it is not enough simply to acknowledge the enormity of the debt burden that low-income African countries carry; finding a just solution to the crisis should begin with a recognition of the fact that the debt escalated in the first place during the period when the economies of the countries concerned were micro-managed by the IMF and the World Bank. Aid and debt contracted in the heyday of structural adjustment was mainly for budget support and meeting debt service obligations; the assistance received did nothing to enhance domestic capacities and was anchored on the philosophy of rolling back the frontiers of the state. It is also not enough to want to 'make poverty history'; we need to ask why poverty escalated during the period of the detailed management of the economies of the low-income countries by the Bretton Woods institutions. Similarly, while it is important to support access to education and expand immunisation coverage, we still need to ask why the human development index for many of the developing countries was lower in 2002 than in 1960 (UNDP 2004) – again in the same period of the micromanagement of African economies by the Fund and the Bank. And to avoid doubt, it must be pointed out that the poor performance of African economies was not for want of compliance with the prescriptions of the IMF and the World Bank. Indeed, as Mkandawire (2005) reminded us, many of these countries were rated 'good adjusters' by the World Bank several times between 1981 and 1998. Malawi, for instance, was rated a 'good adjuster' seven times (2005, p.12).

The demands for a more intensive macro-economic 'reform' or the agenda of global trade liberalisation to which the Annan, Sachs and Blair Commission reports subscribe fly in the face of other reports by different UN and non-UN agencies, and of the views of African countries themselves on trade-related matters and how they might be managed to secure the development interests of the developing countries. The Annan Report, for instance, in fully embracing the WTO process disregarded the findings of specialised UN agencies like UNCTAD (2004a) and the International Labour Organisation (ILO) (2004) which cautioned against an unbridled liberalisation agenda that is oblivious of the specific needs of the least developed countries. In spite of the sanctimonious noises that come out of Downing Street, and the concession of the Blair Commission Report to the right of countries to liberalise at their own pace in line with their development needs, the British government under Prime Minister Tony Blair has been firm in its insistence that the developing countries should accelerate trade liberalisation, including services and official procurement, and has continuously reaffirmed its commitment to advancing the interests of British transnational corporations in this regard (Curtis 2004).

Trade or development discourse?

When carefully considered, it soon becomes obvious that much of the debate around the reform of trade-distorting subsidies, non-tariff barriers, and the increased flow in 'official development assistance' is a distraction from the fundamental developmental objectives that African countries ought to be pursuing, even as important as the issues of trade distortion may be. The critical challenge that many African countries faced in the 1970s was one of an unreformed, inherited, colonial political economy. More than twenty years of structural adjustment has resulted in the reinforcement of commodity dependence and vulnerability to external shocks on account of a failure to promote structural changes in the economies. As important as the reform of trade-distorting policies in the OECD countries may be, a debate structured around 'market access', especially for primary-commodity-producing countries, is a patently false debate. Nothing that we know in theory or practice suggests that a dynamic and sustainable economy can be built around primary commodities, especially agricultural commodities. While the 'market access' debate may gratify those who want to be seen as lending helping hands to Africa, their good will does not amount to very much precisely because of their failure to address the fundamental structural problems that define the character of the political economy of African countries and the mode of their integration into the global economy.

When Uganda's Yoweri Museveni argues that what Africa needs is not aid but to 'trade [its] way out of poverty', the pertinent question to ask is: 'Trade with what? Coffee?' It is not only what we know about the secular decline in the terms of trade inherent in primary (agricultural) commodity export that makes this option an unviable one: the outcomes associated with the operationalisation of (Ernst) Engel's Law and the fact that, generally, demand for primary agricultural products is income inelastic, when it is not being easily substituted, are additional factors that make it important to address Africa's development concerns in terms that go beyond simple issues of market access.[6] No one drinks more cups of coffee in the morning in proportions related to the rise in his or her income. Taken with the oligopsonistic nature of primary commodity markets, increased productivity and output do not lead to increased income but a glut in the market. This has meant sharp declines (or fluctuations) in the earnings of farming households. One implication of this, among many, is that across a wide range of primary commodity products, prices are not policy responsive. To restate the point again: in the absence of a coherent and explicit industrial policy to move up the value chain, the demand for greater market access becomes a distraction. Such a coherent industrial policy is the one viable path by which Africa can hope to couple its trade policy with a development strategy. The reluctance of the leading industrial countries to address the demands of the Africa Group at the WTO for a fundamental review of the current global trade regime to incorporate their yearnings for building their industrial base will need to be overcome.

The Blair Commission Report argued that Africa needs to reduce its dependence on primary commodity exports (2005, pp. 89, 93). It pointed to the experience of the Western world and most recently China and India and would seem to acknowledge a shift into manufacturing as the basis for this shift, but its logic is also defined by a trade discourse rather than a development discourse; 'trade', it argues, 'has been a key driver of economic growth over the last 50 years' in these regions (Blair Commission Report 2005, p. 89). It was, however, trade rooted in manufacturing exports developed as an industrialisation strategy that the neo-liberal mindset insisted was an anathema to free trade – and inappropriate for Africa. Not surprisingly, the report does not offer an industrial policy strategy for Africa. The strategy recommended for enabling Africa to overcome its dependence on primary commodities also turned out to be much tamer in the Blair Commission Report than we might have anticipated. 'The biggest single action that Africa could take to reduce its dependency on raw materials is to help large firms and family farms break into new products and activities' (2005, p. 93). The Commission recommends that the EU and G8 countries should help with rebuilding Africa's infrastructure: 'help Africa develop the capacity to process agricultural products and improve the productivity and quality of raw materials ... fund the development of organisations to help small farmers market their produce.' Supermarkets, it argues, 'could do more to make it easier for household farmers to become suppliers' (ibid.). Everything but an acknowledgment that a dynamic industrial policy is the basis for shifting the dependence of the economy away from primary commodity export; that doing so would require rolling back the one-way and high-velocity global trade liberalisation regimes that have been established since the Uruguay Round negotiations. The lead authors of the Report – who demand rapid movement on the Singapore Issues at the WTO – fail to acknowledge that this will further undermine the capacity of African countries to shift into the production chain that makes trade a 'driver of economic growth'. Further, the report was oblivious to the fact that improved agricultural commodity productivity in a market environment does not produce the same outcome as in manufacturing. Increased commodity productivity in a product market that is neither income elastic nor policy responsive would be disastrous for the producers whose governments cannot afford uneconomic subsidies. This dilemma has been the experience of African commodity producers. Yet, these are issues that UNCTAD has addressed persistently and, in so doing, put them in the public domain; they are also issues reflected in several chapters in this book.

The Blair Commission Report calls for a developmental state but, when carefully scrutinised, this amounts to a call for a developmental state without a development agenda! In this respect, the Commission duplicates the same shaky premise on which the NEPAD document is founded. In spite of Trevor Manuel's claim that the Blair Commission Report is an African agenda, the paper submitted to the 2003 WTO negotiations by seven African countries is utterly clear on what their experience has been under the regime of structural adjustment.[7] Part of the paper is worth quoting at length:

> Most African countries have undertaken, in the past two decades, wide-ranging economic reform measures in the context of the structural adjustment programmes under the tutelage of the World Bank and International Monetary Fund. The main emphasis of these reforms has been on trade liberalisation. These reforms have lowered trade barriers but the broad-based development that was expected to ensue has remained elusive.... Indeed, empirical studies show that industrial growth has fallen behind in a number of African countries being associated with trade liberalisation. (WTO 2003, cited by Hardstaff 2005)

The argument for reducing the cost of trading among African countries might have the sound and feel of regional initiatives such as the LPA and the AEC envisaged under the 1991 Abuja Treaty, but the idea of internal 'trade liberalisation' in the LPA and the AEC was conceived as part of a regional development strategy and industrial policy, not the current predatory global environment. South Africa's part in making the case for increased trade liberalisation in Africa is easily seen as self-serving (Keet 2002). The South African fiscus has benefited significantly from the proceeds that accrue from the operations of its transnational private and state-owned companies in other parts of Africa. As Gelb (2002) acknowledged, this was an important consideration in the articulation of South Africa's strategy. Those who hold the 'realist' approach to South Africa's post-apartheid international relations were convinced that 'the core interest now (at least with regard to Africa) was the promotion of increased trade and investment flows from South Africa to SADC and the rest of Sub-Saharan Africa, with a view to enhancing domestic growth and employment creation' (2002, p. 13). A senior official argued:

> [We need to] make a substantial contribution to our government's Reconstruction and Development Programme. By actively encouraging and assisting with trade promotion in the region, we are ensuring that new employment opportunities are created in South Africa. The latter objective is also being achieved by promoting and facilitating the active involvement of the South African private sector in development and construction projects in the region. (cited by Gelb 2002, pp. 13–14)

Governance: degrading the democratic project
Much like NEPAD, both the Blair Commission Report and the Annan Report took 'governance' as a point of departure in terms of what African countries need to focus upon in order to overcome their development problems. For the Blair Commission Report, governance is 'the *inability* of government and the public services to create the right economic, social and legal framework which will encourage economic growth and allow the poor to participate in it' (2005, p. 24, emphasis mine). Apart from the definitional crisis inherent in this notion of governance,[8] reducing governance to how well the state creates the right environment for economic activities degrades the democratic project in Africa and highlights, again, the trade logic of the report's development discourse. This definitional problem is one the Blair Commission Report shares with NEPAD. Gelb (2002) has argued further that in so far as NEPAD is concerned, the primary concern for South African officials was less about democracy as such and more about fixing Africa's 'governance image'. For the South African authors of MAP, 'poor governance across sub-Saharan Africa (both political and economic) creates negative perceptions for investors – foreign and domestic, portfolio and direct – which directly affects investment levels throughout the region, including

[in] South Africa' (2002, p. 23). The disappointing investment flow into South Africa after 1994 was explained by the 'contagion effect' of being located in a 'bad neighbourhood' (*ibid.*). Fixing Africa's governance crisis, at least in compliance with the neo-liberal mantra, was considered crucial for South Africa's investment prospect. Gelb should know: he was the research coordinator for the South African government's MAP team, served until July 2001 as head of research for the economic unit in President Mbeki's office, and was arguably the lead author of MAP.[9]

Governance, for the Blair Commission, is about providing an enabling environment for economic activities. The additive element of 'poor people', which increasingly has become gestural, fails to comprehend the location of 'poor people' in most underdeveloped economies – as wage-workers, involved in marginal survival activities, or a mass of economically inactive people struggling with long-term unemployment and under-employment. The current misuse of the concept of 'good governance' embraces the creation of authoritarian enclaves within the liberal democratic polity: an independent central banker that is not accountable to the parliament or the electorate; a policymaking process that is hidden from parliamentary oversight and/or the participation of the full complement of cabinet ministers, and the outright subversion of the constitutions of the emerging multiparty democracies.[10] This instrumental abuse of the idea of 'good governance' is far removed from the intentions of the African activists and scholars who, in the first place, put the idea into the public domain in the 1980s in the hope that it would both result in the enlargement of local democratic space and enrich the public policy process. As Mkandawire (2004) recently reminded us:

> The general understanding within African intellectual circles then was that the main challenge of development was the establishment of state–society relations that are (a) developmental, in the sense that they allow the management of the economy in a manner that maximises economic growth, induces structural change, and uses all available resources in a responsible and sustainable manner in highly competitive global conditions; (b) democratic and respectful of citizens' rights; and (c) socially inclusive, providing all citizens with a decent living and full participation in national affairs. Good governance should therefore be judged by how well it sustains this triad. The urgency of the democratic aspect of good governance was highlighted by the clamour for democracy by social groups that had opposed misgovernment and the imposition of policies by unelected institutions – national or foreign.

The degradation of the democratic project in Africa through a lop-sided global governance discourse is creating a bizarre situation where gross abuses of human rights and massive electoral fraud in a country like Nigeria, to cite one example, are tolerated by the international -

proponents of 'good governance' while Zimbabwe, to cite another example, faces massive condemnation, the difference being the acquiescence of one with the global neo-liberal project while the other is in full rebellion. There is no current or historical evidence to support the claims made by the Blair Commission Report that 'good governance', however understood, is a condition for economic growth. As Ha-Joon Chang (2002) has noted, most of what the neo-liberals claim as essential elements of 'good governance' did not exist in the periods that the Commission identified as marking the phase of the structural transformation of the economies of the Western world, the East Asian Tigers, or contemporary China. The democratic project must be seen as an end in itself and for a purpose different from simply facilitating economic growth: the right of people to be treated with dignity and their right of full participation in their own governance is an independent project, not an instrumental appendage of 'higher' economic goals, nor a residual category to be thrown in for purposes of appearing to be politically correct. The paradox of a degraded discourse on governance is that it arms those who wish to reverse the scant democratic gains of the last two decades in Africa on account of poor economic growth or increasing inequality.

Debt, aid, and development

By far the most significant aspect of the Blair Commission Report is the acknowledgment – at last – of the validity of arguments that several scholars, activists, civil society organisations and the OAU/AU had made for years, namely that debt cancellation is a prerequisite for Africa's development. As late as 2003, the idea of debt cancellation was still being dismissed on the grounds of the 'moral hazard' attached to such a venture – debt relief or rescheduling were possibilities, but not cancellation. The 450-page final version of the Blair Commission Report released in May 2005 was particularly elaborate in arguing that the debt, for most part, was no longer collectable and it was time that 'creditors' owned up to that. The debt cancellation it envisaged should include 'debt stock and debt service buy-up to 100 per cent, and cover multilateral and bilateral debt' (2005, p. 109). In January 2005, during his visit to Cape Town, the British Chancellor Gordon Brown had firmly declared to an audience at the National Assembly that the objective was 100 per cent debt cancellation. For a report that repeatedly called for 'bold and comprehensive action', there were early warnings concerning the promise. Several caveats were entered into the agenda, ranging from offering 100 per cent cancellation to 'poor countries in sub-Saharan Africa *which need it ...*' [italics mine], to debt cancellation 'as soon as possible', and limiting the cancellation to debt service due before countries on the enhanced Highly Indebted Poor Countries (HIPC) programme reach the completion point.

In the run-up to the May 2005 British general elections, the Chancellor spoke of the moral obligation of the New Labour government to end misery and poverty, as well as the crushing debt burden that poor countries feel. As he put it, 'to insist on the payment of these debts offends human dignity – and is therefore unjust. What is morally wrong cannot be economically right.'[11] The Blair Commission Report was held up as evidence that the government has not lost its 'radical' instinct. Brown affirmed to the audience in a London church that Britain would 'not force poor countries to liberalise as a condition for our aid or our trade negotiations'. There were more electioneering statements like Brown's talk of allowing 'poor countries …to participate on equal terms in the international economy'. It was a speech designed to inspire an audience with strong social justice campaign credentials. But even in that speech, there were ambiguities and caveats – ranging from the casual, interchangeable use of 'debt cancellation' and 'debt relief', to a predetermined idea of what the resources released would be spent on.

Whatever the intention and the promises, what emerged at the end of the 2005 G8 conference was considerably less than what had been promised. Rather than 100 per cent debt cancellation for the 'poor countries in sub-Saharan Africa which need it', the cancellation applied to only the countries that were at the completion point of the enhanced-HIPC process. The 'deal' covered debt owed to the multilateral institutions like the World Bank, IMF, and the African Development Bank, not the debt owed to governments (such as the British government). It applied to 18 countries, 14 of which are in sub-Saharan Africa, not all poor countries. More important, because the debt was linked to the enhanced-HIPC process, the conditionalities attached to that process remain in place as eligibility criteria for current and future beneficiaries – the same conditionalities that Chancellor Brown claimed were an affront on decency. The deal contradicted the promised end to telling African countries what to do and how to do it! In announcing the G8 agreement at the end of the summit, Brown was clear on what the money released by the cancellation could be used for. The beneficiaries must maintain their commitment to deepening economic reforms to 'boost private sector development and … the elimination of impediments to private investment, both domestic and foreign'.[12]

It could be argued that the outcome of the G8 summit reflected the vagaries of negotiations with countries that were not party to the Commission for Africa. This does not, however, explain Britain's position on bilateral debt. For instance, the Blair Commission Report identified Nigeria as a country outside the HIPC framework whose debt situation needed attention (May 2005, pp. 319–20). Eighty-five per cent of Nigeria's external debt stock of about US$36 billion is bilateral. According to its Debt Management Office, the total amount of loan that the country took – as verified by its central bank – over a period of 38 years was US$13.5 billion. Over that same period, the country had paid back US$42 billion but still owed about US$36 billion (CBN 2005).[13] In the preliminary debt negotiations with the Paris Club of creditor countries, in June 2005, Nigeria was required to make an upfront payment of US$12 billion in order to qualify for an US$18 billion debt write-off. In the period 2000 to 2004, annual external debt service payment averaged US$1.7 billion; the 'debt write-off deal' amounted to collecting in one year what might have taken a little over 7 years to collect! After making the upfront payment, the country's outstanding debt stock would be US$18 billion. Measured against the federal expenditure for 2004, the upfront payment that the Paris Club was demanding would be the equivalent of nearly 10 years' spending on 'social and community services' – education, health, etcetera.[14] The gap between the claimed objective of 'making poverty history' and action could not be wider. The consensus among commentators in the country was that the victory that President Obasanjo and his Finance Minister claimed over the 'deal' was a sham.[15] It is worth noting that a significant portion of Nigeria's bilateral debt is owed to Britain.

The debt negotiation strategy adopted by the leading African advocates of NEPAD (Presidents Olusegun Obasanjo, Abdoulaye Wade, and Thabo Mbeki) is instructive, and in opposition to the position announced by the African Union at the end of the first Conference of African Ministers of Economy and Finance (CAMEF) in early May 2005, in Dakar, Senegal (AU 2005). The AU statement maintained a long-held position that any debt cancellation initiative must cover *all* African countries. By contrast those concerned with partnership with the G8, including the 2005 Chair of the AU (President Obasanjo), took a line that undermined the collective position of the organisation to which they belong. The debt cancellation announced after the 2005 G8 meeting at Gleneagles, Scotland, continued on the path of the HIPC initiative, and covered only 18 of the 27 countries that were expected to reach the completion point in 2005. It was a position that greatly compromised Africa's development option and the credibility of the AU. The HIPC conditionalities contain the same policy instruments that have created the problem of Africa's 'maladjustment' (Mkandawire 2005) and the failed adjustment programme of the past 25 years.

The aid discourse shared by the three reports fails to distinguish between short-term aid flow to bridge initial 'resource gap', which is why it is referred to as 'official *development* assistance', and the aid dependence that arose since the 1980s in sub-Saharan Africa. Further, they do not engage with the institutional processes that have produced this dependence. It is this that has made the contemporary ideas of ODA *non-developmental*. Unlike the case of Botswana, which is often cited as evidence of the graduating out of aid dependence, the current crisis is inherently driven by the same macro-economic policies that all the reports (including the NEPAD document) endorse. First, the policy of aggressive liberalisation subverted the fiscal base of the state in much of sub-Saharan Africa. Under the adjustment programme, trade liberalisation alone imposed a cost of US$272 billion on African countries (Christian Aid 2005, Dembele 2005). The fiscal base of governments has been further weakened by the strategies that many of the countries adopt in order to attract investment – generous tax holidays and concessionary access to social and municipal services.

Second, the policy instruments deployed under adjustment failed to target or address the core problems associated with the inherited colonial political economy. These core problems include excessive dependence on primary agricultural and mineral commodities and low levels of industrial manufacturing activities. The balance-of-payment crisis of the late 1970s and early 1980s is widely blamed on the excessive vulnerability to external shocks that the inherited colonial economy created. This is why the growth rate achieved between 1960 and 1980 is often classified as 'perverse growth'. Third, aggressive liberalisation in sub-Saharan African countries, in the context of continued trade-distorting subsidy in the OECD countries, made the countries even more vulnerable. The result has been a persistence of current account deficit in countries like Ghana, Uganda and Mozambique that are normally considered successful adjusters (Adesina 2004a). Much of what counts for aid was used to bridge the budgetary gaps created by this increasingly endemic macroeconomic disequilibrium. The result has been aid flows to patch the fractures created by the neo-liberal policies rather than development assistance. Much of what the Sachs and Blair Commission reports propose is a continuation of this pattern of aid flow. Fourth, apart from the widely acknowledged abuse of aid, by donors and recipients, the increasing indebtedness experienced since the 1980s involved the combined use of further debts and aid to finance new debt. Between 1980 and 1995, 'official long-term debt' increased more than four-fold and the indebtedness to the multilateral institutions rose more than six-fold (UNCTAD 2004b). In its current form the aid discourse, which seeks a re-engineered state, envisions a deformed developmental state: one without a development agenda. The key to effective poverty reduction is raising the productive capacity of the African countries in a sustainable manner. Sustainable improvements in social policy have to be under-pinned by an increasingly productive and dynamic economy; it cannot depend on aid or charity. Such an economy would require that we return to the foundational developmental issues. It cannot be based on an army of Bretton Woods and associated 'donor' officials setting up parallel ministries across Africa or second-guessing and steering policies from

Washington, London, or Paris. The Sachs Report, which seeks to widen the remit and hold of the Bretton Woods officials, is precisely the kind of assistance the continent does not need. Africa's sustainable development future lies in a different direction. It would require a state–citizens nexus that African intellectuals and activists envisaged in the 1980s when they demanded the opening up of the democratic space and a new compact between a responsive and accountable state and its citizens.

Conclusion

Much of this book is concerned with the broad contours of the development challenges facing Africa and contained in the NEPAD initiative. In addressing the questions arising, the concern has been to focus on policy content, not declaratory statements. The latter is the ground on which the promoters of NEPAD have tried to sell it. But these statements cannot disguise the fact that NEPAD's policy instruments of choice fail to target most of what the contributors to this collection consider the fundamental development challenges facing Africa. The recent outpouring of international sentiments about the need to act decisively to overcome Africa's development problems is not something that the authors in this book will dismiss. But the point must be stressed again and again that policy, not sentiment, is the important item for consideration; the heart of the matter. As with NEPAD, the acid test is a rigorous examination of the policies that are meant to give force to the sentiments.

A starting point will be a fundamental reworking of NEPAD. This is something the sponsors of NEPAD allowed themselves. The MAP/NEPAD document was drafted when the South African government was still in its phase of infatuation with the neo-liberal project. The 10-year review that South Africa commissioned between 2002 and 2003 has resulted in significant shifts in policy choice and orientation. Most discernible is a wrestling of the centre of policymaking away from the Treasury and the Economic Team within its Presidency, and a shift towards a more active role for the state in its economy and society (SA Government 2003). The paradox of the programme sold to the rest of the continent is that while the country that authored the text has moved on to embrace a more active role for the state, NEPAD is trapped in a time warp – of South Africa before 2004 and the world before 9/11.

The task of reconstituting an African development agenda must move beyond the impasse that is presently in evidence, and which several of the chapters in this book allude to. At an institutional level, CODESRIA has developed a number of initiatives designed to move the African social research community on a forward march to chart new terrains in development thinking. Of critical importance in this regard is the research project it has launched with *Rethinking Africa's Development*, the scholarly exchanges it plans to undertake in support of the project, and the Advanced Policy Dialogue programme it will undertake in order to promote improved interaction and dialogue between African policy-makers and researchers. TWN-Africa's role in facilitating a greater synergy, mutual support, and coordination among African trade negotiators will complement this effort and will also ensure that a permanent dialogue is made between the continent's academic and its civil society intellectuals. But these are all initial steps in a long journey and there is an awareness that the tasks that have been defined, as well as the ambitions underpinning them, will require a considerable commitment of resources. The important thing, however, is that the trip has started and there is a determination to go long haul to get to the desired destination.

NOTES

1   In spite of the conflicting use of the idea (Hardt & Negri [2000], Mann [2003], Harvey [2003], Allen [2005]) or the attack on the concept (Shaw 2002), we use 'new imperialism' to refer to the post-1980 phenomenon of global imperial rule by stealth, policed largely by an army of enforcers from the Bretton Woods institutions and within ostensibly multilateral bodies like the WTO. Behind the 'consultation' and 'advice' is the metal fist of global capital and the state to enforce compliance. It is distinct from classical imperialism in the absence of 'direct rule' and the geographically specific empires associated with colonial rule. Domination is at 'arms length' (Allen 2005) and not easily associated with individual countries. It is equally distinct from what used to be called neo-colonialism, a term which refers to the mechanisms of 'indirect rule' enforced by functionaries of state and capital mainly associated with former colonial rulers or the US. Contemporary 'new imperialism', like all forms of domination, is contradictory, 'incoherent' (Mann 2003), and subject to the counter-hegemonic projects of those it seeks to dominate. Harvey (2003) would refer to it as a phase of 'neoliberal imperialism'. We are inclined to think that its objectives are more than facilitating penetration by capital; it has distinct geopolitical objectives as well. The invasions of Afghanistan and Iraq marked another phase in the evolving nature of imperialism – what Harvey (2003) refers to as 'neoconservative imperialism'. The latter harks back to the gun boat 'diplomacy' of the nineteenth century rather than simply being associated with the rise of the neoconservatives in the US. Otherwise we cannot explain why France, while opposing the war on Iraq, would join the US in ousting Jean-Bertrand Aristide from Haiti a few months later.

    Shaw's (2002) attack on the continued relevance of the idea of 'imperialism', *sui generis*, is instructive, especially for a paper that was strong on theoretical insight. Shaw mistook his situational experience of capitalism and imperialism for their global reality. Someone based in the UK or US might experience the late-twentieth century imperial state as a democratic polity, characterised by respect for human rights and economic prosperity at home; those at the receiving end of its power – from Northern Ireland to Vietnam, Nicaragua,

Mozambique, Angola, and lately Afghanistan and Iraq – might experience it differently. Indeed, that precisely is the nature of imperial rule – the differential experiences registered by its beneficiaries and its victims.

2 Cf. Craig S. Smith, 'Major Creditors in Accord to Waive 80% of Iraq Debt', *New York Times* (22 November 2005), <http://www.nytimes.com> (accessed 22 November 2004). In a signal of what was to come, the second instalment of 30 per cent write-off of Iraq's (often odious) debt, in 2005, was tied to an IMF-approved package of 'economic reform programmes'. The final tranche, in 2008, is conditional on an IMF-approved score card of compliance with the reform programme! *Plus ça change...*!

3 One should note that Adedeji's ECA is not anything like Kingsley Amoako's ECA. As Randriamaro's chapter shows, and as is central to the Accra conference, the *Compact for African Recovery* produced by Amoako's UNECA (2001) is fundamentally similar to NEPAD (2001) – both driven by the neo-Washington Consensus discourse of Wolfensohn's CDF. Adedeji's ECA produced the *Lagos Plan of Action* and the *African Alternative Framework to Structural Adjustment Programmes* (AAF-SAP). In that sense, it would not be Adedeji's ECA that 'lost out to the OAU' as the new centre of 'policymaking', it would be Amoako's ECA. But this would fly in the face of the genesis of NEPAD. The October 2001 version involved the inputs of ECA staff, who met with the South African and Nigerian officials to undertake the task of 'cleaning up' the original New Africa Initiative, itself a merger of the Millennium Action Plan (MAP) and the OMEGA Plan.

4 The 'Singapore Issues' refer to the foci of the four working groups established at the inaugural WTO Ministerial Conference in Singapore, in 1996: government procurement, competition policy, the protection of investment, and trade facilitation.

5 At the launch of the report of the Commission for Africa in South Africa in March 2005 Trevor Manuel, the South African Finance Minister and a member of the commission, objected to *Our Common Interest* being referred to as the Blair Commission Report. This objection, shared by Tony Blair, would seem more concerned with facilitating the impression that this is an 'African agenda' – as Manuel told the South African parliament. We follow the convention here for naming reports. This after all was the outcome of the British Prime Minister's initiative, funded by the British government, and facilitated with human resources provided by the British government.

6 This awareness is central to the analysis that underscored the LPA and AAF-SAP, and familiar to any student of Raúl Prebisch. Further (Engel's Law), the share of food in a household's budget reduces as its income increases!

7 These are Ghana, Kenya, Nigeria, Tanzania, Uganda, Zambia, and Zimbabwe.

8 The idea that governance is the *inability* to do something subverts the Commission's presumptions about 'good governance'.

9 Making sense of South Africa's engagement with the region requires an appreciation of the contradictory nature and impulses that characterise the engagement. Claims of South African 'sub-imperialism' fail to grapple with these contradictory impulses. They homogenise a diversity or multiplicity of agency: cross the private sector, government, and civil society; and are at work within each of the blocs. Previously colonial transnational companies now wrap themselves up in the South African flag, and proclaim the 'African Renaissance' when operating on the continent. The investment in peacekeeping operations – from the Comoros to the DRC – and efforts in the preservation of the Timbuktu

manuscripts represent another side of the equation. Within the government itself, the Department of Trade and Industry behaves differently from the Department of Defence and those departments oriented towards social services. This does not displace the argument that the South African fiscus is a major beneficiary of the operations of its transnational corporations operating on the continent.

10 For instance, the agreements between the IMF/WB and client countries are hardly ever brought to the attention of the countries' parliaments, and in most cases not even before the cabinet. Oversight and control over the agreements are sometimes limited to the Ministers of Finance and the governors of the central banks. Even more worrying are the treaties that several African countries are entering into with the United States government, in which they undertake not to hand American citizens over to the International Criminal Court. In Nigeria's case, the treaty was never brought to the attention of the National Assembly; it did not discuss or ratify the treaty, which violates the country's 1999 Constitution.

11 Gordon Brown (Sunday 24 April 2005), 'When there is injustice anywhere, it is indeed a threat to justice everywhere'. Speech at St John's Church, Isleworth, London. <http://www.labour.org.uk> (Accessed 24 April 2005). It will be poor analysis (or politics) to assume that these are 'political' statements of a politician in pursuit of votes.

12 BBC (11 June 2005), 'G8 reaches deal for world's poor' <http://news.bbc.co.uk> (15:45 GMT) (accessed 12 June 2005), Sanjay Suri (14 June 2005), 'Privatisation Hangs Over Debt Relief' <http://www.other-net.info> (accessed 17 June 2005).

13 *Punch* Newspaper, 'Obasanjo promises to stop debt payment if …', Thursday 10 March 2005.

14 Author's calculation based on the Central Bank of Nigeria's 2004 *Annual Report* (CBN 2005, pp. 129–30). The CBN put the total central government expenditure (capital and recurrent) on 'social and community services' at 164.42 billion *naira*. The US$12 billion the Paris Club was demanding would be the equivalent of 1,620 billion *naira*.

15 Femi Falana, 'Debt Relief, A Trap' (*Sunday Punch*, 17 July 2005); J. K. Randle, 'The Debt Talk' (*Vanguard*, 24 August 2005); Lanre Banjo, 'Obasanjo "April Fooled" Nigerians in June – No Debt Relief' (*Nigeriaworld* 29 July 2005) (http://nigeriaworld.com) (accessed 2 August 2005).

REFERENCES

Adesina, J., 2004a. 'Africa's Encounter with Neoliberalism: the Making of Endemic Development Crisis'. Paper prepared for the Economics of the New Imperialism International Conference (International Development Economists Associates) 22–24 January 2004, Jawaharlal Nehru University, New Delhi (revised version).
—— 2004b. 'NEPAD and the Challenge of Africa's Development: Towards the Politics of a Discourse', *Society in Transition: Journal of the South African Sociological Association*, 35, No. 1.
African Union, 2005. *The First Conference of African Ministers of Economy and Finance (CAMEF) – Report*. 7 May, Dakar. AU/CAMEF/Rpt (1).
Allen, J., 2005. 'Arm's length imperialism?' *Political Geography*, 24: 525–44.
Annan, Kofi, 2005. *In Larger Freedom: Towards Development, Security and Human Rights for All*.

New York: United Nations (21 March).

Chang, Ha-Joon, 2002. *Kicking Away the Ladder: Development Strategy in Historical Perspective.* London: Anthem.

Central Bank of Nigeria (CBN), 2005. *Annual Reports and Statement of Accounts, 2004.* Abuja: CBN.

Christian Aid, 2005. *The Economics of Failure: the Real Costs of 'Free' Trade.* London: Christian Aid.

Commission for Africa, 2005. *Our Common Interest: an Argument.* London: Penguin Books.

Curtis, M., 2003. *Web of Deceit: Britain's Real Role in the World.* London: Vintage.

Dembele, D. M., 2005. 'Is aid the answer?' *Alliance*, 10, 3 (September) pp. 57–60.

Gelb, S., 2002. 'South Africa, Africa and The New Partnership for Africa's Development'. Johannesburg: Edge Institute.

Hardstaff, P., 2005. 'WDM Media Briefing on the UN Millennium Project report edited by Jeffrey Sachs'. World Development Movement.

Hardt, M. and Negri, A., 2000. *Empire.* Cambridge, MA: Harvard University Press.

Harvey, D., 2003. *The New Imperialism.* Oxford: Oxford University Press.

ILO, 2004. *A Fair Globalization: Creating Oopportunities for All.* Geneva: ILO.

Keet, D. (2002) *South Africa's Official Position and Role in Promoting The World Trade Organisation.* Cape Town: AIDC.

Mann, M. 2003. *Incoherent Empire.* London: Verso Press.

Mkandawire, T. 2004. 'The Itinerary of an Idea', *D+C Development and Cooperation*, 31, 10 (October); <http://www.inwent.org/E+Z/content/archive-eng/10-2004/tribune_art1.html>

Mkandawire, T. 2005. 'Maladjusted African Economies and Globalisation', *Africa Development*, 30, 1&2: 1–33.

Olukoshi, A., 2002. 'Governing African political space for sustainable development: a reflection on NEPAD', in Peter Anyang' Nyong'o, *et al* (eds), *NEPAD: A New Path?* Nairobi: Heinrich Böll Foundation.

Shaw, M., 2002. 'The Problem of the Quasi-Imperial State: Uses and Abuses of Anti-Imperialism in the Global Era'. Paper presented at the conference on The Global Constitution of 'Failed States': Consequences of a New Imperialism? University of Sussex 18–20 April 2001 (revised, mimeo).

South African Government, 2003. *Towards a Ten-Year Review: Complete Report.* Pretoria: The Presidency.

UNDP, 2004. *2004 Human Development Report: Cultural Liberty in Today's Diverse World.* New York: UNDP.

UN Millennium Project, 2005. *Investing in Development: a Practical Plan to Achieve the Millennium Development Goals (The Sachs Report).* London: Earthscan.

UNCTAD, 2004a. *Economic Development in Africa: Trade Performance and Commodity Dependence.* Geneva: UNCTAD.

UNCTAD, 2004b. *Economic Development in Africa. Debt Sustainability: Oasis or Mirage?* Geneva: UNCTAD.

PART 1

NEPAD:
the Debate

1 Development and the Challenge of Poverty

NEPAD, post-Washington Consensus and Beyond

'Jìmí O. Adésínà

The 2000/1 *World Development Report* on global poverty put the total number of people in sub-Saharan Africa living below the World Bank's US$1 per day norm for defining the core poor at 290.9 million in 1998 (World Bank 2001a: 23). Measured against the 1987 figure, 73.7 million more people in the region had dropped below this poverty line in the eleven years up to 1998. While there was a global increase in the number of people living in poverty in the reference period, a greater proportion of people in sub-Saharan Africa were living in poverty than anywhere else in the world: 47.7 per cent and 46.3 per cent in 1987 and 1998, respectively (World Bank 2001a). Even if one were to quarrel with the estimation technique used in the report, the region's association with poverty and its characterisation as a development wasteland is the dominant impression.

Genocidal conflicts, civil war, the HIV/AIDS pandemic, economic stagnation and poverty would seem to characterise sub-Saharan Africa in the eyes of both the media and regional leaders. In its opening eight paragraphs, the New Partnership for Africa's Development (NEPAD) outlines the crisis of sustainable growth, poverty and social exclusion in Africa, as well as the increasing marginalisation of the continent in the global market place. As an agenda for the rejuvenation of Africa, NEPAD represents a major initiative on the part of the African heads of state and government. Such a continental initiative has not been mooted since the 1980 Lagos Plan of Action and the African Alternative Framework to Structural Adjustment Programmes (AAF-SAP) that the United Nations Economic Commission for Africa (UNECA) launched in 1989. However, the NEPAD document is fraught with weaknesses and problems. In this chapter we address these from the perspective of the challenge of poverty for Africa's development: a core aspect of attempts to 'market' NEPAD.

In this chapter, we look at the prognosis of the 'African condition' as outlined in the NEPAD document and examine its core policy options for development and poverty reduction. We argue that, while the sponsors of NEPAD promote it as having poverty eradication as a core value, there is very little guidance in either the NEPAD base document or associated documents on the direction for dealing with the crisis. None of the six task teams established under the NEPAD framework is concerned with poverty reduction specifically; NEPAD addresses the issue of poverty reduction under the rubric of human resource development. The sponsors of NEPAD, it would seem, take the neo-liberal perspective of treating social development concerns as residuals of economic growth. To underscore such a policy focus, NEPAD's concern with economic growth persistently stresses 'sound macro-economic policies', institutional and legal reform, and a greater openness of Africa to the process of globalisation. Where it addresses the strategy for poverty reduction, NEPAD takes the existing policy strategies of the Bretton Woods institutions as its organising framework. It is, we argue, in its combined reading of the economic policy orientation and poverty reduction strategies that NEPAD represents a major misreading of the African experience of neo-liberal policy instruments deployed over the last two decades in Africa and the 'rediscovery of poverty' (Mkandawire 2001a) by the World Bank and the IMF. NEPAD would seem to be suggesting, essentially, that Africa should press on down the path of neo-liberal economic and social policy. This misreading of Africa's late-twentieth-century experience, we also argue, is predicated on an ahistorical reading of Africa's development experience in the four decades since 1960. It is in this context that NEPAD's discourse is better understood as deriving from the post-Washington consensus of the Bretton Woods institutions than as an autonomous engagement with Africa's experience. Against the picture of unremitting development failure that NEPAD suggests, we argue for a more dis-aggregated reading of Africa's post-colonial development experience.

Considering the close alignment of NEPAD and the neo-liberal discourse, we examine the neo-liberal development direction in sub-Saharan Africa and the implementation of the World Bank's Comprehensive Development Framework (especially the IMF-linked Poverty Reduction Strategy Paper) and the IMF's Poverty Reduction and Growth Facility as mechanisms for poverty reduction. The evidence, we argue, does not support the unqualified support that the African sponsors of NEPAD gave these policy instruments. Indeed, the disjuncture between macro-economic policies and poverty reduction is quite stark. Furthermore, several paragraphs of the NEPAD document demonstrate a simplistic reading of the global and domestic difficulties facing many African countries – notwithstanding the fact that the Bretton Woods institutions are themselves the sources of some of the evidence. Indeed, the critical challenge for Africa in addressing the crisis of poverty is in confronting the problems of global equity and an equitable and socially inclusive development framework at the national and continental levels.

NEPAD: discourse and reading of the crisis

NEPAD has its roots in the Millennium African Recovery Programme (MAP)[1] and the Omega Plan for Africa, which was described by its authors as 'an African strategy for globalisation' (Wade 2001). While MAP was promoted as a joint initiative of the presidents of Algeria, Nigeria and South Africa, it dates back to the entrance of the 'African Renaissance' into the South African lexicon, while Thabo Mbeki was still Deputy President. Mbeki's first State of the Nation address as President of South Africa put the idea formally on the agenda of the South African government. On 21 November 2000, the African Renaissance and International Cooperation Fund Act (No. 51 of 2000) was signed into law in South Africa. Its preamble prefigures the content of MAP and NEPAD.[2] In January 2001, Mbeki presented the plan to the World Economic Forum. The wording of the MAP document itself suggests that other African countries who were not among the initiating countries were welcome to buy into it, as long as they were 'prepared and ready to commit to the underlining principles guiding the initiative' (Mbeki 2001). The Omega Plan emerged, arguably, as a counterpart programme to MAP in June 2001, focusing on infrastructure, health, education and agriculture.

At the July 2001 Lusaka Summit of the Organisation of African Unity (OAU), the Omega Plan and MAP were merged into the New African Initiative. The latter document was reformulated into NEPAD at the October meeting of the Heads of State Implementation Committee (HSIC) in Abuja, Nigeria. The communiqué at the end of the October 2001 outlined the structure of NEPAD and its links with various task teams and lead agencies.[3]

Core issues in the marketing of NEPAD focus on the Partnership as:

1 A 'holistic and comprehensive integrated strategic framework for the socio-economic development of Africa', providing a vision for the continent;
2 An African plan conceived and developed by its leaders, with ownership a primary concern;
3 A platform for engaging with the rest of the world in a partnership.

The goals of NEPAD were stated as the promotion of accelerated growth and sustainable development, poverty eradication and ending

Africa's marginalisation in the context of globalisation. The sectoral priorities are defined as bridging the infrastructure gap, human resource development, agriculture, the environment, culture, and science and technology platforms. The vision of resource mobilisation covers capital flow and market access. The principles and objectives of NEPAD include:

- 'African ownership, responsibility and leadership of the initiative;
- Making Africa attractive to both domestic and foreign investors;
- Unleashing the vast economic potential of the continent;
- Achieving and sustaining an annual GDP growth rate of 7 per cent for the next 15 years;
- Ensuring that Africa achieves the International Development Goals (IDGs);
- Investing in human development;
- Promoting the role of women in all activities;
- Promoting regional and sub-regional economic integration;
- Developing a new partnership with the industrial world and multi-lateral agencies;
- Strengthening the capacity to lead negotiation on behalf of the continent at different development forums that require continent-wide coordination;
- Ensuring capacity for accelerated implementation of cooperation agreement and approved projects; and
- Strengthening Africa's capacity to mobilise external resources' (NEPAD 2001).

The conditions for sustainable development are given under three clusters:

- Peace, security, democracy and good governance;
- Economic and corporate good governance;
- Sub-regional and regional approaches to development.

While the prospect of a sustained 7 per cent growth rate for the next 15 years may be questioned, this and other issues represent desirable objectives for a continent that is characterised as having experienced unremitting economic, social and political adversity. It is difficult to quarrel with a document that sets peace, security and 'good governance' as conditions for sustainable development or the accelerated reduction and elimination of widespread poverty. What needs further discussion is the context in which that discourse is located and the policy directions that NEPAD's sponsors consider for achieving these desirable ends.

However, what is new about NEPAD – contrary to much of the media representation – is not the issue of a continental focus on peace and security, peer review, or a regional approach to development. Issues of peacekeeping and enforcement as responses to regional conflict have previously been articulated within the structures of the OAU, with a formal unit within the organisation focusing on this. For instance, at sub-regional level, the Economic Community of West African States (ECOWAS) deployed a military force (ECOMOG) in Liberia to end the carnage of civil war in that country. A regional approach to development was fully articulated in the Lagos Plan of Action in 1980. The 1991 Abuja Treaty on the African Economic Community flowed directly from the Lagos Plan of Action and the African Alternative Framework to Structural Adjustment Programmes (AAF-SAP). What is unique about NEPAD is the macro-economic objective – an attempt to take ownership of policy instruments that the Bretton Woods institutions and the Group of Eight countries (G8) had contentiously foisted on most African countries since the 1980s. It is the idea that there is no alternative to neo-liberal social and economic agenda an idea at the heart of the 1996 policy shift in South Africa – which is being extended to the rest of the African continent. This becomes obvious when we consider the discourse and policy orientation that defines NEPAD.

Policy directions

The NEPAD document locates itself within a broad international development debate, while emphasising local ownership as an African driven and Africa-focused initiative. In locating itself within the international development debate, NEPAD proceeds on a claim of global consensus in the wake of several initiatives. This is located around UN-based initiatives and bilateral initiatives: from the UN's New Agenda for the Development of Africa and the Copenhagen Declaration on Social Development, to multilateral initiatives such as the World Bank-led Strategic Partnership for Africa and Poverty Reduction Strategy Paper, and bilateral efforts such as the Tokyo Agenda for Action, the US African Growth Initiative, or the G8 Okinawa Declaration. Ohiorhenuan (2002) has tried to link NEPAD with the United Nations Millennium Development Goals (MDGs) using a matrix of policy proclamations contained in both. This is to be expected since the UN Assembly that ratified the MDGs and the Copenhagen Declaration involved the participation of the same countries that produced NEPAD. We will argue, however, that NEPAD has stronger links with the neo-liberal side of the 'global consensus' on development – characterised by the Bretton Woods institutions and the creditor cartel countries – than the UN bodies. Both as regards its targets and the mechanisms it advocates for achieving its goals, NEPAD differs fundamentally from the MDGs.

For instance – no minor area of difference – where the UN's MDGs set the goal of debt cancellation, NEPAD argues for 'accelerated debt reduction for heavily indebted African countries' and 'improved debt relief strategies for the middle-income countries' (NEPAD 2001, para. 185). More importantly for our discussion of development and the challenge of poverty, NEPAD proceeds on the basis that Africa needs 'to develop the capacity to sustain growth at levels required to achieve poverty reduction and sustainable development' (para. 64). The programme recognises that growth, by itself, does not reduce poverty, but rather that poverty reduction results from sustained growth levels. Sustainable development, the document notes, is dependent on 'infrastructure, capital accumulation, human capital, institutions, structural diversification, competitiveness, health and good stewardship of the environment' (para. 64). The economic premise for achieving sustained growth is:

> Restoring and maintaining macro-economic stability, especially by developing appropriate standards and targets for fiscal and monetary policies and introducing appropriate institutional frameworks for achieving these standards.

> Instituting transparent legal and regulatory frameworks for financial markets and the auditing of private companies and the public sector (para. 49).

A stable macro-economic environment is a desirable goal in any context, but what gives NEPAD's version a distinct character is the twinning of such a stable environment with fiscal and monetary targeting. It is within this context that economic and corporate governance, and good governance broadly, are integrated. The accent on peace, security and political governance, while involving concern for the negative impact on ordinary people, is perhaps more concerned with the perception of Africa as an unfavourable destination for foreign direct investment – the anchor of resource inflows for NEPAD.

It may be legitimate to argue that, as an initiating document, we could not expect NEPAD to provide detailed mechanisms on every aspect of its principles and agenda. It is equally legitimate to raise the question of the policy options that NEPAD assumes will be used and the policy instruments that we can discern from such policy options. It is in the area of poverty reduction that this, perhaps, becomes most apparent.

Poverty reduction is presented in NEPAD as a core policy concern. However, NEPAD takes sustained economic growth as precedent to targeted anti-poverty measures, which is itself within the framework of existing Bretton Woods initiatives. NEPAD calls on member countries to:

> Work with the World Bank, the International Monetary Fund (IMF), the African Development Bank and the United Nations (UN) agencies to

accelerate the implementation and adoption of the Comprehensive Development Framework, the Poverty Reduction Strategy and related approaches (para. 116).

The emphasis on gender in poverty reduction policies that are targeted at women is within the context of asking for compliance with and support for existing Bretton Woods initiatives.

While NEPAD's sponsors argue that it is not about going to the industrial countries of the Organisation for Economic Cooperation and Development (OECD) with a begging bowl, it does call for an increase in development aid to 0.7 per cent of the GNP of each developed country. The increased aid flow would be disbursed to 'complement funds released by debt reduction for an accelerated fight against poverty' (para. 185). While NEPAD recognises the problem of market access for the products of African countries and seeks the 'negotiation of more equitable terms of trade for Africa countries within the WTO', still it suggests bilateral initiatives for addressing the problem of trade access. One assumes that it is clear that, while South Africa may negotiate with the European Union on market access, Sierra Leone, Burundi or Lesotho are not in a similar position. These are positions that are far weaker than those UN agencies such as the United Nations Conference on Trade and Development (UNCTAD) or the Economic and Social Council are advocating, but within current thinking at the World Bank and IMF.

In other words, while the idea of some kind of partnership with Africa is not a new one in either the World Bank or the United Nations, it is the Bretton Woods institutions' reading that defines NEPAD's discourse and policy focus, which itself emerged after one and a half decades of unremitting challenge and criticism of the Bretton Woods institutions and the creditor cartel countries. It is within this context that we talk of the post-Washington Consensus.

While the idea of a post-Washington Consensus may be associated with Joseph Stiglitz (1998), what actually emerged as the postscript to the Washington Consensus has very little, in content, to do with his more practical interrogation of orthodox neo-liberalism. After being forced out of the World Bank, Stiglitz remains an outsider to the Bretton Woods institutions and their political handlers. What we refer to here as the post-Washington Consensus has very little to do with his prescriptions and critique. Rather, it is in the evolving narratives and discourse of the Bretton Woods institutions that we locate the post-Washington Consensus, which emerged in the late 1990s over the approach to policy conditionalities attached to debt negotiation and access to international lending facilities. Orthodox adjustment had very little to say about democracy, good governance, institutions, or the social consequences of neo-liberal policy instruments being implemented. The orthodox neo-liberal agenda was concerned with stabilisation, extensive deployment of market liberalisation, and the retraction of the state. Budget and capital account balancing (with healthy foreign reserves), divestment of state assets, trade, exchange rates and labour market liberalisation are central to orthodox adjustment.

The shift in modes of representation of orthodox adjustment followed two separate lines of encounter. By the mid-1980s, mounting evidence of the severe damage that the implementation of orthodox neo-liberalism was causing had become palpable and impossible to ignore. The sources included the works of scholars and activists, UN agencies like the United Nations Children's Fund (UNICEF), the United Nations Development Programme (UNDP), and UNCTAD; the international non-governmental organisation (NGO) sector, including Oxfam, Bank Check, and the Bretton Woods Project; the bohemian anti-Bretton Woods and anti-globalisation protesters in the West; and the anti-SAP (Structural Adjustment Programme) riots in Africa and elsewhere. The initial response was the Social Dimension of Adjustment programme ware-housed by the World Bank (1987–1992).[4] The resistance to adjustment on the continent took the form of a resurgence of civil society and a demand for the democratic reform of the post-colonial state. The demand for or actual launch of sovereign national conferences in Zaïre (now the Democratic Republic of the Congo) and Benin were only the more dramatic expressions of a much wider response. Alongside the popular response was the work of the Public Choice School that provided the basis for the Bretton Woods institutions' reading of the governance issue in Africa. As Olukoshi noted (1998: 22), 'the World Bank, given the resources at its disposal and its wide reach, came to set the pace for other donors, including many of the bilaterals, on the governance question'. As with the Public Choice School, the World Bank defined the crisis of governance as being at the heart of Africa's development crisis.

We argue that in both its linkage to the choice of economic policies for redeeming Africa and its reading of the post-colonial African experience, the discourse of NEPAD owes a lot to this branch of the governance debate in Africa. Good governance, while seemingly focused on empowering the civil society, was defined by the agenda of restructuring the African state to becoming a vehicle for neo-liberal economic restructuring:

> The Bank had no doubt that there is an organic linkage between the institution of a system of 'good' governance and the prospect for the successful implementation of structural adjustment. By encouraging the rule of impersonal forces of the market and instituting economic 'rationality' into the process of resource allocation, a system of open and accountable government would be encouraged. The nurturing of open and transparent governance will, in turn, make it difficult to justify 'irrational' economic decisions (Olukoshi 1998: 25).

Good governance is defined by the provision of a stable environment for private capital, ensuring the sanctity of contracts, and guaranteeing that expropriation would not happen (Beckman 1992; Adésínà 2002). The guarantee of independence for central bankers meant monetary policies could be made without the policy makers worrying about being politically accountable. Indeed, the argument for the so-called independence of central bankers and the transfer of monetary policies to them was precisely to shield macro-economic policies from the accountability criterion to which politicians are subject in a democracy (cf. Rogoff 1985; Berger *et al.* 2002).[5] Central bankers could act in the interest of capital without bothering about the backlash from an electorate that may feel short-changed. Key economic policies are made in committees (of central banks) that are not accountable to the electorate, remaining outside the public domain and the oversight powers of an elected legislature.

Actual experience of this notion of governance in Africa produced neo-liberally inclined political leaders who became increasingly authoritarian. A distinct aspect of this orientation was the wave of conditionalities and cross-conditionalities to which many countries were subjected – even as macro-economic policy making was shut away from the arena of public debate. NEPAD shares this approach to policy making.

Renewed campaigns against the debt overhang, neo-liberal globalisation, the debilitating impacts on social lives, rethinking in some donor sectors (Japan being an important player here), and the activities of UN agencies,[6] forced further rethinking: 'There is now a global discourse insisting on economic policies that are socially sensitive' (Mkandawire 2001a: 1). The result was 'the rediscovery of poverty'. James Wolfensohn's internal World Bank memorandum of 21 January 1999 sought to codify the lessons and how these could be integrated into the operations of the international financial institutions as a 'balance sheet with two sides' (Wolfensohn 1999: 5).[7]

The memorandum argued for a Comprehensive Development Framework into which the World Bank's Poverty Reduction Strategy Papers (PRSP) and the IMF's Poverty Reduction and Growth Facility (PRGF) are integrated. The World Bank (2000a) defined the CDF as 'a holistic approach to development that balances macro-economic with structural, human and physical development needs'. It emphasises country ownership, 'strategic partnership among stakeholders … and accountability for development results'. Six of the twelve pilot sites for implementing the CDF are African countries.[8] It is, however, instructive that in both the Wolfensohn memorandum and the World Bank's practice, economic growth and social development issues are seen as 'two sides of a balance sheet' – if economic growth falls on the asset side, does that make social development a deficit item? Again, the perspective that there is a trade-off between growth and equity remains at the core of the apparent shift in the Bretton Woods institutions' discourse.

What separates the orthodox Washington Consensus from what we call the post-Washington Consensus is the shift from an earlier position that 'obviated the need for comprehensive social policies to accompany the growth process' (Mkandawire and Rodriguez 2000: 19). The re-discovery of poverty and of the 'two-sidedness' of development involved the renewed attachment of conditionalities to accessing World Bank and IMF facilities – social conditionality is added to political conditionality. Access to the Highly Indebted Poor Countries (HIPC), PRGF and PRSP initiatives is conditional on what the Bank euphemistically calls 'an adequate policy and institutional framework' (2000b: 4). The extent to which the double entry accounting of Wolfensohn's balances is suggest-ive of a recourse to orthodox thinking in neo-liberalism is a topic to which we will return. Suffice it to say that the forced resignation from the World Bank of Ravi Kanbur (as director of the 2000/1 *Development Report*) and Joseph Stiglitz (as Senior Vice-President and Chief Economist) is emblematic of the limit of consensus on the cause of poverty, its true nature, and how it can be ended.

To this emerging post-Washington Consensus of an apparently com-prehensive understanding of development NEPAD owes its language, assumptions and orientation. The private sector is seen as the engine of growth and the emphasis is on market-friendly institutions to provide the 'sound' macro-economic framework for such a development path.

Misreading of the African experience

NEPAD's reading of Africa's economic and social post-colonial experience replicates the evolving discourse of the Bretton Woods institutions outlined above. The effect is that it allows little or no disaggregation of phases and factors accounting for the current crisis that is the immediate concern of the sponsors of NEPAD. A more disaggregated understanding of the African experience would have focused attention on a different set of problems and policy options for addressing them.

What comes through in NEPAD's reading of the post-colonial experience is an unremitting picture of 'poverty and backwardness' (NEPAD 2001: para. 2). While colonialism failed to produce entre-preneurial, professional and middle classes, many African governments did not help matters because they 'did not empower their peoples to embark on development initiatives to realise their creative potential' (para. 23). 'Poor leadership, corruption and bad governance' were pervasive forces further undermining weak states and dysfunctional economies inherited from colonialism. The post-colonial 'rate of accumulation' was too low to rebuild societies after the damage done by colonialism (para. 25). Africa, since its post-colonial emergence, has been caught in a 'vicious cycle, in which economic decline, reduced capacity, and poor governance reinforce each other' (para. 26). Neo-liberal reforms of the 1980s are credited with having removed 'serious price distortions, but gave inadequate attention to the provision of social services'; the latter was responsible for the failure of these countries to 'achieve sustainable higher growth under these programmes' (para. 24). The assumption by the sponsors of NEPAD that structural adjustment was a development programme is intriguing. So is the idea that the missing link in Africa's achievement of sustainable growth was adequate provision of social services. This one-sided reading of the post-colonial experience reproduces the neo-liberal reading of Africa.

Africa's development and social policies (poverty reduction, human capability enhancement) are more differentiated than NEPAD allows. We address this briefly because it has implications for how we assess the viability of the macro-economic policies preferred by the sponsors of NEPAD and the Bretton Woods institutions' poverty reduction mechanism favoured by the Partnership. In borrowing from the analysis of the African state that was inspired by the Public Choice School, NEPAD falls into the same trap. First, to assume, at an analytical level, a total bankruptcy in the capacity of African states to be developmental – however vaguely defined – and yet, at the prescriptive level, to insist on the same state having to do all that is required to engineer Africa's development: this absurd proposition is what Mkandawire (2001b: 289) memorably calls 'the pessimism of the diagnosis and the optimism of the prescription'.

Table 1.1 (p. 45) shows some African growth statistics, relative to those of Latin America and Asia, over the period 1967–80. As Mkandawire notes, 'despite the many distortions of import substitution, until the second "oil" crisis many African economies had performed relatively well' (2001b: 303). Compared to the period under neo-liberal adjustment, when an average annual growth rate of 6 per cent is considered a target, Mkandawire notes that, if we were to take this as the measure of a successful growth rate, ten of the of the top 27 best performers in 1967–80 were sub-Saharan African countries. These ranged from Botswana, which topped the global league with an average growth rate of 14 per cent during the period, to Kenya, Cotê d'Ivoire, and Seychelles at 7 per cent. The Republic of Congo, Rwanda and Nigeria had a growth rate of 6 per cent.

As Van Arkadie (1999, cited in Mkandawire 2001b: 305) notes:

A significant part of the development budget was locally financed, balance of payments were in a reasonable order, exchange rates were not out of line, and inflation appeared only occasionally and then in modest form. An indicator of the order of the macro-economic environment was the cosy relationship between the IMF and most African countries before the first oil shock.

As Table 1.2 shows, between 1964 and 1980, mean rates of saving in sub-Saharan Africa were on the increase; the proportion of countries in the region with a savings rate of more than 25 per cent rose accordingly. What is instructive is the decline of 6.76 per cent in the average saving rate in 1980–91, and the 75 per cent drop, in the same period, in the proportion of African countries that had saving rates of over 25 per cent. The rates of saving and investment of the top-performing countries in sub-Saharan Africa, as Mkandawire argues, compare well with those of the 'developmental states' of East Asia (2001b: 304). The relative lower yield in the rate of growth also does not lend itself to a simplistic explanation.

Table 1.3 shows selected social development indicators of 19 sub-Saharan African countries, mainly for the period 1960–82. Again, contrary to the idea of pervasive development failure that the discourse of NEPAD and the Bretton Woods institutions suggests, there were clear improvements across these indicators. The same picture is replicated in the case of Zimbabwe in the post-independence decade.

Africa's deepening crisis of development and poverty

At this stage, the point is not to argue that Africa's first twenty years of post-colonial growth and social development were an unqualified success. The vulnerability of many of the economies to external shocks, and the severity of the balance of payments and current account crisis in the early 1980s in many African countries, indicate problems that are more fundamental. The nature of the crisis and the solution were, we will argue, grossly misjudged by the neo-liberal orthodoxy. While it is difficult for the World Bank and IMF to own up now, many of the African countries implemented development policies that were dominant within the Bank at the time. Furthermore, the shift from a private-sector-led economic growth strategy to a state-led one was, for many African countries, not an ideological issue. The experience of Nigeria is illustrative of this (Adésínà 1994). The shift to a state-led industrialisation strategy in the Second National Development Plan followed an extremely disappointing private sector response to all the investment incentives that were on offer in the late 1950s and 1960s.

What is described as a 'binomial' crisis in the NEPAD base document also fails to contextualise the origin and nature of the debt crisis. The sustainability of foreign debt – which had been promoted by the Bretton

Table 1.1 Selected growth statistics, 1967–80

Statistics	Latin America	Sub-Saharan Africa	Asia
Mean	4.5	4.3	4.7
Median	4.8	4.1	5.5
Standard deviation	2.2	2.7	4.5
Variance	4.9	7.1	20.6
Percentiles			
20	2.6	2.0	2.3
40	3.5	3.3	4.8
60	5.2	4.7	6.2
80	6.8	6.2	7.6

Source: Mkandawire 2001b: 304.

Woods institutions as a needed direction for accelerating growth – did not become a problem until 1980. Real interest rates rose from an average of 1.3 per cent in the period 1973–1980 to 5.9 per cent between 1980 and 1986. This was 'the direct result of the economic policies followed by the new conservative governments installed in the major industrial countries after 1979' (Toye 1994: 21). The deflationary policies pursued by governments in the industrial world were an important factor which undermined the growth of developing countries' exports in the 1980s.

In addition to lost exports, developing-country growth collapsed in the 1980s as deflation in the developed countries triggered a severe crisis of indebtedness. This crisis had been building up throughout the period 1973–80, largely unnoticed by the commercial banks, developing country borrowers and international organisations for economic cooperation (Toye 1994: 20). The impact of the stabilisation programmes of the IMF in many of the countries manifested in the contraction of the economy

Table 1.2 Savings rates in sub-Saharan African countries

	1964	1973	1980	1991
Mean	16.38	18.48	21.47	14.71
% of countries with savings greater than 25%	25.0	29.0	31.6	9.5

Source: Mkandawire 2001b.

Table 1.3 Selected social development indicators of some sub-Saharan African countries

	Life expectancy at birth (years)		Child death rate (aged 1–4)		Adult literacy (%)		Primary school enrolment* (% age group)		Basic needs index	
	1960	1982	1960	1982	1960	1985	1960	1981	1960	1982
Botswana	40	60	23	13	33	72	42	102	48	80
Cameroon	37	53	28	16	19	56	65	107	48	73
Chad	35	44	60	37	6	25	17	35	25	42
Congo (Brazzaville)	37	60	23	10	16	63	78	156	52	78
Côte d'Ivoire	37	47	40	23	5	43	46	76	37	61
Gabon	36	49	34	22	12	62	100	202	54	72
Ghana	40	55	27	15	30	53	38	69	45	66
Kenya	41	57	21	13	20	59	47	109	47	76
Lesotho	42	53	29	17	59	73	83	104	64	77
Madagascar	37	48	45	23	34	68	52	100	45	73
Malawi	37	44	58	29	22	41	30	62	33	55
Niger	37	45	45	27	1	14	5	23	25	39
Nigeria	39	50	50	20	15	42	36	98	35	68
Somalia	36	39	61	47	2	12	9	30	22	34
Sudan	39	47	40	23	13	20	25	42	34	49
Swaziland	38	54	33	27	29	68	58	110	48	74
Uganda	44	47	28	22	35	57	49	54	50	59
Zaïre	40	50	32	20	31	61	60	90	50	70
Zambia	40	51	38	20	47	76	42	96	48	76

* Figures for 1981 primary school enrolment include students above primary-school age.
Source: Ghai 1987: 124.

and a mounting social development crisis: in health, education, and social welfare. Increased liberalisation of the economies carries the added effect of weakening the capacity of the state to respond to the increased frequency and severity of financial crises globally (Stiglitz 1998: 13). The perception that countries have to compete to produce policies that are 'credible' in the financial markets has put the deflationary bias at the heart of economic policy making (Elson 2001: 9). Yet more African countries, with weakened resource bases, are being forced into a policy arena that makes them more vulnerable to the heightened instability in the global financial market. The impact of the economic contraction and deflationary bias in many countries is the heightening of labour market crisis and dislocation. NEPAD speaks of the removal of price distortions as a positive outcome of structural adjustment. Yet the neo-liberal misreading of the African labour markets is central to the policies that created so much labour market dislocation (Adésínà 1994). The escalating crisis of unemployment is a major contributor to the crisis of poverty (Wuyts 2001).

If the economic crisis of the early 1980s arose out of a severe balance of payments and capital account crisis, the experience of many countries since 1980 has been the escalation of the debt crisis, not its reduction. The escalation in the debt crisis in the period that African countries and treasuries were subjected to the most detailed supervision and control by the Bretton Woods institutions raises a host of questions about the nature of neo-liberal programmes and the real functions of the World Bank and IMF when administering these programmes. In 2000, 94.86 per cent of long-term debt and 76.13 per cent of the total debt stock of the sub Saharan African countries was public or publicly guaranteed (World Bank 2001a: 258) – roughly the same figures as in 1980.

As Table 1.4 shows, the rates of investment and savings across the board remain at a level lower than they were in the period 1975–9, at the onset of the 'crisis'.

As Figure 1.1 shows, Africa continues to experience a severe deterioration in terms of trade: 'Between 1970 and 1997, cumulative terms of trade losses for non-oil exporting countries in SSA amounted to 119 per cent of the regional GDP in 1997 and 51 and 68 per cent of the cumulative net resource flows and net resource transfers to the region, respectively' (UNCTAD 2001: 35–36).

Table 1.5 suggests that for every US$1 net capital inflow, Africa loses 25 cents to net interest payments and profit remittances. Terms of trade losses alone account for 51 cents. The effect is a net resource outflow from the continent. The UNCTAD report (2000: 36) argues that:

> The addition of such resources would have raised the investment ratio by nearly 6 percentage points per annum in non-oil-exporting countries of

Table 1.4 Investment and savings in sub-Saharan Africa, 1975–99

	1975–9	1980–4	1985–9	1990–4	1995–9
Sub-Saharan Africa					
Investment	23.1	17.7	16.0	17.4	19.1
Savings	19.3	13.6	13.7	13.8	15.3
Sub-Saharan Africa (excluding Nigeria)					
Investment	21.0	17.4	16.3	16.7	18.9
Savings	15.8	11.2	13.0	11.6	13.1
Sub-Saharan Africa (including South Africa)					
Investment	22.2	19.5	15.7	15.5	18.0
Savings	20.6	17.6	16.5	15.3	16.5

Source: UNCTAD 2001.

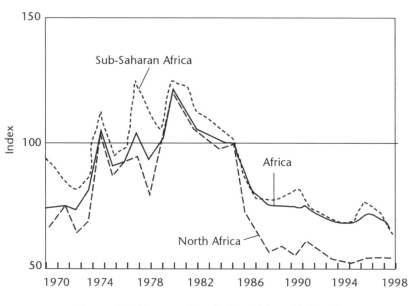

Figure 1.1 Terms of trade for Africa, 1970–98

Source: UNCTAD 2001.

Table 1.5 Breakdown of sub-Saharan African net resource flows

For every US $1 net capital inflow:	
Net interest payment & profit remittances abroad	25c
Capital outflow and reserve build-up	30c
Terms of trade losses	51c
Net resource flow	−6c

Source: UNCTAD 2001: 36.

Africa and added to annual growth by 1.4 per cent per annum. This would give a *per capita* GDP of $478 for 1997 instead of the actual level of $323. In other words, if non-oil-exporters in Africa had not suffered from continued terms of trade losses in the past two decades, the current level of *per capita* income would have been higher by as much as 50 per cent.

The paradox is that the terms-of-trade losses are not some immutable economic law, but the direct result of trade policies pursued by the same OECD countries that form the creditors' cartel to which sub-Saharan Africa 'owes' US$206.1 billion (2000 figures). In 1997, the estimated cost of the agricultural subsidies in the OECD countries was US$470 billion or $1.287 billion a day. Some of the already weak and insufficient provisions on special differential treatment that some of the African countries enjoyed under the Lomé Convention and the generalised system of preferences 'have been eliminated ... by the conditionalities imposed by Bretton Woods institutions and creditors' (UNCTAD 2001: 42)! The elimination of agricultural protection in the OECD countries would have meant an estimated gain for the sub-Saharan African economies of US$6 *per capita* or US$3,857.4 million, using 1999 population figures.

The essence of the discussion so far shows that the past twenty years of neo-liberal policies in Africa have failed to tackle important structural impediments to global trade. The argument in the NEPAD document, that what Africa needs to do is to integrate more fully into the global marketplace, mirrors the erroneous characterisation of African economies as 'closed'. The problem is not being averse to global integration; rather, it is that the trade regimes and practices of the powerful countries continue to deny African countries access to these markets – precisely in areas where Africa has the comparative advantage.[9]

The capacity of many African states to govern and regulate their societies and economies was severely undermined in the enforced retreat of the public sector in the heady days of neo-liberal orthodoxy. After years in which neo-liberal policies led to the severe contraction of the civil service, which was supposed to be bloated and unproductive, the World Bank has rediscovered that the size of the African civil service is insufficient for its population. After years of civil servant demoralisation and loss of prestige,[10] the Bank is devising programmes to rebuild the capacity that its policies destroyed in the last two decades. Either way, Bank staff and consultants win.

The paradox of adjustment is that the countries that have done fairly well by it (like Ghana and Uganda) have done so because of a quite unorthodox response to donor pressure and the relatively hegemonic nature of their regimes (cf. Hutchful 2002).

The post-Washington Consensus and the challenge of poverty

During the first wave of the deployment of neo-liberalism, extensive studies were undertaken on the social impact of the stabilisation and adjustment regimes. Some optimism has been expressed over the apparent shifts in the dominant representations of the neo-liberal agenda – especially in the rediscovery of poverty and expressions of social concern – in the centres of global capitalism. However, the underlying tendency remains the advancement of the neo-liberal programme. While it would be unfair to suggest that there has been no shift within the Bretton Woods institutions or the G8, for example, it is perhaps better to understand the apparent shift as something in the nature of a revolution – and neo-liberalism as an intensely successful (counter-) revolution. First generations are often extremely brash and 'bloody-minded', while successor generations are more likely to be more moderate in their orientation, and more media-conscious.

As Cheru (2001: 11) notes concerning the HIPC Initiative and the PRSP: 'the broad macro-economic objectives are inconsistent with the poverty reduction goals'. Although there are important differences between the original HIPC Initiative and the enhanced Initiative,[11] the fundamentals have hardly shifted. In the same way, the IMF's PRGF is a re-tagging of its earlier Enhanced Structural Adjustment Programme. In other words, we are dealing with different delivery vehicles for the same goods, but this shift in modes of representation is not new.

The implementation of such 'poverty-conscious' initiatives as HIPC and PRGF belie their representation. While the Bretton Woods institutions made concessions to Oxfam and UNICEF on greater 'involvement' of civil society (cf. Figueredo and Cheru 2000), a review of the implementation shows that 'the "template" for preparing the PRSP ... is designed by donors, which says very little about the authenticity of national ownership' (Cheru 2001: 14). In several cases, consultation with civil society around policy design was either ignored or a mere gesture, and even where there has been extensive consultation, the design of the macro-economic policies that underscore these 'poverty-conscious' projects was excluded from discussion.

A crisis at the heart of the new 'debt relief' and 'poverty reduction' programmes is that they are most unlikely to achieve these objectives. An Oxfam report, cited by Cheru (2001: 15), suggests that:

> Annual budget savings for most countries receiving HIPC debt relief would be modest. Some countries, including Senegal, Tanzania and Zambia, will emerge from the HIPC debt relief process in the perverse position of paying more in debt servicing. Debt payments will continue to absorb a disproportionately large share of government revenue, amounting to more than 15 per cent in six countries and to over 40 per cent in Zambia, Cameroon and Malawi.

The unsustainable level of debt even in the acclaimed success stories of structural adjustment, such as Ghana, continues to defy the logic of what can reasonably be defined as a success story. Between 1996 and 2000, Ghana's total debt escalated from a little over 120 per cent of GDP to over 185 per cent in 2000, before falling back slightly in 2001: the 40 percentage point escalation between 1999 and 2000 is accounted for by foreign debt. Ghana continues to experience a negative trade balance: US$1,246 million in 1999 and US$823 million in 2000 (IMF 2002: 31). Even by the rather optimistic projections of the IMF staff, the trade deficit will remain between US$775 million and US$822 million well into 2005. This picture applies across a range of macro-economic indicators (IMF 2002). Two decades into the micro-management of Ghana's economic and social life, the economy remains tied to primary products as sources of export earnings: cocoa and gold account for 74.5 per cent of export earnings. In 2000, cocoa prices were at a 27-year low, while oil prices (a major import) were at US$30 per barrel (IMF 2002: 8); in 2000, the same set of external shocks that plagued Ghana's economy in the 1960s and the 1970s remained.

An important example of the contradiction between macro-economic objectives and poverty reduction objectives is illustrated by the privatisation of water in Ghana. Two conditions were set for the release of new tranches under the HIPC Initiative: 'full cost recovery in the public utilities with automatic tariff adjustment formulae for electricity and water' (IMF 2002, para. 22). The IMF argued that this 'pricing reform is necessary to safeguard macro-economic stability, and hence the authorities have agreed that its implementation should be a condition for completion of the fifth review' under the PRGF Initiative (*ibid.*). An initial increase in water tariffs from 400 cedis to 800 cedis was implemented in May 2001. It is estimated that tariffs will escalate by another 300 per cent under the 2002 conditionality of the Bretton Woods institutions (Bretton Woods Project 2002). The conditionality of full cost recovery and automatic adjustments in tariffs protects international capital at the expense of ordinary Ghanaians. Under the terms of the privatisation of the management of water, the government of Ghana will still have the responsibility of raising an estimated US$500 million for upgrading the water infrastructure! Eight European transnational companies are bidding to lease the Ghanaian water infrastructure: four French, two British, one Dutch, and one Swedish companies (ISODEC, n.d.). This in a country where over 60 per cent of the population earn less than US$1 a day, 68 per cent lack sanitation services, and 35 per cent lack access to safe water (Africa Action 2002).

The demand for the privatisation of water delivery services is not made by the Bretton Woods institutions alone – the UK's Department for International Development has made the privatisation a condition for the release of a grant of £10 million to the government of Ghana (Christian Aid 2002: 2). The paradox is that building an inclusive globalisation project was the theme of UK Prime Minister Tony Blair's speech at the 2001 Labour Party Conference. He insisted that globalisation would fail if it only works for the few!

As the Coalition Against Privatisation argued, the privatisation of water services is not in the national interest of Ghana, much less the poor. It is 'the result of very deft political manoeuvrings by a consortium of donor countries committed to promoting the interests of their own corporate citizens' (Bretton Woods Project 2002). A public monopoly is being converted into a private monopoly under the control of European transnational water companies. The term imperialism, like class, does not seem fashionable anymore, even among the old left, but it is difficult to think of a more apt description.

Figueredo and Cheru (2000) have extensively covered the negative impact of stabilisation and adjustment in Zambia, especially in relation to the HIV/AIDS pandemic. The projected debt-service cost to the Zambian treasury, they argued, will increase from US$291 million in 1998 to US$392 million in 2000 and US$621 million in 2001. Debt service costs in 2001 are more than three and a half times the total social expenditure of the Zambian government in 1996.

The Nigerian case is no less disturbing. Between the end of 1999 and June 2001, when Nigeria's standby agreement with the IMF was up for renewal, a range of macro-economic conditions had deteriorated. The value of the naira had dropped 30 per cent, and inflation rose from 0.2 per cent in December 1999 to 18 per cent in March 2001. The central bank tried to rein in the run on the naira in the foreign exchange market by selling off dollars, only to find itself in a situation where the banks buy the dollars with one hand and sell it off with the other. Indeed, as early as the late 1980s, intermediation in the foreign exchange market was a major source of profit for banks and less formal currency market speculators. Efforts to control money supply ended up pushing up the cost of borrowing, and compounding imported inflation in an economy whose dependency was reinforced by trade liberalisation. Interest rates in the interbank market rose from 17 to 20 per cent for most of 2000, to between 30 and 40 per cent in 2001 (IMF 2001: 21). The IMF's assessment was to blame the government for not controlling spending, without any awareness of the effects of its capital account liberalisation and the very tight monetary policy recommended by Michel Camdessus at a public forum in Abuja in March 1999 – 'even if,' in his words, 'initially it gives rise to high interest rates' (quoted in the IMF Survey, 28, 7: 100).

The paradox of the debt overhang is quite striking in the Nigerian case. Of the total external debt stock of US$31,935 billion (78 per cent of GDP), 76.95 per cent (US$24 573 billion) is classified as bilateral debt. Of the bilateral debt, 99.44 per cent is owed to the Paris Club. More remarkably, US$21,589 billion (88.35 per cent) of the amount owed to the Paris Club is made up of the consolidation of arrears, penalties or capitalised moratorium interest, rather than new loans taken out by the country. In 1999 alone, interest payments accounted for 45.6 per cent of the total federal budget, and 59.6 per cent of all recurrent spending. Around US$1.9 billion was paid out to service external debt at the end of 1999; another US$1.5 billion was allocated for 2000. For 2002, US$1.7 billion was paid out in debt servicing.

In 1999, the federal government spent on interest payments 16.5 times its total spending on health, and 8.5 times its total spending on education. For 2002, the budget provision for debt servicing (a 'first call' budget item) is nearly 13 times more than total spending on health and almost eleven times the spending on all tiers of education. The debt-service-to-export ratio is expected to rise from 10 per cent in 2000 to 21 per cent in 2002, and 25 per cent in the medium term. By the IMF's estimation, Nigeria's external debt situation will worsen even in the medium-to-long term. Under an assumption that debt will not be rescheduled, it was expected that outstanding external debt would rise to 85 per cent of GDP in 2003 (IMF 2001: 70). Even under its best scenario – the rescheduling of 67 per cent of the net present value of the debt – the debt service will consume 18 per cent of total export earnings. Nigeria can expect to face 'a surge in debt service payments in 2005' and thereafter (IMF 2001: 72).

If foreign direct investment was to be the reward for macro-economic policies that are severely undercutting social development issues, evidence of the flow of foreign direct investment does not provide any room for optimism. Between 1995 and 2000, which were years of considerable difficulties, Africa's share of global FDI fell from 2 to 0.7 per cent (Basu and Srinivasan 2002: 6).

Africa's development and the challenge of poverty: beyond NEPAD

As noted at the beginning of this chapter, NEPAD is an initiative that requires serious engagement, precisely because it claims an African pedigree. The challenge of poverty for development needs to top the agenda of any serious African initiative. So far, we have argued (1) that NEPAD owes more to the Bretton Woods discourse than to other initiatives from United Nations agencies; (2) that the macro-economic orientation suggested in NEPAD is a call to persevere on the same path that Africa has been on for the past two decades; (3) that, where it suggests specific policies for poverty reduction, NEPAD has adopted the existing initiatives of the Bretton Woods initiatives; and (4) that, while it claims that it is not asking for more aid, we have shown that increased official development assistance (ODA) is an important component of its financing.

So what do we do with NEPAD? Not a lot, we will suggest, and this applies both to its content and to the nature of its politics. In its politics, NEPAD is donor-focused; it makes very little attempt to engage with Africans on whose behalf the initiative was supposed to have been designed. Precisely because it is donor-focused, NEPAD has not been able to address some important issues regarding trade regimes and policies. As shown earlier, about 50 per cent of the net resource loss to Africa is trade-related. While NEPAD acknowledges difficulties with trade access, this problem does not receive sufficient prominence. Yet the comparative advantage of an initiative such as NEPAD is to tackle what UNCTAD (2001: 47) called the 'asymmetries and imbalances in the global trading system', and some of the existing WTO agreements.

What Africa needs, and NEPAD seems incapable of providing, is a coherent platform for pooling the resources of the African countries for focused and effective trade negotiations, as well as a challenge to the prevailing norms within the WTO. For instance, several of the development policy options that were available to the East Asian developmental states are today illegal under the WTO rules: the agreements on trade-related investment measures (TRIMs) and trade-related intellectual property rights (TRIPs) are two such cases. While NEPAD refers to inherent inequities in the existing global trade regime, the behaviour of South Africa, its main sponsor, has in fact served to undermine the negotiating position of African countries within the WTO (cf. Keet 2002).

While debt cancellation is a stated Millennium Development Goal (MDG), NEPAD's preference has been to walk away from this in preferring the enhanced HIPC Initiative. Under Section 15 of the United Nations Millennium Declaration, the cancellation of all official bilateral debt was a commitment made to the heavily indebted poor countries 'in return for their making demonstrable commitments to poverty reduction' (United Nations 2000). More specifically for Africa, Section 28 of the Declaration involved a stated commitment to taking 'special measures to address the challenges of poverty eradication and sustainable development in Africa, *including debt cancellation*' (emphasis added). The failure to press for the declared goal secured at the level of the United Nations (and to which the G8 countries are morally bound) demonstrates a failure of policy on the part of those who drafted the NEPAD document. The silence on debt cancellation as a stated MDG is mirrored by the World Bank.[12]

The debt overhang remains a major drain on African economies and efforts to tackle the social sector crisis facing many African countries. The crises are themselves not separate from the enforcement of the liberalisation agenda of the Bretton Woods institutions and the debt crisis. A situation where an ostensibly Africa-focused and Africa-owned champion walks away from such an important (if limited) gain as the cancellation of bilateral debt seems incomprehensible. The impact in Nigeria's case of securing this advantage would have been significant: it would have meant the cancellation of 77 per cent of its debt overhang. The failure of policy that NEPAD embodies – concerning the debt and poverty issues, for instance – owes much to the macro-economic policies of South Africa since 1996. While internal policy is important, not laying to rest the issues of debt and trade regimes will continue to undermine the efforts of African countries. Neither will African countries need the type of ODA that continues to nurture dependency of a subordinate nature.

The enthusiasm expressed for neo-liberalism and the amount of effort being devoted to preparing the institutional framework for a market-friendly investment environment seem naïve in the light of available evidence about the practical working of neo-liberal globalisation. The 2001 UNCTAD report shows clearly that in almost all the African countries, except Mauritius, Egypt and South Africa, there was widespread erosion of real wages (between 25 and 45 per cent) between 1985 and 1998. The South African figure may hide the considerable instability within the labour market. For instance, between 1994 and 1997 there was a net loss of 423,000 jobs, and between June 1998 and March 2001 a further loss of 300,130 jobs (Adésínà 2001). This is in the context of an increase in the working-age population from 20.86 million in 1994 to 27.64 million in February 2001, and a declining proportion of economically active people (Statistics South Africa 2001). A significant aspect of this trend is what looks like a shift in the structure of the labour market: while 394,432 full-time jobs disappeared in the industrial sector between June 1998 and March 2001, 92,302 part-time jobs were created. The labour market crisis is inexorably linked to issues of livelihood and poverty. We raise this because the South African economy is one of the most robust and by far the biggest on the continent. Yet its labour market experience has been compounded by increased volatility in the exchange rate, due in part to the same exposure to the forces of neo-liberal globalisation that NEPAD is promoting.

While a private-sector-led development trajectory may be the concern of the Bretton Woods institutions and their handlers, the development of capitalism takes diverse forms. The narrowing of the role of the state to tending the stable for private capital flies in the face of past and present lessons for successful growth economies. Privatisation is not necessarily the *sine qua non* for successful economic performance. The contrasting experiences of Russia and China are quite compelling:

> China extended the scope of competition without privatising state-owned enterprises .... Chinese policymakers not only eschewed a strategy of outright privatisation, they also failed to incorporate numerous other elements of the (orthodox) Washington Consensus (Stiglitz 1998: 22).

As Stiglitz further noted, if the thirty provinces of China were separate countries, they would account for the twenty fastest-growing economies in the world between 1978 and 1995. Russia, on the other hand, under the pressure of the Bretton Woods strategy of forcing through policies before the window of opportunity for reform closed, was stampeded into a programme of privatisation without an adequate regulatory environment or competition. The result was that Russia's output in 1998 was below the level of the previous decade of the Soviet Union. The widespread collapse in social indicators and the upsurge in poverty are two consequences of a reform that was driven more by ideology than common sense.

Nigeria's recent experience with the privatisation of its national telecommunications carrier is also a lesson in how not to privatise. The external and internal promoters of the privatisation programme were more concerned with selling off the state-owned enterprise than with recognising the severe recession in the global telecommunications industry. Five months after the sale of 51 per cent equity to a consortium, the deal fell through because the consortium could not raise the necessary funds to cover the US$1.3 billion.

Finally, the experience of taking the rhetoric of liberalisation at face value is that governments tend to lose control over their own macro-economic programmes, in terms of policy choice and the social agenda they could pursue. The drive to knock down every obstacle to the unrestricted movement of capital is not inherent in globalisation; it is when globalisation becomes a weapon in the hands of global financiers that self-interest is presented as something in the interests of humanity. It is one of the abiding intellectual crises of the authors of the NEPAD document that they confused global interconnectedness (via information technology) with the demand for unrestricted access by transnational capital to all national economies (pervasive trade liberalisation). The latter is both a distinct phase in the evolution of capitalism and an attempt to deal with the crisis of over-accumulation in the North. Furthermore, the authors of NEPAD confused neo-liberal ideology with its practice, yet the actual practice of the countries and agencies insisting on developing countries implementing full liberalisation is to practise the reverse where they perceive their 'national' interests to be at stake. Nowhere is this more apparent than in the US and EU policies on agriculture.

The deflationary bias inherent in neo-liberalism does not serve national or continental interest when embedding poverty reduction in macro-economic policies is an objective. Even at the level of macro-economic policy making, the deeper the level of liberalisation, the fewer the policy options available to the state. It is paradoxical that at the time that NEPAD seeks to re-make African states' development, it recommends a framework that weakens the capacity of the state to deliver. Yet the structure of many of these economies is fundamentally different from those at the heart of a neo-liberal regime. Stiglitz (1998) makes for interesting reading on how a US government took a very unorthodox approach to the management of its own economy, at the same time as staff of its Treasury Department (most notably Lawrence Summers) were acting as enforcers for the Bretton Woods programme of orthodox neo-liberalism. The example of the privatisation of the management of water projects in Ghana demonstrates the gap between the claims of poverty reduction as an inherent part of the neo-liberal regime and facilitating the penetration of African markets – even in the provision of water. The idea of automatic adjustments of tariff for full cost recovery is tied to the exchange rate, which is not a tradable (a commodity that can be exported or imported). The objective is essentially to protect the European companies that will run the water services against inherent instability in the Ghanaian exchange rate.

Meeting the challenge of poverty is multifaceted. While current practice within the World Bank and IMF is to use targeting and a safety net approach to poverty alleviation, an African agenda needs to move beyond this approach. Poverty reduction in Africa is as much about raising the productive capacity of economies as it is about specific social policy. Neo-liberalism, with its deflationary bias, would seem inappropriate. In 1994, we argued that much of what the World Bank and IMF were doing in Africa qualified as relentless social vivisection (Adésínà 1994: viii). For instance, policies that create massive contraction in the labour market will be poverty-inducing. The regime of targeting as a means for accessing social services also undermines social inclusion and equity. We are unaware of any study that compares the cost of erecting the infrastructure of targeted anti-poverty measures with universal entitlement, but it would be a useful comparison. Universal entitlement to social services not only removes the stigma of accessing the services (Elson 2001), but has the advantage of enhancing a socially inclusive milieu in the country or community. While the issue of financing almost always comes up when the idea of universal entitlement is raised, the experience of several African countries in the period 1960–80 demonstrates how much can be done with so little in terms of social service delivery. Moreover, the link between economic growth and human development is much more than the two sides of the balance sheet that Wolfensohn suggests. Investment in education and health nurtures growth; growth improves the capacity to expand and deepen social policy.

Conclusion

NEPAD is both an opportunity and a challenge. It is an opportunity because, in putting the idea of a continental development agenda on the table, it renews debate about Africa's development future. However, NEPAD remains a challenge because it is driven by a discourse that is based on a distorted reading of Africa's post-colonial experience and the current challenges. Its origin in South Africa may explain the considerable concern with global engagement and its neo-liberal macro-economic orientation, but that would not account for the number of African governments that have joined the initiative. It may reflect the new corps of African heads of state whose politics is defined by the global neo-liberal counter-revolution. Our argument is that the seeming embrace of neo-liberalism demonstrates a weak reading of the continent's experience of the past two decades as well as the variety of experiences with capitalism. The very policy framework that has deepened the crisis and widened poverty cannot be the platform for meeting the challenges of development and poverty. In spite of NEPAD's marketing as an anti-poverty development agenda, neither poverty reduction nor human resource development, broadly, features on its list of priority sectors. Historically, success in combating poverty has required a highly focused approach that transcends the 'equity/growth' trade-off thinking of the neo-classical economists, which is immanent in NEPAD itself.

The politics of NEPAD, expressed in its marketing, remains the greatest concern. From inception, the programme has seemed donor-focused. There would seem to be more awareness about its content in the donor community than among the people the initiative is supposed to serve. This is not simply a problem of access or communication; awareness of what it contains and actually says is as limited in South Africa as elsewhere on the continent. It is partly because its authors are driven by the same technocratic approach to policy making that the Bretton Woods institutions have favoured since the early 1980s – shutting the public away from the arena of macro-economic policy formulation. Policy crises are thereafter defined as matters of communication and marketing: to get the public on board a wagon they did not help to construct in the first instance. NEPAD is itself rooted in this illiberal approach to making neo-liberal economic policies.

NOTES

1 See <http://www.dfa.gov.za/events/map.htm>. MAP, it seems, stands as an acronym for several things: Millennium African Renaissance Partnership Programme; Millennium Action Plan, etcetera The NEPAD Secretariat website (<www.nepad.com>) suggests that MAP went through at least three drafts.

2 The Act aims to establish a fund 'to enhance cooperation between the Republic and other countries, in particular African countries, through the promotion of democracy, good governance, the prevention and resolution of conflict, *socio-economic* development and integration, humanitarian assistance and human resource development' (RSA 2000; emphasis in original).

3 According to the NEPAD document (NEPAD 2001: paras 200–1), the Implementation Committee comprises the heads of state of Algeria, Egypt, Nigeria, Senegal and South Africa, plus ten others (two from each of the AU's five regions). It is responsible for (a) 'identifying strategic issues that need to be researched, planned and managed at the continental level'; (b) setting up mechanisms reviewing progress on agreed targets and standards, and (c) 'review(ing) progress on implementation of past decisions' to rectify problems and eliminate delays. Five task teams were established: on capacity building in peace and security; economic and corporate governance; infrastructure; a central bank and financial standards; and agriculture and market access.

4 The Social Dimension of Adjustment programme was supposed to be a joint programme of the World Bank, UNDP and African Development Bank, but it was effectively taken over by the World Bank. A programme that emerged out of the policy impacts of this action was meant to audit the policies that were implemented by it – undermining the intention of independence in the assessment of the social consequences of structural adjustment.

5 As Rogoff (1985: 1187) puts it, 'society' is better off having a central banker that places '"too large" a weight on inflation rate stabilization' relative to social welfare. The case for an independent and conservative central banker with considerable discretionary power to move beyond fixed monetary targets was made on the grounds that such an individual is shielded from public pressure.

The impact of central bank conservatism on trade unions has been a major component of the debate. As Berger *et al.* (2002: 3) put it, the move amounted to 'delegating monetary policy to an independent and conservative central bank, which cares less about unemployment than the government does'.

6 These include the 1990 World Summit for Children, the 1992 UN Conference on Environment and Development and, more significantly, the 1995 World Summit for Social Development, as well as the 2000 Social Summit (Copenhagen + 5) in Geneva, all of which built up to the Millennium Summit (Ohiorhenuan 2002).

7 'On the left,' he argued, 'is the macro-economic presentation .... There is, however, a clear need for a second side which reflects more adequately an analytical framework that presents the structural, social, and human aspects ... beyond the familiar statistics of infant and maternal mortality, unemployment and children in school, to address fundamental long-term issues of the structure, scope and substance of societal development' (Wolfensohn 1999: 4–5). Sustainable growth and poverty alleviation were (re-)adopted by the IMF and World Bank.

8 These are Ghana, Côte d'Ivoire, Uganda, Ethiopia, Eritrea and Morocco.

9 The main actors in these trade regimes are the same G8 countries that the sponsors of NEPAD appeal to, as if these regimes were mere outcomes of nasty-mindedness of the heads of the government of these countries rather than matters of *realpolitik* and internal political interests.

10 Up to the late 1970s in Nigeria, the civil service would not employ a university graduate in the administrative cadre unless s/he graduated in the First or Second Class (Upper) Divisions. The private sector did not bother employing anyone who graduated in the First Class Division: the university (public sector) would have been the natural direction of employment. Both the civil service and the universities have now suffered a considerable loss of prestige, making them unattractive to most who graduate in the First or Second Class (Upper) Division.

11 This is mainly in connection with the length of the period of compliance with the conditionalities set by the Bretton Woods institutions before a country becomes eligible (from six years to three years), and the seeming commitment to a more socially inclusive policy design mechanism.

12 The World Bank's website devoted to the MDGs (<http://www.develop-mentgoals.org>) fudges the debt cancellation aspect of the MDGs. While acknowledging the goal of cancellation of bilateral debt, it subsumes all debt issues under the HIPC Initiative. There is no acknowledgment of Section 28 of the Millennium Declaration. While one can understand this in an institution that survives on the proceeds of debt repayments, it is difficult to understand why the leaders of countries for which Section 28 was a landmark gain would fail to press the advantage home.

REFERENCES

Adésínà, 'J., 1994, *Labour in the Explanation of an African Crisis*, Dakar: Codesria.
—— 2001, 'Labour Market and the Challenge of Development', keynote address to the Provincial Consultative Conference on Labour Market Information and Skills Development, East London, South Africa, 16 August.
—— 2002, 'Neoliberalism, Labour and the Dilemma of Democracy: the Nigerian

Case', paper presented at the CASS/OSIWA conference on 'Democracy in Nigeria: the Journey so Far', Abuja, Nigeria, 18–20 February.

Africa Action, 2002, 'Ghana Water Privatization: Update', 14 March, <http://www.africaaction.org/docs02/wat0203.htm>.

Basu, A. and K. Srinivasan, 2002, *Foreign Direct Investment in Africa: Some Case Studies*, Washington DC: International Monetary Fund.

Beckman, Bjorn, 1992. 'Empowerment or Repression? The World Bank and the Politics of African Adjustment', in P. Gibbon, Y. Bangura and A. Ofstad (eds.), *Authoritarianism, Democracy and Adjustment*, Seminar Proceedings No. 26, Uppsala: The Scandinavian Institute of African Studies, pp. 83–105.

Berger, H., C. Hefeker and R. Schöb, 2002, *Optimal Central Bank Conservatism and Monopoly Trade Unions*, Washington DC: International Monetary Fund.

Bretton Woods Project, 2002, 'Ghanaians Contest Bank-backed Water Privatisation', <http://www.brettonwoodsproject.org/topic/privatesector/p2701ghanawater. html>.

Cheru, F. 2001, 'The Highly Indebted Poor Countries (HIPC) Initiative: a Human Rights Assessment of the Poverty Reduction Strategy Papers (PRSP)', Independent Expert Report to the 57th session of UN Commission on Human Rights, Geneva: Unesco.

Christian Aid, 2002, *Master or Servant*, London: Christian Aid.

Elson, D., 2001, 'For an Emancipatory Socio-Economics', draft paper prepared for the UNRISD meeting on 'The Need to Rethink Development Economics', Cape Town, 7–8 September.

Figueredo, R. and F. Cheru, 2000, 'Debt Relief and Social Investment', Report of the Special Rapporteur and Independent Expert to the 56th Session of the UN Commission on Human Rights, Geneva: Unesco.

Ghai, D., 1987, 'Successes and Failures in Growth in Sub-Saharan Africa: 1960–1982', in Louis Emmerij (ed.), *Development Policies and the Crisis of the 1980s*, Paris: Organisation for Economic Cooperation and Development.

Hutchful, E., 2002, *Ghana's Adjustment Experience: the Paradox of Reform*, Oxford: James Currey.

International Monetary Fund, 1999, 'Camdessus Sees Governance as Key to Nigeria's Reform, Pledges IMF's Support', IMF Survey, 28, 7.

—— 2001, *Nigeria: 2001 Article IV Consultation – Staff Report; Staff Statement; and Public Information Notice on the Executive Board Discussion*, Washington DC: IMF.

—— 2002, *Ghana: Fourth Review under the Poverty Reduction and Growth Facility, Request for Waiver of Performance Criteria and for Extension of the Commitment Period – Staff Report; Staff Statements*, Washington DC: IMF.

ISODEC, n.d., 'Why Water Privatization in Ghana Must Be Stopped', London: Christian Aid.

Keet, D., 2002, *South Africa's Official Position and Role in Promoting the World Trade Organisation*, Cape Town: AIDC.

Mbeki, T., 2001, 'Millennium Africa Renaissance Program: Implementation Issues Briefing at the World Economic Forum Meeting', 28 January. Available at <http://www.nepad.com>.

Mkandawire, T., 2001a, *Social Policy in a Development Context*, Geneva: UNRISD.

—— 2001b, 'Thinking about Developmental States in Africa', *Cambridge Journal of Economics*, 25.

Mkandawire, T. and V. Rodriquez, 2000, *Globalization and Social Development after Copenhagen: Premises, Promises and Policies*, Geneva: UNRISD.

NEPAD, 2001, The New Partnership for Africa's Development (NEPAD), Midrand: NEPAD Secretariat.

Ohiorhenuan, J., 2002, 'The Management of African Development: Some Questions about NEPAD', public lecture delivered at the Rhodes University 'Public Policy Dialogue Series', East London, South Africa, 18 April.

Olukoshi, A., 1998, The Elusive Prince of Denmark: Structural Adjustment and the Crisis of Governance in Africa, Uppsala: Nordic Africa Institute.

RSA (Republic of South Africa), 2000, 'African Renaissance and International Cooperation Fund Act (No. 51), 2000', Government Gazette, Vol. 425.

Rogoff, K., 1985, 'The Optimal Degree of Commitment to an Intermediate Monetary Target', Quarterly Journal of Economics, 100, 4 (November).

Statistics South Africa, 2001, (http://www.statssa.gov.za/u&e/Chapter_ 2.htm).

Stiglitz, J. E., 1998, 'More Instruments and Broader Goals: Moving towards the Post-Washington Consensus', WIDER Annual Lecture, UNU World Institute for Development Economics Research, Helsinki.

Toye, J., 1994, 'Structural Adjustment: Context, Assumptions, Origin and Diversity', in Rolph van der Hoeven and Fred van der Kraaij (eds.), Structural Adjustment and Beyond in Sub-Saharan Africa, Oxford: James Currey.

UNCTAD, 2001, Economic Development in Africa: Performance, Prospects and Policy Issues, Geneva: United Nations Conference on Trade and Development.

United Nations, 2000, 'Resolution adopted by the General Assembly: 55/2. United Nations Millennium Declaration', New York: United Nations.

Wade, A., 2001, Omega Plan for Africa: an African Strategy for Globalisation, Dakar: Republic of Senegal.

Wolfensohn, J. D., 1999, 'A Proposal for a Comprehensive Development Framework: a Discussion Draft', Memorandum to the World Bank, 21 January, mimeo.

World Bank, 2000a, Comprehensive Development Framework, Washington DC: World Bank.

—— 2000b, 'The Cost of Attaining the Millennium Development Goals', mimeo.

—— 2001a, World Development Report 2000/1: Attacking Poverty, New York: Oxford University Press.

—— 2001b, Global Development Finance: Building Coalitions for Effective Development Finance, Washington DC: World Bank.

Wuyts, M., 2001, 'Inequality and Poverty as the Condition of Labour', paper prepared for discussion at the UNRISD meeting on 'The Need to Rethink Development Economics', Cape Town, South Africa, 7–8 September.

2 NEPAD and the Global Political Economy

Towards the African Century or
Another False Start?

Ian Taylor

In the last few years, a developmental agenda has been advanced by leading African élites aimed at revitalising Africa's place in the global political economy. This culminated in the launch on 11 July 2001 at the last OAU (soon to be the African Union) summit in Lusaka of the so-called New African Initiative. This was subsequently renamed, in Abuja on 23 October 2001, the New Partnership for Africa's Development (NEPAD). The leaders of Algeria, Egypt, Nigeria, Senegal and South Africa have been at the forefront of this movement and have been advancing what may turn out to be an interesting new period in Africa's relations with the developed world, particularly in the post-Seattle period.

This chapter aims to investigate what exactly this new developmental agenda stands for and what is 'new', if anything, about the positions being advanced by leading exponents of this group, as crystallised by NEPAD. The role of South Africa's Thabo Mbeki is examined, although not exclusively, as his voice has been among the loudest in promoting the project around the globe. The chapter contends that NEPAD is granted a hearing precisely because the message communicated fits the neo-liberal discourse and avoids blaming particular policies or global trade structures for Africa's marginalisation but rather, if pushed, simply assigns the blame to 'globalisation'. In addition, the leading African élites promoting NEPAD have gained the North's seal of approval regarding their outward commitment to liberal democracy and market economics, and are held up as models from which the rest of the continent should learn. It will be indicated why this is problematic.[1]

This does not mean that I see no merits in the New Partnership for Africa's Development. In many respects, it is one of the best documents to emerge from the African political élite for a considerable time. In particular, its publicised commitment to the developmental needs of the African people is appreciated, as are the attempts being made to penetrate the shield of sovereignty behind which too many corrupt leaders have hidden. But I fear that these noble goals may be undermined by the broader global power games that the G8 countries are clearly out to play with this new generation of African leaders. I am also concerned that there is no obvious strategy to be found in NEPAD to counter these power games, and that some of the language used, and some of the economic measures proposed in the document, play into the hands of the G8 strategists. Indeed, as South Africa becomes 'just another country' in terms of its foreign policy, and bearing in mind its leading role in pushing NEPAD forward, concern is expressed over the 'policy fit' between Northern élites and their counterparts in *some* African states.[2]

NEPAD and the global political economy

Thabo Mbeki has been lauded as a leading light in promoting the run-up to the launch of NEPAD: according to the *Mail and Guardian* of 14–20 July 2000, 'as a result of his recent interventions, Mbeki has emerged over the past six months [January–June 2000] as the developing countries' single most important voice in the world economy'. This voice frequently resonates with a chorus of well-identified African allies. According to one report, 'a tough triumvirate of African leaders ... South Africa's Thabo Mbeki, Nigeria's Olusegun Obasanjo and Algeria's Abdelaziz Bouteflika ... dominate Africa's continental club, the Organisation of African Unity (OAU). With their good political and diplomatic track-records, the three [are] taken seriously in Africa and in the West' (Smith 2000).

As chair of the Non-Aligned Movement (NAM), South Africa has led this organisation in a series of negotiations with the G8 countries, trying to convince them, along solidly orthodox lines, to improve the conditions for Africa's place in the global economy.[3] For instance, South Africa used its statement at the Africa–EU Summit, held in Cairo in April 2000, to make an impassioned plea for an end to Africa's economic marginalisation and to human suffering on the continent. In a similar way, Mbeki used his speech at the 54th Session of the United Nations General Assembly in September 1999, and particularly his address as chairperson of the NAM at the opening of the South Summit in Havana in 2000, to develop an eloquent plea for the introduction of what he calls a global 'caring society' to soften the harsher aspects of global capitalism. Such activism has fitted Mbeki's much-touted African Renaissance, which, although devoid of any meaningful content (uplifting rhetoric aside), has underpinned post-apartheid South Africa's foreign policy, particularly since Nelson Mandela stepped down (Taylor and Williams 2001; Ajulu

2001). However, this renaissance has been criticised, much as NEPAD has, for fitting the Northern-dominated hegemonic order rather too snugly. As one critical commentary put it,

> The African Renaissance suggests a continental effort led by South Africa to advance the familiar 'end-of-history' thesis … South Africa's African Renaissance (this choice of words is important) is anchored in a chain of economies which, with time, might become the African equivalent of the Asian Tigers…. In this rendition, the African Renaissance posits Africa as an expanding and prosperous market alongside Asia, Europe and North America in which South African capital is destined to play a special role through the development of trade, strategic partnerships and the like. In exchange for acting as the agent of globalisation, the continent will offer South Africa a preferential option on its traditionally promised largesse of oil, minerals and mining. (Vale and Maseko 1998: 279)

Mbeki and other African élites are increasingly playing a prominent role in discussions relating to reform of the international political economy. Indeed, the presence of Mbeki, Obasanjo, and Bouteflika at the Group of Seven Countries (G7) Okinawa summit in July 2000, Mbeki's guest appearance at the EU summit in Portugal in late 2000, and the prominent role these leaders played at the United Nations Millennium Summit in September 2000 – as well as at the Davos 2001 meeting of the World Economic Forum (notable for the lack of attendance by assembled élites during Mbeki's session) and the Genoa G8 summit – all illustrate the status that they currently enjoy. The fact that President Bouteflika was the first active president to give a presentation at the closing session of the 53rd Annual UN Conference is an indication of the high-profile role members of this reformist group have assumed in recent months. Indeed, it seems as if the twenty-first century is starting with a concerted push by key African state élites to put development back on the international agenda after a decade of post-Cold War neglect and marginalisation. One source claimed that such dialogue 'represented a growing consensus among countries of the South to engage with the wealthiest countries … on the need to examine, collectively with the South, the global economic system and its impact on developing countries' (Mahatey 2000).

Having incorporated Senegal's Abdoulaye Wade's Omega Plan into the Millennium Africa Renaissance Programme, NEPAD now seeks to cultivate some sort of fellowship with the North. This idea of a 'partnership' between the North and Africa, aimed at reversing the growing income disparities in the world, has been readily endorsed by various world leaders.[4] In his report aimed at the United Nations Millennium Summit of Heads of State and Government in September 2000, Kofi Annan also endorsed the idea of a 'partnership' between North and

South, specifically aimed at the target of halving the proportion of people living in extreme poverty, and lifting more than one billion people out of it, by 2015.

At first glance, the high-energy diplomatic initiatives pursued by NEPAD's promoters, either singly or in concert, suggests a positive development for the continent. After all, rather than continuing to place the blame for the continent's woes on the colonial legacy or on a philosophy underpinned by *dependencia* – both 'explanations' having lost their currency in the North – this grouping is engaging the developed world on its own terms, arguing for liberalisation and free trade and for globalisation. This engagement and the calls for partnership are far more likely to gain a hearing in London or Washington than the rhetoric of anti-imperialism and appeals for special treatment. But it is this very acceptability, this 'fit', that carries within it the danger that the message of this group will serve to legitimise (perhaps unwittingly) existing global power relations rather than restructure them. Asserting that Africa must 'gel' with the world, as one report put it, without interrogating the structural situation within which the continent (and the South in general) finds itself, is highly problematic (see 'Mbeki: SA Must "Gel" with World', *Citizen*, Johannesburg, 12 February 2001). Furthermore, the agenda that they seek to push holds within it the seeds of the further marginalisation of the majority of Africa's peoples, while granting a highly privileged stratum of African élites the potential to benefit from the ongoing globalisation process. Indeed, a main criticism of the initiatives being advanced is that they serve the interests of externally oriented fractions within key (comparatively developed) African states, while leaving the rest of the continent to sink or swim, as it were, with the globalisation current. Motives for their activism were summed up by one source as being 'drawn together because these middle-income developing countries were all feeling the pinch of Northern projectionist trade policies' (Khan 2000). Making neo-liberalism somehow 'work for all', rather than rethinking the overall global trading system, is the key strategy of South Africa particularly and NEPAD more generally (Taylor 2001a). We now turn to the link between globalisation, export-driven trade policies and a nascent transnational élite in Africa.

Globalisation and an emerging transnational élite

Concomitant with notions of globalisation is the three-fold domination of the world, by (a) transnational capital, (b) the hegemony of neo-liberalism, and (c) the emergence of a global historic bloc (Harris and Robinson 2000: 2). This last feature of our contemporary world is led by what may be termed an emergent transnational capitalist class: 'Today, transnational class relations cannot be ignored. Just as capital, production, labour and culture have become globalised, classes too are increasingly becoming transnational' (Embong 2000: 990). This fraction does not openly admit itself as a class *per se*. However, it would be accurate to say that it has 'attained a clearly distinctive class consciousness' with an 'awareness of a common concern to maintain the system that enables the class to remain dominant' (Cox 1987: 358–9). This global élite comprises transnational executives and their affiliates; globalising state bureaucrats; capitalist-inspired politicians and professionals; and consumerist élites (Sklair 1997). Originating in the capitalist core, this transnational élite is increasingly developing linkages with like-minded parties in the South to form a truly global élite. The élites promoting NEPAD may be seen as key representatives of this phenomenon.

Having said that, it is important to recognise that this is no monolithic bloc advancing a unified and uncontested agenda. The fractions from which this transnational historic bloc are drawn share a fundamental principle – the maintenance of global capitalism – but outside of this core concern, tensions and disagreement mark their interactions with one another. Indeed, 'fierce competition among oligopolist clusters, conflicting pressures, and differences over the tactics and strategy of maintaining class domination and addressing the crises and contradictions of global capitalism make any real internal unity in the global ruling class impossible' (Robinson 1998). Nevertheless, such a transnational élite has become increasingly aware of shared values and interests that transcend petty and immediate strategies. This has been facilitated by an emerging network made up of 'transformed and externally integrated national states, together with ... supranational economic and political forums' (Harris and Robinson 2000: 27). The economic forums are institutions such as the World Bank, the IMF, the WTO and regional banks. The political forums include the G8, the G22, the OECD, the European Union, the United Nations system, and so on: 'It is through these global institutions that the [transnational élite] has been attempting to forge a new global capitalist hegemonic bloc' (ibid.: 28). The developing world's élites have been inexorably drawn into this process, with the 'leading capitalist groups in the Third World [having] transnationalised by integrating into global circuits of accumulation through a variety of mechanisms, ranging from subcontracting for global corporations, the purchase of foreign equity shares, mergers with corporations from other countries, joint ventures and increasing foreign direct investment (FDI) abroad of their own capital' (ibid.: 4).

However, as this brave new world has been built, tensions and contradictions have been increasing and cracks in the monolith (the unity of which was always exaggerated) have now developed into potential cleavages. The crowning moment so far in this ongoing process was at the WTO meeting in Seattle in November 1999, but previous open disagreements between the IMF and World Bank already hinted that the Washington Consensus was increasingly under threat (see Naim 2000). Indeed, for perhaps the first time, the voices of the South, which had long criticised the one-size-fits-all programmes of the international financial institutions, were now no longer disregarded: much of their criticism seemed to be taken on board. This was graphically shown at the 2001 meeting of the World Economic Forum (WEF). Whereas in the main, previous WEF meetings had been summits of the great and the good converging in a celebratory (if not self-congratulatory) jamboree in praise of globalisation and the free market, concern over the direction globalisation was taking now marked out clear differences at this conference of the transnational élite. This consciousness, sensitised post-Seattle, has meant that a certain space has opened up for (limited) questioning of the globalisation litany. As *Business Day* newspaper of 29 January 2001 put it,

> the greater receptiveness to the developing world's concerns has everything to do with the WEF's realisation of a widespread backlash against globalisation.... It recognises the belief amongst the world's poor that globalisation has brought more benefits to the richer developed countries than to the poorer developing countries.... This year's Davos gives more attention to this backlash against globalisation, recognising that earlier ... expressions of intent to narrow wealth discrepancies have not yet borne much fruit.

Similarly, the July 2001 G8 summit in Genoa, with the much-publicised welcoming stance towards NEPAD, did seem to indicate that the North's élites were now somewhat concerned. Tellingly, and in a perhaps unintentional – but still damning – indictment of the G8's track record on priorities, Italian foreign minister Renato Ruggiero claimed that 'the G8 is, *for the first time in its history* [emphasis added] dealing with the questions of poverty [and] access of the commodities from the developing South to international markets' (as quoted in *Business Day*, 24 July 2001). But equally, as one commentator in the *Mail & Guardian* newspaper (27 July–2 August 2001) put it, 'it was inevitable that [NEPAD] would be well received by the G8 since it was spot on in terms of timing and political correctness. When you have rioters trashing Genoa in the name of kinder Third World treatment, no politician is going to say it is a bad idea.'

Is the seeming ready response to the NEPAD genuine or not? Certainly, widespread political unease among African élites at the social cost of liberalisation and economic restructuring, as well as growing protests against globalisation in all its myriad forms by massed ranks of protesters at every transnational meeting point mean that global élites must contend with a number of major issues at the turn of the new millennium. Whilst opposition to globalisation has also been building in the North, it has been relatively well contained – trashings of downtown Seattle, Prague, Gothenburg and Genoa notwithstanding. Such protests and riots should not be belittled, however: they have, by all appearances, rattled the composure of the Northern élites. The fact that African élites now also give voice to some of the concerns, although arguably as incoherently as the masked anarchists do, means that issues surrounding the continued thrust and direction of globalisation need to be taken seriously in the global power centres. Indeed, a number of African leaders have been quite active in the debates surrounding strategic questions related to the world order. Having said that, the inherent limitations for Africa within such a debate are important if we are to understand the potential within the agenda professed by certain African élites. Although South African spin doctors claimed that Thabo Mbeki was 'at the helm of the most imaginative and resolute plan yet to emerge from Africa', other commentators have remarked that NEPAD was 'not the most radical documents ever but, because of that, there is more chance that the G8 leaders will buy into it' (quoted in the South African newspapers Business Day of 24 July 2001 and Sunday Independent of 22 July 2001). So, various tensions, both within readings of the potential of the NEPAD's agenda, as well as intra-élite strains, are of intense interest. Interrogating such tensions demonstrates a profound weakness in any optimistic assessment of the project and certainly places in perspective any appraisal that seeks to cast the emerging project as symbolised by NEPAD as a new international economic order for our post-hegemonic era.

North versus South? Not quite

Although media coverage at Seattle was given over to the antipathies displayed by élite delegations from the developing world, it is clear that the objections raised by these delegations were a pot-pourri of – often contradictory – agendas, ranging from the demand for global reform, to special or equal treatment for Southern exporters. Frustration at the North's apparent haughtiness in its treatment of the South, particularly African representatives, contributed to the build-up of pressure at the meeting –which eventually boiled over and caused the abortion of the summit. However, it must be emphasised that, in the main, what élites from the South were advocating was not a radical restructuring of the global capitalist order, despite the more optimistic accounts advanced by their self-proclaimed allies (largely Northern-based 'solidarity' groupings). Instead, what most Southern delegations were pressing for was increased access to the world market for externally oriented fractions of the South, as well as a greater part in administering the world system. Far from stopping globalisation, the élites were actually pushing for greater integration into the global capitalist order, but on renegotiated terms that favour externally oriented Southern élites. The actual neo-liberal underpinnings of the global market are presumed to be sacrosanct. As Trevor Manuel (1998), South Africa's finance minister, asserted, 'There is a new resilience and a new will to succeed in the African continent. We in South Africa have called it a renaissance, a new vision of political and economic renewal. It takes the global competitive marketplace as point of departure.'

This position, an essential acceptance of the basic tenets of the world order, reflects the actuality that élites from Africa are, in the main, just as interested in maintaining the global system as their colleagues in the North. Reflecting on the monumental sea-change of the 1980s regarding macro-economic common sense, one account has remarked that:

> Third World élites were not the passive victims of the US liquidation of the development project. At least some fractions of such élites were among the strongest supporters of the new Washington Consensus through which the liquidation was accomplished. To the extent that this has been the case, Third World élites have been among the social forces that have promoted the liberalisation of trade and capital movements. (Silver and Arrighi 2000: 66–7)

Thus, imagining that resistance to neo-liberalism might be located in the élites of the South is, to put it mildly, naïve. As if to prove my point, the reforms being advocated by the supporters of NEPAD are increasingly cast as sensible strategic choices to defend worldwide neo-liberalism from some sort of populist reaction. The United Nations Secretary-General (quoted in Business Day, 16 February 2001) has made this quite explicit, stating that 'the unequal distribution of benefits and the imbalance of global rule making which characterises globalisation today inevitably will produce backlash and protectionism'. In turn, he continued, this 'threatens to undermine and ultimately unravel the open world economy that has been so painstakingly constructed over the past half-century'.

Thus, defending globalisation and the advancement of specific externally oriented interests and values, whilst ameliorating excessively negative aspects of this project, is the new message. Certainly, one analysis in the South African media (Business Day, 23 March 2000), referring specifically to South African involvement in this project, asserted that 'for President Thabo Mbeki, the Renaissance means, essentially, the promotion of Western political and economic values'. This is somewhat problematic, for, as Thompson and Leysens (1996: 8) point out, 'there is quite obvious tension between on the one hand supporting global free trade, and on the other committing oneself to changing the rules of the system to ensure greater equity'.

Internally oriented nationalist projects heading in the direction of de-linkage (or couching their rhetoric in such terms) that characterised much of Africa in the pre-globalisation era, have evaporated as the global economy has experienced a profound restructuring and as the developing world has been on a full-scale retreat from the heady days of the new international economic order (NIEO). With the lost decade of the 1980s marking out Africa's fortunes, debt and decay have left a legacy which has hollowed out the ideological and material bases of the old nationalist and inward-looking programmes – whether capitalist or socialist. At the same time, the opportunities afforded to those national bourgeoisies (and state élites) in Africa with the vision to 'ride the globalisation wave' mean that those pushing integration or accommodation with global capitalism have had their positions emboldened in quite phenomenal terms. As this process has occurred, divisions between inward-looking and externally oriented fractions of national élites have emerged: the root cause of much of the contradictions and political struggles within national spaces in recent times.

In Africa, dominant élite fractions have increasingly effected this transnationalisation process through locking into the global. They have indulged in mergers or cooperative pacts with transnational corporations (TNCs), moved their portfolios offshore, engaged in financial specu-lation, diversified their holdings outside the national space, and invested abroad. For instance, from March 1995 until mid-September 2000, the South African Reserve Bank approved R7.85 billion worth of direct investment by South African companies in southern Africa, while globally, South African companies received approval for a total of R74.5 billion in foreign direct investment overseas (Mboweni 1999). One analyst remarked that 'South African big companies listed themselves in London and New York with the purpose to collect capital more efficiently. To sum up, South Africa is now firmly integrated within the international financial and business network' (Hirano 2000: 8). This process is played out, to varying degrees, throughout Africa. Élite fractions have continued to integrate themselves into international financial and business networks and have played the role of agent-on-the-ground for foreign direct invest-ment. It is interesting to note that between 1993 and 1998, the three countries in Africa receiving the most FDI also happen to be among the three key promoters of NEPAD: Egypt, Nigeria and South Africa.[5]

The point is that outward-looking élites, having bought into the glob-alisation discourse, actively encourage FDI from transnational companies. This in itself may not be problematic as all developing states need capital to finance development, setting aside for one moment the fact that there is actually a net outflow of capital from Africa. It is the type of FDI that is welcomed and the manner in which this is managed and guided by the host country that is crucial: the question is how to make those corporations engaging in FDI in Africa development-oriented. Problematically, the proponents of NEPAD are those state élites who have embarked on profound liberalisation projects that aim to further open up their domestic economies to external capital with little or no control, whilst abetting the wider process of connecting to the globalising world market. As such, fractions of African élites are in themselves emerging as vital sections of a wider transnational capitalist class. Such sections have increasingly attempted to make use of the global capitalist system in a strategy aimed at bolstering their own position within the global historic bloc. In general, they come from countries whose economies have 'a magnitude that cannot be sustained only by regional running but requires more openness to the world economy ... [thus compelling] a strategy for combating marginalisation and adapting to globalisation' (Hirano 2000: 12). The close fit between interests of externally oriented élites and the type of project advanced by NEPAD is evident. In South Africa, for instance, according to the *Cape Argus* of 19 February 2001,

> President Mbeki is on a marketing mission for his economic plans for South Africa and the continent. Mbeki and several top cabinet ministers met twenty members of the President's Big Business Working Group ... to elaborate on [his] envisaged economic programme.... In response, the business leaders applauded the President and the government's strong emphasis on matters economic.'

Reformist impulses that do emerge from this fraction of African élites emanate from a sense that the rules of the game within global trade (not, mind, the wider overarching architecture) are 'unfair' to them and their national allies.[6] Thus,

> IMF-bashing is back in style [in Africa] – even if the rhetorical flourishes of their leaders have different origins.... Self-evidently, the trajectory chosen ... amounts at best to attempting to join the system, to play by its rules and, having discovered that the game is set up unfairly, to adjust these rules somewhat in the Third World's favour. (Bond 1999: 339)

The strategic choice made by NEPAD is to challenge the North at its own game. This is not a North vs South engagement, however, and is not an attempt á la NIEO to re-write the global rules. Rather, it is a broadly Southern attempt to use the North's rules. As an analyst in the *Mail & Guardian* (27 July–2 August 2001) noted, 'Free trade is the only issue that [Africa] can beat the G8 over the head with; and [we] must do so by shaming them in front of their voters.' The increasing usage of anti-dumping strictures is a case in point. Certainly, South Africa, India and Brazil since 1995 have been consistently among the main initiators of anti-dumping measures, invariably against Northern exporters.[7] This in itself reflects the changes that have occurred within the global economy and in particular mirrors the dominant ideology that is an integral part of the ongoing order. As Kufuor (1998: 194) argues, 'the history of the developing countries in the world trading system reveals initial hostility to a regime that was controlled by advanced and industrialised countries. However it is obvious that the developing countries' attitudes [have changed].' This attitudinal change has coincided with the rise to hegemony among the transnationalised élites of the neo-liberal discourse.

Yet such challenging of the North takes place within a milieu in which the essential underpinnings of the global order are unchallenged. NEPAD's message, like South Africa's broader trade strategy, is very much linked to the discourse of globalisation and the workings of the 'free market' (see Taylor 2001b). After all, South Africa's finance minister is chairperson of the joint IMF/World Bank Board of Governors. Indeed, commenting on NEPAD, one analyst remarked that:

Nothing here [in NEPAD] would dismay the World Bank or the International Monetary Fund, although reform of these institutions is also a priority. The latest buzzword in the corridors of these institutions is 'authorship' – jargon for a hands-off approach to reform. The plan chimes with this new approach by encouraging African governments to claim 'ownership' of reforms which, just a few years ago, foreign lenders were happy to prescribe from Washington. (Ashurst 2002: 37)

It is apparent that leading fractions within key states in the South regard the integration of their territories into the global economy as crucial and inevitable. Thabo Mbeki (2000) summed up this attitude when he proclaimed that 'the process of globalisation is an *objective* outcome of the development of the productive forces that create wealth, including their continuous improvement and expansion' [emphasis added], while Nigeria's Obasanjo stated (in the *Middle East Times*, 23 July 1999) that 'we must get used to the idea that globalisation is a fact of life. It's a reality of the new age.' However, as Philip Cerny (1999: 152) remarks, 'globalisation is driven not primarily by some inexorable economic process, but rather by politics: by ideology, by the actions, interactions and decisions of state actors, their private-sector interlocutors and wider publics'.

In the NEPAD base document, it is stated that SAPs 'provided only a partial solution', removing serious price distortions but giving 'inadequate attention to the provision of social services', resulting in a situation where 'only a few countries managed to achieve sustainable higher growth'. Patrick Bond (2001) asks a number of important questions about such statements, worth repeating here:

- What if structural adjustment represented not a partial solution but instead, reflecting local and global power shifts, a profound defeat for genuine African nationalists, workers, peasants, women, children, manufacturing industry and the environment?
- What if promoting reforms really amounted to the IMF and World Bank imposing their cookie-cutter neo-liberal policies on desperately disempowered African societies, without any reference to democratic processes, resistance or diverse local conditions?
- What if the removal of 'price distortions' really meant the repeal of exchange controls (allowing massive capital flight), subsidy cuts (pushing masses of people below the poverty line), and lowered import tariffs (causing widespread de-industrialisation)?
- What if inadequate attention to the provision of social services in reality meant the opposite: excessive attention to applying neo-liberalism not just to the macro-economy, but also to health, education, water and other crucial state services?
- And what if the form of IMF/Bank attention included insistence upon greater cost recovery, higher user-fees, lower budgetary allocations, privatisation, and even the disconnection of supplies to those too poor to afford them, leading to the unnecessary deaths of millions of people?

Ignoring such fundamental questions, NEPAD puts forward an agenda that demands that global integration be facilitated by a working relationship with transnational capital and corporations, an aggressive liberalisation policy and an essentially prostrate attitude towards the international financial institutions. Hence, at Seattle such élites came out in favour of the activities of the TNCs and the TNCs' continued presence within their countries:

> In Seattle they fought hard to maintain … advantages for themselves and their transnational partners. Arguing for low wages is not a plan for national development, but a defence of Nike paying 25 cents an hour, and Third World sub-contractors running industrial zones for the TNCs that drive the global economy. (Harris and Robinson 2000: 4)

It is, of course, no coincidence that the élites promoting NEPAD most energetically spring from states at the forefront of advancing liberalisation and the neo-liberal package within their own territories: South Africa is currently busy implementing its own self-imposed structural adjustment programme known as GEAR (Growth, Employment and Redistribution) (Taylor and Williams 2000). Indeed, according to one account, 'it is only a small exaggeration to say that [NEPAD] prescribes for an entire continent the kind of policies already pursued in South Africa' (Ashurst 2002: 37). Under Obasanjo, Nigeria has pushed ahead with deepening reform and is currently a favourite in Washington (Odife 1999). Setting itself the goal of attracting $10 billion worth of FDI per annum, opening up the telecommunications, oil, transport, and energy sectors, and pushing for a free trade area with Ghana to broaden the market for investors, Obasanjo's Nigeria is determinedly seeking to lock into the global economy after years of marginalisation and neglect. Cairo, likewise, is following orthodox policies – approved by the core – in an attempt to restructure its economy as a site of foreign investment and a welcoming destination for transnational capital (Mitchell 1999). Although beset with internal insurrection, Algiers has also been pursuing a liberalisation policy since 1995, intensifying on the accession of Bouteflika.

These projects have been advanced at the behest of the global powers and have been encouraged by the transnational élites, with bail-out packages, new loans, and so on acting as lubricants to ease the process. Such processes stand to benefit specific factions. Although talking of Asia, Gill's (1999: 3) comments can be equally applied to Africa when he asserts that 'deregulation, privatisation, and liberalisation are a means of strengthening a particular set of class interests, principally the power of private investors'. He adds, 'Structural adjustment allows for a redistribution of claims on future profit-flows that enable foreign capital to gain power and control over regional development patterns.'

On the ground in Africa, however, such reforms have generated considerable social conflict and threaten the position of the African globalisers. Key leaders promoting NEPAD are in place to advance a liberal democratic project, however uneven (Mkapa in Tanzania, Wade in Senegal), or 'liberators' from past oppression (Obasanjo, Mbeki's African National Congress). Their mandate was to improve the lot of the marginalised and dispossessed, not to deepen social conflict and exacerbate the insecurity of the poorest whilst opening up markets for their own élites and transnational counterparts.[8] This has resulted in a profound contradiction as there is 'an inconsistency in … requiring both democratic reform and continued economic adjustment and austerity. It is unlikely that the newly enfranchised citizens will actually vote for further austerity' (Riley 1992: 549). The compromise they have made with the North now seems to be increasingly one-sided and, instead of rising prosperity and stability brought about by the globalisation message, increased discontent and even questions regarding their legitimacy are emerging. While this occurs, the Northern élites have to date seemed oblivious to the social tensions their neo-liberal nirvana has reaped in the margins. The message of NEPAD and other reformist impulses is that it is the South that has had to shoulder much of the burden for global restructuring, and it is the élites in the South who have to face the wrath of the affected. To ameliorate these conditions, some of Africa's élites are claiming a much greater input in managing the global economy and in evening the playing field.

Such impulses were graphically illustrated at the Seattle WTO meeting, where African élites in particular expressed outrage at the cavalier fashion in which they were treated at a supposedly global forum. It was this feature of the negotiations that primarily contributed to the collapse of the Seattle talks – an important point to remember when reflecting on the latest WTO round. Certainly, the breakdown of negotiations was not triggered by any monumental clashing of economic agendas or philosophies: Seattle was not the battleground of North vs South. Rather, it was the form and procedure of the negotiations that stimulated such discord and antagonism. Competing agendas surfaced and interests were not common across the board, but what was evident was that the substance of global trade and the neo-liberal underpinnings of international commerce were not under attack by the assembled élites of the South, and most certainly not from those African delegates from countries later to advance NEPAD. While the headlines back home may have portrayed the élites as 'standing up' to the developed world, amid paragraphs mentioning neo-imperialism and colonialist arrogance, the substance of the talks remained untouched and will frame any subsequent WTO rounds. In that sense, for all the drama, Seattle did not mark a 'victory' for Africa; rather, it reflected the hegemonic status that neo-liberal economics had achieved among the transnational historic bloc. As one commentator in the *Mail & Guardian* (2–8 February 2001) cynically put it,

> getting the rhetoric right is one thing, changing behaviour is quite another. It's easy to make all the right noises about making globalisation inclusive, but what does this mean when the rich countries of the North spend $1 billion a day subsidising their farmers, with an annual subsidy three times as large as the entire amount spent on aid budgets? Not a lot.

The launch of MAP at Davos and later NEPAD merely underscored this point.

MAP and NEPAD: another false start?

The launch of the Millennium Africa Renaissance Programme (also known as the Millennium African Recovery Plan) at the WEF in late January 2001, and NEPAD's launch in October 2001 were the first concrete crystallisations of what key African élites have in mind in advancing their cause. The background to NEPAD is of interest. Essentially, in 2000 the OAU meeting in Lomé, Togo agreed (under lobbying from Nigeria and South Africa) that Africa should draw up and agree on an African Recovery Programme, authorising the presidents of Algeria, Nigeria and South Africa to work on this programme. The New African Initiative (as

NEPAD was known for a time) is a merger of MAP and the Omega Plan, proposed by Senegalese President Abdoulaye Wade. NEPAD was unanimously adopted by the OAU's Lusaka Summit on 11 July 2001, being promoted as a blueprint for the regeneration of Africa. According to This Day (23 July 2001), MAP was 'designed to present a common front when Africa deals with the developed world, seek aid and investment in return for good governance, and unite African countries against social and economic problems like AIDS'. On the other hand, 'the Omega Plan, drawn up by the Senegalese president, sets goals and defines financial means to narrow infrastructural gaps'. Only hard bargaining managed to prevent the Omega Plan from sabotaging African unity before it had even begun, particularly when Wade began claiming (in Gaborone's Daily News of 28 June 2001) that his plan was 'a practical initiative for overcoming Africa's economic difficulties' while MAP was 'more of a manifesto'. Yet Wade's plan was extremely problematic and did not deserve the status that it was given (though no doubt satisfying the ego of its author). It involved obtaining repayable treasury bonds from the North to finance a pan-continental infrastructure scheme which, Wade admitted, would advantage Northern contractors. As Wade asserted in an interview with allafrica.com in 2001,

> I will show how the West will benefit. To carry out all this infrastructure work we will need foreign and European firms, which are technically more advanced than ours and which can build roads much faster than we could do ... two-thirds of the resources I'm talking about would go to Western companies to carry out the work.

After a 'fusion' with MAP, the Davos document is now somewhat different from the one presented in Lusaka and Genoa.

Although MAP was then still in its embryonic stage, Mbeki announced, as Johannesburg's Citizen of 30 January 2001 reported, that its advocates would seek to enrol like-minded élites across the continent: 'participating African leaders would form a compact committing them to the programme and a forum of leaders who would make decisions about subprogrammes and initiatives'. The contents of both MAP and NEPAD (which effectively replaces it) are recycled from previous 'visions' and statements that have marked off Africa's post-independence experience at regular intervals. A commentator in Mmegi/The Reporter (2–8 February 2001) noted that 'there have been a number of African initiatives, like the African Human Rights Charter, to deal with its [the continent's] problems, and agreements and instruments have been approved, signed and even ratified, without being used effectively to deal with wars, human rights violations, genocide, and also with prevailing under-development and poverty'.

Perhaps what is new about NEPAD is its very mainstream approach to development, which can relatively easily settle into the hegemonic norms that stake out the global political economy, as well as promoting a greater role for the international financial institutions in Africa. One analyst in the *Mail & Guardian* (2–8 February 2001) noted that, with MAP, 'while calling for African leaders to assume ownership of economic development, Mbeki in the same vein calls for World Bank-led strategic partnerships with Africa and the International Monetary Fund Poverty Reduction Programme. This is despite the role the two organisations have played in wreaking havoc to the economies in Africa.' Indeed, according to a *Business Day* report (19 February 2001), Bouteflika, Obasanjo and Mbeki flew to Bamako in Mali to meet Horst Kohler, head of the IMF, and World Bank chief James Wolfensohn, to discuss how to construct a 'global partnership for African development' and advance 'its integration into the world, with the help of developed countries, the private sector and multilateral institutions' such as the Bretton Woods bodies. As the director of the South African Council of Churches' ecumenical service for socio-economic transformation, Mongezi Guma, noted in the *East London Daily Dispatch* (2 March 2002), 'NEPAD correctly states that current "globalisation" policies fail to lift Africa out of socio-economic decline but then goes on to say that Africa therefore needs more of the same policies.'

It is self-evident that Mbeki has been highly active in touting his 'global initiative on Africa' (Taylor 2001b). This enthusiasm to position himself as the 'voice of Africa' evidenced itself in the overt public relations attempt by the ANC to craft Mbeki as some sort of philosopher-king, centred around the African Renaissance. Ironically, Mbeki is only able to pass himself off as such a visionary because of the receptivity in Northern capitals to his reformist message that remains well within – and indeed legitimises – the current hegemony of neo-liberalism. As Dot Keet asked (quoted in Khan 2000), 'is it that they are representing the developing world to the WTO or legitimising the WTO to the developing world?'

Certainly, the apparently sympathetic hearing that Mbeki and others have received in various global power centres is precisely because the message they are communicating eases responsibility for growing world inequality and African immiseration. Any particular policies that cause such processes are passed over and, instead, the blame is pinned on the amorphous phenomena known as 'globalisation'. Even this is embraced by NEPAD: it is the way in which globalisation acts on Africa, and not the very contents of it, that are the source of Africa's woes. As Patrick Bond (2000: 8) put it, writing on Mbeki's global strategy:

> There is never to be found, in Mbeki's repertoire of explanations, the dangerous notion that the gulf between rich and poor widens *precisely because Northern capital enjoys ever-growing capacity to source inputs ever more cheaply from*

the South, thanks to asymmetric trade relations, debt peonage and currency crashes generated by regular bouts of financial-speculative raiding. That possibility, and the policy implications it suggests, can never be considered, much less stated in polite discourse.

This problem lies at the heart of NEPAD's agenda and is derivative of the fact that its apparent credibility with transnational élite counterparts in the North is predicated on the shared acceptance and advancement, within African national spaces and beyond, of precisely the hegemonic agenda that Mbeki et al. (unintentionally?) cast as undermining their own domestic legitimacy. The promoters of NEPAD cannot openly reject the neo-liberal thrust of globalisation because that would entail a rejection of their own position, as well as calling into question their own individual compromises with externally oriented capital from which they draw much of their advice and support (Taylor and Vale 2000). Bridging the gap between their popular constituency, which in the main is far more critical of – if not openly hostile to – the continued ravages of globalisation, and their élite class allies in big capital, the promoters of NEPAD remain caught within a web of contradictions and send out mixed signals vis-à-vis their own positions regarding the future ordering of the global political economy.

Already, tension over particular countries' roles has threatened to undermine unity. We have already mentioned Abdoulaye Wade's apparent solo attempt to represent the whole of Africa. Nigeria and South Africa's growing cosy relationship has also been noted. One report in Mmegi/The Reporter (2–8 February 2001) asserted that when Pretoria and Abuja were negotiating about MAP in its initial stages, 'it seem[ed] a little undiplomatic to have excluded Egypt, which is said to resent what it sees as South Africa's pretensions to the leadership of the African continent'. This dispute is over form not substance, however, as the Egyptians have been as enthusiastic about neo-liberal solutions to Africa's developmental impasse as Pretoria. Indeed, one senior Egyptian official, in advocating the African Renaissance, asserted:

> The need to recognise and realise the importance of economic integration, open markets and free trade among African countries as a prerequisite to achieve economic development ....
>
> The goals of [the African Renaissance] should be ... empowering the private sector as an engine of economic growth ... and achieving sound macro-economic indicators and creating an environment that is invesment-friendly. (Khattab 2000: 6)

Certainly, relatively petty diplomatic spats aside, the contents of NEPAD's agenda are highly problematic if a new vision for North–African relations (and NEPAD claims just that) are being advanced as some sort of new consensus on how the global political economy is to be re-ordered. This is particularly so if such visions see the adoption of neo-liberalism as a prerequisite for development.

In the post-Seattle era, as growing disenchantment with the panacea of globalisation emerges, particularly in the South, space does seem to be opening up for a strategic intervention by key African élites on how the world may be run on more equitable lines. However, the overall thrust, exemplified in spirit at Seattle and other élite meeting points, and crystallised in some sort of shape by NEPAD, leaves the agenda advanced very much in line with ongoing global hegemonic norms centred around neo-liberalism and standard approaches to export-driven development paths. As Malley (1999: 364) remarked, 'where once there was talk of curbing the power of multinational corporations and promoting self-reliance, now one hears only of lifting restrictions and increasing trade'.

This reality undermines the potency of NEPAD's message and suggests that the call from Africa is crafted by and for an externally oriented élite who recognise, with their transnational allies in the North, that cosmetic changes may be required if the whole house of cards is not to collapse in on itself. This process would most probably start in the developing world, where the position of the liberalising élite remains precarious and more open to domestic (and volatile) unrest than their Northern counterparts. Hence the call from NEPAD can be cast as a defensive measure to protect key African élites' positions in the face of withering domestic criticism of the path on which they have chosen to take their home polities. While this call may temporally placate critics who may believe that at last 'their' governments are doing something to ameliorate the negative effects of globalisation, the very narrowness and limited nature of the NEPAD agenda reveal fundamental shortcomings. These shortcomings are rooted in too narrow a conception of the global political economy, and too easy an acceptance of, if not naïve belief in, the willingness of the North to compromise its power. This limited reading of the current world order belies any real potential for the necessary changes required for a more equitable world.

Limited reformism and NEPAD

Clearly, the major factor absent from NEPAD's message is a coherent analysis of the organising principles of the current global order. These organising principles stipulate that sovereign states are the ultimate building blocks of a cooperative order, and that power differentials between states are unavoidable: all one can do is to try to mitigate some of the effects of these differentials. On a structural level, thus, no analytical attention is paid to other sources and loci of power and privilege in global affairs, such as transnational classes or multinational corporations. Such a restricted focus on power and privilege can lead to nothing more than a programme aimed at partial and piecemeal change, the core features of any reformist tendency. Although a great deal of emphasis is placed on the phenomenon of globalisation, the absence of any sustained structural analysis of global interaction is also evident in the failure of the NEPAD to interrogate the structural effects that globalisation, driven by the liberalisation of the markets for goods, ideas and capital, has had on the very nature of the state. The problem with globalisation is not so much that it has restricted state autonomy or eroded sovereignty, but rather that its logic induces states to opt for being instruments of competition, rather than instruments of development.

One of the marked features of NEPAD's promoters is their apparently supine position before the globalisation juggernaut. Exemplifying this, Nelson Mandela (cited in Bond 1998) remarked, 'globalisation is a phenomenon that we cannot deny. All we can do is accept it.' However, instead of having 'no alternative' but to embrace globalisation and then embark on reformist measures, a variety of policy choices and strategic instruments remain unused. This, naturally, helps craft a convenient blind spot for NEPAD's authors and promoters. Their own policies aid and abet the very marginalisation and immiseration they now decry. Options that may include real attempts to change the very dynamic of globalisation by restricting the 'openness' of specifically financial markets are largely ignored.

Indeed, by raising essentially reformist questions and negating the very possibility of alternatives, many African élites contribute to the acceptance of neo-liberalism as the only macro-economic framework and development strategy within which they (and by implication, all others) can work. The best option one can pursue in such a scenario is hence to work via a 'tactical' engagement policy to maximise benefits. This essentially self-reinforcing policy has occurred within the context of a globalised international political economy and the concomitant rise to hegemony among the transnational élite of neo-liberalism. Not only is this linked to the material benefits that this transnational élite and its externally oriented allies can expect to reap from a liberalisation strategy, but it also reflects an ideological climate in which the élite in all international financial institutions and most multilateral bodies and national administrations earnestly believe that neo-liberalism is the best and only way to promote growth and development (in that significant order). As one analyst remarked,

> Core interests have supported neo-liberalism not only for material gain but also because there has been a genuine belief that it will lead to development. For peripheral interests (LDCs as well as the 'emerging

market economies' of central and eastern Europe), consent has been given with conviction that participation in the global marketplace will benefit them. (Lee 1995: 156)

This helps account for the acceptance of the broad principles of neo-liberalism within whose framework NEPAD proffers support within the global order. The agenda for change pursued by NEPAD is thus clearly a restricted, reformist agenda and not one aimed at a transformation of global relations, which is obviously a precondition for the drastic reduction of global poverty. Yet this lack of a real agenda for fundamental change suits the transnational élite, in both the North and the South. The post-Seattle order, as evidenced by NEPAD, will almost certainly not be marked by a rejection of the liberalisation discourse and orthodoxy; rather, in future the North will have to tread more carefully in pushing the neo-liberal agenda. Sceptics would assert that this will simply be 'spin' on an older and more established orthodoxy, and parallels with Blair's rhetoric around the 'Third Way' may lead to some clues as to how this more 'caring' neo-liberalism may be cast. After all, it has been said (in *Business Day*, 23 March 2000) that 'Blair is a new-style social democrat who promotes a Third Way. Its chief proponent in Africa is Mbeki.' Yet critics point out that the Third Way is no more than spin-doctored neo-liberalism. As Callinicos (2001: 121) reminds us, 'far from breaking with the neo-liberal policies of the New Right, it has continued and, in certain ways, radicalised them. The Blair government has carried privatisation further than its Tory predecessors dared.'

Advancing this (admittedly cynical) scenario, cooperative élites in Africa will be needed to sell the message. This is where NEPAD fits in. Having taken on board the discourse of globalisation, liberalising élites in the developing world are the best candidates for pushing a more cooperative posture on their part in trade negotiations, whilst at the same time winning a degree of latitude from the global powers-that-be. This in itself reflects the changes that have occurred within the global economy and in particular mirrors the dominant ideology that is an integral part of the ongoing order. However, the danger of being co-opted by the holders of power is one that a reformer always has to be aware of, and develop a strategy against. So far, there has been little sign of such a counter-strategy on the part of NEPAD. As Thompson and Leysens (1996: 9) framed it,

> supporting free trade while at the same time insisting that [Africa] must attempt to change the rules of the system in a non-confrontational manner [and within the neo-liberal discourse] amounts to a one-way traffic bridge. It accepts that the end of history, or for that matter ideology, has indeed been reached.

It is for this reason that any celebratory mood that was, momentarily, felt in the aftermath of Seattle, and that is wrapped around the NEPAD banner, needs careful reflection and interrogation. Africa-based initiatives are vitally needed, but it seems clear that what is emerging is a nascent reformism, emanating from key élites in the developing world, that, far from ushering in a twenty-first-century NIEO, remains rooted in an orthodox discourse that benefits only a small élite. Unfortunately:

> African officials are so conditioned by the neo-liberal 'development' paradigm, or, alternatively, they are so conditioned by their own class interests, that ... [alternatives cannot be envisioned] without pressure from below. At the end of the day, it is the people, especially the working people in mines, factories, farms, and the service sector, that must take upon themselves the responsibility to protect their own jobs, income, family welfare, the environment and national patrimony. (Tandon n.d.)

Certainly, according to the *Mail & Guardian* (16–22 February 2000), 'recent South African politicians have sung the global neo-liberal tune. President Thabo Mbeki often talks left but acts right; Minister of Finance Trevor Manuel and Minister of Trade Alec Erwin don't even bother to talk left anymore.' Such tendencies are not restricted to South Africa, but increasingly mark the behaviour of the élites promoting NEPAD, with their rhetoric of reformism staking out the limited boundaries from which they engage the North. Despite Mbeki's claims that NEPAD reflects 'the sovereign will of the people' and the 'aspirations of the masses' (quoted in *The Sowetan*, 24 July 2001), the initiative has been remarkable for its lack of consultation with civil society in Africa. If it did have the popular base it claims, then irritating questions over the WTO's project of advancing a corporate-dominated world and the related pressure to commodify might have been raised. But such questioners were not consulted during NEPAD's formulation. If this is the best hope for Africa, then the future looks bleak indeed for the continent and its peoples.

NOTES

1 For comment on this orthodox 'recipe' for 'good governance', see Taylor 2000.
2 For a critique of the 'just another country' thesis, see Vale and Taylor 1999.
3 For a good discussion of this, see Bond 2001.
4 Former US President Bill Clinton's advocacy of the African Growth and Opportunity Act must be seen in this light.
5 Figures taken from various UNCTAD reports and cited in Loots 2000.
6 For how this relates to broader South African foreign policy, see Taylor 2001.
7 Figures adapted from WTO Secretariat, Rules Division Antidumping Measures Database, cited in Miranda *et al.* 1998; figures for 1998 cited in *Financial Times* (London), 6 May 1999.
8 On South Africa's role in this, see Taylor 2002.

REFERENCES

'A New African Initiative: Merger of the Millenium Partnership for the African Recovery Programme (MAP) and Omega Plan', July 2001. Available online at <http://www.polity.org.za/govdocs/misc/mapomega.html>.

Ajulu, R., 2001, 'Thabo Mbeki's African Renaissance in a Globalising World Economy: the Struggle for the Soul of the Continent', Review of African Political Economy, 87.

Ashurst, M., 2002, 'Taking the Initiative', BBC Focus on Africa, January–March.

Bond, P., 1998, 'Global Financial Crisis: Why We Should Care, What We Should Do', Indicator SA, 15, 3.

—— 1999, 'Global Economic Crisis: a View From South Africa', Journal of World-Systems Research, 5, 2 (Spring).

—— 2000, 'Can Thabo Mbeki Change the World? Strategies, Tactics and Alliances Towards Global Governance', Inaugural Frantz Fanon Memorial Lecture, University of Durban-Westville School of Governance, 17 August.

—— 2001, 'What is Pretoria Planning for Africa?', Kabissa-Fahamu-Sangonet Newsletter, 45 (December 2001).

—— 2001, Against Global Apartheid: South Africa Meets the World Bank, IMF and International Finance, Cape Town: University of Cape Town Press.

Callinicos, A., 2001, Against the Third Way, Cambridge: Polity Press.

Cerny, P., 1999, 'Globalising the Political and Politicising the Global: Concluding Reflections on International Political Economy as a Vocation', New Political Economy, 4, 1.

Embong, A. R., 2000, 'Globalisation and Transnational Class Relations: Some Problems of Conceptualisation', Third World Quarterly, 21, 6.

Gill, S., 1999, 'The Geopolitics of the Asian Crisis', Monthly Review, 50, 10 (March).

Harris, J. and W. Robinson, 2000, 'Fissures in the Globalist Ruling Bloc? Seattle and the Politics of Globalisation from Above', Third Wave Study Group paper.

Hirano, K., 2000, 'Globalisation and African Renaissance', unpublished paper.

Khan, F., 2000, 'South Africa Criticised for "Ploughing its Own Path"', Inter-Press Services (Johannesburg), 1 June.

Khattab, M., 2000, 'An Egyptian View of the African Renaissance', Africa Dialogue, Monograph Series No. 1.

Kufour, K. O., 1998, 'The Developing Countries and the Shaping of GATT/WTO Antidumping Law', Journal of World Trade, 32, 6 (December).

Lee, K., 1995. 'A Neo-Gramscian Approach to International Organisation: An Expanded Analysis of Current Reforms to UN Development Activities' in A. Linklater and J. Macmillan (eds.), Boundaries in Question: New Directions in International Relations, Basingstoke: Macmillan.

Loots, E., 2000, 'Foreign Direct Investment Flows to African Countries: Trends, Determinants and Future Prospects', Mots Pluriels, 13 (April).

Mahatey, N., 2000, 'Official View', Global Dialogue, 5, 2 (July).

Malley, R., 1999, 'The Third Worldist Moment', Current History, November.

Manuel, T., 1998, Keynote Address at a Deutsche Stiftung für internationale Entwicklung meeting on 'A Policy Dialogue: IMF, DSE Forum', Berlin, 1–3 December.

Mbeki, T., 2000, Keynote Address to the National General Council of the ANC, Port Elizabeth, July.

Mboweni, Tito, 1999, 'The Role of the South African Reserve Bank in Economic Integration in the Southern African Development Community', Statement at

Africa Dialogue Lecture Series, University of Pretoria, 21 September.

Miranda, J., R. Torres and M. Ruiz, 1998, 'The International Use of Antidumping: 1987–1997', Journal of World Trade, 32, 5 (October).

Mitchell, T., 1999. 'No Factories, No Problems: The Logic of Neo-Liberalism in Egypt', Review of African Political Economy, no. 82.

Naim, M., 2000. 'Fads and Fashions in Economic Reforms: Washington Consensus or Washington Confusion?' Third World Quarterly, 21, 3.

NEPAD, 2001, 'The New Partnership for Africa's Development (NEPAD)', Midrand: NEPAD Secretariat. Available online at <http://www.dfa.gov.za/events/nepad. pdf>.

Odife, D., 1999, 'Economic Policies, Democratisation and Investment Inflow in Nigeria', Africa Economic Analysis, <http://www.afbis.com/analysis/investment. htm>.

Riley, S., 1992, 'Political Adjustment or Domestic Pressure: Democratic Politics and Political Choice in Africa', Third World Quarterly, 13, 3.

Robinson, W., 1998, 'Capitalist Globalisation and the Transnationalisation of the State', paper presented at a workshop on 'Historical Materialism and Globalisation', University of Warwick, 15–17 April.

Silver, B. and G. Arrighi, 2000, 'Workers North and South', in L. Panitch and C. Leys (eds.), Socialist Register 2001: Working Classes, Global Realities, London: Merlin Press.

Sklair, L., 1997. 'Social Movements for Global Capitalism: the Transnational Capitalist Class in Action', Review of International Political Economy, 4, 3 (Autumn).

Smith P., 2000, 'Africa Lowers its Handicap', The Economist: the World in 2000, London: The Economist, 2000.

Tandon, Y., n.d., The Role of Foreign Direct Investments in Africa's Human Development, <http://attac.org/fra/list/doc/tandon.htm>.

Taylor, I., 2000, 'Globalisation and Democracy: Rethinking the Link Between Africa's 'Democratisation', Aid, and Neo-Liberalism', in L. Thompson (ed.), Development, Democracy and Aid in Southern Africa, Bellville: University of the Western Cape.

—— 2001a, Stuck in Middle GEAR: South Africa's Post-Apartheid Foreign Relations, Westport: Praeger.

—— 2001b, 'The "Mbeki Initiative": Towards a Post-Orthodox New International Order?', in P. Nel, I. Taylor and J. van der Westhuizen (eds.), Promoting Change? Aspects of Reformism in South Africa's Multilateral Diplomacy, Aldershot: Ashgate.

—— 2002, 'South Africa's Promotion of "Democracy" and "Stability" in Southern Africa: Good Governance or Good for Business?', in S. Breslin, C. Hughes, N. Phillips and B. Rosamond (eds.), New Regionalism in the Global Political Economy: Theories and Cases, London: Routledge.

Taylor, I. and P. Vale, 2000, 'South Africa's Transition Revisited: Globalisation as Vision and Virtue', Global Society, 14, 3.

Taylor, I. and P. Williams, 2001, 'South African Foreign Policy and the Great Lakes Crisis: African Renaissance Meets Vagabondage Politique?', African Affairs, 100, 399.

Thompson, L. and A. Leysens, 1996, 'Comments: South African Foreign Policy Discussion Document', unpublished paper.

Vale, P. and I. Taylor, 1999, 'South Africa's Post-Apartheid Foreign Policy Five Years On: From Pariah State to "Just Another Country"?', Round Table: Commonwealth Journal of International Relations, 352 (October).

Vale, P. and S. Maseko, 1998, 'South Africa and the African Renaissance', International Affairs, 74, 2.

3 NEPAD and Its Critics

Eddy Maloka

Five years ago, the Nordic Africa Institute and the Development Institute of the African Development Bank, with the support of the Swedish Ministry for Foreign Affairs, published a book entitled *A New Partnership for African Development: Issues and Parameters* (Kifle et al. 1997). The book's primary focus was Sweden's relations with Africa, but the organisers of the seminar from which the papers and the title for the book came could not predict that one day the title of their collection would refer to an initiative that would be known by the acronym NEPAD.

The New Partnership for Africa's Development (NEPAD) developed out of a merger of the Millennium African Recovery Programme (MAP) and the Omega Plan. NEPAD is intended to be a framework and programme of action for the renaissance of the continent. The initiative has three components: first, it is a set of principles and commitments that African leaders make on matters of democracy and good governance; second, it is a three-pronged strategy that rests on the identification of preconditions for sustainable development in the continent, priority sectors to be targeted, and strategies for resource mobilisation; and, finally, it is a follow-up mechanism with the Heads of State Implementation Committee as the overseeing authority and the Secretariat as an implementing agency.

The unveiling of NEPAD generated a lot of attention globally and, at least from January 2002, in the aftermath of the meeting of the African Social Forum in Bamako, Mali, the initiative has been inundated by critiques from sections of African civil society. These critiques gained momentum as the Kananaskis summit of the G8 approached, as African leaders were perceived to be dealing with this group of industrialised countries behind the backs of their people, who were being kept in the dark. Canada also contributed to this debate on the continent as its tiermondist NGO sector, through contact with sections of the African NGO community, created the impression, at least in that part of North America, that NEPAD was being widely rejected by African people.[1] The G8's package of support for NEPAD, known as the 'G8 Action Plan for Africa', and a comparatively insignificant financial commitment that the summit made towards the plan, also contributed to this debate. Processes towards the inauguration of the African Union were also a factor, especially with regard to the perception that there was a conflict and duplication between NEPAD and institutions of this continental organisation. Not surprisingly, whereas some observers could conclude that NEPAD 'is arguably the most profound policy formulation to have emerged from African leadership, and is certainly the most important since the socialist prescriptions of the 1950s and 1960s' (Mills and Hughes 2001/2: 139), others could declare that 'We do not accept NEPAD!! Another Africa is Possible!!' (African Civil Society Declaration 2002). One positive factor to emerge from this debate over NEPAD is that the critique has generated a wealth of intellectual activity across the continent, in the form of conferences, workshops, symposia and Internet discussion fora, as well as published material such as scholarly papers and declarations.[2] This debate is healthy and will contribute to the enrichment of reflections on the development direction that the continent should take. Nor has a development document produced by African leaders sparked such a heated debate across the continent since the Lagos Plan of Action in 1980.

Critiques of NEPAD can be grouped into two categories. In the first category is the culturalist argument, popular among Northern political scientists, whose intellectual source, as exemplified by Patrick Chabal (2002), is the belief that 'contemporary politics in Africa is best understood as the exercise of neo-patrimonial power'; and that 'the neo-patrimonial [political] system is deeply embedded in the African socio-cultural matrix'. According to this view, 'African political systems today exhibit three intriguing characteristics which deserve careful analysis, if only because they go against prevailing expectations. They are increasingly informal; they appear to "retraditionalise"; and they have signally failed to spur sustained economic development'. This neo-patrimonial form of government 'rests on well-understood, if unequal, forms of political reciprocity which link patrons with their clients along vertical social lines'. Therefore, 'unless these considerations [the neo-patrimonial nature of the post-colonial African state] are seriously taken into account, there is a risk that NEPAD will fail to live up to expectations'. For Chabal (2002), 'NEPAD must, in large measure at least, be understood as a commitment on the part of the current (not so new) élites in Africa to the present "democratic orthodoxy" in order to guarantee a transfer of resources [that are necessary for the dispensing of patronage] to Africa: a continuation with, rather than a break from, the type of relations that has guided the continent's engagement with the international community since independence'.

The second category of critiques – emanating mainly from constituencies on the African continent such as trade unions, the intelligentsia, debt cancellation and trade NGO networks, women's organisations, churches, and rural and urban development NGOs – is informed by critical questions relating to the post-Washington consensus and the terms of Africa's integration into the global economy. The arguments in this category can be clustered around six issues. The first issue is, of course, a concern about lack of consultation with African civil society, or what has been described as the top-down approach that the NEPAD process followed. This concern dominates civil society discussions of NEPAD, as well as debates at the Kananaskis summit. For example, the African Scholars Forum for Envisioning Africa, meeting in Nairobi in April 2002, noted that 'although NEPAD was to be "prepared through participatory processes involving the people", the lack of serious and thorough consultation with African citizens, as well as particular stakeholders such as academia, civil society and women's organizations during the process of developing the NEPAD is alarming' (African Forum 2002).

The second group of issues, probably amounting to the most fundamental critique of NEPAD, revolves around conceptual and ideological assumptions associated with the NEPAD base document. To be fair, some of the critics who raise conceptual and ideological concerns with NEPAD do acknowledge the significance of the initiative. For example, for Dani Nabudere (2002: 3), NEPAD 'is a product of the continuing search by African people and their leaders to create pan-African structures that can lead to the social and economic transformation of the continent in a rapidly "globalising world"'. The initiative is, according to Nabudere, 'an instrument of contestation between Africans seeking self-determination in their development efforts and those forces that seek the continuation of the exploitation of the continent's resources upon which the accumulation of their wealth depends'. For Yash Tandon (2002), some of the 'positive features of NEPAD' include 'the need to negotiate a new relationship with their development partners, which is the central idea behind NEPAD; also central to the spirit of NEPAD is the idea that through the "African Renaissance" project, the African continent that has been "plundered for centuries" will "take its rightful place in the world"'; and the 'focus on "African ownership and management"'. Similarly, the African trade union conference on NEPAD, held in Dakar in February 2002, prefaced its critique of the initiative by 'accepting the concept of, and the need for, partnership with Africa's development partners', and reiterated 'our commitment to programmes that would emancipate African economies from the doldrums of stagnation, among them the NEPAD' (African Trade Union Conference 2002). Scholars at the Forum for Envisioning Africa, however,

> were of the view that neo-liberalism and classical economics is the framework that informs the NEPAD, though there has been an attempt (rather faint) at capturing the African reality. An examination of other models besides that of classical economics would have assisted those behind the NEPAD proposal to develop an alternative development framework, which is citizen-centred. (African Forum for Envisioning Africa 2002)

Similarly, a meeting of African scholars and development activists, held in Accra in April 2002, noted in its final declaration that 'the most fundamental flaws of NEPAD ... reproduce the central elements of the World Bank's *Can Africa Claim the Twenty-First Century?* and the ECA's *Compact for African Recovery'*. Among the fundamental flaws noted in the declaration are 'the neo-liberal economic policy framework at the heart of the [NEPAD] plan, which repeats the structural adjustment policy packages of the preceding two decades and overlooks the disastrous effects of those policies', and that 'in spite of claims of African origins, its main targets are foreign donors, particularly in the G8' (Joint Conference 2002). The Central Committee of the Congress of South African Trade Unions (COSATU) also raised 'concerns about the economic proposals in NEPAD' at its meeting of April 2002: 'We need to ensure that macro-economic governance does not stray too far towards stabilisation, at the cost of growth and employment creation. Moreover, emphasis on privatisation in the section [of the NEPAD base document] on infrastructure ignores the reality that privatised services will not serve the poor on our continent.'

Another concern is the definitions of 'democracy' and 'good governance' used in the NEPAD base document. According to the final declaration of the Accra meeting mentioned above, NEPAD's 'vision of democracy is defined by the needs of creating a functional market'. The African Forum for Envisioning Africa meeting declared that 'the architects of NEPAD appear to have transplanted the assumption of the concept of good governance of the World Bank, thus the document is lacking a comprehensive understanding of the structure of African society'. The critics have also taken issue with what is perceived to be the NEPAD base document's casual treatment − nay, tacit support − of the HIPC debt relief programme (as opposed to debt cancellation) and the Poverty Reduction Strategy Paper (PRSP) approach. Equally important is the issue of gender, an issue that has been raised in a number of scholarly papers.[3] Besides what is viewed as a lack of mainstreaming of gender in the NEPAD base document, including the strategies and priority sectors on which the initiative is anchored, there is also a concern that the base document 'adopts the social and economic measures that have contributed to the marginalisation of women' notwithstanding 'its stated concerns for social and gender equity' (Joint Conference 2002).

The third issue revolves around how the NEPAD base document conceptualises the substance of Africa's integration into the global economy. There is a recurring theme in the NEPAD base document that Africa is 'marginalised' and that therefore one of the solutions to the continent's predicament should be sought in its 'integration' into the global economy. This view has not been well received, not least because of the wealth of studies of Africa's political economy suggesting that the continent is the most integrated region in the global economy; the problem is not 'exclusion' or 'marginalisation', but rather the form and terms of the integration of the continent into the global economy. Viewed from this perspective, the NEPAD base document subscribes to a conformist approach to the international trade regime, anchored by the WTO. According to this critique, therefore, the focus should be on challenging the form and terms of Africa's integration into the global economy, including relations with the Bretton Woods institutions and transnational corporations. Furthermore, the Nairobi Forum of African Scholars 'viewed with suspicion' the 'enthusiasm with which the NEPAD proposal is receiving [sic] from the North ... particularly in connection to the call within the document "for more aid and free trade"'. The former Executive Secretary of the United Nations Economic Commission for Africa, Adebayo Adedeji (2002: 5), raised this point sharply in his keynote address to the Forum: 'Why has the new NEPAD initiative, unlike the five African initiatives of the 1980s and 1990s, been so well received by the donor community and the Bretton Woods institutions ...? Is it because it is in line with the DMS [development merchant system][4] or has there been a dramatic change of heart and attitude on the part of the merchants of the DMS? Are they going through a paradigm shift?'

The fourth issue is the conditionalities that are at the core of the NEPAD process. It is well known that the structural adjustment packages of the World Bank and the IMF entailed a set of conditionalities pertaining to macro-economic issues, public finance management and, from the late 1980s, insistence on a minimalist notion of 'democracy' and compliance with a technocratic definition of 'good governance'. For this reason, NEPAD's insistence on commitments that African leaders must first make on matters of corporate, political and economic governance is viewed as tantamount to the reintroduction of adjustment conditionalities through the back door.

The fifth issue is a view that the thinking in NEPAD is not informed by the wealth of development experience that the continent has accumulated since independence, and that the NEPAD base document makes no reference at all to landmark pan-African documents such as the Lagos Plan of Action of 1980, Africa's Priority Programme for Economic Recovery (APPER) of 1985, the United Nations Programme of Action for Africa's Economic Recovery and Development (UN-PAAERD) of 1986, the African Alternative Framework to Structural Adjustment Programmes for Socio-Economic Recovery and Transformation (AAF-SAP) of 1989, the African Charter for Popular Participation for Development of 1990, the Abuja Treaty of 1991 and the United Nations New Agenda for the Development of Africa in the 1990s (UN-NADAF) of 1991. What is important here is that the 'cardinal principles' at the core of these documents were, according to Adedeji (2002), 'self-reliance, self-sustainment, socio-economic transformation, holistic human development and the democratisation of the development process'. Indeed, Adedeji warned that 'NEPAD must not compromise these cardinal principles'; and, informed by his experience at the ECA, he notes that the key pre-NEPAD, non-DMS initiatives were 'undermined and jettisoned by the Bretton Woods institutions and Africans were thus impeded from exercising the basic and fundamental right to make decisions about their future'.

The final issue revolves around the relationship between the NEPAD process and the African Union institutions. There was a very strong view, especially around the time of the launch of the African Union in Durban, that NEPAD was a process running parallel to the latter and therefore posed a threat to the pan-African unity that the Organisation of African Unity (OAU) has built since its formation in 1963. Some critics even think that the role of NEPAD duplicates that of the Conference on Security, Stability, Development and Cooperation in Africa (CSSDCA).

Why the critique?

Before proceeding to an appraisal of the critiques under discussion, it may be necessary to reflect on why some of the issues arose in the NEPAD debate. The first factor is due to how the NEPAD initiative has been popularised until recently. As reflected in the 'NEPAD Progress Report: July 2002' presented at the inaugural summit of the African Union, hitherto the campaign for the popularisation of NEPAD has been confined to the private sector and Africa's development partners, including the G8 countries and multilateral institutions. The highly publicised meetings that the NEPAD process held with the private sector and leaders of the G8 and Bretton Woods institutions, without comparable attention being accorded to the popularisation of the initiative among African civil society, contributed to creating the suspicion that NEPAD was a 'deal' with the North and transnational corporations. Admittedly, this short-coming has been recognised, and hence it could be reported to the African Union in the NEPAD 'Initial Action Plan: July 2002' that 'now that the implementation of the NEPAD is ready to take off, the role of communications and marketing becomes very important'. To this effect, 'in-country' and 'regional' NEPAD communications structures are to be established not only for keeping 'the NEPAD initiative and all its projects and programmes alive in each and every country' and to 'ensure harmony in information dissemination throughout the continent and internationally', but also to take the initiative 'to schools, to communities, to the business sector, to religious institutions, to the youth and women's associations and the civil society at large' (NEPAD 2002: 8).

As well as the problem of suspicion outlined above, the NEPAD com-munication strategy that is now being implemented will have to address the confusion arising from stories making the rounds in the continent about the origins of the initiative. For Patrick Bond (2002: 9), for example, NEPAD was initiated by Thabo Mbeki in the form of the 'secretive Millennium African Recovery Plan [MAP]' marketed among the G8 countries and the Bretton Woods institutions during the course of 2000. Subsequent to that, 'Mbeki managed to sign on as partners two additional rulers from the crucial North [Abdelaziz Bouteflika of Algeria] and West [Olusegun Obasanjo of Nigeria] of the continent'. For Leon Pretorius and Saliem Patel (n.d.), the MAP 'was drawn up by a team of African and international economists under the auspices of a six-member steering committee headed by Professor Wiseman Nkuhlu from South Africa'.

A second obstacle is the extent to which decades of experience with authoritarian rule in most parts of the continent have eroded the trust that African people had in their leaders. To be sure, African scholars at the Nairobi Forum could observe: 'The distrust and absence of confidence that the people of Africa have in the leaders should not be taken lightly.' From this perspective, it is difficult for many sections of African civil society to accept that NEPAD could be a sincere effort by African leaders to address the development and political predicament of the continent.

Third, the critique of NEPAD is informed by contestations taking place within African countries. For example, the critique of NEPAD that is coming out of South Africa is essentially a critique of the ruling African National Congress (ANC) government, and particularly of the country's macro-economic policy. Hence, some of these critics, as exemplified by Bond, use 'NEPAD' and 'Mbeki' interchangeably. According to Bond (2002: 5), 'NEPAD's public reading of globalisation is blinkered and unrealistic, and so are Mbeki's plans for reform [of the global economy].

Here, South Africa's own experience is instructive, both in relation to lessons learned and actions taken to combat the excesses of global apartheid.' For Trevor Ngwane (2002), a Soweto-based anti-NEPAD activist, 'Mbeki calls for good governance and an end to corruption in NEPAD but in his own backyard his ANC comrades are busy enriching themselves through ill-gotten government contracts and kickbacks.' Similarly, for Mohau Pheko, a Johannesburg-based gender and trade network NGO activist: 'My question is, before we can even get to NEPAD, what has GEAR [the South African government's macro-economic strategy] done for us? What fundamental transformation has it brought to our lives? GEAR is too market-driven and export-oriented for the good of many. So before I embrace NEPAD, I want to know what it is that GEAR has done for me and my people?' (quoted in an interview in *Soweto Sunday World*, 11 August 2002). The secretary-general of the South African trade union federation, COSATU, also added his voice to the critique: 'COSATU will not accept any programme aimed at giving capital a free rein. What NEPAD amounts to is the Africanisation of the GEAR strategy. How can NEPAD hope to take us out of our ugly past if it's happening above our heads?' (cited in *Business Report*, Johannesburg, 29 April 2002).

The same can be said of the critique that has been coming out of Zimbabwe, which, for its part, is informed primarily by the crisis that the country is currently experiencing. Some Zimbabwean critics have argued that 'Zimbabwe's case could perhaps turn out to be the test case for NEPAD's governance agenda. It remains to be seen what Obasanjo and Mbeki's response will be faced with an increasingly recalcitrant regime in the former British colony' (as seen in a contribution by Innocent Nkata to an e-conference on NEPAD). This angle to the critique is also popular outside the continent: for example, the *Washington Post* (6 May 2002) wrote in a lead editorial entitled 'Africa's Challenge': 'Africa's leaders ... theoretically are committed to something called the New Partnership for Africa's Development.... But Africa's leaders need to demonstrate that they mean to live up to their rhetoric. Zimbabwe suggests that they may not. Zimbabwe is a textbook case of the link between governance and development.' The International Crisis Group (2002) took a similar line in its country report on Zimbabwe, with the sub-title 'G8 Should Link NEPAD to Progress on Zimbabwe Crisis': 'The EU, US and other friends of Zimbabwe can also help. They should toughen and extend targeted sanctions and make clear there will be no progress on NEPAD and the [Kananaskis] G8 summit ... unless African leaders put more pressure on ZANU-PF.'

Fourth, the legacy of the struggle against the structural adjustment programmes of the World Bank and the IMF is another factor, and so is the process of the transnationalisation of civil society. Not only have these experiences shaped the character of African civil society, but they have also contributed to the production of a wealth of 'counter' and 'alternative' development thinking across the continent. Nor has the credibility of the Bretton Woods institutions been left untainted by these contestations over structural adjustment. Indeed, a related factor is the struggle that is being waged by the 'anti-globalisation' forces against African debt and the international trade regime, as symbolised by the WTO. Therefore, any initiative that reads like another structural adjustment package (with its conditionalities) and is perceived to be advocating the 'integration' of Africa into the global economy will face stern opposition from these constituencies.

Finally, there is a significant shift taking place on the continent on the role of member states *vis-à-vis* the United Nations Economic Commission for Africa in the development and implementation of initiatives such as NEPAD. Adedeji (2002) was right to argue that many, even most, of the initiatives that preceded NEPAD were 'initiated and led by the ECA'. Since its inception in 1958, the ECA, as one of the regional commissions established by the United Nations Economic and Social Council, has played a critical role in the building of pan-African institutions, articulating development plans and strategies, advocating policies and providing technical cooperation, and supporting the OAU's anti-colonial struggles, especially in Southern Africa. It is thanks to the efforts of the ECA that institutions such as the African Development Bank were established, and that sub-regional communities like the Economic Community of West African States (ECOWAS) and the Common Market of Eastern and Southern Africa (COMESA) became a reality.

However, recently, and especially since the 2001 summit of the OAU in Lusaka, there is a growing determination by some states on the continent to take the initiative and give leadership on critical pan-African matters, rather than leave these to the ECA. It is partly for this reason, and contrary to what is commonly believed in some civil society quarters, that the ECA was not involved in the early conceptualisation and development of the NEPAD base document. In fact, the ECA's reaction to the unveiling of MAP was to develop its own *Compact for African Recovery: Operationalising the Millennium Partnership for the African Recovery Programme*. The non-involvement of the ECA in the early phases of the NEPAD process may have affected the extent to which the NEPAD base document could dialogue with previous initiatives, of course, but perhaps this is also a signal of the beginning of a new power relationship between the ECA and the continent's states. It may be better, as is the case in most parts of the world, that critical continental development issues should be politically driven (by organs that represent constituencies) rather than left to United Nations agencies.

Back to basics

What is the origin of NEPAD, and how did the process evolve? Nigeria's President Obasanjo recently reported in his 'Progress Report' on behalf of the NEPAD Heads of State Implementation Committee.

> As you will recall, the mandate for the [NEPAD] initiative had its genesis at the OAU Extraordinary Summit held in Sirte, Libya, during September 1999. The Summit mandated President Mbeki and President Bouteflika to engage Africa's creditors on the total cancellation of Africa's external debt. Following this, the South Summit of the Non-Aligned Movement and the G77, held in Havana, Cuba, during April 2000, mandated President Mbeki and myself to convey the concerns of the South to the G8 and the Bretton Woods institutions. Realising the correlation between the two mandates and the fact that debt relief forms one critical aspect of the overall development agenda for Africa, our [OAU] Summit in Togo in July 2000 mandated the three of us to engage the developed North with a view to developing a constructive partnership for the regeneration of the Continent.[5]

It is important to note here that the NEPAD mandate originates from the same summit that set in motion the process of the establishment of the African Union and its related organs. This was no accident; the two initiatives, the African Union and NEPAD, are central to the pan-African drive for the realisation of the continent's recovery.

Contrary to what is suggested in some of the critiques, the NEPAD process was a culmination, rather than the beginning, of energies that were invested into efforts aimed at finding solutions to the continent's development predicament. This section will try to problematise a claim raised in one of the NGO declarations on NEPAD: 'While conscious of the importance of joint endeavours for the development of Africa, this "new international partnership" initiative [NEPAD] ignores and sidelines past and existing programmes and efforts by Africans themselves to resolve Africa's crises'. The declaration cites as examples of sidelined programmes the Lagos Plan of Action and the Cairo Agenda, and then continues:

> In contrast to such programmes, NEPAD is mainly concerned with raising external resources, appealing to and relying on external governments and institutions. In addition, it is a top-down programme driven by African élites and drawn up with the corporate forces and institutional instruments of globalisation, rather than being based on African people's experiences, knowledge and demands. A legitimate African programme has to start from the people and be owned by the people. (African Civil Society Declaration 2002)

This section of this chapter will argue that Africa is yet to see a programme that will 'start from the people'; even the OAU declaration and the celebrated Lagos Plan of Action, as well as the United Nations Millennium Declaration, followed a top-down approach, and were all driven by the political élite.

Nor did NEPAD invent the idea of a 'partnership' with the North, amid a recognition that the post-1990s had introduced new challenges and constraints for the continent that were not there in the late 1970s and early 1980s when the Lagos Plan of Action was developed. UN-PAAERD (1986–90) was the first systematic programme aimed at creating a 'compact' or 'partnership' with the international community. Indeed, the then UN Secretary-General was very optimistic about this programme which, according to him, represented a

> unique agreement between African states and the international community, with both sides committing themselves to serious far-reaching efforts to accelerate Africa's development process. It was the first such programme to be adopted by the United Nations, and it created major expectations for better prospects for Africa. (Cited in Centre for Southern African Studies 1991: 1)

UN-PAAERD, as a 'compact' between African leaders and the international community, was based on the principles of mutual commitment, responsibility and cooperation. The international community, through the UN, committed itself to mobilising resources through aid, and African leaders, for their part, committed themselves to implementing a 'sharply focused, practical and operational set of activities, priorities and policies' at national, sub-regional and regional levels.[6]

The end of the Cold War presented the continent with a set of new challenges, and the OAU at its summit of July 1990 in Addis Ababa, Ethiopia, adopted a declaration 'on the Political and Socio-Economic Situation in Africa and the Fundamental Changes Taking Place in the World'. This declaration noted 'fundamental' changes which, 'we found, constitute major factors which should guide Africa's collective thinking about the challenges and options before her in the 1990s and beyond in view of the real threat of marginalisation of our continent'. African leaders at the summit were also 'concerned that, in addition to these problems [challenges] there is an increasing tendency to impose conditionalities of a political nature for assistance to Africa'. Nonetheless, the summit conceded that 'democracy and development should go together and should be mutually reinforcing', and that 'the achievement of … objectives [listed in the declaration] will also require an international cooperation and solidarity as well as fundamental changes in the international economic system'.

Similarly, the Final Review and Appraisal of the Implementation of UN-PAAERD, presented to the UN General Assembly in December 1990, introduced its preamble with a loaded assessment: 'the Programme of Action proved to be too optimistic in two basic senses. First, the concept of a global compact at the continental level was difficult to achieve. Specific arrangements were not always directly related to the goals and targets of the Programme of Action. Second, hopes for a favourable external economic environment for Africa during the period 1986–1990 were not fulfilled.' For its part, the United Nations Conference on Trade and Development (UNCTAD), in its very detailed Review and Appraisal of UN-PAAERD, reached a depressing conclusion: 'Progress has been uneven and insecure.' For this reason, the UN launched another programme in 1991, because 'the circumstances which led to the adoption of the Programme of Action are as valid today as they were in 1986'. UN-NADAF had as its priority objectives into the 1990s 'the accelerated transformation, integration, diversification and growth of the African economies, in order to strengthen them within the world economy, reduce their vulnerability to external shocks and increase their dynamism, internalise the process of development and enhance self-reliance'. UN-NADAF was founded on two key principles: shared responsibility and full partnership. Notwithstanding the mid-term and final reviews of UN-NADAF in 1994 and 2000 respectively, the impact of this initiative on the continent is yet to be seen.

It was from the mid-1990s that African leaders started defining, in concrete terms, how the continent should tackle its post-Cold War challenges, and the operationalisation of the relationship between democracy and development. The 'Relaunching Africa's Economic and Social Development: the Cairo Agenda for Action' document, adopted at the OAU summit of 1995, was one of the biggest efforts in this regard. The Cairo Agenda for Action, as a 'compact', is a programme constructed around 'What we can do for ourselves' and 'What we require from our development partners'. Among the commitments that African leaders make in the Cairo Agenda for Action are 'democracy, governance, peace, security, stability and sustainable development' and the 'structural transformation of African economies'. The issues that are entailed in the latter commitment include 'the need for Africa to be competitive, if it is to participate in the world economy', and a call on African governments to 'launch a programme to restructure Africa's exports and expand intra-African trade in particular through trade liberalisation programmes'. The Cairo Agenda for Action calls on African governments to 'ensure the speedy promotion of good governance, characterised by accountability, probity, transparency, equal application of the rule of law, and a clear separation of powers, as an objective and a condition for rapid and sustainable development in African societies'. Furthermore, for the Cairo Agenda, 'it is essential to clearly define the role of government and the private sector in development. Governments should make special efforts to encourage the participation of the private sector in the development process.'

As to what is required from the continent's 'development partners', the Cairo Agenda for Action calls for the 'democratisation of the international system', and raises a concern that 'development aid that had been provided had not always been used for the priority programmes of countries assisted. What is more, we are witnessing an increasing marked trend of rivalry between African governments and non-governmental organisations (NGOs). Sometimes the governments were even robbed of their responsibilities.' On the debt issue, the programme notes that

> for economic reforms to succeed in Africa, all creditors including multi-lateral institutions should adopt enhanced measures which should go beyond debt rescheduling. International commitment to Africa's recovery can be shown by reducing the debt burden to a point where it ceases to inhibit investing in Africa.

Some of the issues entailed in the Cairo Agenda for Action were raised again at the OAU's millennium summit in July 1999, in the form of the Algiers Declaration. The declaration notes that

> despite the hopes generated by the end of the Cold War and the attendant prospects of peace, development and integration in the world economy, we note that the post-Cold War era is fraught with new and grave uncertainties, serious risks of marginalisation and new challenges that pose numerous threats to our continent.

Of course, while the Declaration reiterated the leaders' 'commitment to the protection and promotion of human rights and fundamental freedoms', it also called upon 'the international community to ensure that they [the latter principles] are not used for political purposes'. Indeed, the Declaration also called for 'a mutually beneficial and genuine international partnership; a partnership based on a balance of interests and mutual respect; a partnership, the most crucial and immediate ingredients of which are the genuine democratisation of international relations'. It was left to the summit in Lomé, Togo, in July 2000, to develop 'a set of common values and principles for democratic governance' in its 'Declaration on the Framework for an OAU Response to Unconstitutional Changes of Government'. For the first time, the OAU tried with this declaration to develop a common standard for what constitutes 'democratic governance' and a definition of 'unconstitutional changes of government', and these ideas were to be incorporated into the NEPAD process.

The year 2000 was probably one of the most productive years for the OAU in as far as matters discussed in this chapter are concerned; the year not only witnessed the consolidation of the NEPAD mandate and the adoption of the declaration on unconstitutional changes of government, there were also other important developments which were to impact on the NEPAD process. Important in this regard was the adoption by the OAU and the European Community of the Cairo Plan of Action, a commitment made in April 2000 'to work towards a new strategic dimension to the global partnership between Africa and Europe'. The partnership envisaged in the Cairo Plan of Action is to rest on five pillars, including 'integrating Africa into the world economy' and 'human rights, democratic principles and institutions, good governance and the rule of law'. Under 'integrating Africa into the world economy', the two regional bodies agreed to 'deepen the link between trade and development in the multilateral trading system'; 'enhance the capacity of African countries to derive maximum benefits from opportunities offered by the WTO'; 'support the efforts of African countries in continuing to adopt sound macro-economic and other policy reforms, including adjustment policies, as well as the effort of the public sector in creating the enabling environment for the development of the private sector activity'; 'commit ourselves to the creation of a conducive environment in Africa for an enhanced private sector development, including macro and micro economic foundations of competitiveness'; and 'work with governments and private sector in order to improve a regulatory framework for the business community'.

The consolidation of the acceptance of the concept of a triangular relationship between democracy, peace/security, and development, an idea that developed strongly in the course of the 1990s and influenced the NEPAD base document, was achieved in the Solemn Declaration of the CSSDCA, which was adopted at the Lomé summit of July 2000. The Solemn Declaration, based on the CSSDCA concept as developed by President Obasanjo in the 1990s, is anchored by a recognition of 'the interlinkage between peace, stability, development, integration and co-operation'. In an effort to operationalise this concept, the CSSDCA is organised around four 'calabashes' for Security, Stability, Development and Cooperation. Each of the four calabashes has a set of principles and a plan of action. The CSSDCA, as outlined under the Development Calabash, was not intended to compete with the NEPAD process, which was already in place: 'An effective solution to Africa's external debt problem including total debt cancellation in accordance with the mandate given to Presidents of Algeria and South Africa, is crucial to supporting Africa's programme on poverty eradication.' Nor did the Solemn Declaration deviate from the acceptance of the importance of democracy for the continent; the Stability Calabash notes that 'stability requires that all States be guided by strict adherence to the rule of law, good governance, people's participation in public affairs, respect for human rights and fundamental freedoms, the establishment of political organisations devoid of sectarian, religious, ethnic, regional and racial extremism'.

Therefore, when African Ministers of Finance met in November 2000 under the auspices of the ECA to prepare for the UN High-Level Meeting on Financing for Development and the Third UN Conference on Least Developed Countries, not only was the process of the drafting of the NEPAD base document already in place, but the concept of a 'compact' or 'partnership' with the North based on some trade-offs was already entrenched in the continent's development thinking. Indeed, the ECA conference of African finance ministers resolved to develop a 'New Global Compact with Africa' in which 'the developed countries would invest the necessary resources, through aid, debt relief and market access, in order to give African countries the needed impetus to sustained growth. In turn, Africa would intensify its efforts at political and economic reforms' (ECA 2000). However, the ECA's work on the compact was affected and reoriented by the NEPAD process, which had been taking place for over a year. According to the ECA, 'as the process of articulating the Compact and the related consultations evolved, it emerged that the Presidents Mbeki of South Africa, Obasanjo of Nigeria and Bouteflika of Algeria were developing an initiative known as the Millennium Partnership for African Recovery Programme (MAP)', and therefore the compact was 'conceived as a technical input to the elaboration and implementation of MAP', and published in April 2001 as the *Compact for African Recovery: Operationalising the Millennium Partnership for the African Recovery Programme* (ECA 2001).

From this perspective, the 2001 summit of the OAU in Lusaka not only consolidated all these developments, some of which had been running parallel to each other, but also set in motion an implementing mechanism for the NEPAD process in the form of the Implementation Committee which was to report to the summit. This decision was not aimed at marginalising the OAU at all. The NEPAD Progress Report to the African Union in July 2002 addressed this matter: 'The management structures of NEPAD are not designed to be a new bureaucracy or to compete with OAU/AU structures, but are designed to ensure follow-up and implementation in the phase of transition from the OAU to the AU.' The inaugural summit of the African Union did not bring to an end this status quo as the transition is ongoing, and this includes the transformation of the OAU Secretariat into the Commission of the African Union. Indeed, in the Durban declaration African leaders vowed to 'rededicate ourselves to the objectives of the ... NEPAD, as a programme of the African Union for strengthening inter-African cooperation and integration in a globalising world and to overcome the prevalence of poverty and strive for a better quality of life for all the peoples of Africa' (African

Union 2002). And as part of the continent's ongoing search for and effort to develop common norms and standards for the improvement of governance in Africa, the summit also adopted a Declaration on the Principles Governing Democratic Elections in Africa, which not only defines the role of the Union, but also puts forward principles of democratic elections and the responsibility of member states.

Another important achievement of the Durban summit was the adoption of the Declaration on Democracy, Political, Economic and Corporate Governance as an instrument that will facilitate accession by member states to the NEPAD process and ensure compliance with the principles contained therein. This declaration is organised around four objectives: democracy and good political governance, economic and corporate governance, socio-economic development, and the African Peer Review Mechanism. Whereas the latter, according to the declaration, 'will entail an undertaking to submit to periodic reviews [by an independent agency], as well as to facilitate such reviews, and be guided by agreed parameters for good political governance and good economic and corporate governance', each of the three other objectives has a set of principles and an action plan.

The NEPAD declaration should be read together with the NEPAD base document; the two documents are complementary. The NEPAD process, as already suggested, began in 1999, and the drafting of the base document, first as MAP and later as the merged version, took place between July 2000 (the Lomé summit) and July 2001 (the Lusaka summit). For its part, the Declaration on Democracy, Political, Economic and Corporate Governance is not only aimed at taking the NEPAD process forward, but is also an attempt to engage some of the responses to and critiques of the NEPAD base document. There are a number of areas where the declaration demonstrates an attempt to cover ground that could not be covered in the base document. For example, in the first place the declaration pays tribute to a long list of pre-NEPAD initiatives, none of which is mentioned in the NEPAD base document. Second, there is an attempt, arising from the previous point, to locate NEPAD firmly in the tradition of the OAU, particularly in how declarations are formulated and issues are raised. There is also an attempt to mainstream the thinking already in existence within the OAU into the declaration. For example, the section on 'Democracy and Good Political Governance' draws strongly on the declaration on unconstitutional changes of government, especially in the definition of core values and common standards for democracy and good governance. There is also an effort to reaffirm the approach, principles and plan of action outlined in the CSSDCA Solemn Declaration. Third, there is an attempt to re-emphasise gender equity and mainstream gender into NEPAD thinking, especially in the section on 'Socio-Economic Development':

'The marginalisation of women remains real despite the progress of recent years. We will, therefore, work with renewed vigour to ensure gender equality and ensure the full and effective integration of women in political and socio-economic development.'

Fourth, there is an attempt to put socio-economic rights at the centre of the NEPAD objectives as part of the effort to ensure that the plight of people remains the central objective of development. Part of this is the emphasis on the role of the state: 'Globalisation and liberalisation does not mean that there should be no role for government in socio-economic development. It only means a different type of government.' Finally, while the declaration 'welcome[s] the strong international interest in and support for NEPAD', it nonetheless calls for 'new forms of international cooperation in which the benefits of globalisation are more evenly shared'; the creation of 'a stable international economic environment in which African countries can achieve growth through greater market access for their exports; the removal of trade barriers, especially non-tariff barriers and other forms of protectionism'; and 'debt cancellation'.[7]

Conclusion: the way forward

The debate sparked by the release of the NEPAD base document has mobilised constituencies across the continent and put Africa's development at the top of the agenda. At the same time, some elements of the critique are due to a limited and selective reading of the development literature emanating from the OAU, especially since the 1990s. The NEPAD process is an attempt to bring together all the strands of thinking that have been running through the OAU since the end of the Cold War, especially the triangular interlinkage between democracy, development and peace/security. There has also been an effort within the OAU throughout the 1990s to develop common values and standards for the improvement of governance on the continent, and this entails accepting self-imposed 'conditionalities' while at the same time calling on the North not to use these for political gain. Also, there has been consensus within the OAU on the substance of the challenges facing the continent in the post-Cold War era, and on how these should be tackled. The NEPAD process, itself a product of this consensus on the approach to take in the 'globalising' world, is a further elaboration of this consensus.

What is new about the NEPAD initiative, however, is the attempt to develop an effective mechanism for the enforcement of compliance with some key principles that African leaders have been committing themselves to in OAU declarations for more than two decades. The thinking in NEPAD, as a product of deliberations among the continent's political élite, will inevitably reflect the character and limitations of this élite in particular and the post-colonial state in general, and this includes contradictions between African countries. To try to read NEPAD as a socialist programme or a party-political plan is to miss the point. It is through a careful and patient engagement with the NEPAD process that non-state actors, including critics, can advance their own agenda. For example, the Peer Review Mechanism can be used effectively by organs of civil society, especially those with grassroots support, to advance the democratic consolidation process within countries and hold leaders accountable. And likewise with the emphasis in the NEPAD declaration on socio-economic rights: this can be used to advance micro and macro struggles around the right to development. Those non-state organs involved in struggles on the international trade front can use to their political benefit issues that are being taken up in the NEPAD process around market access, the transformation of the international trade regime and the Bretton Woods institutions, and the call for debt cancellation.

There are many ways in which the NEPAD process can be used to advance struggles by non-state actors on a number of fronts, and this will benefit the continent's recovery efforts.

NOTES

1 For this debate, see, for example, Africa-Canada Forum 2002; *Au Courant* 2001.
2 Most of this material and information is available electronically: for an attempt to bring it together, see Bond 2002.
3 See, for example, Longwe 2002; Butegwa n.d.
4 By DMS, Adedeji (2002: 4) refers to a system 'under which foreign-crafted economic reform policies have been turned into a new kind of special goods which are largely and quickly financed by the operators of the DMS, regardless of the negative impact of such policies on the African economies and polities'.
5 This report was incorporated into the 'NEPAD Progress Report: July 2002' which was submitted to the inaugural summit of the African Union.
6 UN-PAAERD and other landmark documents can be found in *Africa's Development Thinking Since Independence: a Reader*, 2002.
7 This declaration is contained in 'Summary of NEPAD Action Plans: July 2002'.

REFERENCES

Adedeji, A., 2002, 'From the Lagos Plan of Action to the New Partnership for African Development and the Final Act of Lagos to the Constitutive Act: Whither Africa?', Keynote Address at the African Forum for Envisioning Africa, Nairobi, Kenya.

Africa-Canada Forum, 2002, 'The New Partnership for Africa's Development (NEPAD): a Commentary', April.

African Civil Society Declaration on NEPAD, 2002, Durban, 4–8 July.

African Forum for Envisioning Africa, 2002, Executive Summary of the proceedings, Nairobi, Kenya.

African Trade Union Conference, 2002, 'Dakar Declaration on the Role of African Workers and Trade Unions in the New Partnership for Africa's Development', 20 February.

African Union, 2002, 'Durban Declaration', Durban: African Union, 10 July.

AISA, 2002, *Africa's Development Thinking Since Independence: a Reader*, Pretoria: Africa Institute of South Africa.

Au Courant, 11, 1 (2001).

Bond, P. (ed.), 2002, *Fanon's Warning: a Civil Society Reader on the New Partnership for Africa's Development*, Trenton: Africa World Press.

Butegwa, F. n.d. 'Popularising NEPAD Among Women in Africa', paper prepared for the United Nations Fund for Women (UNIFEM).

Centre for Southern African Studies, 1991, 'Extracts from: Economic Crisis in Africa: Final Review of the Implementation of UN-PAAERD', Cape Town: University of the Western Cape.

Chabal, P., 2002, 'The Quest for Good Government and Development in Africa: Is NEPAD the Answer?', *International Affairs*, 78, 3.

COSATU, 2002, Media Statement of the Central Executive Committee, Johannesburg: Congress of South African Trade Unions.

ECA, 2000, Eighth Session of the Conference of African Ministers of Finance, 'Statement on the Third UN Conference for the Least Developed Countries', Addis Ababa: UN Economic Commission for Africa, 21–22 November.

—— 2001, *Compact for African Recovery: Operationalising the Millennium Partnership for the African Recovery Programme*, Addis Ababa: UN Economic Commission for Africa.

International Crisis Group, 2002, 'Zimbabwe: Risk of Internal Conflict Imminent: G8 Should Link NEPAD to Progress on Zimbabwe Crisis', 14 June.

Joint Conference on Africa's Development Challenges in the Millennium, 2002, 'Declaration on Africa's Development Challenges', Accra: Council for Development of Social Research in Africa (CODESRIA) and Third World Network-Africa, 23–26 April.

Kifle, H. et al. (eds.), 1997, *A New Partnership for African Development: Issues and Parameters*, Uppsala: Nordic Africa Institute.

Longwe, S. H., 2002. 'Assessment of the Gender Orientation of NEPAD', paper presented at the African Forum for Envisioning Africa, Nairobi, Kenya.

Mills, G. and T. Hughes, 2001/2, 'MAPing a New Future: Towards a New Development Paradigm for Africa?', *South African Yearbook of International Affairs*, Johannesburg: South African Institute of International Affairs.

Nabudere, D., 2002, 'NEPAD: Historical Background and Its Prospects', paper presented at the African Forum for Envisioning Africa, Nairobi, Kenya.

NEPAD, 2002, 'Initial Action Plan: July 2002', Midrand: NEPAD Secretariat.

Ngwane, T. 2002. 'Should African Social Movements Support NEPAD?', Notes from a speech to the African Social Forum's Seminar, World Social Forum, Porto Alegre, Brazil, 2 February.

OAU, 1990, 'Declaration on the Political and Socio-Economic Situation in Africa and the Fundamental Changes Taking Place in the World', Addis Ababa: Organisation for African Unity, 9–11 July.

Pretorius, L. and S. Patel, n.d. 'The New Partnership for Africa's Development (NEPAD): a Critical Review', *Labour Research Service*.

Tandon, Y., 2002, 'NEPAD = SAP+GATS+DSB', *Seatini Bulletin*, 5, 4 (28 February).

PART 2

Sectoral Challenges

4 Africa's Agrarian Transformation
The Efficacy of the NEPAD Agriculture Strategy

Sam Moyo

Objectives and goals of NEPAD

This chapter provides a brief appraisal of the efficacy of the agricultural development strategy of NEPAD. The New Partnership for Africa's Development (NEPAD) purports to be 'a renewed commitment by African leaders to eradicate widespread poverty in the region and put the African continent on a path of sustainable growth and development and accelerate the integration of the continent into the global economy' (NEPAD 2001: 17). This objective is laudable and indeed a timely starting point from which to reverse Afro-pessimism and resist the continued inequitable exploitation of African rural resources and labour, and through which to focus the African Union on fighting for equitable global governance, resource allocations, consumption and trade relations.

The programme of action for NEPAD was endorsed by all heads of state who attended the African Union Summit in July 2002 in South Africa. Belatedly, a deliberate effort has begun to broaden the consultative process with civil society and to ensure greater participation of more governments and Africans. This chapter attempts to promote this process. The recent emergence of various civil society, research and community-based organisations and state forums debating NEPAD is laudable. The need to digest and incorporate their concerns is critical, yet engagement also needs to be structured in a way that brings maximum benefit.

The long-term objectives of NEPAD suggest a commitment to focusing development efforts on rural development. These objectives include the eradication of poverty and placing the African countries, both individually and collectively, on a path of sustainable growth and development, thus ending the marginalisation of Africa in the globalisation process and promoting the role of women in all activities (NEPAD

Table 4.1 Matrix of goals and objectives of NEPAD agriculture sector plan

Goals	Objectives
Increased food security	• To achieve food security in African countries, through increased food production, thus raising nutritional standards
Better access to markets	• To promote measures against natural resource degradation and encourage production methods that are environmentally sustainable • To integrate the rural poor into the market economy and provide them with better access to export markets • To develop Africa into a net exporter of agricultural products • To become a strategic player in agricultural science and technology development
Increased rural incomes	• To increase rural people's purchasing power and stabilise rural incomes
Rural infrastructure	• To improve rural infrastructure
Institutional environment	• To improve the agricultural institutional environment, through institutional support in the form of research centres and institutes, and the provision of extension and support services
Resource mobilisation	• To lobby bilateral donors and multilateral institutions for financial support for African agriculture • To mobilise internal resources (public and private financing)

Source: NEPAD 2001.

2001: 29). The main goals of NEPAD are clearly specified as being focused on high growth rates and less clearly but implicitly concerned with promoting equity, through a commitment to advancing the social development aims of the Millennium Development Goals (MDGs). The goals are to achieve and sustain an average GDP growth rate of above 7 per cent per annum for the next fifteen years, and to ensure that the continent achieves the MDGs (NEPAD 2001: 29). To tackle these goals and objectives, NEPAD has set up sectoral priorities: infrastructure, especially information and communication technology and energy; human resources; health; agriculture; the environment; and market access initiatives. The plan does not state whether the priority areas are ranked in order of importance, but the importance of agriculture in Africa cannot be overemphasised. The sector accounts for about 35 per cent of the continent's GDP, 40 per cent of its exports, and 70 per cent of total employment (Townsend 2000).

Since the overall focus of NEPAD is implicitly on eliminating rural poverty, it is essential that any assessment of NEPAD's efficacy should examine the real commitment of its objectives to the rural populace and disaggregate the expected growth and development impacts in this framework. A synthesis of NEPAD's agricultural strategy objectives shows that the programme seeks to achieve the range of goals outlined in Table 4.1.

This chapter examines the nature and efficacy of the NEPAD agricultural strategy in terms of delivering transformation that can ensure rural development, poverty reduction and regional integration. Specifically, the chapter identifies, from scattered sections of the NEPAD base document, the basis of its agricultural strategy, and tries to bring descriptive coherence to it.

Status of agriculture in Africa

To ensure an appropriate strategy is developed, a thorough understanding of the underlying status of African agriculture is necessary. The agriculture sector plan of NEPAD provides an extensive assessment of the state of African agriculture and rural poverty, but is limited in its treatment of the structural forces and external (global) causes of rural and agricultural underdevelopment. In focusing on internally based weaknesses, NEPAD does identify some crucial features of African poverty. The majority of Africa's population are rural-based, and thus heavily dependent on agriculture for their livelihood and survival. Rural areas are home to some eighty per cent of the total population, which includes seventy per cent of the continent's extreme poor and undernourished (NEPAD 2002a). Agriculture contributes a significant

Table 4.2 Importance of agriculture in selected national economies

Country	Agriculture as % share of GDP (1995)	Agricultural labour as % of total labour force (1990)
Angola	17.8	75
Botswana	4.2	46
Burundi	52.1	92
Comoros	38.7	77
Eritrea	11.2	80
Ethiopia	50.0	86
Kenya	29.7	80
Lesotho	11.0	40
Madagascar	33.8	78
Malawi	44.2	87
Mauritius	9.4	17
Mozambique	34.9	83
Namibia	13.6	49
Rwanda	37.8	92
Seychelles	4.0	11
South Africa	4.4	14
Swaziland	12.5	39
Tanzania	46.2	84
Uganda	49.5	85
Zambia	18.7	75
Zimbabwe	17.1	68

Source: IFAD 2001.

share to the continent's GDP and the majority of Africa's labour force is employed in agriculture (see Table 4.2).

Poverty in Africa has reached alarming levels: half of the population, or 340 million people, live on less than US$1 per day, the international poverty line (NEPAD 2001). On the global scene, of 1.2 billion people in extreme poverty, 25 per cent are from sub-Saharan Africa. An examination of poverty statistics in Eastern and Southern Africa indicates that the majority of Africa's rural people live below the national poverty line, as shown in Table 4.3. The proportion of rural people below the national poverty line is as high as 90 per cent in Malawi and Rwanda. Proportions of urban populations below the national poverty line are less than of rural people. There exists a wide rural–urban gap.

Table 4.3 Prevalence of poverty by country

Country	Population living on less than $1 a day, %	Population living below national poverty line, %		
		Total	Urban	Rural
Angola				65
Botswana	35	28		55
Burundi	36	60	66	58
Comoros		33		
Eritrea		31	62	83/52
Ethiopia	46	55	32	34
Kenya	50	42	29	46
Lesotho	48	49	28	54
Madagascar	72	70	47	77
Malawi	42	54		90
Mauritius		11		12
Mozambique		51	62	69
Namibia		27	67	70
Rwanda	46	51	7	93
Seychelles		19		
South Africa	24	20		
Swaziland		27		50
Tanzania	11	51	20	50
Uganda	69	55	8	57
Zambia	85	68	46	88
Zimbabwe	41	26	39	75

Source: IFAD 2001.

Rural poverty in Africa has been attributed to various root causes, both internal and external. Table 4.4 presents a framework of some of the major causes of poverty for the rural people of Africa. Sub-Saharan Africa is home to some of the world's hungriest and most undernourished people. On a country basis, *per capita* dietary energy supply (calories per day) is decreasing in most countries. Compared to other regions, child malnutrition for children under five years is greatest in Africa: about a third of all children under five years are undernourished, compared to an average of 8 per cent in Latin America and the Caribbean, Europe and Central Asia. In addition, Africa has a very high infant mortality rate, of 106 per 1,000 live births, compared to the world average of 58 per 1,000 live births (World Bank 2001; Esterhuysen 2002).

Table 4.4 Causes of poverty among Africa's rural people

Cause	Description
1 Marginalisation of African farmers from the land	There is widespread inequitable land distribution biased against small-scale farmers. Research has shown a direct relationship between land holdings and poverty: poverty increases as land holdings decrease.
2 Marginalisation through system of exchange	Agricultural policies during the colonial era were heavily biased against rural African farmers, e.g. in some instances African farmers were not allowed to sell their surplus agricultural produce through the legal marketing channels, but were forced to sell to neighbouring large-scale commercial farmers or through informal channels. Smallholders were accorded little or no production support in the form of finance, extension, and so on.
3 Guided development after independence	Top-down approaches to policy formulation and implementation by the new governments, which largely ignored input from small-holders and thus their economic interests.
4 Incomplete adjustments	Structural adjustment programmes (SAPs) have had limited success on the African continent, in many cases incapacitating African rural agriculture through the removal of state support (input subsidies, production finance, price supports, etc.).
5 Internal small-scale farmer constraints	This problem mainly manifests itself in a shortage of labour for agricultural production. Labour-intensive production systems are still dominant in smallholdings in Africa.

Source: Derived from IFAD 2001.

Although there was an increase in the daily per capita dietary energy supply in sub-Saharan Africa from 2,120 kcal to 2,190 kcal between 1990–2 and 1997–9, the number of chronically undernourished people rose from 108 million to 194 million people during the same period (NEPAD 2002a). The problem of hunger in Africa is rooted in an inability to produce enough food to feed its growing population. Compared to other regions in the world, African agriculture uses predominantly traditional technologies and is heavily undercapitalised; for example, less than 7 per cent of cropped areas is irrigated and capital stock per hectare is about one quarter of that in Latin America (World Bank 2000). Fertiliser usage in Africa averages 19 kg per hectare, compared to 100 kg in East Asia and 230 kg in Northern Europe. It follows that Africa lags behind in farm productivity: for the year 2000, cereal yield averaged 1,230 kg per hectare, compared to 3,090 kg in Asia and 3,040 in Latin America (NEPAD 2002a). Indeed, Africa lags behind all other regions in the world in cereal production (see Figure 4.1). In 1999 alone, there was a production gap of almost 900 million metric tonnes between Africa and Asia. Moreover, cereal yields in Africa have remained stagnant at an average of between half to one metric tonne per hectare, while yields in the developed world have grown to more than three and a half metric tonnes per hectare between 1961 and 2001 (FAOSTAT Database).

Other constraints identified regarding the poor performance of African agriculture include inadequate infrastructure, unstable market opportunities, small markets and lack of current market information, uncertain policy environments and poor competitiveness of African products on the international market. The huge subsidies provided to Northern farmers are a major cause of the poor competitiveness of Africa's agricultural products. In the European Union and the USA, maize and sugar are priced well below what it costs to produce them; they are sold at between 20 and 25 per cent of their production costs, because of the huge subsidies accorded to farmers (Mather 2002). Compared to other regions in the world, the benefits derived by Africa from global agricultural trade are low because of the unfair trading practices of the North; ironically, trade among African states themselves and other developing countries is also very low. The majority of African countries' trade is with the North and thus heavily exposed to the double standards of the developed world. The World Trade Organization (cited in Oxfam 2002) notes that 70 per cent of Africa's merchandise exports were destined for Northern Europe, North America or Japan in 2000. South Africa exports 70 per cent of its citrus fruit to the EU, and faces a threat from the lobbying of one of the biggest citrus exporters, Spain, of a ban on fruit exports from South Africa. However, as Mather (2002) points

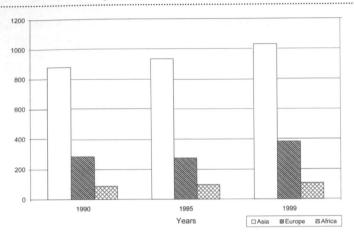

Figure 4.1 Cereal production (million metric tonnes)
Source: FAOSTAT Database.

out, Spain's problem is not about diseases or other health concerns, but about international competition.

Agricultural development is crucial to poverty reduction, to developing an agro-industrial strategy, and to promoting intra-country, inter-country and continental development linkages based on improved trade and balanced development.

NEPAD's agricultural development plan

NEPAD's agriculture strategy is placed within the framework of a specific developmental philosophy. As with most previous African development initiatives, NEPAD stays with the tradition of emphasising the promotion of agricultural development in Africa's future.

The NEPAD agricultural plan can be understood in terms of those elements directly specified as being the framework for agricultural development and other elements in the plan, which indirectly support agricultural development. The direct agricultural plan is composed of three key areas: land productivity and water management, food security and supply, and rural infrastructure and market access.

Land and water management

The NEPAD agricultural strategy seeks to address the problem of declining soil fertility in Africa's arable land, and the constraints associated with the continent's climatic variability through investment in new irrigation schemes and the rehabilitation of dormant schemes for increased agricultural production. About 725 million hectares, or 83 per cent of Africa's arable lands, have serious soil fertility or other limitations and will require costly improvements to attain high and sustained productivity. Nutrient depletion in the continent has been estimated to cost about US$1 billion to US$3 billion in natural capital loss. Due to the widespread problem, the plan proposes investments in the protection and improvement of the soil. The focus is also on the promotion of sustainable integrated soil fertility and land management approaches among farmers. An estimated total of US$3.7 billion is required for such investments in soil and water conservation.

Only 7 per cent of arable land is irrigated in Africa, but 40 per cent of this is in North Africa, whilst in the developing world the lowest percentages are 10, 29 and 41 per cent for South America, South-East Asia and South Asia, respectively. The agricultural strategy advocates strategic public and private investment in water management. Investments are estimated to increase the area under irrigation by close to 60 per cent, or 7.4 million hectares, to 20 million hectares by 2015. The plan identifies three categories of water and land developments: farm and small-scale irrigation development; humid lowland development and land improvement activities; and upgrading/rehabilitation of existing large-scale irrigation systems and development of new large-scale schemes. The whole programme is estimated to cost US$37 billion dollars over a 14-year period.

Food security and supply

Africa is home to the world's poorest people. One of the key objectives of NEPAD's agricultural strategy is to eradicate food insecurity and hunger on the continent, and ultimately poverty. To improve food security, the plan clearly articulates the need for vigorous large-scale community-based programmes to improve the performance of small farms throughout the region. The plan will encourage governments to provide a policy and incentive framework that is conducive to agricultural growth, including well-functioning and lucrative markets for agricultural products. Getting the policy and incentive framework right, it is thought, will induce farmers to make a contribution to the required investment in raising production.

Expanding food production by small farms alone will not be enough to eradicate hunger and poverty. According to the plan, governments will need to introduce targeted complementary measures to broaden the access to food by persons who are unable to meet their dietary requirements through their own production or have no access to resources to purchase it. These will take the form of targeted food safety nets. Another key component of the food supply plan is the need to strengthen partnerships within Africa and between Africa and the developed world in support of the food security problem. Within the continent, government, the private sector, and rural communities need to set up cooperation deals that are mutually beneficial.

The plan also outlines the necessity of taking advantage of existing regional programmes for food security, prepared by regional organisations in collaboration with the Food and Agriculture Organisation (FAO). The FAO's Regional Programme for Food Security (RPFS) is mainly composed of the following components: trade facilitation, harmonisation of agricultural policies and support of the national Special Programmes on Food Security (SPFS) adopted by all member countries of the FAO. The SPFS will be implemented in two phases, focusing on household and community-level food security issues (such as water control, intensification of sustainable production systems, diversification of farming activities, participatory analysis and resolution of socio-economic constraints that restrict farm-level profitability and food security). The funding estimates for food supply are estimated to rise from US$345 million in 2002 to US$710 million in 2015.

Rural infrastructure and market access

With the anticipated growth in agricultural production, the plan outlines the need for complementary investment in rural infrastructure, particularly roads, storage, processing and market facilities. The poor state of Africa's rural infrastructure is blamed on paltry investment in the sector. Between 1990 and 1996, external investments in economic infrastructure in sub-Saharan Africa were US$26.7 billion, or just over one-third of East Asia's US$71.9 billion dollars. Resource mobilisation will play a major role in investment in rural infrastructure through lobbying for concessional loans and grants from the international community. In addition, a mix of public and private financing alternatives will have to be considered. The plan also states the need for institutional support for capacity building and training in support of all organisations responsible for the planning, design, construction and continued operation, maintenance and management of both productive and rural infrastructure.

Under market access, the plan aims to reverse Africa's declining share of world exports. The continent's share of world exports decreased from about 8 per cent in 1971–80 to just 3.4 per cent in 1991–2000. International lobbying assistance is expected to play a key role in ameliorating domestic supply-side constraints, which include a high dependence on a limited number of exports, weak technological capacities, an inadequate legal and regulatory framework, and trade policies that fail to encourage agricultural exports.

The other objective under market access is investing in both human resources and facilities to meet technical standards for export products, in the context of WTO sanitary and phytosanitary standards. A wide gap exists between the developed world and Africa in product standards, especially in value-added processed products rather than primary products. Also of importance is intra-African trade: the plan articulates the need for the development of regional or continent-wide technical standards – in line with WTO agreements – for various sub-sectors within agriculture. Another major constraint facing Africa's trade is the unwillingness of the developed world to open up its markets to Africa's exports. The plan thus seeks to engage the developed world in constructive dialogue to reform restrictive trade practices that are biased against Africa. Estimates for funding requirements amount to some US$90 billion over the 14-year period.

Implementation strategy

The background sectoral documents of NEPAD (2002c) set out the basic framework through which the agriculture sector plan will be implemented. The proposed implementation will be based on a three-pronged strategy, which encompasses capitalising on natural resource management, strengthening economic and trade reforms, and focusing on rural development and poverty. For the successful implementation of the strategy, the steps and actions have been outlined at national, regional and international levels. These are summarised in Table 4.5.

The implementation plan also articulates issues that are to be addressed to advance the NEPAD agricultural strategy. These include getting agricultural and other economic policies right through policy reform and harmonisation, improving access to and investment in land and water resources, facilitating investment and resource mobilisation, and capitalising on existing initiatives that have endorsed NEPAD. Some of these initiatives include the Forum for Agriculture Research in Africa (FARA), the Southern African Centre for Cooperation in Agricultural and Natural Resources Training (SACCAR), the Association for Strengthening Agricultural Research in Eastern and Central Africa (ASARECA), the African Centre for Agricultural Research and Development (CORAF) in North Africa, the Consultative Group on International Agricultural Research (CGIAR) and its partners, the World Bank, FAO and the Global Forum for Agricultural Research.

Indirect agricultural plan components

Perhaps an inadequate consultative and integrative process of developing the agricultural sector development plan explains the tenuous and often implicit way in which various other components of NEPAD are expected to promote this sector. The indirect ways in which agricultural transformation is to be achieved largely involve the promotion of economic

Table 4.5 NEPAD agricultural strategy implementation

National level	Regional level	International level
• Increase public sector capacity to support farmers by reviewing national research and extension systems	• Review existing structures and programmes of regional and sub-regional institutions	• Develop renewed partnerships with donors, multilateral institutions and creditor governments
• Establish public and private sector partnerships (PPPs) for increased investment	• Establish crop-/livestock-specific research programmes or institutions	• Improve standards of produce and access to international markets
• Increase efficiency and use of water supply for agriculture	• Put in place strategies for food emergencies	• Network with external partners in areas of technological know-how, extension services and rural infrastructure
• Improve security of land tenure for traditional and modern farming	• Promote intra- and inter-regional trade by adopting international sanitary and phytosanitary standards and eliminating tariffs on cross-border trade	• Invest in research into high-yield crops, durable preservation and storage methods
• Enhance agricultural credit and finance schemes especially for smallholders	• Harmonise agricultural policies in the region	• Multilateral trade negotiations including sanitation and other agricultural trade regulations

Source: NEPAD 2001.

and agricultural policies and broader institutional change. Various NEPAD components that will have an indirect bearing on the agricultural strategy are synthesised in Table 4.6.

Critique of NEPAD agricultural sector plan

Development philosophy and framework
The NEPAD agriculture strategy is placed within a specific development philosophy and strategy. Although the NEPAD documents do not coherently explain the philosophical, theoretical and strategic basis of NEPAD's development strategy, it can be derived from the different sections of the report. The political context is one of seeking stability within the existing world order, based upon the rule of law within a liberal democratic political framework. The approach to development and change is based upon the evolution of markets and a liberalisation process supported by limited state intervention.

The major criticism regarding NEPAD is the efficacy of its development philosophy. The lack of an explicit commitment to promoting equity in general and in the agricultural sector is not only surprising but also indicative that NEPAD is theoretically founded on a 'trickle-down' framework. While it is notable that the agriculture-based rural development policies of NEPAD are directly concerned with poverty, references to equity and redistribution are lacking. Some of the implicit concerns with equity can, however, be explored from its sectoral plans.

Our analysis shows that the NEPAD agricultural strategy is steeped in a market-led framework to development management, which requires a minimalist role for the African state. This approach to promoting agricultural development is, however, fundamentally counter to existing practices of global agrarian development. While this approach to agricultural policy conforms to the dominant paradigm espoused by the Bretton Woods institutions, its major limitation is that the agricultural, trade and monetary policies of Northern states directly undermine the goals of weaker states. This is because agricultural development policy management in the northern hemisphere is based on extensive state intervention in product and factor markets in favour of an agrarian structure comprising mainly protected owner-operated family farms, dominated by private sector transnational firms. This relationship is reinforced and protected by the dominant position held by these states in key multilateral financial, aid and trade institutions. Some of the analytic, philosophical and strategic deficiencies of NEPAD's agricultural development strategy will be summarised in this section.

First, the overall analytic framework of the problems of agriculture and policy weaknesses are steeped in the Bergian and Batesian discourses

Table 4.6 NEPAD indirect agricultural plan components

NEPAD component	Objectives	Implications for agriculture
Infrastructure	• Expand cross-border infrastructural development • Improve access to infrastructural services	• Facilitate marketing within, across and between countries
Resource mobilisation	• Increase resource mobilisation through domestic savings, effective tax collection and private capital inflows • Debt relief • Push for reform of ODA delivery system	• Increase resource flows to agriculture and thus investment in the sector
Market access/trade	• Remove non-tariff barriers between countries • Improve competitiveness of African products through better production	• Increase intra-African trade and thus avoid risks associated with Northern markets
Human resources	• Poverty reduction • Improve skills training • Reverse the brain drain	• Availability of skilled labour base for the agricultural sector
Technology	• Promote cross-border cooperation in technology development and knowledge dissemination • Information analysis to support productive activities • Generate critical mass of technological expertise	• Ensure appropriate skills • Design and appraise appropriate technology for agriculture
Environment	• Environment and natural resource conservation	• Sustainable agricultural production

Source: NEPAD 2001.

(Mkandawire n.d.), whose factual and theoretical groundings have been refuted by two generations of African scholars (see Adésínà, Chapter 1). Moreover, the NEPAD agriculture strategy is based on a market-dominated approach to agricultural development management. While its focus on improving infrastructure is refreshing, it mainly follows SAP-type policy prescriptions because of the anti-state tendency. While it pretends to argue for a neutral and generic principled framework to redress specific agricultural production bottlenecks, the wider NEPAD macro-economic policy assumptions that inform the agricultural strategy do not provide for a proactive role for state intervention in enhancing agricultural development through the subsidisation of entrepreneurs and retaliation against Northern agricultural subsidies.

The major systemic weakness of the NEPAD agricultural strategy is its neglect of the primacy of Northern trade-related constraints to African agriculture. The double standards and effects of issues such as protectionism, subsidies, agricultural production and dumping are not articulated in a strategy to defend the African agricultural sector and to nurture the market potential repressed by external dumping.

In addition, the NEPAD rural strategy views rural poverty more as a by-product of improved market-based growth in agricultural production than as a direct product of the inefficiencies of capitalist agrarian systems, the negative effects of direct exploitation of rural labour and the wider effects of inequality. The strategy generally laments the lack of market access, but does not adequately specify how this deficiency operates or how African agriculture could more radically influence improved access to Northern markets. Instead, the strategy focuses on improving infrastructure and product quality, which could improve access to markets. The strategy is biased towards diplomatic dialogue and negotiation in international fora, while improving internal conditions for market access.

As a result, the strategy does not articulate issues of social justice or demands for reparations in general, which could form a basis for reviving African agriculture. This weakness is evident in the particular context of the land question in vast parts of the continent. It is a concern that the governance and economic policy framework omits the central problem of social justice, despite the widespread demand for social policy to be based on these concerns and the growing popular militancy that focuses on redistributing and seizing control of land resources. The strategy also calls for institutional reforms directed at internal national regulatory systems as the route to improved agricultural development, with little concern expressed for the improved regulation of the trans-national agrarian market system, or the reform of the international multilateral governance systems which affect agriculture.

Importantly, the strategy recognises the importance of agriculture in the larger development context, especially with respect to improving production and productivity. Nonetheless, the strategy lacks coherence in terms of setting targets for agricultural production that are linked to an industrialisation plan and other critical areas such as broader natural-resource-based economic activity and environmentally friendly, sustainable development. The role of domestic food security, local industrial inputs and markets, and the relationship between these and external markets as part of the wider development plan are not articulated, either.

So, too, the strategy recognises the importance of improving the income distribution structure of rural communities in order to enhance their consumption capacities and to reduce poverty – yet it does not have a vision for land and agrarian reform linked to an industrial development strategy that could cumulatively lead to development, especially for rural area populations. The strategy is loud about developing infrastructures such as irrigation infrastructure, energy, transportation, research and extension. But the organisation and targets for this are not specified, and appear to be based on market delivery systems. Table 4.7 shows the dominant models versus the desired models in NEPAD's development philosophy framework.

Food security

The main purposes of agricultural production are to meet food security needs, supply inputs to agricultural industry and earn foreign currency. As outlined earlier, hunger and malnutrition are increasing in Africa at an alarming rate. Agricultural exports are also decreasing. As can be seen in Table 4.8, at least half of the commodities exported by African countries declined in the last decade. There are also some crops that have increased in export quantities: the most notable is tea in Morocco. In Nigeria, for all the crops outlined, export quantities have fallen by more than 90 per cent, except for cocoa. At this point, Africa is increasingly depending on food aid and imports to feed its people and provide input requirements for agro-industry. African countries' dependency on food aid has serious connotations.

As noted by Oxfam (2002), in 1996 the United States Agency for International Development (USAID) was very proud of the fact that 90 per cent of the countries importing agricultural products from the USA were former recipients of food aid. Oxfam went on to note that there is a negative relationship between food aid availability and recipient country needs. Food aid is abundant when prices on the international market are depressed and vice versa.

The agricultural import bill is growing at a faster rate than export receipts. The African economy is increasingly relying on food imports to

Table 4.7 NEPAD's dominant model versus the desired model

Dimension	Dominant model	Desired model
Aid	• conditional	• humanitarian only
Loans	• high interest debt	• low interest
Trade	• unequal trade • unfair trade • externally oriented	• equitable trade • fair trade • internal logic
Investment	• privatisation • capital-intensive • minimal/deposit (counter-flows) • speculative • extractive	• employment-focused • internal investment focus • external concrete • material • value adding
Poverty focus	• growth then equity • inequality • impoverishing	• equitable redistribution • development then growth
Reform	• financial/macro-economic restructuring	• economic restructuring
Markets	• land enclosures • privatise/deregulate capital • withdrawn state	• redistribution • state support
Social unit	• private firms • NGOs	• pan-African • state

feed its people, as can be seen in Table 4.9. Food imports grew by nearly 20 per cent, while food exports increased by 13 per cent. The agricultural resource gap (the difference between agricultural exports and imports) is widening, having grown by some 44 per cent in the last decade.

Table 4.8 Changes in quantity of agricultural exports between 1990 and 2000, %

Country	Maize	Cotton	Tobacco	Beef	Cocoa	Coffee	Bananas	Tea	Rice
Algeria						−100.00			
Egypt	2,269.84	60.30	513.69	−93.90		−100.00		4,323.81	
Ethiopia		−100.00		−100.00		55.30		−40.65	
Ghana			790.67		44.70	719.24	12,463.00		
Malawi	−91.73	101.66	227.06		−51.58	−51.58		69.70	51.13
Morocco	−100.00	−83.35	−40.00					16,100.00	
Nigeria		−93.18	−98.87		−6.03	−100.00	−100.00	−100.00	
Senegal		32.04	701.21	−92.86				−99.61	600.00
South Africa	−69.17	−16.47	326.47	36.13		78.77	60.69	1,046.37	
Uganda	−98.83		2,626.45	−10.64		−22.62	−93.39	30.57	360.00
Zimbabwe	−85.69	−73.84	55.96	817.33	−80.00	−46.77	50,157.14	47.01	

Source: Calculated from FAOSTAT Database.

Table 4.9 Agricultural trade in Africa (US$000)

	1990	1995	2000	% Change 1990–2000
Food exports	6,950,093	7,836,503	7,884,732	13.4
Food imports	12,705,138	17,572,462	15,229,443	19
Agri-exports	12,193,472	15,305,689	13,546,248	11
Agri-imports	15,992,092	21,660,627	19,046,810	19
Resource gap	3,798,620	6,354,938	5,500,562	44.8

Source: FAO Database.

The main reasons for the purportedly poor performance of African agriculture are mainly internal, even if some external reasons are identified. According to NEPAD's assessment, these factors are among those crucial to the weakness of African agriculture in an interrelated and dynamic context:

External factors: these are largely defined as physical or environmental factors, such as climatic uncertainty; 'unstable world commodity prices' are also cited, albeit as more or less natural processes rather than outcomes of specific Northern economic policies, multilateral rules, and the particular operations of private transnational actors in the global system.

Internal factors: these are biases in the economic policies of the African states; to a lesser extent, the document cites the neglect of the agricultural sector by multilateral institutions.

The NEPAD agricultural strategy takes as its starting point a narrow perspective, which suggests that production decline in absolute terms defines the continent's agrarian problem. The decline in production is thus the cause of declining rural incomes and thus the main source of rural poverty. This internalist and physicalist explanation of the African agricultural crisis ignores the more fundamental global, systemic and complex character and causes of the African agricultural and rural poverty problem. The more appropriate complex problem needs to be articulated as follows:

1 The relative decline of agricultural production for domestic food and industrial requirements, relative to demographic changes (population growth and urban relocation of vast segments). This has led to increased food insecurity and impoverishment.

2 The increasing cost of food for the poor and the concentration of consumption among the relatively wealthier and better-endowed countries, regions and social groups.

3 Continued or proportionate decline in food production versus production for exports and even for local agro-industrial activities, as a result of the concentrated allocation of resources towards raw material exports and because of the de-industrialisation of basic agro-industrial concerns.

4 The declining earnings from agricultural exports as a result of declining terms of trade and the protection of Northern markets. This has constrained foreign currency earnings and rural incomes.

However, the analysis of internal factors focuses on the purported omissions of multilateral institutions in the area of lending, rather than on their sins of commission, such as protection and subsidies, and exploitative lending policies. Thus the NEPAD agricultural strategy is more preoccupied with reversing the decline of World Bank credit to African agriculture – from 39 per cent to 7 per cent over the last twenty years – than with the negative effects of their SAP-based agricultural conditionalities, or with proposing a fundamentally different policy framework.

Land and water

One of the problems that the plan neglects is the inequitable distribution of land and water resources. The legacy of colonialism created dual agrarian structures in Africa. The problem of inequitable distribution of land is most profound in Southern Africa.[1] For other parts of Africa, the problems associated with land are mainly to do with insecurity of tenure and traditional property regimes. Most small farmers throughout Africa have land use rights and ownership is vested in the state. Many authors (Platteau 1996; Binswanger and Deninger 1993) argue that land reforms that involve redistribution are not needed in most parts of sub-Saharan Africa; instead, reform should aim at strengthening indigenous land rights. Furthermore, they recommend the implementation of market-based land reform for redistribution (Moyo 2000).

Table 4.10 shows the distribution of land by various types of land tenure in Southern Africa. The NEPAD agricultural strategy concentrates on solving the soil fertility problems and increasing the area under irrigation under the land–water initiative. It does not address the problems of inequities with respect to both land and water, nor does it discuss the historical basis of such inequitable distribution.

Lack of access to water for agricultural purposes is most pronounced in North and Southern Africa. Although the NEPAD agricultural sector plan shows that only 7 per cent of the total arable land is irrigated, it is also important to recognise that most of the land under irrigation is in the hands of minority social groups. In Zimbabwe in 1991, about 104,500 hectares was under irrigation, with 68 per cent of this on large-scale

Table 4.10 Land tenure in Southern Africa (approximate % of national territory)

Country	Freehold and leasehold	Communal, tribal, customary land	Conservation, minerals, water, catchments, reserves and other state land
Angola	6.0	51.0	43.0
Botswana	6.0	71.0	23.0
DR Congo	8.9	28.0	63.1
Lesotho	22	77.2	0.8
Malawi	27.4	65.0	7.57
Mauritius	77.4	9.8	12.8
Mozambique	22.5	32.4	45.1
Namibia	36.3	41.0	22.7
Seychelles	22.0	69.0	9.0
South Africa	44.3	53.0	2.67
Swaziland	43.2	49.8	7.0
Tanzania	6.6	47.4	46.0
Zambia	6.0	58.0	36.0
Zimbabwe	41.0	43.0	16.0

Note: The formerly privileged group mainly dominates freehold/leasehold, while the black majority mainly dominates customary/tribal tenure.
Source: Moyo 2001.

commercial farms mainly owned by minority whites, and only 6 per cent on smallholders' farms (Rukuni and Eicher 1994). Thus redistributive reforms of these two key resources (land and water) are a necessary but not sufficient condition for boosting agricultural production and peace and stability in Africa. Land conflicts, through land occupations in Zimbabwe and other countries, demonstrate how the inequitable distribution of land can threaten peace and stability in an economy.

Trade/market access
The major threat facing the NEPAD agricultural strategy is that it is heavily reliant on the North's commitment to eradicating trade policies that are biased against Africa. Although Africa has to a large extent embraced market reforms promoted by the Bretton Woods institutions, farmers in the developed world still receive huge production subsidies. OECD

subsidies for agriculture total some US$300 billion a year, almost equivalent to Africa's GDP (World Bank 2000). Recently, the USA caused an uproar when it passed a new Farm Bill that almost doubled the subsidies received by farmers. In addition, Africa's exports are subjected to some punitive non-tariff barriers, a case in point being the quantitative controls and special taxes applied to coffee exports from Africa in several EU countries (Ng and Yeats 1996). Although Africa has to make great strides to meet standards under the WTO agreements, it is important to note that sanitary and phytosanitary standards are open to abuse by the North in repelling the continent's agricultural exports.

There is controversy regarding Africa's agricultural terms of trade with the rest of the world. According to Townsend (2000), sub-Saharan Africa's external terms of trade have been on the increase for most countries during the period 1989–96, as can be seen in Table 4.11. Only a few countries have experienced declining terms of trade for agriculture (Mali, Niger, Ghana, Malawi and Zimbabwe). Nigeria and Uganda, in turn, experienced tremendous growth rates of 7 per cent. The increasing external terms of trade have been attributed mainly to lucrative prices on the international market in recent years (Townsend 2000). But sources outside the World Bank's sphere of influence note that prices of most primary agricultural commodities have been on a downward trend in the last two decades (Oxfam 2002). This can be seen in Table 4.12. Prices are a key component in the calculation of terms of trade. The highest slump was recorded for sugar, which decreased by about three-quarters. For the overall economy, external terms of trade have been declining. According to Adésínà (Chapter 1), cumulative terms of trade losses between 1970 and 1997 for non-oil exporting countries amounted to 119 per cent of regional GDP in 1997, whereas Townsend (2000) estimated the growth rate of external terms of trade to be −0.87 per cent between 1990 and 1996. It is important to note, however, that the reliance on traditional agricultural exports exposes the continent to international price fluctuations, usually the result of a slump in demand from the North, Africa's major trading partner. It thus makes sense to invest in product diversification and search for new, non-Northern markets.

While it is widely acknowledged that Africa's trade is heavily biased towards the developed world, there should be a great drive to promote intra-African trade. Africans have the highest non-tariff barriers among their countries, with tariff levels on all imports in sub-Saharan Africa averaging 27 per cent, while those of OECD countries and fast-growing exporters from the Far East are 3 per cent and 9 per cent, respectively (Townsend 2000). Thus, the trade initiative's success will to an extent depend on the commitment of African countries to removing barriers to trade and addressing domestic supply constraints, which have resulted in

Table 4.11 External terms of trade in sub-Saharan Africa, 1990–6

Country	Barter terms of of trade (agriculture) growth rate p.a.	Net income terms of trade (agriculture) growth rate p.a.	Barter terms of trade (economy) growth rate p.a.
Sub-Saharan Africa	1.63	4.21	−0.87
Burkina Faso	4.2	0.9	1.4
Cameroon	11.9	12.9	−4.4
Côte d'Ivoire	3.9	6.8	3.2
Ethiopia	0.7	10.9	−1.7
Ghana	−5.9	−2.7	0.13
Kenya	1.4	3.4	7.2
Madagascar	7.4	3.4	1.6
Mali	−1.4	1.4	1.8
Malawi	−2.3	−0.8	−3.1
Mozambique	−0.8	6.6	−
Niger	−5.1	−10.2	−4.1
Nigeria	7.0	10.5	−4.5
South Africa	4.6	0.7	0.6
Tanzania	1.9	8.7	−0.8
Uganda	8.3	22.2	5.3
Zimbabwe	−1.9	9.6	−1.5

Source: Townsend 2000.

Table 4.12 Declining prices of agricultural commodities, 1980–2000

Decrease by 0–25%		Decrease by 26–50%		Decrease by over 50%	
Bananas	−4.4	Coconut oil	−44.3	Cocoa	−71.2
Tea	−23.1	Cotton	−47.6	Coffee	−64.5
		Fish meal	−31.9	Palm Oil	−55.8
		Groundnut oil	−30.9	Rice	−60.9
		Maize	−41.6	Rubber	−59.6
		Soyabean	−39.0	Sugar	−76.6
		Wheat	−45.2		

Source: Oxfam 2002.

the continent's ballooning food import bill. In five years from 1990, Africa's food import bill increased from US$12.7 billion to US$17.5 billion, whilst exports increased by less than US$2 billion (FAOSTAT Database).

The opportunity costs of unfair trading practices on the African continent are also onerous. The developing world could remove 128 million people from the poverty trap, if only it could increase its share of world exports by just 1 per cent. In monetary terms, trade barriers cost the developing world US$100 billion per year, which is double what the developing world receives as aid. Sub-Saharan Africa alone incurs trade losses in excess of US$2 billion per year (Oxfam 2002). It is important to note that these are only short-term opportunity costs; the long-term opportunity costs in terms of investment are much higher. This chapter thus advocates a radical shift in the international trading system and a vigorous promotion of intra-African trade. There are many benefits to be derived from increasing trade within the continent.

Infrastructure and finance

The NEPAD agricultural strategy will require an annual investment of some US$12 billion, excluding maintenance costs, for the next fourteen years. This will require vigorous resource mobilisation from both domestic and international sources. For most countries, the investment capital will have to be sourced mainly from the developed world. Yet the plan comes at a time when aid flows to Africa are dwindling rapidly. The President of the World Bank summed up the situation:

> It is a supreme irony that just at the time when African leaders are putting the right policies in place and are showing results, overseas aid to Africa has fallen from US$32 per person in 1990 to US$18 per person in 1998. We must reverse that trend. I join Horst [Kohler, President of the International Monetary Fund] in saying that it is time for a concerted appeal to the heads of government and major aid donors to make it clear, once and for all, that development assistance is not charity, but a vital investment in global peace and security. Current levels of foreign aid, at some 0.24 per cent of annual GDP, fall far short of the 0.7 per cent target developed countries promised to meet. The difference between these two figures is worth US$100 billion a year. For millions of people, this is the difference between life and death. And it is surely an amount that, if correctly used, could make the achievement of global objectives possible. (Wolfensohn 2001: 3–4)

The major threat facing NEPAD in mobilising resources is dependency on the Bretton Woods institutions and donor countries for its investment finance, against a backdrop of dwindling development assistance from donor countries, bilateral and multilateral institutions, a

Table 4.13 World Bank lending to borrowers in Africa by sector, 1992–2000 (US$ million)

Sector	1992–7 (annual average)	1998	1999	2000
Agriculture	322.1	176.9	188.1	173.5
Economic policy	527.1	330.1	676.6	426.3
Education	235.7	372.3	194.1	159.7
Electricity	181.4	380.3	0.0	42.9
Environment	47.1	71.8	15.0	16.4
Finance	213.1	5.0	29.4	60.4
Mining	10.7	5.0	15.0	0.0
Multisector	38.9	0.0	0.0	65.0
Oil and gas	31.4	0.0	17.5	116.6
Population, health and nutrition	133.3	227.0	172.1	110.0
Private sector	204.5	44.4	78.1	200.6
Public sector	96.4	180.5	121.2	283.4
Social protection	118.9	114.7	129.6	139.4
Telecommunications	14.9	0.0	10.8	10.2
Transportation	294.4	770.1	236.6	256.2
Urban development	132.3	85.0	110.9	10.8
Water supply	124.6	110.7	75.0	87.7
Total	2,726.7	2,873.8	2,070.0	2,159.1

Source: World Bank 2001.

ballooning food import bill, and growing external debt. World Bank support to borrower countries in Africa has been on the decline, as can be seen in Table 4.13.

Most donor countries have pledged to support NEPAD and high hopes were riding on the outcome of the G8 summit in Kananaskis, Canada, in June 2002. But the summit proved a slap in the face to NEPAD and Africa. No financial support was forthcoming, only a pledge to give Africa more time on the agenda for the meeting in 2003. Africa, with a huge debt burden, was offered US$1 billion in extra debt relief, compared to the US$20 billion given to Russia for disarmament at the end of the summit (Ologa 2002).

NEPAD faces the threat of grinding to a halt if the funds required to close the huge resource gap are not forthcoming. The current situation looks gloomy, as can be seen in Tables 4.14 and 4.15. The resource gap in

Table 4.14 Resource flows in Africa (% of GDP)

Country	Gross domestic investment		Gross domestic savings		Resource balance		Overall deficit/ surplus	
	1990	1999	1990	1999	1990	1999	1990	1999
Algeria	29	27	27	30	−2	3		2.9
Cameroon	18	19	21	19	3	0		−5.9
Côte d'Ivoire	7	19	11	25	5	6	−2.9	−1.3
Egypt	29	23	16	14	−13	−8	−5.7	−2.0
Ethiopia	12	19	7	4	−5	−14	−9.8	
Ghana	14	22	5	4	−9	−18	0.2	
Kenya	20	15	14	7	−5	−8	−3.8	−0.9
Mozambique	16	35	−12	11	−28	−24		
Nigeria	15	11	29	0	15	−11		
South Africa	12	16	18	18	6	3	−4.1	−2.9
Zimbabwe	17	18	17	15	0	−2	−5.3	−5.0

Source: World Bank 2001.

most countries is widening. Gross domestic savings follow a similar trend; the sharpest fall was recorded in Nigeria, from a level of 29 per cent of GDP to zero per cent in 1999. Although net private capital inflows and foreign direct investment increased during the same period, the growth rate has been outstripped by external debt, which sky-rocketed by more than US$1 billion in some countries. The largest positive movement of FDI was encountered in Nigeria, with a surge of 79 per cent or US$463 million. Net private capital inflows were only 6.85 per cent and 5 per cent for 1990 and 1998 respectively.

The externalisation of foreign currency to pay debts greatly reduces the capacity to support agriculture against a ballooning agricultural import bill. The majority of foreign currency is earned from agriculture. Compared to other regions, such as the EU and USA, subsidies to support agriculture are very low in Africa. Subsidies and current transfers to the whole economy in high-income countries averaged 56 per cent of total expenditure in 1990, compared to 11 per cent in North Africa and the Middle East, and 10 per cent in sub-Saharan Africa (World Bank 2001). Wilmot (2002) estimates that more than US$200 million flows out of Africa on a daily basis to meet debt obligations and other commitments, which amounts to more than double the annual investment flows of US$64 billion that African leaders are seeking for NEPAD.

Table 4.15 Resource flows in Africa (US$ million)

Country	Net private capital inflows		Foreign direct investment		External debt		Balance of payments on current account	
	1990	1998	1990	1998	1990	1998	1990	1998
Algeria	−424	−1,321	0	5	22,887	30,665	1,420	
Cameroon	−125	1	−113	50	6,679	9,829	−196	−235
Côte d'Ivoire	57	181	48	435	17,251	14,852	−1,100	−207
Egypt	698	1,385	734	1,076	32,947	31,964	−634	−2,762
Ethiopia	−45	6	12	4	8,634	10,352	−244	−520
Ghana	−5	42	15	56	3,881	6,884	−223	−350
Kenya	122	−57	57	11	7,058	7,010	−527	−363
Mozambique	35	209	9	213	1,653	8,208	−415	−429
Nigeria	467	1,028	588	1,051	33,440	30,315	4,988	−4,244
South Africa		783		550		24,712	2,065	−1,936
Zimbabwe	85	−217	−12	76	3,247	4,716	−140	

Source: World Bank 2001.

Commitment among African leaders to agriculture as the main driver of economic growth on the continent is also unconvincing. Budgetary allocations to the agricultural sector remain very low on the continent. In Zimbabwe during the period 1990 to 2001, the agricultural sector's budgetary allocation averaged 4 per cent – one and a half times less than the vote allocated to the non-productive defence sector (Government of Zimbabwe, various years). Africa's public spending in agricultural research stagnated in the 1980s and 1990s at about $1,148 million per year. Previous studies have shown that investment in agricultural research is important in increasing agricultural productivity, household incomes and overall economic growth. Moreover, Delgado *et al.* (1998) and Block and Timmer (1994) estimate that growth in agriculture as a result of yield-increasing technologies can have multiplier effects on overall economic growth of about two to three times the initial agriculture growth rate.

Investment by the private sector in funding agricultural research has also been minimal, and is estimated at about 2 per cent of total agricultural funding. It is thus imperative for the public sector and the private sector to craft mutually beneficial private–public partnerships (PPPs) by increasing their commitment to agricultural research rather looking outward for investment in this field. It is also good economics to strengthen existing regional research initiatives and promote the creation of new ones.

Other than looking to the North to be forthcoming with investment finance for NEPAD, Africa surely needs an alternative. The starting point will be for Africa to demand total debt cancellation from the North. African leaders have to get their investment priorities right. South Africa provides a good example: while the country is at the forefront of seeking funds for NEPAD, it plans to spend US$11 billion on a new defence acquisition plan from the North (Abdul-Rahman 2002). Resource mobilisation should start on the continent itself, after investment finance is raised in Africa.

Human resources initiative

NEPAD's human resources initiative is silent on the skilled labour requirements for the implementation of the agricultural strategy. The NEPAD agricultural strategy is under threat from the critical exodus of skilled professionals to the developed world, where incentives are lucrative, and from the HIV/AIDS pandemic, which is wreaking havoc on the continent. It is positive to note that the initiative seeks to address the problem of the brain drain.[2] The developed world is benefiting from the brain drain and it will be difficult to reverse unless the incentive gap between the North and Africa is drastically reduced. An alternative that has to be considered would be to ask the North to contribute towards the training of skilled labour on the African continent.

Technology

The main threat facing NEPAD's agricultural strategy in terms of technology initiatives has to do with transfer and pricing. Especially with the onset of structural adjustment programmes, which were accompanied by the removal of state subsidies on key agricultural inputs such as seed, credit and fertiliser, yield-enhancing technologies have become very costly for smallholder farmers. In Zimbabwe, smallholder fertiliser usage declined from 25.8 per cent before the introduction of the SAP in 1991 to 24.86 per cent between 1991 and 1995 (Oni 1997). The decline in fertiliser usage has been attributed mainly to the removal of the government subsidy on fertiliser.

Some scholars (such as Pingali 2001) argue that the differential between the industrialised countries and the developing world is mainly attributable to the gap in farming technologies. Maize yields in the developed world average above eight tonnes per hectare, whilst those in the developing world are at barely three tonnes per hectare. Matnon and Spencer (1984) argue that in many instances the unavailability of appropriate technologies, not policy constraints, is the major factor limiting agricultural production in Africa. In the developing world, more than half of the total area allocated to maize is sown with traditional low-yielding varieties (Pingali 2001). In this way, poor access and the unavailability of appropriate technologies are hindering agricultural growth in Africa.

NEPAD's technology initiative is silent on increasing access to appropriate technologies among smallholder farmers in Africa. Research has shown that smallholder farmers are capable of adopting new yield-enhancing technologies, although at a slower rate than their large-scale commercial counterparts (Ellis 1988).

Implementation plan

The strategy does not present itself in any structured way that defines the entry point for far-reaching reform, or which provides a framework for prioritising certain elements, linking others, or sequencing the interventions. In other words, the strategy is more of a listing of some of the objectives and approaches to achieving these, without any strategic approach that specifies how cause–effect relationships can be manipulated by the state in order to meet specific targets.

The NEPAD document's section on implementing the agricultural strategy is surprisingly casual and narrow. Having noted the importance of agriculture to the livelihoods of the poor in rural areas, it does not accord this sector the priority it deserves. Whereas the cancellation of debt and improving market access are indeed appropriate priorities for the overall NEPAD programme, the absence of agriculture among the four areas for immediate implementation undermines the substantive and material basis of the programme. The lack of a framework in which to set agricultural production and servicing targets deprives the NEPAD agriculture strategy of any concretely defined implementation process.

More importantly, the strategy is watered down by the fact that its implementation is applied to two existing projects that both owe their structure to the input of external multilateral institutions:

1 Expanding the Integrated Land and Water Management Action Plan (this prioritises irrigation and fragile resource management practices);
2 Strengthening Agricultural Research and Extension Systems (this focuses on diffusing technology and innovations).

The emphasis of the NEPAD agriculture strategy on using the same multilateral and bilateral aid organisations in implementing these two projects represents an institutionally narrow and conservative approach. Rather than focusing on existing and new indigenous African institutions, and calling for a major structural and policy reform of these dominant external institutions, the NEPAD agricultural strategy allows itself to be entangled in an institutional framework that – lacking an internal strategic purpose and effective implementation strategies – has for many years overseen the demise of African agriculture.

It is striking how the implementation action plan is only structured around universal or generic principles of strengthening capacity rather than on collaborative transnational projects. The action plan does not propose any concrete inter-state or sub-regional agricultural projects or refer to any transnational infrastructure projects that could shift the orientation and costs of specific forms of domestic production to fill widely known gaps in food security and local agro-based industrial shortfalls. This vague approach to project facilitation appears to close the space for concrete action planning. There is a need for this agricultural development strategy to be opened to and guided by concrete output plans or targets emanating from the participating countries, each within its sub-regional context.

Conclusions

An alternative vision to that proposed by NEPAD for agricultural development is required. It is more likely to emerge from a more broadly based land and agrarian reform project, based on an industrialisation strategy built around the key sub-regional integration blocks as defined in the Lagos Plan of Action and subsequent endogenous planning initiatives. This requires the revitalisation of the agrarian planning and development promotion activities of organisations such as the Food, Agriculture and Natural Resources Directorate of the Southern African Development Community (SADC) to ensure a more focused commitment to intervening in sub-regional development, based on an equitable distribution of benefits and trade-offs from existing trade and investment balances.

Africa needs an agrarian transformation to be collectively planned in the context of an integrated rural development strategy. The five key elements of such a strategy are land reform, integrated transectoral rural production (agriculture, mining, natural resources, rural industry), rural infrastructure development, institutional reform and regional integration.

Most crucially, an agricultural development plan must be developed around clear-cut inter-state obligations to structure production, outputs and incomes in a manner that optimises regional income distribution and promotes value-adding processes in industry and other related sectors. Such a strategy should above all be based on redressing historic and contemporary social and economic injustices, in a truly social democratic model of development management. The development of agriculture itself will only be feasible in the context of promoting the

Box 4.1 Elements of agrarian transformation and integrated rural development

I   *Land reform*
Land redistribution, tenure reforms and sustainable land use promotion.

II *Integrated rural production strategy*
1 Agrarian reform
  (i)   Production and land productivity improvements and coordination
  (ii) Rural financial systems restructuring
  (iii) Agricultural trade and marketing reforms
2 Natural resources management/utilisation reforms
  (i)   Tourism diversification and democratisation strategy
  (ii) Forest, industries expansion, and productivity growth strategy
  (iii) Biotechnology and related resources industrial development
3 Agro-industrial and mining development strategy
  (i)   Processing and manufacture policy and support systems

III *Rural infrastructure development*
1 Transportation, communication system, development
2 Energy
3 Water policy and redistribution systems

IV *Rural institutional reform and rural resources deployment*
1 Improved rural policy institutions, restructuring, coordination and efficiency
2 Devolution of local government natural resources control and financing
3 Integration of human resources and development and civil society into rural local governance

V   *Regional and sub-regional production and trade integration strategy* interactive improvement of productivity, access to land, renewed agricultural financial support, reoriented trade systems and relations and the effective mechanisation and irrigation of agriculture.

The author would like to acknowledge the assistance rendered by Walter Chambati in the preparation of this paper.

NOTES

1 Zimbabwe, Namibia and South Africa are the worst-affected countries (Moyo 2001). In South Africa, 5 per cent of the population, mostly white farmers, own almost 87 per cent of the land. In Namibia, white farmers own around 70 per cent of the most productive agricultural land. In Zimbabwe, approximately 4,000 white commercial farmers (0.03 per cent of the population) control 42 per cent of the agricultural land.

2 It is estimated that 130,000 university graduates leave the continent each year (Wilmot 2002).

REFERENCES

Abdul-Rahman, T., 2002, 'Who Needs the G8?', News Africa, 1, 28.
Adésínà, 'Jimi, (in this volume), 'Development and the Challenge of Poverty: NEPAD, the post-Washington Consensus and Beyond'.
Block, S.A. and Timmer, C.P., 1994. 'Agriculture and Economic Growth: Conceptual Issues and the Kenyan Experience', in Consulting Assistance on Economic Reform (CAER) Project, Cambridge, MA: Harvard Institute for International Development.
Binswanger, H. and K. Deninger, 1993, 'South African Land Policy: the Legacy of History and Current Options', World Development Report, 21, 9 (September).
Delgado, C., Hopkins, J., Kelly, V., Hazell, P., McKenna, A., Gruhn, P., Hojjati, B., Sil, J., Curbois, C., 1998. 'Agricultural Growth Linkages in Sub-Saharan Africa', IFPRI Research Report No. 107, International Food Policy Research Institute, Washington DC.
Ellis, Frank, 1998, Peasant Economics: Farm Households and Agrarian Development, Cambridge: Cambridge University Press.
Esterhuysen, Pieter (ed.), 2002, Africa at a Glance: Facts and Figures 2001/02, Pretoria: Africa Institute of South Africa.
Food and Agriculture Organisation, FAOSTAT Database <http://www.fao.org>.
Government of Zimbabwe, various years, Budget Estimates, Harare: Government of Zimbabwe.
IFAD (International Fund for Agricultural Development), 2001, Assessment of Rural Poverty: Eastern and Southern Africa, New York: Oxford University Press.
Mather, C., 2002, 'The Double Standards of World Trade', Mail & Guardian (Johannes-burg), 2–7 August.
Matnon P. J. and M. Spencer, 1984, 'Increasing Food Production in Sub-Saharan Africa: Environmental Problems and Inadequate Technological Solutions', American Journal of Agricultural Economics, 66.
Mkandawire, Thandika, n.d., 'African Agrarian Capitalism from Colonialism to

Adjustment', unpublished paper.

Moyo, Sam, 2000, *Land Reform under Structural Adjustment: Land Use Change in the Mashonaland Provinces*, Uppsala: Nordiska Afrikainsitutet.

—— 2001, 'The Politics of Land Distribution and Race Relations in Southern Africa', paper presented at UNRISD Conference on Racism and Public Policy, Durban, September.

NEPAD, 2001, 'The New Partnership for Africa's Development (NEPAD)', Midrand: NEPAD Secretariat. Available online at <http://www.dfa.gov.za/events/nepad.pdf.>

—— 2002a, *Agriculture Strategy Document No. 1: Underpinning Investments in African Agriculture and Market Access*, Midrand: NEPAD Secretariat.

—— 2002b, *Agriculture Strategy Document No. 2: Extending the Area under Sustainable Land Management and Reliable Water Control Systems*, Midrand: NEPAD Secretariat.

—— 2002c, *Working for Household Food Security and Economic Prosperity in Africa*, Midrand: NEPAD Secretariat.

Ng, I. and I. Yeats, 1996, *Open Economies Work Better! Did Africa's Protectionist Policies Cause Its Marginalization in World Trade?* Washington DC: World Bank.

Ologa, G., 2002, 'Hope for a New Africa', *News Africa*, 1, 28 (July).

Oni, Stephen, 1997, *The Impact of ESAP on Communal Areas of Zimbabwe*, Harare: Friedrich-Ebert-Stiftung.

Oxfam, 2002, *Rigged Rules and Double Standards: Trade Globalisation and the Fight against Poverty*, Oxford: Oxfam. Available online at <http://www.marketradefair.com.>

Pingali, P. L., 2001, 'World Maize Facts and Trends. Meeting World Maize Needs: Technological Opportunities and Priorities for the Public Sector', Mexico: CMMYT.

Platteau, J., 1995, *Reforming Land Rights in Sub-Saharan Africa: Issues of Efficiency and Equity*, Geneva: UNRISD.

Rukuni, I. and C. Eicher, eds, 1994, *Zimbabwe's Agricultural Revolution*, Harare. University of Zimbabwe Publishers.

Townsend, Robert F., 2000, *African Agricultural Research and Development: Increasing Effectiveness and Financial Sustainability*, Washington DC: European Commission and World Bank.

Wilmot, P., 2002, 'A Future That Works', *News Africa*, 1, 28 (July).

Wolfensohn, James D., 2001, 'The Challenges of Globalization: the Role of the World Bank', address to the Bundestag, Berlin, April.

World Bank, 2000, *Can Africa Claim the Twenty-First Century?*, Washington DC: World Bank.

—— 2001, *World Bank Annual Report 2000: Annual Review and Summary Financial Information*, Washington DC: World Bank.

5 Industrialisation of Africa
A New Approach

Sekou Sangare

In the period 1980–3, the growth of industrial added value in Africa was only 3 per cent on average per year in real terms. This growth rate fell continually from 3.7 per cent in the first half of the 1980s to a little more than 1 per cent at the beginning of the 1990s. This poor performance is not only below that of other developing countries, but is also proof of the stagnation and indeed the decline in industrial production in many African countries, and in particular those south of the Sahara. The share of African exports in the world's manufactured products remained very low and continued to drop at a time when other developing regions were rapidly increasing their market share. Similarly, the flow of direct investments in Africa remained very low and was concentrated on a few countries with raw materials. The dependence on imports remained high, while the signs of a technological expansion were very weak.

This tendency persisted in the 1990s, while many African countries were experimenting with structural adjustment programmes marked by the stabilisation and liberalisation of their economies. Results show that these programmes are inappropriate to halt the African crisis, give a new impulse to the flow of investments or become carriers of industrial growth – contrary to experience, for example, in the South-East Asian countries. This also shows the difference in development strategies undertaken by the two regions. While the development of the 'Asian Tigers' was dependent on investment, that of African countries seems to be more aid-dependent. Economic policies in the two regions reacted to the different problems posed by two development strategies: in Africa, policies satisfied the macro-economic concerns of sponsors and donors; in South-East Asia, they responded to the micro-economic criteria of investors. To learn from the South-East Asian countries, industrialisation in Africa should focus on conditions that attract foreign investment.

The backdrop

Industrial structure in Africa is as diverse as its resources, and depends a great deal on the geographic situation of the country. Generally defined, the industrial sector comprises the mines, oil, construction, public infrastructure and manufacturing. The share of industrial production in the gross domestic product of African countries with natural export resources can sometimes reach 60 per cent. In contrast, considered strictly in the sense of manufacturing, the industrial sector remains marginal in Africa. In most countries, industrial added value is below 10 per cent. In the course of the past twenty years, only countries such as South Africa, Mauritius and Swaziland have registered regular growth in industrial added value, boosting its share of their economies to more than 20 per cent.

African economies, and consequently their industries, have suffered the negative effects of monetary and real shocks because of their excessive dependence on primary production oriented to outside markets. The agricultural sector, which still employs about 70 per cent of the active population in most countries, is dependent on climatic shocks and the price fluctuations of international markets. The possibility of adjusting to these shocks is limited by the reduced size of the economies of African countries and their weak horizontal integration. For the most part, these shocks have broken the momentum of industrial development, even in countries that experienced a strong growth rate after independence, such as Côte d'Ivoire and Kenya.

The absence of an economy of scale linking adjacent African markets prevents the industrial redeployment of the large companies, since the low revenues of small countries do not allow companies to produce a critical mass of goods to compensate for heavy investments. Strangely, this inherited situation of colonial balkanisation was ratified by the African heads of state when the Organisation of African Unity was set up, mainly in its clause on territorial integrity. The resulting protectionist tendencies within various countries prevent wider trade and confine firms to working within the limits of these states.

Tariff and institutional protection within states also explains the present weakness of infrastructure in the fields of transport and communication between African countries. This, moreover, contributes to the extroversion of industrial structure in Africa and its vulnerability to outside shocks. It is in this context that, in April 1980, the Lagos Plan of Action was born. As stipulated in the founding statement of this plan, African countries committed themselves to reinforcing existing economic communities and to establishing other economic groupings with a view to eventually setting up an African common market (see UNECA, OAU and UNIDO 1982). Twenty years later, in October 2001, the New

Partnership for Africa's Development (NEPAD) was set up to advance projects and develop common infrastructures aimed at African economic integration.

The Lagos Plan of Action pointed out that the post-independence institutionalising of colonial structures perpetuated the dualisation of African economies, with a marginal industry oriented to outside consumption and a disconnected agricultural sector. This discouraged integration and modernisation of the continent's economies. Moreover, the industries established under the import substitution approach specialised in the production of products derived from a foreign consumption style and requiring outside inputs, which contributed to the deterioration of the terms of trade. Moreover, these industries were more capital-intensive, which could not be advantageous to the recycling of the large workforce. Thus, the structural transformation of sectorial employment in Africa was not able to follow the classical tendency which was seen in industrialised countries: progressive migration of the workforce from the primary sector to the secondary sector in a first stage, and towards the tertiary sector in a second phase.

In contrast, everywhere in Africa the migration of the labour force short-circuited the secondary sector by going straight from the primary sector to the tertiary sector. Official statistics in 1996 put the average employment of the active population at 62 per cent, 15 per cent, and 23 per cent, respectively, in the primary, secondary and tertiary sectors (ILO, 1997). But reality is completely different because there has been excessive growth in the informal services sector in almost all African countries, alongside increased poverty, criminality and AIDS in the cities.

One of the major obstacles to industrial development in Africa is the lack of physical infrastructure on which inter-African exchanges can be built. NEPAD clearly addresses this problem by emphasising the multilateral financing of trans-border infrastructure, including roads, railways and information technology.

The structural adjustment programmes of the last twenty years failed to address the problems of a specifically African industrialisation. The stabilisation policies which resulted emphasised liberalisation within African countries, whereas the major constraint was rather the narrowness of internal markets. It is true that privatisation has given a certain efficiency to management and has improved the performance of previously profligate companies. However, if this improved performance soothed the pockets of the new shareholders, it did not benefit consumers in African countries. Instead, the substitution of private monopoly for public monopoly brought with it an increase in the price of goods and services, without necessarily improving the quality of what was offered. The next section shows how thinking in academic circles and multilateral development institutions was influenced by the macro-economic stabilisation approach, with a limited explanation of industrialisation problems in Africa.

Economic theory and development

Economic theory focuses on risk and uncertainty as determining factors when making decisions about investments (Dixit 1989; Dixit and Pindyck 1994). Explicitly stated, investment seems to be explained by four groups of factors, as follows:

$$I = f(Em, f, q, u)$$

where Em is expectations for future market conditions; f the company's financial constraints; q the value of the company on financial markets; and u political and economic uncertainty. This hypothesis has been through many stages of development, theoretical as well as empirical, which we can summarise in three research axes: irreversibility, selection of markets, and financial constraints. We will analyse the results of these studies below and their relevance in explaining the state of industrialisation in Africa.

The irreversible nature of investment, which is long-term, presupposes that capital cannot be invested productively without being affected by the physical and sometimes human costs which are not recoverable or only transferable with difficulty from one sector to another or from one region to another (Bernanke 1983; Pindyck 1988). Consequently, private investors will be less inclined to commit themselves to expenses in the form of physical investments when they are unsure of the economic, social and political environment. It can thus be seen that changes causing uncertainty, which are often associated with unpredictability, the instability of the incentive structure, and a lack of a sustained and credible economic policy, can have a significant impact on the decision to invest in a country.

Research undertaken on the link between uncertainty, economic policy and the decision to invest originates in the theory of rational anticipation, according to which macro-economic stability sends out signals to private investors on the direction taken by policies and the credibility of the government's commitments in the efficient management of the economy. As Barro (1974) has shown, the excessive volatility of macro-economic variables or uncertainty as to the future of these variables sends signals that relative prices are going up. This idea has been verified by empirical studies on the instability of inflation, budgetary deficits and the exchange rate by Blejer and Khan (1984), Greene and Villanueva (1991), Serven and Solimano (1993), Mlambo and Elhiraika

(1997) and Mlambo and Oshikoya (2001). However, what is not explained by these studies is the fact that the level of investment remains low even in African countries that have a relatively stable monetary system, like those of the CFA zone, whereas investments flow into other regions of the world in spite of a rather more expansionist economic policy.

Another causal factor investigated in recent studies is the impact of political instability – in terms of revolutions, *coups d'état*, political assassinations, constitutional reviews and changes of government or cabinet reshuffles – on investment decisions (Serven 1997; Gyimah-Brempong and Traynor 1999). The results of this work show a circle of causality: a low growth rate causes political instability, which in turn leads to economic stagnation. One could ask questions as to whether political instability is not due, in the final analysis, to low levels of investment.

Market selection models are based on the premise that, in a competitive environment, only high-performance businesses will survive. Consequently, the decision to enter or withdraw from a given industrial sector will depend only on productivity. This possibility, first suggested by Lucas (1978), and later confirmed by Lippman and Rumelt (1982), presupposes that managerial talents can explain differences of productivity among companies. This difference emerges from the fact that the imitation of production techniques does not appear to be perfect because of the unity, intangibility and indivisibility of production factors. For Jovanovic and MacDonald (1994), for example, even if perfect imitation is possible, the difference in productivity will remain because of the costs and time of imitation.

Another common characteristic in market selection models is the existence of a critical level of productivity which defines the point of equilibrium between entry into and exit from an industrial sector. In this case, the selection process is such that less productive firms have to leave the sector, whereas those able to enter are those in a state of high productivity.

Empirical verification of the hypothesis of market selection has branched out in three directions. The first, looking at growth turnover, consists of testing the age effect and the size effect in the entry, exit and growth of a company. The second category of tests analyses 'productivity turnover', comparing the relative productivity of those companies entering, exiting or remaining in an industrial sector or export market. Finally, the third approach, on productivity reallocation, tries to verify the process of reallocation of the resources of less productive firms to more productive firms in time, within an industrial sector or an economy.

Empirical tests verifying these possibilities, and carried out for the most part in developed markets, confirm that (1) the probability of survival depends on the initial size and age of a firm (Evans 1987; Dunne *et al.* 1989; Dunne and Hughes 1994); (2) productivity is more mediocre and average in firms going in or coming out than those which are established in the sector (Baily *et al.* 1992); and (3) exporting companies are more productive than non-exporting companies, and productivity increases with the level of exports in exporting firms (Bernard and Jensen 1999).[1]

Similar results have been found in developing markets, especially in Asia (Aw, Chung and Roberts 1999) and Latin America (Liu 1993; Liu and Tybout 1996), but with less certain conclusions. In Africa, only the Moroccan and Ethiopian industries have been the subject of an empirical investigation in this direction (Mengistae 1998). Another significant study was carried out by Pattillo (1999), who tested the general irreversibility hypothesis and discovered that the differences in the rate of investment between Ghanaian companies could be explained by differences in terms of irreversibility and by perceptions of risk.[2] Such studies need to be continued to obtain clearer results, in terms of verifying hypotheses in developing markets.

Financial constraint in the choice of investment is a well-known hypothesis of economic research. The idea of the rationing of credit presupposes, for example, that decisions of companies to invest remain constrained by access to external financing in developing countries. However, the results of studies undertaken by Collier and Gunning (1999) and Fafchamps and Oostendorp (1999) have not been able to confirm this possibility in explaining the bad performance of African industries. This, moreover, relativises the idea according to which economic growth is hampered by a lack of development of the financial sector (King and Levine 1993). In fact, this causal factor can strengthen according to the level of development. At a low level of development, growth, and therefore investment, should condition financial development – but this link can be reversed when the economy reaches a tenable level of development.

Too much debt is considered to be another source of uncertainty and difficulty for investments. External debt can have various effects on private investment. First, the future reimbursement of the debt and payment of interest due depends on the development of the global interest rate, the terms of exchange, and the parity of buying power which calls into question the ability of the country to honour its commitments on time. Second, debt repayment can be a kind of additional tax on domestic investments. Third, a country which has too much debt can face liquidity problems on the international capital market in the case of arrears in debt servicing.

Many studies have proved that excessive debt can reduce the incentive to invest because of the anticipated tax on future revenue and the yield of internal investments (Eaton 1987; Sachs 1988; Borensztein (1990). More-over, the securitisation of these debts can reverse this tendency by giving a boost to the movement of investments in debtor countries, as a result of the transformation of the share structure of companies (Sangare 1993). However, this market solution, which is reinforced by the Brady Plan,[3] even if it positively transformed certain economies that were heavily in debt (Chile, Brazil, Philippines), has only had very limited success in African countries because of a general lack of interest in Africa by foreign investors.[4]

New directions for industrial theory and policy

In the face of the failure of industrialisation policies in Africa and the inability of traditional economic analysis to explain the poor industrial performance of African countries, the following new research fields should be explored: specific investment, sustainable investment, public investment and the industrialisation of complementarity.

Specific investment

In market selection models, innovative inter-firm imitation appears to be imperfect because of differences in managerial talents. This hypothesis is associated with the theory of asset specificity in the new company theory, according to which a company is a collection of specific assets that are difficult to transfer (Holmstrom 1999; Rajan and Zingales 2000). The combination of production factors (work, capital) as well as groups of relationships within these factors could explain the differences in the performance of companies. This line of research, which assumes that the company can be a source of creation as well as destruction of value, deserves to be investigated as an explanation for the low level of indus-trialisation in Africa.

When the relationship between the different actors in a company (shareholders, directors, staff, state, creditors, suppliers, clients) is not arranged in an optimal way, one ends up with painful conflicts of interest that prevent the company from creating value on a long-term basis. This situation can also be characterised by the entrenchment strategies of directors who make less-than-optimal investment choices. In Africa, businesses are often headed by teams of people who have relationships with politicians; company boards are connected among themselves and linked with the government ministries in power. The lack of real competition on the directors' market as well as the network of relation-ships of these directors with those in power creates a situation where each one is looking for personal gain to the detriment of other actors in the business. The governance structure of African businesses is then in a situation where it generates a destruction of value, thus explaining the poor performance of industries on the continent.

Sustainable investment

The chronic instability of African countries gives rise to uncertainty, which undermines long-term investment decisions. This situation relegates African markets into the hands of short-term investors motivated by concerns of liquidity, to the detriment of long-term investments, which are a condition of industrial development. This hypothesis, which we call the Grenshaw investment law, assumes that bad investors will chase away good investors in Africa (Sangare 2001). African markets would then be purely speculative markets with a high level of endogenous risk.

Thus the high risk associated with the business environment in Africa creates an adverse selection, to the benefit of short-term investors whose objective is the immediate viability of their projects. This attitude also brings about a lack of support investments such as professional training. Consequently, the transfer of technology and know-how between industrialised countries and Africa remains low, because foreign businesses that are supposed to guarantee this transfer are not very keen to do so.

Owing to the high level of political and economic risk, the high-performing companies in industrialised countries propose short-term offers, which tend to be expensive. They are also less inclined to enter into situations that might involve collusion in corrupt practices, especially when bidding for highly competitive tenders. Rather, they would prefer sectors that tend to attract less competitive tenders in the bid to gain control over the public sector. This explains, for example, the poor performance of privatised companies in the majority of African countries.

Public investment

Devarajan, Easterly and Pack (2001) have shown that, historically, the level of investment has been far from low in Africa. The question, then, is quite simple: have finances been directed towards economic projects or 'white elephants'? Moreover, the structural adjustment programmes have resulted in the rolling back of the state from involvement in state economic activities in many African countries, manifested by the private wheeling and dealing of civil servants and members of government to the detriment of public investment. For all that, from French Colbertism to the Asian Tigers (World Bank 1993), industrial development seems to have been boosted and accompanied by strategic state planning. In various different countries, the public sector has played and continues to play a role as the catalyst of private investment. Public investment in the form of optimal allocations of public resources towards the training of human resources, applied research, the setting up of infrastructure, and fiscal advantages are all requirements for industrial development.

The first years of independence in Africa were characterised by public investment encouraged by planning policies. The bad management resulting from the cost of the government-run monopoly structure resulted in most cases in bankruptcy for these young economies. From the 1980s, structural adjustment programmes, put into practice to counteract the economic crisis in African countries, chose macro-economic equilibrium over a micro-economic explanation of poor industrial performance. This tendency was accentuated with the ending of the Cold War. The failure of socialist planning was associated with a perceived need to reduce public intervention. In the majority of African countries, a transition occurred quickly from 'all state' to 'no state'. What resulted was the dismemberment and selling off of public investments, for the most part in sectors necessary to industrial development (water, electricity, telecommunications). The deficiency of these support investments before and after privatisation has prevented industrial redeployment in African countries.

The industrialisation of complementarity

The post-colonial industrialisation strategy was based on import substitution. The majority of African countries followed the experiment in the Latin American countries, under the influence of Raul Prebisch at the United Nations Commission for Latin America (CEPAL). According to this theory, the unfavourable position of developing countries in the export of primary products and the lack of competitiveness of these countries in exporting manufactured products, prevents these economies from reaching a high growth rate based on exports. Consequently, these countries would do well to set up substitution industries for imported products, to orientate internal demand towards manufactured products at a national level.

This idea led many young countries into a costly industrialisation exercise, characterised by protectionism, the building of factories, and the orientation of internal demand towards an imitative local production, even though these industries used inputs not to be had in the national market. The lowering of prices of primary products in international markets (when revenue from these products was vital to finance national investments) as well as the simultaneously rising prices of foreign inputs necessary in substitution industries, resulted in a deterioration in the terms of trade and, as a corollary, a drop in the competitiveness of these economies, an excessive reliance on external debt, and the bankruptcy of substitution industries dependent on a reduced internal demand. Moreover, the turnkey factories needed a continuous transfer of technology and know-how between North and South because of the low level of education in developing countries. This was not encouraged in an ideological context characterised by activism against multinational firms and the effect of the eviction of short-term investors.

The alternative to import substitution for African countries would be the industrialisation of complementarity. This approach attempts to capitalise on the synergy between, on the one hand, the transnational industrial sector and local resources (agricultural, mineral) and, on the other hand, industries from developed countries and partners in African economies through subcontracting, outsourcing, and other forms of industrial alliance. This approach is based on the Ricardian theory of comparative advantage (Ohlin 1933).

The industrialisation chain would then be developed downstream from the natural resources of African countries. This form of industrialisation would minimise the costs of external shocks (drops in the prices of primary products, increases in interest rates, etcetera) at the same time as accelerating the horizontal integration of African countries and their insertion in the global economy through competition between international firms to invest in this value chain.

Conclusion

This chapter sets out the background and the theory in explaining industrial investment factors, and suggests new approaches that could be considered to the problem of African industrialisation. It seems that earlier work on the industrialisation of Africa has been influenced far more by macro-economic considerations as a reply to questions arising from stabilisation policies. Considering the factors that explain industrialisation in developed countries and in the new industrial countries, it is important to investigate further the micro-economic foundations, sometimes endogenous, that prevent the industrial development of Africa. These new lines of thought coming from experiences in development in other regions of the world, and specific factors pertaining to the African continent, could contribute to the success of initiatives promoted by NEPAD.

NOTES

1 Regional integration and the opening of outside markets to African products would be more cost-effective for African economies than foreign aid.
2 This theory was also suggested by Fielding (1993) and Bigsten *et al.* (1999).
3 Named after the former US Secretary of State in the Treasury, Nicholas Brady. This plan was implemented in 1990 in Mexico, the Philippines, Costa Rica and Venezuela.
4 In Africa, only Morocco applied this plan.

REFERENCES

Aw, B. Y., S. Chung and M. J. Roberts, 1999, 'Productivity and Turnover in the Export Markets: Micro Evidence from Korea and Taiwan', mimeo, Philadelphia: Pennsylvania State University.

Baily, M., C. Hulten and D. Campbell, 1992, *Productivity Dynamics in Manufacturing Plants*, Washington DC: Brookings Institution.

Barro, R. J., 1974, 'Are Government Bonds Net Wealth?', *Journal of Political Economy*, 82.

Bernanke, B. S., 1983, 'Irreversibility, Uncertainty, and Cyclical Investment', *Quarterly Journal of Economics*, 98.

Bernard, A. and J. Jensen, 1999, 'Exporting and Productivity', mimeo, New Haven: Yale School of Management.

Bigsten, A., P. Collier, S. Dercon, M. Fafchamps, B. Gauthier, J. W. Gunning, A. Oduro, R. Oostendorp, C. Pattillo, M. Soderbom, M. Sylvain, F. Teal and A. Zeufack, 1999, 'Adjustment Costs, Irreversibility and Investment Patterns in African Manufacturing', mimeo, Washington DC: Götebord University, IMF and World Bank.

Blejer, M. I. and M. S. Khan, 1984, 'Government Policy and Private Investment in Developing Countries', *IMF Staff Papers*, 31, 2.

Borensztein, E., 1990, 'Debt Overhang, Credit Rationing and Investment', *Journal of Development Economics*, 32.

Collier, P. and J. Gunning, 1999, 'Explaining African Economic Performance', *Journal of Economic Literature*, 37, 1.

Devarajan, S., W. Easterly and H. Pack, 2001, 'Is Investment in Africa Too Low or Too High?', *Journal of African Economies*, 2.

Dixit, A., 1989, 'Intersectoral Capital Reallocation under Uncertainty', *Journal of International Economics*, 26.

Dixit, A. and R. Pindyck, 1994, *Investment under Uncertainty*, Princeton: Princeton University Press.

Dunne, P. and A. Hughes, 1994, 'Age, Size, Growth and Survival: UK Companies in the 80s', *Journal of Industrial Economics*, 12.

Dunne, P., M. Roberts and L. Samuelson, 1989, 'The Growth and Failure of US Manufacturing Plants', *Quarterly Journal of Economics*, 104.

Eaton, J., 1987, 'Public Debt Guarantees and Private Capital Flight', *World Bank Economic Review*, May.

Evans, D., 1987, 'Tests of Alternative Theories of Firms' Growth', *Journal of Political Economy*, 95.

Fafchamps, M. and R. Oostendorp, 1999, 'Investment', in J. W. Gunning and R. Oostendorp (eds.), *Industrial Change in Africa: Micro Evidence on Zimbabwean Firms under Structural Adjustment*, London: Macmillan.

Fielding, D., 1993, 'Determinants of Investment in Kenya and Côte d'Ivoire', *Journal of African Economies*, 2.

Greene, J. and D. Villanueva, 1991, 'Private Investment in Developing Countries: an Empirical Analysis', *IMF Staff Papers*, 38, 1.

Gyimah-Brempong, K. and T. L. Traynor, 1999, 'Political Instability, Investment, and Economic Growth in Sub-Saharan Africa', *Journal of African Economies*, 8.

Holmstrom, B., 1999, 'The Firm as a Subeconomy', *Journal of Law, Economics, and Organization*, 15, 1.

ILO. 1997. *Yearbook of Labour Statistics 1996*, 55th Issue. Geneva: ILO.

Jovanovic, B. and G. MacDonald, 1994, 'Competitive Diffusion', *Journal of Political*

Economy, 102.

King, R. G. and R. Levine, 1993, 'Finance, Entrepreneurship and Growth: Theory and Evidence', *Journal of Monetary Economics*, 32.

Lippman, S. and R. Rumelt, 1982, 'Uncertainty Imitability: Analysis of Inter-firm Differences in Efficiency under Competition', *Bell Journal of Economics*, 13.

Liu, L., 1993, 'Entry-exit, Learning, and Productivity Change: Evidence from Chile', *Journal of Development Economics*, 42.

Liu, L. and J. Tybout, 1996, 'Productivity and Growth in Chile and Columbia: The Role of Entry, Exit and Learning', in M. J. Roberts and J. R. Tybout (eds.), *Industrial Evolution in Developing Countries*, Oxford: Oxford University Press.

Lucas, R. E., Jr, 1978, 'On the Size Distribution of Business Firms', *Bell Journal of Economics*, 9.

Mengistae, T., 1998, 'Ethiopia Urban Economy: Empirical Essays on Enterprise Development and the Labor Market', D. Phil thesis, Oxford University.

Mlambo, K. and A. B. Elhiraika, 1997, *Macroeconomic Policies and Private Saving and Investment in SADC Countries*, Abidjan: African Development Bank.

Mlambo, K. and T. W. Oshikoya, 2001, 'Macroeconomic Factors and Investment in Africa', *Journal of African Economies*, 12.

Ohlin, B., 1933, *Interregional and International Trade*, Cambridge: Harvard University Press.

Pattillo, C., 1999, 'The Impact of Uncertainty on the Investment Behaviour of Ghanaian Manufacturing Firms', in P. Collier and C. Pattillo (eds.), *Investment and Risk in Africa*, London: Macmillan.

Pindyck, R. S., 1988, 'Irreversible Investment, Capacity Choice, and the Value of the Firm', *American Economic Review*, 83, 1.

Rajan, R. G. and L. Zingales, 2000, *The Governance of the New Enterprise*, Cambridge: National Bureau of Economic Research.

Sachs, J. D., 1988, 'The Debt Overhang of Developing Countries', in G. Calvo, J. B. de Macedo, R. Frindlay and P. Kouri (eds.), *Debt, Growth, and Stabilisation: Essays in Memory of Carloz Diaz Alejandro*, Oxford: Basil Blackwell.

Sangare, S., 1993, 'Stratégies financières face à l'endettement international: les options de swaps', PhD thesis, University of Aix-Marseille.

—— 2001, 'Efficience des marchés financiers au centenaire', University of Cocody-Abidjan.

Serven, L., 1997, 'Irreversibility, Uncertainty and Private Investment: Analytical Issues and Some Lessons for Africa', *Journal of African Economies*.

Serven, L. and A. Solimano (eds.), 1993, *Striving for Growth after Adjustment: the Role of Capital Formation*, Washington DC: World Bank

UNECA, OAU and UNIDO, 1982, *A Programme for the Industrial Development Decade for Africa*, New York: United Nations Economic Commission for Africa, Organisation of African Unity and United Nations Industrial Development Organisation.

World Bank, 1993, *East-Asian Miracle*, Washington DC: World Bank.

6 The Character and Role of Trade within NEPAD

Critical Challenges and Questions

Dot Keet

An examination of the trade dimensions within NEPAD, and their direct and indirect implications, has to be undertaken at three levels:

- specific proposals on trade;
- trade-related proposals in other spheres;
- perceptions and proposals on Africa's approach to and location within the global trade system.

These all pose a number of significant challenges and questions for Africa.

Trade-related dimensions of NEPAD

Infrastructural interlinkages within Africa
NEPAD (2001) points out that the building of cross-border and trans-African road networks, railways, and other means of transport and communication, and the consolidation of joint energy, water and other systems, will be far more effective by benefiting from 'economies of scale' (para. 93). The creation of such essential regional public goods and inter-linkages are, in fact, essential to enhancing regional cooperation and trade and crucial to integrated African development. These have to be 'addressed on a planned basis – that is, linked to regional integrated development – [without which] the renewal process of the continent will not take off' (para. 197). NEPAD sees the major aim of such infrastructure to be 'improving productivity for international competition', and enabling 'the international community to obtain African goods and services more cheaply' (para. 101).

However, the first problem is that such huge infrastructural projects, spanning regions and even the entire continent, are not primarily conceived as developmental instruments tailored to the needs of specific sectors, regions or sub-regions in Africa. This would entail careful joint cross-country and cross-border planning and inter-governmental negotiations. NEPAD, however, is basically promoting these as the main attractions to be marketed to draw foreign investment into Africa. These are offered as great opportunities for investment, together with the guarantee of governmental support, particularly through public–private partnerships (PPPs), and with promises of lowering the risks facing private investors (paras 105–6). However, with PPPs it is usually the private sector that reaps the fullest benefits, while the public side carries the burdens and risks.

In addition to having to provide essential support facilities and – on current international investment terms – to guarantee favourable or 'flexible' labour conditions within such 'joint' endeavours, African economies and peoples would also have to carry the related financial costs arising from the profit 'repatriations' or capital exports by such investors. The bigger the project and the foreign investment involved, the greater the possible adverse pressures on Africa's external balance of payments, and on its external indebtedness. Foreign 'credit' or loans will add to these costs, even if ODA grants are also applied. And, as history has shown, net financial outflows will prevail for long periods before the creation of such infrastructure begins to have a developmental impact and generates positive financial returns.

Furthermore, the building of such essential 'sinews' for development in Africa will undoubtedly be evaluated, taken up, and located by gigantic transnational technological, construction and service corporations within the framework of their own global investment strategies in these and related sectors. With vastly greater financial and technological resources, management and other skills than the whole of Africa combined, it is such international corporations and investors that will determine not only the technical features but also the very functioning, the commercial orientation and overall character of such projects as profit-making enterprises; whatever may be the other – declared – intentions of African governments.

In addition to the above problems, the most fundamental question to be posed concerns the sequential and functional relationship between such infrastructural provisions and the economic development and trade that it is presumed will therefore be created and stimulated. The question is whether the provision of sophisticated transport, communication, power and other infrastructures will provide the means to economic 'renewal' in Africa, or whether such infrastructures themselves have to be created out of real economic development: do they not have to be an organic part of substantive economic needs, reflecting and accompanying, as they unfold, the forms and levels of economic activities within countries, regions and the continent? Setting up sophisticated structures in advance of and to stimulate such economic processes, without the necessary systems and appropriate infrastructure to maintain and service them, and without the economic agents and activities to fully utilise or effectively employ them, could simply create more vast 'white elephant' projects in Africa. The interrelationship or interaction between infrastructural provisions and general economic or specific trade development entails much more complex development dynamics than seem to be acknowledged in NEPAD's simple correlations.

The encouragement of capital flows within Africa

There is certainly much to be done within and between the respective African countries and regions to eliminate procedural and bureaucratic impediments to productive capital flows, particularly to geographic regions and sectors deficient in the necessary financial resources. NEPAD (2001: para. 95) recommends 'the promotion of intra-African trade and investments' through 'the harmonisation of economic and investment policies and practices'.

However, although NEPAD devotes a considerable section to mobilising resources (paras 147–55), it offers little in the direction of mobilising domestic resources within Africa. This reflects its *a priori* conviction that 'the bulk of the needed resources will have to be obtained from outside the continent' (para. 147), although elsewhere it points to 'an urgent need to create conditions that promote private sector investment by both *domestic* and foreign investors' (para. 148; emphasis added). In the section specifically devoted to private capital flows (paras 153–5), NEPAD defines the priorities as offering the necessary incentives to international investors, especially with respect to their concerns over 'security of property rights' and the need to provide them with governmental insurance schemes, and other guarantees that go with PPPs. Furthermore, all of these incentives are located in the context of 'the deepening of financial markets within countries, as well as cross-border harmonisation and integration' (para. 154). Thus, such measures will not only draw foreign investors into Africa but facilitate the movement of capital around Africa, with the entire continent turned into a vast integrated and secure field for international investors.

In addition, it must be noted that such financial 'harmonisation' or liberalisation will in particular be advantageous to South African companies and investors and, through the repatriation of their profits back to South Africa, will contribute to the further heavy preponderance of the South African economy within Africa. South Africa alone already accounts for more than two-thirds of the combined GDP of sub-Saharan Africa, and a third of the GDP of the whole continent. Financial liberalisation within and between African countries could, conversely, also encourage the flow or 'flight' of domestic capital from other African countries to the (relatively) greater security and profitability of South African financial markets, and thus reinforce the imbalances.

In the light of such polarising tendencies reinforcing the existing imbalances within Africa, it is also significant to note that NEPAD attaches no importance to the active and proactive role of the kind of regional and continental development funds and other public financial instruments that both the African Alternative Framework to SAPs (AAF-SAP) and the plan for the African Economic Community (AEC) propose. These could provide the compensatory and redistributional mechanisms to redirect or at least influence the nature of capital flows towards disadvantaged geographic areas or social groups, or into strategically important sectors – a vital requirement for more balanced development, equity and stability in Africa.

In similar vein, NEPAD makes no recommendations on the role of public investment strategies and agencies, in and of themselves, as central players in driving and directing major projects and targeting key areas or sectors requiring development. NEPAD only sees such a role for the state in supporting and empowering private investors, whether in PPPs or not. Thus, although at various points apparently promoting the role of government, NEPAD's conception of this is the kind of 'enabling role' for private capital and market forces that the World Bank also now recommends, as it has gradually moved to recognise (and promote its own version of) 'the role of the state' in development in Africa.

Common and coordinated regulatory frameworks

NEPAD recommends that agreed public regulatory terms will be important to facilitate cross-border cooperation and the 'coordination of national sector policies and effective monitoring of regional decisions'; as well as 'the promotion of policy and regulatory harmonisation to facilitate cross-border interaction and market enlargement' (paras 105–6). Thus, regulations would deal with manufacturing processes and standards and trade regulations, such as agreed rules of origin, and the harmonisation of economic and investment policies and practices (para. 95). Such regulatory supervision by designated national and regional public regulatory bodies is necessary in all technical spheres, from maritime, rail and road traffic, and telecommunications regulations, to environmental controls; and in all social service spheres, such as labour rights and conditions and safety regulations, education and health standards, especially the monitoring of human diseases and animal pest controls, and so on. NEPAD clearly recognises the importance of harmonised and coordinated regulatory frameworks for intra-regional and inter-regional cooperation and integration.

What would be most significant is the actual content of such regulations, not only in technical but in comprehensive developmental terms. Will such regulations also be designed to encompass the monitoring of the business operations and general economic, social, labour and environmental impacts of corporations and other private agencies, to make them more financially transparent, socially and environmentally responsible and democratically accountable? This is what trade unionists and other civil society campaigners demand when they call for obligatory corporate codes of conduct through the democratic public (re)regulation of all corporations and other economic agencies, nationally, regionally, and globally. NEPAD is not at all clear on this.

There could also be potential tensions between concerns about designing and promoting a wide range of joint national, regional, and continental regulations, appropriate to the situations within Africa and the needs for planned African developmental integration, on the one hand, and, on the other hand, the observance of existing international regulations to achieve more effective external trade. In terms of the latter, NEPAD seems to be concerned to 'improve the standards of exports', by conforming to international standards and by generally measuring up to the − pervasively biased − rules and regulations set in the WTO (paras 158, 161). These include, for example, terms in the Agreement on Trade Related Investment Measures (TRIMs) specifically constraining governments from setting what are defined as internationally 'distorting' developmental regulations on FDI, meaning obligatory labour rights and conditions, labour training, technology transfer, local content inputs and so on.

Complementary or combined cross-border production

NEPAD observes the long-recognised dilemma of most African economies of being 'vulnerable because of their dependence on primary production and resource-based sectors, and their narrow export bases [and that] there is an urgent need to diversify production' (para. 156). In this regard, it notes the importance of African countries 'pooling' or combining their resources within regional production strategies, 'cross-border interactions among African firms' and cross-border inter-sectoral linkages (paras 94, 156, 168). NEPAD proposes 'the alignment of domestic and regional trade and industrial policy objectives, thereby increasing the potential for intra-regional trade, critical to the sustainability of regional economic arrangements' (paras 171–2).

NEPAD's proposals for industrial development stand in clear contrast to the plan of the African Economic Community to explicitly prioritise collective self-reliance and employment generation – rather than export competitiveness, as NEPAD does. And, in the AEC plan, such industrial development is to receive public financial and technical support, drawing on local components and other inputs, and to be characterised by 'industrial specialisation in order to enhance the complementarities of African economies, and expand the intra-community trade base [with] due account being taken of national and regional resource endowments' (OAU 1991). NEPAD avoids any suggestion of state subsidies and other supports to industrialisation, other than through PPPs, and these basically towards the support of the private sector.

It is also significant that, where NEPAD does elaborate on modalities for economic diversification, these are based on 'harnessing Africa's natural resource base' and increasing 'value-added in agro-processing and mineral beneficiation [and] a broader capital goods sector' (para. 156). These certainly all have a role to play in internal production dynamics within all economies, but these sectors tend to be based on larger-scale, capital-intensive and even very high-tech enterprises. NEPAD's vision seems to emulate the economic and technological patterns of the most industrialised economies, aimed as it is at 'bridging the gap between Africa and the developed countries' (para. 98). Its proposals in the sphere of industrial development within Africa do not explicitly prioritise labour-intensive projects and will not, in practice, necessarily encourage employment creation. NEPAD does not stress economic development and diversification, deliberately based on human resource mobilisation and capacitation – which both the AAF-SAP and the AEC plans prioritise.

In so far as NEPAD does deal with the human factor in development, it is to focus on promoting the private sector. There are some useful pointers to 'both micro enterprises in the informal sector, and small and medium enterprises in the manufacturing sector [as] the principal engines of growth and development' (para. 156). However, it is not so much these but larger internationally connected enterprises that will inevitably be the main beneficiaries of the partnerships proposed between African and non-African firms. In dealing with broader human resource development, this is mainly based on the poverty reduction (not eradication!) policies of the International Monetary Fund and World Bank for the masses, and mainly concerned with reversing the brain drain of skilled professionals from Africa (paras 124–5). The latter is indeed yet another serious resource outflow from Africa to the rich countries. But, although NEPAD also deals with expanding education and skills training, its approach seems to be based not on the inherent human rights of the people of Africa in these spheres, but rather on the view of the World Bank that people are 'factors of production' and that more skilled people will attract and service more productive foreign direct investment.

Agricultural development and food security

NEPAD states that an '(i)mprovement in agricultural performance is a prerequisite of economic development on the continent'. The base document adds: 'The resulting increase in rural people's purchasing power will also lead to higher effective demand for African industrial goods. The induced dynamics would constitute a significant source of economic growth' (para. 134). It notes the structural constraints affecting the sector, such as uncertainties in climatic conditions, and it refers to the necessity of infrastructural and institutional support, and even direct governmental support, such as in the provision of irrigation, but only 'when private agents are unwilling to do so' (para. 135). It also provides some pointers to the crucial issues of access to land, water and rural credit, although it does not spell them out in detail. And while it makes some important references to small-scale and women farmers, the weight and significance of these references have to be evaluated in the context of an emphasis on larger-scale 'intensive agriculture based on a significant flow of private investment', with a call for donor aid to go to 'individual high profile agricultural projects' (paras 135, 158).

Moreover, in the section on market access, NEPAD makes it clear that its aim is to 'integrate the rural poor into the market economy and provide them with better access to export markets' in terms of the broader aim 'to develop Africa into a net exporter of agricultural products' (para. 157). Not only is there totally inadequate detail on how this is to be achieved, but NEPAD's writers seem oblivious to the well-known fact that there are clear tensions between such a cash crop export orientation, on the one hand, and, on the other hand, the production of food crops for family, community, national and regional food security, although the latter is apparently a NEPAD concern.

Similarly, while actively promoting increased commodity exports from Africa, NEPAD's brief reference to 'the instability in world commodity prices' does not even try (as the AEC plan does) to provide counter-proposals to this (para. 132).[1] Nor does NEPAD seem to recognise the increased vulnerability of African economies to external price shocks that will accompany the increased dependence on agricultural exports, or the downward pressures that have been exerted upon commodity prices by ever-increasing volumes of agricultural exports from the poor South into the rich North. Once again, NEPAD seems in tune with World Bank instructions to African countries to increase and diversify their agricultural production, while endeavouring to service and please the needs and tastes of the consumer markets in the rich countries.

More broadly, NEPAD is not only weaker than many existing governmental and non-governmental plans and programmes for agricultural and general rural development in Africa, but it does not even acknowledge, endorse or try to benefit from the important proposals and demands being jointly posed by the Africa Group in their endeavours in Geneva within the WTO negotiations on the Agreement on Agriculture. This also reflects the more general inconsistencies and weaknesses in NEPAD's recommendations on how Africa should engage with the multilateral trade system, and more specifically with the World Trade Organisation.

NEPAD even lags well behind the widely accepted arguments of European NGOs, and major institutions such as the World Bank, which deplore and call for an end to the dumping of EU, US and other industrialised economies' subsidised agricultural exports into Africa and elsewhere in the Third World. The impacts of such export dumping are as damaging as the other internal structural constraints within Africa that NEPAD notes. Furthermore, the forced removal of agricultural tariff and quota protection in Africa against such unsustainable competition will actually pre-empt effective solutions to internal problems. NEPAD's silence on such Northern government agricultural policies is a clear indication of the diplomatic constraints required in dealing with the policies of governments that NEPAD's promoters would like to welcome as aid 'partners' with Africa.

Specific trade dimensions within NEPAD

The explicit NEPAD proposals on trade illustrate even more directly the influence of the dominant neo-liberal trade and other economic theories within this programme.

The promotion of trade within, and between, African regions
NEPAD supports the promotion of intra-African trade and investments, and the need to promote and improve regional trade agreements; it even refers to 'the creation of a single African trading platform' (para. 155). It seems to understand the developmental potential in promoting intra-African trade 'with the aim of sourcing within Africa, imports formerly sourced from other parts of the world' (para. 169). It recognises the potential for creating backward and forward linkages within and between African economies (although it does not use these terms) through 'increased intra-regional trade via promoting cross-border interactions among African firms' (para. 168). It even suggests at one point, although rather tentatively, that 'consideration needs to be given to a discretionary preferential trade system for intra-African trade' (para. 171). This, if acted upon, could provide some tariff policy support to encourage inter-African trade, and more internally oriented economic interactions.

But there is a major challenge posed to such potential internal African trade and mutual development by two other dimensions of NEPAD's strategy. The first is that, while apparently aiming to create larger and more integrated markets within Africa to stimulate African producers and provide larger and guaranteed markets for African traders, NEPAD also explicitly offers up Africa as 'a vast and growing market for producers across the world' (para. 176). This offer would have to be based on generous access to African markets as a *quid pro quo* or reward for the increased foreign aid that NEPAD is seeking from the home governments of such companies and international exporters. But an expanding market for world manufactured products, intermediate goods and services would create further competitive pressures on African producers and providers of goods and services. The tensions are once again evident within NEPAD, between intra-African developmental proposals, on the one hand, and, on the other hand, susceptibility to the requirements of international partnerships.

There are other tensions within this plan, reflecting differences on the ground in Africa. As with financial market liberalisation, which will create more favourable conditions in Africa for South African – and not only international – investor interests, the inter-regional trade liberalisation proposed in NEPAD will, without other deliberate countervailing programmes and corrective measures, also work mainly to the benefit of the relatively stronger economies in Africa – such as Egypt, Kenya, Mauritius and, above all, South Africa. This happens with 'free trade' everywhere, and the effects of the 'freer' trade imposed under SAPs are already evident in the vast and rapidly growing trade imbalances in favour of South Africa in relation to all its neighbours in Southern Africa and further afield in the rest of Africa.

In recognition of such country differences, and different vulnerabilities to trade liberalisation, provisions for the promotion of intra-regional trade have to be internally designed for differing rates of tariff reduction between diverse economies, with respect to different sectors, and even for specific products, according to the needs of the respective member states, and especially for the least-developed countries and small-island and landlocked states. This is what the AEC plan, for example, proposes (AEC Treaty 1991). Member states of specific regions need to design their tariff policies to give preferential, if qualified and transitional, treatment to fellow members' trade. This is what is proposed in the Maseru Protocol on trade interactions within the Southern African Development Community. Such an approach is important in order to prioritise inter-African trade in relation to exporters from outside Africa, which is a legitimate development strategy. However intra-regional preferential trade also affects exports into such regions from other countries or regions within Africa. Thus, similarly negotiated inter-regional preferential trade arrangements are also required. NEPAD does not enlarge on these challenges and, even more significantly, is almost totally silent on the various forms and phases of trade integration on the continent, which the AEC plan outlines in great detail.

It has also not been lost on African observers of South Africa's energetic promotion of NEPAD that even the 'preferential' trade terms suggested for African exporters within Africa could, in fact, serve to make Africa a privileged reserve for the few stronger African economies (and those of their companies that are not internationally 'competitive'). If that is what Africa is to be turned into, it would confirm the claims of neo-liberal theorists that such preferential policies are exploited by the strong to the disadvantage of the less strong.[2] In this light, too, the proposed 'sourcing' of imports and intermediate inputs 'from within Africa' and 'the higher effective demand for African industrial goods' would also be most advantageous to the production and export sectors of more industrialised South Africa (paras 158, 161). This is precisely why, contrary to neo-liberal trade prescriptions, it is imperative that such intra-regional and inter-regional trade liberalisation within Africa – even if gradual and assymetrical – has to be accompanied by broader complementary and counterbalancing investment and development programmes. It is only through such negotiated and strategically designed development and diversification programmes that the inherited or initial economic imbalances and the inevitably uneven gains from trade liberalisation can be mitigated and countered. Moreover, it is only through such multi-directional approaches that increasingly open trade between African economies can be turned into re-balancing strategies rather than processes creating further uneven development and economic polarisation.

'Market access' for the increase of international trade from Africa

NEPAD stresses the 'importance of increased investment in order to strengthen Africa's external trade' (para. 166). In this regard, it identifies 'market access to the developed countries for African exports' as one of its top priorities, and concludes that this is one of 'the programmes to be fast-tracked in collaboration with our development partners' (paras 97, 189). With respect to the trade policies of these 'partners', NEPAD notes that '(a)lthough there have been significant improvements in terms of lowered tariffs in recent years, there remain significant exceptions on tariffs, while non-tariff barriers also constitute major impediments'. In addition, '(p)rogress on this issue would greatly enhance economic growth and diversification of African production and exports. Dependence on ODA would decline and infrastructure projects would become more viable as a result of increased economic activity' (para. 173). NEPAD would thus seem to be making important proposals to ensure that Africa's development is supported by the expansion of its external trade.

The adoption of 'improved market access' has become the new glib answer to Africa's development problems. After many years of argument on this by African governments in their separate and joint official positions, more recently this has been picked up and promoted by Northern development NGOs and even the 'new' World Bank. From all directions, however, this is a thoroughly inadequate response. In the apparent acceptance and most practical expression of this by various European governments and by the EU, market access is not what it seems to be in the Brussels propaganda. Even the generous tariff-free and quota-free access to the EU for all exports of all LDCs – the much-publicised Everything But Arms (EBA) agreement, which NEPAD welcomes – is actually hedged around with exceptions and postponements until the year 2006, and in some cases until the end of the year 2009. And safeguards will continue to protect European producers against the threat of import surges from the weakest and poorest countries in the world, whose export trade is supposedly being encouraged by the EU.

What is more, even such qualified access is not on offer to the non-LDC or so-called developing countries in Africa. Yet, even were they included, and even under the most optimal market access, this is not the simple solution to Africa's economic problems that it is presumed to be, even by NEPAD. Although trade barriers are discriminatory and are a serious impediment, the more basic problems for most African countries reside in their supply capacities, their low levels of production, volumes, quality and price competitiveness, infrastructures, trade financing and commercial information, and so on. NEPAD seems to recognise this (para. 171). What NEPAD does not explicit emphasise is that market access may be necessary but is certainly not a sufficient answer to the needs of African countries. The problems of African countries are much more about all-round development than trade. The former drives the latter and, although trade in specific sectors can be useful under certain circumstances, it does not, in and of itself, create development. Furthermore, as authoritative studies from UNCTAD (2002) and the UNDP (2003) show, trade does not necessarily even create quantitative growth.

NEPAD does see that there are other impediments to effective African export trade, but its solutions focus on technical and marketing deficiencies, and at one point it even seems to blame Africans' trade limitations on their own 'low standards'. However, what NEPAD does not enlarge on are the high tariffs in the richest countries, and their deliberate tariff escalations that are increased in proportion to the degree of processing or manufacture of African exports. These high protectionist barriers are constantly criticised by African trade analysts and representatives in international meetings such as the WTO rounds, but NEPAD does not even endorse, let alone build on such public African positions. The inadequate observations by NEPAD on the long-standing role of such policies in deliberately impeding industrial development and diversification within Africa reflect either a lack of appreciation of this by the creators of NEPAD, or – yet again – a diplomatic reluctance to confront Northern partners with the fuller realities of their active role in placing barriers in the way of economic diversification and development in Africa.

Although NEPAD appears to support trade diversification, it tends to focus Africa's external trade on those traditional areas of export in which it has, according to the World Bank and NEPAD, comparative advantage (paras 162, 171, 173). NEPAD promotes more trade in African food and agricultural products, although also in processed form (para. 158). But this commodity export orientation affects not only trade, but the kind of agricultural policies and programmes being promoted by NEPAD.

And this NEPAD approach goes further to reinforce Africa's attention not only on its traditional exports but also on its traditional trading partners – mainly the countries of Europe. Although NEPAD at one point recommends negotiations to 'facilitate market access for African products to world markets', and it even makes a token reference to encouraging South–South partnerships, the main focus and orientation of its recommendations to African heads of state is that they do all they can to secure and stabilise what it calls 'preferential treatment by key developed country partners' (paras 169, 172, 185).

Such tariff preferences, together with financial and technical aid from Europe to their African, Caribbean and Pacific (ACP) partners under the auspices of the Lomé Convention, have reflected and reinforced the long-standing orientation and heavy dependence of these countries on Europe. Yet NEPAD calls on African leaders to defend and extend such relations of dependency – not only through the Cotonou Agreement that is now replacing Lomé, but also under Washington's African Growth and Opportunity Act (AGOA). Although NEPAD makes a passing mention of the fact that there may be 'deficiencies in their design and application' (para. 172), it has not even begun to take on board the more developed positions of the ACP countries in their negotiations with the EU, let alone the more advanced positions of ACP civil society organisations, particularly in challenging the 'reciprocal trade liberalisation' that the EU is demanding. Nor does NEPAD's position remotely begin to question the outrageous invasions of African policy rights and political autonomy by Washington in return for the limited 'special' access to the US market that it offers under AGOA.[3]

NEPAD apparently fails to understand the ways in which these agreements reflect the real aims and self-interests of the most powerful industrialised countries. Such agreements cannot be viewed or treated as benign 'partnership' agreements; nor are they about mere diplomatic relations. The extremely weak engagement of NEPAD on such centrally significant economic agreements between Africa and its major investment, trade and aid partners raises profound doubts and holds out little hope for the continent. This thoroughly questionable approach may, in fact, reflect the realities of how African governments would deal with the 'new partnerships' with these Northern governments within the framework of this plan. Similar cautious accommodations are to be expected, and are already indicated in how NEPAD advises that Africa engage with the same 'partners' in the context of the multilateral trade system and the World Trade Organisation.

Locating Africa within the multilateral trade system and the WTO

In touching on the multilateral trade system at various points, the NEPAD document makes reference to the 'absence of fair and just rules' and the 'unfavourable terms of trade' facing Africa, and it even mentions the 'biases in economic policy and instability in world commodity prices' that affect Africa negatively (paras 33–34, 132). It calls for active participation by African leaders to ensure 'open, predictable' market access for Africa's exports (para. 170), the usual code words referring to the multilateral system of trade under WTO rules. In Section VI on 'A New Global Partnership', NEPAD declares that 'African leaders envisage the following responsibilities and obligations of the developed countries and multilateral institutions'; including, *inter alia*, their obligation to 'negotiate more equitable terms of trade for African countries within the multilateral framework' (para. 188). NEPAD is, therefore, encouraging an active engagement by African governments within the multilateral system of rules and regulations being created by and implemented under the WTO.

In the half dozen brief sentences focused specifically on the multilateral system and the WTO, NEPAD exhibits what has to be termed an inadequate grasp of the nature, functioning and effects of this system. Despite some passing observations on the inequities of the global system, NEPAD welcomes 'the new trading opportunities that emerge from the evolving multilateral trading system' (para. 169). This new system is evolving, and has been given an enormous boost by the Uruguay Round Agreements created out of the General Agreement on Tariffs and Trade (GATT) negotiations finalised in April 1994. But, already in the penultimate stages of that round, UNCTAD (1994a, 1994b, 1994c, 1995) warned that, despite the predicted vast expansion of global trade, Africa would actually lose out to the tune of some US$2.5–3 billion in the years immediately following. This has since been borne out in experience, and even accepted, in general terms, in studies by other reputable mainstream institutions such as the World Bank and the OECD (UNDP 1996/Oxfam 1999).

In the years following the signing of the dozens of Uruguay Round Agreements, and the establishment of the WTO in 1995, it soon became clear to governments throughout the developing world, as they tried to implement these agreements, and as the detailed terms of the agreements were subject to meticulous examination by both governmental and independent trade lawyers and development analysts, that there were gross imbalances, deficiencies and inconsistencies within and between the respective agreements (Das 1998). These not only militated against the interests and needs of the developing countries but reflected the pervasive bias towards the interests of the most developed.[4] NEPAD, however, simply refers to the need for the rules and regulations of the WTO to be implemented, and makes no mention of the almost 100 specific implementation issues relating to problems within virtually all the agreements. The governments of the developing countries, individually and collectively, have been trying over the past five or six years to make these issues the priority matters on the agenda of the WTO for review, revision and rectification, only to be intransigently blocked by the more powerful players in the WTO, particularly the notorious Quad consisting of 'The Majors': the EU, the USA, Canada and Japan.

Even when it mentions problems of implementation, NEPAD does not in any way bring out the fact that these are not only about the difficulties facing the weaker developing countries, especially in Africa, in implementing the legal and institutional requirements of the WTO. It is such 'failures' that the powerful governments and the WTO Secretariat constantly criticise. At the same time, NEPAD ignores the fact that it is the most powerful industrialised country governments, themselves, that have tactically avoided implementing those Uruguay Round terms they consider inimical to their interests. A particularly blatant case is the USA's skilful evasion of its undertakings to remove tariff and quota restrictions on textile and clothing exports from developing countries. With regard to both the USA and the EU, such protectionism is most notoriously evident in their resistance to removing direct and indirect agricultural production and export subsidies, in contravention of the letter and spirit of WTO agreements and undertakings. NEPAD diplomatically avoids any explicit mention of these implementation issues.

These countries – the proposed 'partners' in Africa's development – have also postponed the fulfilment of their undertakings to provide financial and technical assistance to the LDCs and other countries that would (or, as the Quad insisted, might) be adversely affected by the new global regime. Such compensatory measures were promised by the powerful governments at the last moment before the signing of the Marrakech

Treaty that concluded the Uruguay Round. These were part of the *quid pro quo* terms of the deal to secure the acceptance of the whole package – about which many developing country governments had strong reservations, even at that stage. Such evasive tactics by the rich and powerful governments reinforce serious doubts about their preparedness for an honest and supportive partnership with Africa. But NEPAD's failure even to note the tendentious manoeuvres and blatant failures of the governments of the richest countries in the WTO points, once again, to the inevitable political constraints placed on the promoters of partnership, entailing aid from such governments.

Alternatively, or in addition, it can be concluded that the technical formulators and political promoters of NEPAD are unaware of such outrageous abuses. But, if they are unaware, then it has to be said that they are ill-equipped to formulate a historic strategy for the whole of Africa. For example, NEPAD blandly suggests that the expansion of the WTO 'must recognise and provide for the African continent's special concerns, needs and interests in future WTO rules' (para. 169). It repeatedly calls on African heads of state to ensure this, and urges them to persuade the developed countries to 'negotiate more equitable terms of trade for African countries within the WTO multilateral framework' (para. 188). But the writers of NEPAD patently fail to understand the real nature of the WTO. It is an extremely tough negotiations arena where ruthless hard bargains are driven by powerful corporate and national vested interests, and it is characterised by unprincipled arm twisting and barely veiled threats – not the polite diplomatic position-taking of heads of state. And, with the WTO Secretariat clearly biased towards the interests and demands of the most powerful member states and the expansion of the liberalised global trade regime, the WTO is not a neutral open forum or assembly of nations where world leaders gather to debate and influence each other's positions.

On the other hand, in addressing itself to African heads of state in this connection, NEPAD cannot acknowledge that it is precisely certain political leaders of African countries, far removed from the realities and extreme complexities of the WTO negotiations in Geneva, who frequently undermine African efforts in the WTO. This is also because many top political leaders in Africa are far more susceptible to the pressures and persuasions of their Northern aid and trade partners, who are known to contact them directly and confidentially outside of the negotiations processes and behind the backs of the African negotiators on the front line, in order to counter and undermine African negotiating positions and negotiators. Even many African trade, industry, agricultural, environmental and other ministers are often less in touch than are their own WTO negotiators with the full complexities of the negotiating issues and arguments, and the delicate tactical positionings and strategic alliances being created in Geneva.

Such disjunctures and divisions within and between African governments, between the negotiating teams in Geneva and their home ministries, and between detailed technical, legal and economic arguments on the one hand, and broad political or diplomatic positions, on the other hand, are also evident in NEPAD's approach to the WTO. It refers to 'strategic areas of intervention' in the abstract (para. 171) but does not, for example, acknowledge the concrete Africa Group positions in Geneva, such as the comprehensive and ground-breaking proposals on the review and revisions of the WTO Agreement on Trade Related Aspects of Intellectual Property Rights (TRIPs), or on the Agreement on Agriculture. The latter has direct implications for NEPAD's agricultural development projects, but it may be that it is ignored in this document because South Africa identifies with the Cairns Group of big agricultural exporting countries, led by Australia, New Zealand, Canada, Chile and other larger, more developed countries in the WTO. Nor (unsurprisingly) does NEPAD acknowledge the even more advanced positions of many Third World peasant organisations and small farmer organisations, and development NGOs from South and North, arguing that small-scale agriculture, and production for food security and food sovereignty be placed outside the demands and trade disciplines of the WTO.

But NEPAD's failure to endorse, or even acknowledge, the specific collective African positions in the WTO may also reflect the position of the South African government towards the Africa Group in Geneva, and their degree of distance and independent positioning vis à-vis the officially endorsed positions of the rest of Africa (AIDC 2002). The major difference between South Africa and the jointly agreed African positions – both for the Third WTO Ministerial in Seattle, in December 1999, and the Fourth Ministerial in Doha, in November 2001 is that Africa officially opposed and collectively resisted the introduction of a range of new issues for negotiation in the WTO. However, South Africa's more ambiguous official position was to accept most of these as legitimate and necessary bargaining issues, or at least as matters to be bargained over as trade-offs for other needs. Similarly, the issue of industrial tariff liberalisation in the WTO, which the joint African position opposes but which South Africa supports, is nonetheless subtly alluded to in NEPAD as the need for 'further liberalisation in manufacturing' (para. 171). It would seem that South Africa has also tried to use the NEPAD programme to gain endorsement – in what is a key African document – for the introduction of a multilateral investment agreement into the WTO. This is carefully coded as 'transparency and predictability as a precondition for increased investment', and offered as a trade-off with the governments of the industrialised countries 'in return for boosting supply-side capacity and enhancing the gains from existing market access' (para. 170). It has to be seen how the Africa Group in Geneva and African governments in general will interpret and respond to this apparent NEPAD ploy. It is, however, not lost on other African countries that South Africa – with its banks, private companies and even parastatal corporations keenly looking for investment opportunities in Africa and elsewhere – could see it as in its own national interest to go along with the regime – globalised rights for corporations in all countries and (almost all) sectors – at which an investment agreement in the WTO is aimed.

In response to African complaints about the pressures of the day-to-day functioning of the WTO, and especially the extreme difficulties with which a complex new round of negotiations would confront them, NEPAD proposes 'technical assistance and support to enhance the institutional capacities of African states to use the WTO and to engage in multilateral trade negotiations' (para. 170). Such offers are a standard Quad and WTO Secretariat inducement and misleading reassurance to African governments in order to get them to accept proposals contrary to their own considered judgements. After the Doha Ministerial, South Africa proudly reported that it had obtained 'a strong commitment' by the powerful countries to provide such technical assistance, an expectation flying in the face of their long delays in fulfilling such promises (DTI n.d., Keet 2002). It also ignores the fact that many countries had and have objections to the nature and implications of the new issues, and the dangers of the proposed expansion of the remit of the WTO. Their problem is not merely one of lack of capacity to understand or negotiate the issues. But the further problem with such technical assistance is that it is never neutral, and the content of the instructions and advice given will reflect the opinions and orientations of the pro-WTO institutions and agencies selected to provide the capacity building.

Alongside the failure of NEPAD to take up and support established African positions in and on the WTO, there is another omission in the NEPAD plan that is particularly significant in a document that claims to be providing the guidelines and basis for regional integration between and development within the countries of Africa. NEPAD is totally silent on the terms and constraints imposed on regional trade arrangements (RTAs) as they are defined by the WTO. These constraints are designed to ensure that RTAs, or what are conceived as regional economic communities (RECs) in African plans, do not raise barriers that discriminate against third parties in the world economy. And countries in the RECs that are foreseen or already under way in Africa are further advised to lower their separate and joint tariff provisions, and remove other external barriers, to 'integrate into the global economy ... for their own good' (World Bank

1991). What this means, in practice, is that the kind of preferential trade terms and common external tariffs that such groupings of countries might wish to use for their mutual benefit, and to reduce heavy pressures from external third parties, are severely limited by the WTO's Article XXIV. The African Ministers of Trade call for this contentious article to be reviewed and revised in terms of the development needs and aims within African RECs and on the basis of the special and differential terms (SDTs) that the WTO supposedly allows for the special needs of LDCs and other developing countries. Improving and using such potential WTO 'rights' to legally secure the RECs as effective 'spaces' for internal and intra-African development is hardly a radical position. Yet NEPAD's perspective on Africa's engagement with the global trade regime and rules does not even extend to this.

Although NEPAD ignores the details of Africa's officially agreed positions on the WTO, the writers of the NEPAD programme have had to take care not to be seen to be explicitly supporting the launch of an ever-wider new multisectoral round of WTO negotiations. Thus NEPAD carefully suggests that 'if' a new round of multilateral trade negotiations is started, African countries must be prepared. But it also states, without qualification, that African governments must give 'broad-based support' to the WTO (para. 171). The fact is, however, that many African government ministers, and most African civil society organisations engaged on issues around the WTO, are very dissatisfied with both the substance and the functioning of the WTO. NEPAD, however, encourages African governments to see the WTO as a 'forum in which developing countries can collectively put up their demands' (para. 170), and does not point to the extreme difficulties the governments of Africa and the rest of the developing world face in engaging with the powerful governments in formal and informal WTO negotiations. This is due not only to the imbalances of power between the different players but to the untransparent, inaccessible, exclusionary and thoroughly undemocratic nature of this byzantine organisation. This is reinforced by the blatant bias within the WTO Secretariat towards the demands of the global powers and the assumptions of the neo-liberal trade paradigm. Yet although NEPAD makes at least one small mention of the need for reform in the multilateral finance institutions (para. 188), there is no equivalent reference to the equally urgent need for reform of the WTO.[5]

NEPAD and the integration of Africa into the global economy
In all the above positions, NEPAD is seriously lacking in its apparent grasp of the nature of the WTO. This is not merely a trade institution but a new global executive body, and the central component of an emerging but undeclared system of global economic government. The WTO is the

main institutional instrument for the restructuring and (re)regulation of an emerging globalised economy. NEPAD is similarly lacking in its understanding and characterisation of the processes of globalisation, and this is reflected in its proposals on how Africa should relate to these processes.

In its introductory section dealing with the globalising world economy, NEPAD makes some critical comments on the increased costs imposed by globalisation on 'Africa's ability to compete' (para. 28), and observes that the costs of global processes 'have been borne disproportionately by Africa' (para. 30). It even notes that, in the absence of fair and just rules, globalisation has 'increased the ability of the strong to the detriment of the weak' (para. 33), and that 'increasing polarisation of wealth and poverty is one of the number of processes that have accompanied globalisation' (para. 35). These remarks are testimony to the extent to which even the writers of NEPAD have been affected by the exposure by UN agencies, above all the UNDP and UNCTAD, of the uneven, polarising and destabilising impact of globalisation. These and other revelations about the negative as well as the positive effects of globalisation have entered into mainstream discourse. This also reflects, and may be an attempt to outflank, the wide-ranging and increasingly influential criticism from the international movements against the anti-democratic, divisive and damaging effects of neo-liberal governmental and corporate globalisation for people and communities throughout the world.

However, the greater influence of other agencies, such as the World Bank, on the NEPAD writers' fundamental approach to globalisation is expressed in the more pervasive views endorsing globalisation on the grounds of 'the unparalleled opportunities that globalisation has offered to some previously poor countries' (para. 40), and because 'pursuit of greater openness of the global economy has created opportunities for lifting millions of people out of poverty' (para. 32). The significant centrality of such views in NEPAD is evident from its opening statement deploring the 'malaise of underdevelopment' in Africa, caused by its 'exclusion' from the globalising world (para. 1). The supposition that the marginalisation of Africa from the processes of globalisation has been the cause of its underdevelopment, and that 'Africa's potential has been untapped because of its limited integration into the global economy' (para. 16) runs throughout this document. Thus, in NEPAD's view, what Africa needs is to end its 'marginalisation' and 'rapidly integrate' into the global economy (para. 35). NEPAD argues that globalisation is not only the *de facto* context, but also 'provides the means for Africa's rejuvenation' (para. 28).

There are a number of profound misconceptions in NEPAD's approach to globalisation and Africa's location within it, and thus misdirections on what should be done. The so-called 'marginalisation' of Africa is the first misconception, and is actually an inversion of the realities of Africa's location in the international capitalist economy. NEPAD accepts the views of neo-liberal agencies, such as the World Bank, that Africa's internal problems and inhospitable policy environment cause it to be marginalised from the beneficial effects of international flows of investment and trade. On the face of it, Africa does have a minuscule share of less than 2 per cent of international trade and receives an equally minute percentage of the flows of international capital. That more would necessarily be better, as NEPAD unquestioningly accepts, is arguably highly unlikely, as long experience and analysis shows. But the most fundamental problem for Africa is not its exclusion but rather the long-standing subordinate and exploited nature of its inclusion in a profoundly assymmetrical international economy: from its enforced integration into international circuits of trade and finance through colonisation down to the present day. As Samir Amin (2002) observes, 'The concept of marginalisation is a false one which hides the real questions, which are not "to which degree the various regions are integrated" but rather the ways in which they are integrated.'

The consequent necessity, according to NEPAD, for the 'rapid integration' of Africa (para. 52) into the global economy completely misses the significance of the existing forms and extent of the integration of Africa into the global economy. African countries are profoundly dependent upon and locked into the workings of the global economy. Their economies are characterised by contrived and excessive extroversion towards international markets, with extremely limited backward and forward trade and production linkages either within or between African economies. The more commercialised sectors of African production are heavily externally oriented; and, at an average of 43 per cent of GDP (and more than 50 per cent in LDCs), trade carries a much greater weight in African economies than in the supposedly highly globally integrated industrialised economies (where external trade has an average weight of only 20 per cent of their GDPs).

Clearly, it is not external trade *per se* but the role of trade within multi-layered, multidimensional, internally integrated and largely self-sustaining economies that should be the prime concern. The basic character of most African countries, as has long been pointed out by African economists, is that they are internally disarticulated and are mainly shallow trading economies, whereas they need to be transformed into rounded, internally integrated and more soundly based production economies. This concern is reflected to a considerable extent in the AAF-SAP and AEC approach, in contrast with NEPAD's overriding concern with the expansion of 'efficient' production to feed into 'competitive' external trade.

In NEPAD's view, liberalisation and openness are the main instruments for the expansion of trade within Africa and between Africa and the rest of the world, and such openness is both the means and the measure of Africa's integration into the global economy. This misses the fact that it is, in fact, the extensive liberalisation of the external trade and investment policies of most countries in Africa, imposed under structural adjustment programmes, that have been major factors in the de-industrialisation, economic decline and social crises in Africa. It is the enforced opening up of African economies that has made them even more vulnerable to damaging external pressures, reinforcing foreign controls and increasing outside influences within their economies. The connections within NEPAD between liberalisation and openness in order to integrate into the global economy highlight the fact that neo-liberal injunctions about integration *into* are actually and very dangerously about opening *up to* the global economy, meaning the highly competitive trading forces and self-serving investment interests emanating from the rest of the world.

In so far as NEPAD notes the polarisation or 'widening wealth–poverty gap' within and between countries in the globalised world, it refers to such growing inequalities and inequities as being among the outcomes accompanying globalisation (para. 35). In fact, such patterns are not coincidental, nor are they incidental side-effects of globalisation. They are intrinsic to the globalisation of free market economies. The removal of precautionary or protective regulations for the more vulnerable, in order to allow open competition, certainly enables and encourages the already strong, well-endowed, well-placed, favoured, fortunate – or ruthless – to prosper. But this simultaneously plays upon and intensifies the disadvantages of the weaker countries, communities, and social groups. Such uneven effects and social and economic imbalances are intensified and magnified under conditions of unfettered globalised competition. These polarising effects between and within countries (including the richest, such as the USA) have been powerfully and authoritatively documented in the UNDP's Human Development Reports throughout the 1990s. The 'survival of the fittest' and 'devil take the hindmost' attitudes have always been, and are now more than ever, two sides of the same coin of capitalist ideology and practice. Thus, contrary to NEPAD's statement that 'there is nothing inherent in the process of globalisation that automatically reduces poverty and inequality' (para. 40), it is more correct to state that there is much that is inherent in the uncontrolled globalisation of capitalism that automatically *increases* unemployment, human marginalisation, poverty and inequality throughout the world.

In the context of such growing inequalities between Africa and the rest of the world – which it cannot fail to see – NEPAD's response is not to question this system but to suggest a more effectively managed integration of the world. This would create more 'fair and just rules' (para. 33) to ensure a 'more equitable and sustainable' development in Africa (para. 52) and the world. According to NEPAD, this effective management through 'the cooperation of governments and private institutions' will ensure that the 'benefits of globalisation are more equitably spread' (para. 40). NEPAD's writers see that 'governments – particularly those in the developed world – have, in partnership with the private sector, played an important role in shaping the form, content and course of globalisation' (para. 39). In this observation, NEPAD is correct in pointing out that it is not just science and technology that drive globalisation, as is often claimed, but essentially political and economic forces. What NEPAD does not seem to understand is that globalisation reflects the intrinsic expansionary needs of the most highly industrialised economies, and is essential to the very functioning of the capitalist system. The driving motivation for the alliance between the governments of the industrialised economies and their global corporations has been, and is, to restructure international economic relations and re-regulate both international and national economic policies, as required, in order to optimise their advantages and maximise their access and rights all over the world. Thus the 'form, content and course of globalisation' that NEPAD refers to have been determined by and in the interests of the very forces that NEPAD seems to believe will cooperate in the creation of a more just and balanced global system. This reflects NEPAD's belief in its capacity to persuade such neo-liberal and thoroughly self-serving governments (particularly the unilateralist global superpower, the USA) into a 'new partnership' with Africa. This presupposes a far-sightedness and political preparedness in short-sighted, deeply prejudiced, totally self-serving governments – and the corporate forces driving them – to compromise their own economic and political interests and strategic aims and needs in more than token ways in order to respond to the needs of Africa, and indeed of the world.

In the same vein, NEPAD fails to point to the policies and role of the rich and powerful countries in actively contributing to, exacerbating and even creating Africa's extreme problems. To the contrary, NEPAD seems to attribute Africa's failure to benefit from globalisation more to factors and failures within African economies and societies. Thus NEPAD identifies the 'low level of economic activity' in African countries as 'creating a self-perpetuating cycle' that 'severely weakens Africa's capacity to participate in the globalisation process, leading to further marginalisation' (para. 35). It also pursues in some detail the interaction of internal factors in 'Africa's peripheral and diminishing role in the world economy' (para. 26), and there are certainly elements of truth in such observations about internal weaknesses in Africa. But such explanations fail to point to powerful external factors, such as national protectionism in the industrialised economies and their external trade strategies that have deliberately blocked African trade access, and undermined its potential to move up the ladder of productive development. Nor do NEPAD's references to the negative effects of colonialism in Africa touch more than superficially, or give sufficient weight and significance to the profound social disruptions, economic distortions and structural imbalances created in Africa during the processes of colonisation and colonial exploitation (para. 21). Furthermore, NEPAD diplomatically skips over the long decades of direct and destructive neo-colonial economic, political and military interventions by the major powers in post-colonial Africa. Through covert and even open interventions, separately and together – frequently under the umbrella of the Cold War, but always in consideration of their own economic and geopolitical aims – the major powers, and particularly the USA, targeted and actively undermined any African efforts to create national economic strategies to deal effectively with their internal weaknesses, transform their societies, and definitively end their external subordination and exploitation. Yet NEPAD clearly believes in the will and capacity of these same powers and their economic agencies to now be Africa's disinterested partners.

Some questions and challenges

Will NEPAD's proposals for infrastructural projects in Africa be appropriate for the existing development levels and evolving needs within Africa? Or are they mainly intended to attract foreign investment, and will they, in turn, be shaped by the interests of such international investors?

Will NEPAD's proposals on the liberalisation of capital flows within Africa, without appropriate regulatory, corrective and compensatory mechanisms, be conducive to the most effective distribution of public and private investment and more balanced and equitable development between countries and regions, and across the continent?

Are NEPAD's proposals for PPPs a sound means to bring private enterprise into cooperation with the public sector on defined developmental terms? Or will PPPs simply be another means for the state in Africa (as elsewhere) to underwrite and reinforce the operations of private capital, and use public resources to do so?

Will regulatory frameworks in NEPAD be designed to reflect and promote economic, social, labour, environmental and other needs specific to African countries, regions and the continent? Or will these regulations accommodate to (or simply adopt) inappropriate and biased international regulations?

Will the development of agricultural production in Africa serve to increase family and community food security, and national food sovereignty? Or will NEPAD's promotion of ever-greater agricultural exports, on the basis of Africa's so-called comparative advantage, undermine diverse internal agricultural production and instead increase dependence on costly food imports?

Can NEPAD's focus on greater market access for African exports into the richest economies serve as an effective means for increased output and export earnings? Or will the encouragement of Africa's traditional exports into established markets simply reinforce Africa's long dependence and vulnerability to continued external economic pressures and political manipulations?

Will economic diversification and industrial development under NEPAD be based essentially on local resources, and be extensively labour-intensive and designed to generate employment? Or will they rely largely on external financial resources and capital-intensive approaches, with further external costs and pressures on external balances of payments?

Does NEPAD provide for strategically conceived trade policies to be utilised as effective instruments and components of planned industrial strategies? Or does NEPAD subscribe to the neo-liberal theories of liberalised trade as being a necessary and sufficient engine of growth, providing the necessary stimulus of international competition for domestic industrial development?

Is trade integration within Africa seen within NEPAD as an important means to stimulate local producers and provide them with larger and guaranteed markets? Or is liberal international access to such African markets – and accompanying competitive pressures on African producers and providers of goods and services – the quid quo pro that NEPAD is offering in return for international aid and investment?

In so far as NEPAD supports trade liberalisation or preferential trade arrangements to encourage intra-African trade, will this work in equitable and mutually beneficial ways? Or will these trade measures, without accompanying supportive financial and technical programmes, operate to the benefit of the stronger economies and companies within Africa, and especially South Africa?

Will NEPAD further the long-standing African aspirations towards greater self-reliance and more self-sustaining development within the continent? Or will NEPAD reinforce the excessive extroversion of much African commercial production through its support for greater international competitiveness and export-led growth, and excessive reliance on external financing?

Will NEPAD act on its own observations about 'deficiencies in the design and application' of the various reciprocal free trade agreements that are being foisted upon Africa, especially by the EU and the USA? Or will NEPAD's explicit endorsement of such unequal agreements be allowed to reinforce global imbalances through comprehensive trade and trade-related agreements between the strong and the weak?

Can NEPAD continue to promote the WTO as a conducive forum for negotiation with international partners on Africa's needs, despite all the biased uses and blatant abuses by the Quad? Or can NEPAD be fundamentally changed to promote the demands by African and other developing countries for reforms or removal of the dozens of implementation issues in all the WTO agreements, rescinding highly questionable trade-related agreements, and challenging the entire functioning and very role of the WTO itself?

Will NEPAD give prime emphasis and act practically on its observations about the inequities and costs of globalisation for the weak, and especially in Africa? Or will NEPAD follow its more pervasive beliefs in the 'unparalleled opportunities' provided by globalisation, and thus continue to encourage African countries and regions to 'integrate rapidly' into the global economy?

Is the integration of Africa about participating more strategically and selectively in the global economy? Or is integration actually about the opening up of Africa to reinforced penetration and renewed domination by powerful international economic and political forces over the continent; and is globalisation thus more accurately described as 'recolonisation'? And where does NEPAD stand on this?

NOTES

1 The AEC Treaty (1991) suggests 'protecting the prices of export commodities on the international market by means of establishing an African Commodity Exchange', and proposes 'the protection of regional and continental markets primarily for the benefit of African agricultural producers'.

2 Neo-liberal theorists fail to point out that 'free trade' is even more advantageous for the strong over the weak, whereas preferential trade agreements can at least be modulated to take these unevennesses into account.

3 In a significant contrast, the AEC Treaty cautions against such bilateral trade agreements countering intra-Africa trade and development (Article 37).

4 This is even recognised today in some quite mainstream newspapers, such as the *Financial Times* in London, (11 November 2001), and even the conservative *Business Day* in Johannesburg (editorial of 7 November 2001).

5 Not surprisingly, there is no reference at all to the proposals from civil society organisations for the more radical restructuring, reduction and relocation of the WTO under the UN, or closure of the WTO, together with the IMF, World Bank and related undemocratic neo-liberal institutions, which together have assumed the role of a new system of *de facto* global government.

REFERENCES

AIDC, 2002, The Official Position and Role of South Africa in Promoting the WTO, Cape Town: Alternative Information and Development Centre.

Amin, Samir, 2002, 'Africa: Living on the Fringe', New Agenda: South African Journal of Social and Economic Policy, 7.

Das, B. L., 1998, 'The WTO Agreements: Deficiencies, Imbalances and Required Changes', in Trade and Development Issues, Penang: Third World Network.

Department of Trade and Industry (DTI), n.d. 'Report on the Fourth WTO Ministerial Conference, Doha, Qatar, 9–14 November 2001'. Pretoria: DTI.

Keet, D., 2002, South Africa's Official Position and Role in Promoting the World Trade Organisation, Cape Town: AIDC.

NEPAD, 2001, 'The New Partnership for Africa's Development (NEPAD)', Midrand: NEPAD Secretariat. Available online at <http://www.dfa.gov.za/events/nepad.pdf>.

OAU. 1991, 'Treaty Establishing the African Economic Community' (AEC Treaty). Abuja: Organisation of African Unity.

Oxfam. 1999, 'Loaded Against the Poor – World Trade Organisation', Position Paper, November: Oxford.

UNCTAD. 1994a, 'The outcome of the Uruguay Round: An Initial Assessment', Supporting papers to the Trade and Development Report, 1994 (UNCTAD/TDR/14). New York/Geneva: United Nations.

UNCTAD. 1994b, Trade and Development Report, 1994. New York/Geneva: United Nations.

UNCTAD. 1994c, 'A preliminary analysis of the results of the Uruguay Round and their effects on the trading prospects of developing countries' (TD/B/WG.4/13), Geneva.

UNCTAD. 1995, 'Report to the Ad-Hoc Working Group on Trading Opportunities in the New International Trading Context' (Reported in Third World Economics No.124, pp. 1–15, November 1995, Penang, Malaysia).

UNCTAD. 2002, Trade and Development Report 2002. New York/Geneva: United Nations.

UNDP. 1996, Human Development Report 1996: Economic Growth and Human Development. New York: Oxford University Press.

UNDP, 2003, Making Global Trade Work for People, London: Earthscan Publications.

World Bank, 1991, 'Intra-Regional Trade in Sub-Saharan Africa'. World Bank Economic and Finance Division: Africa Region (May 1991). Washington DC: World Bank.

7 Confronting the Digital Divide

An Interrogation of African Initiatives to Bridge the Gap

Y. Z. Ya'u

The unequal access to information and communication technologies (ICTs) has been termed the digital divide. This digital divide exists at various levels, including within countries, between countries and within groups of nations. Africa is presently at the bottom of the ICT ladder. This has serious implications both for the continent and globally. This is because ICTs are propelling the economies of those countries that are ICT-rich faster than those that are ICT-poor, thus further widening the development gap between Africa and the industrialised world.

The realisation of the importance of ICTs in economic development led the UN Commission on Science and Technology for Development (UNCSTD) to devote the years 1995–7 to the study of the linkages between ICTs and development. One of the practical results of that effort was the placing of the digital divide on the global development agenda. Since then, there has been a consensus internationally that there is a need to bridge the digital divide. Flowing from this consensus, there have evolved various bridging strategies, actions and initiatives at international, regional, continental and local country levels.

Learning from these efforts, African countries, under the leadership of the United Nations Economic Commission for Africa (ECA), have been developing national, sub-regional and continental initiatives to overcome the digital divide and to promote the greater inclusion of African communities into cyberspace. The first major step in the African initiative was a meeting of the ECA Conference of Ministers responsible for economic and social development and planning, held in May 1996. The meeting passed resolution 795 on 'Building Africa's Information Highway', which committed member countries to the building of national information and communication networks. It also established a high-level Working Group on Information and Communication

Technologies, which was to prepare an African Strategy for the Information Age. The report of that committee, 'African Information Society Initiatives (AISI)' was subsequently adopted (UNECA 1996). It provided the template for the various National Information and Communication Infrastructure (NICI) plans put up by many countries. AISI and the NICI plans have provided the core of African ICT initiatives, including the bridging strategy as contained in the New Partnership for Africa's Development (NEPAD).

This chapter aims at a critical examination of these efforts and initiatives. It seeks to document them, assesses their level of implementation, and the results, impact and progress made towards achieving the goals of bridging the divide. It provides a coherent explanation of the factors responsible for the present state of affairs in cyberspace and tries to articulate what needs to be learned from these efforts in order to bridge the digital gap.

Africa and the digital divide map

The digital divide, defined as unequal access to information and communication technologies (ICTs) by various communities, has today become a major issue of concern. The reality of the digital divide has been well documented by several reports (see, for instance, ITU 2001, 2002; USIC 2000; Bridges 2001; OECD 2001). Suffice it here to highlight the statistics as they affect Africa.

The digital divide has various dimensions. At the international level, it is the concentration of ICTs and services in the industrialised countries of the North, with few of them in the countries of the South, especially African countries. Recent International Telecommunication Union (ITU) statistics show that whereas the USA alone has more than 180 million telephone lines, the whole of Africa has only 20 million lines. While Africa by 2001 had only 18 landline telephones per 1,000 people, the world average was 146, and that of the high-income countries was 597 lines per 1,000 people (NEPAD 2001: 7).

According to an US Internet Council (USIC) report for 2000, there were approximately 136 million people online in Canada and the USA, with the USA alone having a total global share of almost 36 per cent. The equivalent figure for the whole of Africa is only 2.7 million. In all, Africa, with a population share of about 13 per cent, has only 1 per cent of the total global telephone lines, 1 per cent of the Internet users, 1.2 per cent of the total world Internet sites, and almost zero per cent of global ICT production. With an estimated number of hosts of 274,000 in 2001, Africa represents just 0.19 per cent of total global Internet hosts, while its share of computers stood at 7.5 million, representing 1.53 per cent of the world total. Statistics provided by the International Parliamentary Union show that by 2000, while only fifteen African countries had political parties with websites, in North America and Scandinavia all parties are online, and in Europe only one out of the fifteen EU countries was not represented (IPU 2002).

One other area in which Africa's isolation from cyberspace can be seen is in terms of internal connectivity. Calls between African countries are still being routed through third and fourth parties in Europe and America. Access to the Internet on the continent is often dependent on American and European backbone providers. Even current continental bandwidth projects, such as the Africa One Optical Network, the West African Submarine Cable (WASC) and the South Africa–Far East (SAFE) cable, are dominated by multinational corporations outside Africa.

Within Africa itself, access to ICTs is equally uneven. South Africa has more than one-third of the total telephone lines in the continent. Of just over five million personal computers estimated to be in use on the continent in 2001, 2.1 million are in South Africa, representing a share of about 40 per cent. Similarly, of about 1.6 million Internet users on the continent, more than one million are in South Africa. Even more dramatic is the fact that, of the 150,000 Internet hosts in Africa, 144,000 are in South Africa. Only 27 African countries achieved the ITU minimum of one telephone line per 100 people by 2001, against 22 in the previous year.

But even this limited access to ICTs applies mainly to urban dwellers. This defines the third dimension of the digital divide: unequal access to ICTs between urban and rural people. This dimension is very serious, given that in most African countries the rural population constitutes the majority. In Nigeria, for instance, where the rural population is about 65 per cent, more than 90 per cent of the ICTs are located within a few towns. In fact, the three cities of Lagos, Abuja and Port Harcourt together have more than 60 per cent of the total lines in the country, with Lagos alone having more than 230,000 (NITEL figures, quoted from Aibe 2000). As of 2001, 536 of the 774 local government headquarters had no access to telephone services in the country. In Liberia, 88 per cent of the country's telephone lines are in Monrovia, while in Bangui, the capital of the Central African Republic, the figure is over 90 per cent. In both Eritrea and Guinea, the capitals each have about 97 per cent of the total lines in their respective countries (Chebeau-Loquay 2000).

There is a fourth dimension, which affects virtually all countries of the world, although to varying degrees. This is the gender aspect of the digital divide. Women have less access to ICTs globally but this is likely to be worse in developing countries. Although statistics are not readily available, with the possible exception of South Africa (Bridges 2001), in all African countries women are underrepresented among the online population. As a matter of fact, when ICTs were first introduced in many African countries, they were introduced in the banking and secretarial services sectors, where existing staff, mainly women, were replaced by computer-literate workers, mainly men.

There is another equally global and insidious dimension, which, like the gender dimension, affects virtually all countries. This is the unequal access to ICTs as between workers and ordinary citizens, on the one hand, and those who own capital on the other. In the USA, where the digital divide has taken on a racial dimension, blacks and other poor population groups have less access than whites. The latter constitute 82 per cent of the total online population of the USA, with blacks making up only just over 12 per cent. The United States Internet Council (USIC) report (2000) admits that people with an annual income of $15,000 and below have little chance of access to ICTs in the USA.

But the digital divide is not just about the inadequacy of ICT infrastructure and the diffusion of ICT services. Another gap is opened up by the poor quality and high cost of services in African countries. Several documents have made reference to the relative cost of ICT services on the continent (see, for instance, Zell 2000). The causal factors for high costs include the limited size of the ICT network, the fact that basic equipment such as computers is costly, and the lack of local manufacturing capacity. The problem of poor quality of service relates to the fact that the telephone network is still largely analogue-based in many parts of the continent. Even in the relatively recent domain of cellular technology, in Africa the analogue share is more than 40 per cent. Call completion rates are generally low, while the rate of faults per line is high. This slowness and low bandwidth have affected the rate at which those who have access to the Internet can surf. This is costing the continent a lot of money. For instance, Bell (2002) estimates that Africa's Internet service providers (ISPs) pay about US$1 billion per annum to American and European bandwidth providers for international connectivity.

At another level, there is a critical shortage of skilled ICT workers. Indeed, in most African countries basic computer skills, in terms of being able to use the computer for such applications as word processing, are lacking. This shortage of labour is partly responsible for the low representation of Africans on the worldwide web. This latter aspect, however, has two other dimensions. One is that the language of the Internet, which is still predominantly European, has excluded many Africans who cannot write in these languages. As of now, very few African languages have registered their presence on the Internet. The second is that, given that the majority of the citizens have no access to the Internet, their efforts can leave no trace on the web.

The situation calls for a concerted effort by African countries to address not just the international dimensions of the digital divide but also its internal dimensions. In short, the task is to democratise access to ICTs so that citizens of African countries can have equal access to ICTs. Ironically, except at the level of discussion, the democratisation of access to ICTs has not been given concrete expression in efforts to build the information society in Africa.

African responses to the digital divide

Although a number of African countries have been taking individual decisions with respect to accessing ICTs, it was only after 1999, when the ECA convened the African Development Forum on the Challenge to Africa of Globalization and the Information Age, that African countries took the matter more seriously. The African Information Society Initiative (AISI), which was to provide the framework for the African information technology (IT) renaissance, was to be the vehicle for building an African information society. Its vision is to ensure that by 2010, 'every man, woman, child, village public and private office has secure access to information and knowledge through the use of computers and tele-communication media' (Amoako 1996).

AISI was to be implemented at country level through the NICI plans. NICI was to have four major frameworks: policy development, appli-cations, infrastructure building and technology selection. In terms of *policy development*, each country was to develop an appropriate policy framework for the promotion and regulation of development in the ICT sector. This was to include the setting up of an independent and autono-mous regulatory agency. Under *applications*, each country was to undertake a sectoral needs assessment and prioritise areas in need of immediate attention. *Infrastructure building* would then facilitate these applications. *Technology selection* entailed detailed analysis and selection of appropriate technologies to meet the demands of the applications and the deploy-ment of infrastructure.

Along with these thematic frameworks, there were also cross-cutting issues that were to be addressed in the building of the African inform-ation society. These were gender, youth, community participation, human resource development and research. An elaborate stakeholder spectrum was also defined, including governments, the private sector, NGOs, international development organisations and international ICT companies.

Much of the technology deployment and infrastructure building were undertaken with the assistance of such international organisations as the International Development Research Centre (IDRC), UNDP, UNESCO and the International Telecommunication Union (ITU). The IDRC projects centred on the use of telecentres to provide multi-user access points. Given the poor state of infrastructure and the cost of connection on the continent, telecentres were favoured gifts from many development organisations, although, as business models, they proved to be a failure (Benjamin 2000).

UNESCO has supported the use of ICTs for educational programmes through its Regional Information Network for Africa (RINAF) project, while UNDP has built some Internet backbone in selected African countries. The ITU, along with the African Telecommunications Union (ATU) and the ECA, has given weight to policy development. The ITU was involved in setting up the African Virtual University to train tele-communication experts for the countries using distance learning. The African Connection project of the ATU also has a manpower development component, which involves the setting up of centres of excellence in telecommunications training on the continent. USAID's Leland Initiative has both capacity building for regulators and connectivity components.

Experimentation in technology includes satellite-based connectivity (such as the RASCOM, SAT-2, SAT-3), the IRIDIUM project, submarine cable (such as WASC and SAFE), an optical fibre system (such as Africa One), radio (such as Worldspace receivers), and mobile cellular, which appears to have gained acceptance given its current level of deployment on the continent. Policy planners have also been involved in discussing multi-user access points such as telecentres and cybercafés. The frame-work for policy making is liberalisation and market reforms, whose basic element was the privatisation of state-owned ICT organisations. A number of countries have set up regulatory agencies to regulate as well as end the state monopoly of the sector.

Africa's attempt at building e-commerce capacity also gained the nod of the United Nations Conference on Trade and Development (UNCTAD) in the area of capacity building for policy development and legislation. It has also been involved in capacity building for the participation of small and medium-sized enterprises (SMEs) of developing countries in e-commerce. It has a rich website on e-commerce directed at SMEs. Unfortunately, most SMEs in Africa have problems accessing the Internet.

In preparation for the African Development Forum (ADF '99), the ECA requested all African countries to submit a report on the implement-ation of their NICI plans. These reports provided a continent-wide assess-ment of the ICT situation in each country (UNECA 1999). While it is true that various efforts undertaken by the African countries, at both country and continental levels, have produced some positive results, the report showed that a lot remained to be done. For instance, while there was some growth in the number of telephone lines and Internet users, the position of Africa relative to others remained weak. Africa had a total share of 2 per cent of world telephone lines and contributed nothing to the production of ICTs. About twenty countries had established regulatory agencies in line with the NICI processes, and only fourteen had no mobile cellular telephone services. There was an appreciable level of awareness about the importance of ICTs among policy planners in the countries, despite hardly any awareness among the population at large, who mainly see access to ICTs as a status symbol. Similarly, while, by the end of 1996, only six African countries had an Internet connection, by 1999 only three were without one (Jensen 1999b).

While little was achieved in terms of building the relevant human resources for the African IT revolution, a serious problem came to the fore. This was the issue of the brain drain, a situation in which African skills, especially in the ICT fields, are lured to the developed world. The seriousness of this problem prompted the ECA to set up a committee to study the problems of the African brain drain and how the African diaspora can contribute to the process of building the African information network. As of 1999, it was reported that more than 30,000 Africans with PhDs were living outside the continent (Cogburn and Adeya 1999: 12). The ADF made recommendations on how to utilise these brains as well as how to attract them back home.

The document adopted by the ADF (UNECA 1999b), while reaffirming the participants' commitment to the NICI framework, proposed various initiatives that should be concretised to facilitate the speedy building of the African information society. These included the use of schoolnet and distant education for human resource development, telecentres as a means of access, and e-commerce, among others. It also agreed on programmatic areas and actions to be taken by the various stakeholders in developing the African information society.

The document was presented to African heads of state for their consideration. It formed the core of the African position at the Second Global Knowledge Conference held in March 2000 in Kuala Lumpur, Malaysia, and other ICT fora. It also served as input to the NEPAD section on bridging the digital divide (NEPAD 2001). As a matter of fact, the section was the contribution of the Millennium document, which was drafted by the African Connection secretariat of the ATU. The African Connection has been involved in various post-ADF '99 follow-up programmes. In other words, the NEPAD section on bridging the digital divide is a culmination of various continental African efforts.

The NEPAD document notes that 'Africa has been unable to capitalise on ICT as a tool in enhancing livelihoods and creating business opportunities'. It further observes that while many countries 'have started ICT policy reforms, service penetration, quality or tariffs have not yet improved'. One problem of service penetration is that it is relatively costly in Africa compared to other continents. For example, the connection cost in Africa averages 20 per cent of GDP *per capita*, compared with the world average of 9 per cent, and 1 per cent for high-income countries. Indeed, while in Sweden it is about 0.12 per cent, in Nigeria it is 55.13 per cent and in South Africa – so far the cheapest on the continent – it is 5.26 per cent (Kirkman *et al.* 2002).

Having described the situation on the continent, the document sets out the following objectives:

- To double teledensity to two lines per 100 people by 2005, with an adequate level of access for households;
- To lower the cost and improve reliability of service;
- To achieve e-readiness for all countries in Africa;
- To develop and produce a pool of ICT-proficient youth and students from which Africa can draw trainee ICT engineers, programmers and software developers;
- To develop local content and software based especially on Africa's cultural legacy.

These objectives are to be achieved through this set of actions:

- Work with regional agencies such as the ATU's Africa Connection to design model policies and legislation for telecommunications reform, and protocols and templates for e-readiness assessments;
- Work with the regional agencies to build regulatory capacity;
- Establish a network of training and research institutions to build high-level manpower;
- Promote and accelerate existing projects to connect schools and youth centres;
- Work with development finance institutions in Africa, multilateral initiatives (G8 DotForce, UN Task Force) and bilateral donors to establish financial mechanisms to mitigate and reduce sector risks.

Observations and a critique

In terms of objectives, NEPAD is more specific, although except in the case of one item, there is no timeframe for achieving the rest of the objectives. This is unfortunate, given that the achievement of many of the laudable goals of NEPAD is contingent upon the utilisation of ICTs as development tools. For example, while e-commerce is seen as a tool to increase African trade and to integrate the continent economically, there is no indication as to when NEPAD hopes to see the continent achieve readiness for e-commerce.

Beyond this, there are many gaps in the action-related parts of the document, which would make it difficult for the goals of NEPAD to be achieved, especially in relation to bridging the digital divide. The first is that its understanding of the causes of the digital divide is superficial. In the opening sentence of the section, it says: 'In Africa, poor ICT infrastructure, combined with weak policy and regulatory frameworks and limited human resources, has resulted in inadequate access to affordable telephones, broadcasting, computers and the Internet.' This thinking is circular, in that poor ICT infrastructure is said to be the cause of poor infrastructure! Second, other reasons given for the low penetration of ICT services and infrastructure and the high cost of services are lack of policy and limited human resources – but the fact of the matter is that these are manifestations of the problem rather than its causes. Africa's weak ICT infrastructure is tied to its history of underdevelopment through centuries of exploitation by the Western powers.

Colonial conquest arrested the endogenous development of African people while, at the same time, through brutal exploitation of and surplus extraction from Africa and other colonised societies, it enabled the phenomenal growth of European societies. In the event, Western technology experienced rapid growth and by the early twentieth century communication technology had become relatively mature in Europe and America, laying the foundation for the gap. Modern communication services were introduced in Africa by the colonial powers to enable them to maintain contact with home and to take care of colonial administrative needs. They did not see the need to develop the communication infrastructure beyond these needs. Thus, by the dawn of political independence, African countries inherited a hardly existing communication infrastructure while at the same time lacking the technology to rapidly build this base (Sy 1996). This, coupled with the problems of a postcolonial economy, ensured the deepening of the infrastructure gap.

NEPAD, however, does not claim to offer explanations but solutions, which is not unproblematic. One of the critical ICT problems in Africa is the shortage of relevant skills. This is a global problem, one that even the most advanced countries are experiencing. In Africa, however, the problem is more acute. The indicators of production of engineers and technicians are very low compared to other continents. Apart from the statement that they should 'establish a network of training and research institutions to build high-level manpower' and that a 'task force to accelerate the introduction of ICTs in primary schools would be established', no other concrete measures to tackle this problem are mentioned. There are no targets. While there is an attempt to address the educational system generally, the fact is that seeing education within the framework of market forces would not address these problems, nor produce enough labour for the African information society. Moreover, the challenges ICTs pose in the need for paradigm shift in educational philosophy need to be recognised and addressed.

As an information platform, the Internet in particular is a source of development information as well as a means for expression of cultural identity. As it is, African content is very low on the Internet. An even more serious drawback is that existing content is not accessible to many Africans. While declaring local content production to be an objective, NEPAD does not acknowledge the need to make the content more accessible to people by efforts to create and promote a presence for African local languages on the Internet. No concrete measure to promote African content is offered: what we have in the text is a mere statement of intention.

NEPAD is a development platform, yet it has not articulated how ICTs are to be used to promote development in the continent. Access to ICTs cannot be an end in itself; it must create a tool to use for development purposes. This is why it is important to articulate how these technologies can be deployed for development purposes. They must 'form part of a much broader effort to improve social welfare and economic opportunity within specific national and local contexts' (de Alcantara 2001: 22). In this connection it is important to point out that none of the objectives of the ICT section of NEPAD relates concretely to the issues of ending poverty or even to the use of ICTs for improving healthcare delivery on the continent. Yet ending poverty is supposed to be the overarching objective of the document.

Human resource development is one critical sector in which Africa needs to act urgently and ICTs provide a platform for improving educational accessibility to rural Africa. So far, however, very few African countries have seen the need to deploy ICTs as educational tools. In spite of talk about distant education and the use of ICTs in schools, the performance of African governments in this area is dismal. In fact, in many countries ICTs are regarded more as supporting tools than technologies that should be in the mainstream of the educational process.

Nor does the NEPAD document address itself to the use of ICTs in the promotion of democracy and good governance. In 2000, the African Internet Summit called on all African governments to establish a website, among other measures (NCC 2000), yet today many governments have no websites themselves, not to mention making it a law that all government ministries, parastatals and agencies must set up websites. A survey in 2000 found that, of the 14,492 governance-related websites, only 599 were registered for the countries of sub-Saharan Africa, representing a rate of 12 sites per country, while in Western Europe and North America the rates were 404 and 428 per country (Norris 2002).

In a situation where there are contending needs for funds, the ICT sector has remained largely underfunded. Since ICTs are not locally manufactured, African countries have relied on importation. There have been two main strategies to raise funds for the importation of ICTs. These are development assistance and foreign loans. Both of these have problems and neither has been effective. Consequently, at all African ICT-related meetings, there have been calls for the setting up of ICT development funds or banks. Yet these have not materialised at either state or continental levels. NEPAD has failed to take up this issue. Instead it talks of working 'with development finance institutions in Africa, multilateral initiatives and bilateral donors to establish mechanisms to mitigate and reduce sector risks'.

Over the years, many African countries, as NEPAD observes, have developed or are developing ICT policy frameworks. The basic elements of these policy reforms are liberalisation, ending state monopoly, and opening up the sector to foreign participation. While these have to some extent increased network sizes, they have not made services either cheaper or more accessible to low-income groups. Neither has this regulatory reform led to tangible results in the development profile of the countries. For instance, both Senegal and Uganda are touted as examples of good policy reforms in the ICT sector, yet their economies are still very weak, reflecting no gain from their ICT sectors.

Africa's goal of using ICTs as a means of development will only be realised if access to ICTs is democratised on the continent. This, however, does not feature as an objective in NEPAD. Certainly, the modest aim of raising teledensity to 2 per 100 people cannot amount to democratising access. There is no commitment, explicit or implicit, on universal access. Yet without access to ICTs, even the objective of promoting democracy and good governance can become problematic. ICTs provide access to information, which is a necessary though not a sufficient condition for democracy. This access can only be ensured when we democratise ICT resources. The absence of universal access commitment is an indication of the policy framework that underlines the document. As a market-driven policy framework, its concern is the generation of profit.

In addition to these shortcomings, NEPAD has been a conduit for the dichotomised conception of ICTs, a common conceptual problem of ICT policy making in African countries, and especially in Nigeria and South Africa. This dichotomy arises from separating communications technology from information technology, thus treating each separately and reducing the discourse on ICTs to IT only, and in some instances to just computers and the Internet. In Nigeria, for instance, there are three separate national policies on IT, telecommunications and broadcasting, with two different regulatory agencies (Ya'u 2000). This not only creates problems in terms of coordination between the various agencies and the resulting duplication of efforts, but also prevents the countries from tackling the issues of convergence that ICTs present. These issues are grey areas, which do not fall neatly on either side of the dichotomy and therefore could be ignored by both, resulting in poor e-readiness. Convergence issues require an inclusive and broader view of ICTs and innovative policy making backed by effective legislation. It is not surprising that legislation on ICTs is also in its infancy in African countries. But this is one area they need to tackle in order to create the right framework for the growth of ICTs on the continent.

An interesting illustration of this dichotomy is the fact that, right from the beginning, African telecommunications ministers played very little role in the processes of AISI. Instead, while ministers responsible for economic planning were meeting with the ECA in May 1996 to conceptualise AISI, that same month the ministers responsible for telecommunications were meeting in Abidjan to agree on the Green Paper outlining telecommunications policies for Africa (Aperworkin 2001). Indeed even at the ADF '99 conference many countries were represented by their ministers of planning, education or even communication, but not telecommunications. For instance, Nigeria was represented by the Minister for African Integration while at the same time the Minister for Telecommunications was releasing the National Policy on Telecommunication in Abuja, with no reference to what was going on in Addis Ababa.

What is happening to the gap?

Bridging the digital divide has become an omnibus that every organisation and government wants to catch. Over the years there have been numerous initiatives for bridging the gap. From the various regional and country-based initiatives to those of such organisations as the World Bank, UNDP, the OECD and the DOT Force initiative of the G8, efforts are continuing. As a result of these efforts, there has been a modest improvement in connectivity in most countries. For instance, in 1995, only six African countries had an Internet connection, but now virtually all have access.

In spite of this, however, the digital divide seems to be increasing rather than decreasing. An OECD report (2001), for instance, shows that the gap between North America and Africa rose from a multiple of 267 in 1997 to a multiple of 540 by 2000. The US Internet Council report for the year 2000 also noted that the gap was widening. In a report to the Second Global Knowledge Conference, the Access Working Group of the Global Knowledge Partnership noted that 'there is broad consensus within the international community that gaps in information and knowledge both within and between countries are increasing'. Given this scenario, how can the African countries catch up so that their citizens can take part in cyberspace on a more or less equal footing?

Using what they call the footprint model, Mansell and Wehn (1998: 25) arrive at the conclusion that sub-Saharan Africa will take over a century to reach the 1995 level of Ireland. Even the most promising of the developing countries would take about ten years to reach this position. But this catching up is a mirage, because the industrialised countries will not remain static. They are developing their ICT sectors at much faster speeds. Cogburn and Adeya (1999) have put it better: 'It is an illusion to think that ICT-poor countries can "catch up" or keep pace with advances in the most technologically advanced countries.' But this conclusion can lead to pessimism if not put in context. What Africa needs is not so much to 'catch up' but to use its resources, both human and material, to define and pursue its development goals without having to follow a road that is no longer available, that is, one of colonial exploitation as a basis of development.

Even the most optimistic of the scenarios from the UNCSTD scenario-building workshop (Howkins and Valantin 1997), the Networld, ends up with a world that is afflicted by poverty and deprivation. Although they did not say where this poverty and deprivation would be located, it is certain that it would be both more extensive and intensive in the developing world, and especially African countries. But they also draw the conclusion that the Networld is unlikely to happen because 'its causes and the circumstances that might lead to its coming into existence are fuzzy'. Instead, they see more of the symptoms of the March of Follies, the worst of the scenarios in the current reality. The March of Follies is based on a global community that is exclusive and fragmented.

There are three principal reasons why the gap is increasing rather than decreasing. First, bridging efforts are geared toward producing and capturing new markets for multinational corporations. This, for instance, is why the WTO rules insist that the market should be allowed to drive development in the sector. These market policies are constraining developing countries from providing affordable access to ICTs for their citizens. Any subsidy to citizens by government or national companies is regarded as discriminatory and anti-competitive to foreign companies, who under the WTO regimes must not be discriminated against in any way. And, without a subsidy, no investor would invest in poor communities where teletraffic is very low. This means that under-served communities will continue to be excluded.

Second, the bridging strategies are at best surface-scratching, ignoring the fact that the digital divide is not just about a lack of diffusion of ICTs but both a structural problem and a product of historical phenomena, whose legacies are several other divides in relation to the developed and developing countries. The digital divide cannot be understood outside the dynamics of these other divides, nor can it be bridged without bridging them. Where this is acknowledged, as in the DOT Force report, for instance, the emerging recommendations relate more to how to improve trade in ICTs than to confronting the structural problem that divides the world into rich and powerful countries, on the one hand, and poor and weak countries on the other. Even in the developing countries, as Hamelink (1999: 13) puts it, policy makers 'were concerned with the availability of technological products, rather than with the more complex problems associated with their political, economic and cultural integration', while the emphasis has been 'more on operational choices (procurement and deployment) than on strategic choice (the direction of technological development)'. NEPAD is symptomatic of this thinking. Nowhere in the document is there a discussion of the ways in which ICTs are reinforcing existing global inequalities or of the challenges e-commerce is posing to developing countries. It has also not taken on board such issues as the WTO agreements, negotiations at the level of the World Intellectual Property Organisation (WIPO) and other trade issues.

Third, most efforts locate the problem of the digital divide at the level of consumption. The strategies of promoting access to ICTs in most developing countries are thus centred on how foreign companies can invest in these countries by bringing technologies. The consumerist edge of the policies can be seen from concern about removal of import licences and taxes on imported ICT products and tax breaks for ICT companies that invest in these developing countries. There is no serious discussion or strategising on how to make these countries acquire the capacity to be producers of ICTs. Yet it is known that there is a close symmetry between the diffusion (and hence consumption) of technology and its production. Countries that are producers of ICTs have their ICT sectors moving faster than those that are mere consumers. To bridge the digital divide, we must therefore find a way to globalise the production of ICTs, not just in terms of its spatial distribution but also, and more importantly, in terms of its ownership and control. But NEPAD is silent on a strategy to build African ICT production capacity.

In this connection, it is important to note that the discourse on the digital divide has not taken the issue of control and ownership of the network on board. What effect would it have if every citizen of the developing countries had access to ICTs, which were owned and controlled by a few multinational corporations? Does this necessarily mean that the digital divide is overcome? Ownership must be seen as one of the parameters to measure the digital divide. This is particularly important to the sovereignty of states. The emerging regulatory framework in Africa is to allow multinationals to have control of the sector. NEPAD itself does not see an alternative to this. But what is even more serious is that, as Jensen (1999a: 10) observes, 'the strategic investors in the privatisations to date can be linked to previous colonial ties', with Portugal, France and Britain taking over in their former colonies.

Conclusion

There is no doubt that ICTs are changing the way we do things. However, changing the way we do things does not change the world itself. The world has remained essentially the same. In other words, the basic character of the world in terms of uneven development persists. This uneven development has divided the world into two broad camps; the developed or industrialised world and the underdeveloped or developing world. Industrial and technological developments are concentrated in the developed world while technological dependency, poverty, indebtedness and social instability characterise the developing world.

It is true that the world has, through ICTs, shrunk into a global village. Yet, globalisation, which has brought the world into a single market, has not made the world more democratic or inclusive. Instead, it has reinforced control of the economies of the Third World countries by multinational corporations. Liberalisation has not ended poverty. Instead, it has produced a massive concentration of wealth in the hands of the few while impoverishing the majority. The gap between the rich and the poor both at national and individual levels has been widening. For instance, the ratio of the top 20 per cent of the population to the income of the bottom 20 per cent has moved from 30:1 in 1960 to 78:1 by 1994 (Castells 1998). Today it is worse. The application of ICTs is not bridging this inequality but, as Rodriguez and Wilson (1999) note, is rather reinforcing it:

> Research on the United States and some other developed economies has consistently found that information technology has contributed to substantial increase in the level of domestic inequality; indeed, there is a growing consensus that information technology is one of the driving forces behind the spreading wage inequality gaps in the United States.

While ICT has the potential to address these problems and to help in bridging the technological gap, it has not done so. Instead, ICT development is following the historical pattern of uneven development, with the developing world being ICT-poor. In fact, as Rodriguez and Wilson (1999) observe, despite the fact that some developing economies show very high growth rates of their *per capita* GDP, on average poor countries are not catching up with rich countries.

Essentially, therefore, what ICTs have done is threefold. First, they have provided the technological base for globalisation. Second, ICTs have followed the old pattern of unequal development, resulting in the digital divide. Third, the digital divide, as well as shaping the flow of information and knowledge in the world, has been reshaping the world through the institutional mechanisms of the globalising institutions: what we are seeing is the resurgence of imperialism, this time emblematically represented by knowledge dependence. The restructuring of the world in the image of the new imperialism is taking place within the context of a conscious effort to undermine the role of the United Nations. The UN body responsible for telecommunications is the International Telecommunication Union (ITU). However, since the creation of the WTO, the latter has assumed a more powerful and influential position with respect to telecommunications. The WTO has also undermined the role of UNCTAD, and is affecting the work of such development-related UN bodies as the UNDP, UNESCO and the Economic and Social Council. Systematically, therefore, the globalised world of WTO governance is seeing a decline in UN bodies and therefore in the UN. This should be opposed, because the UN is more open, transparent and representative than the WTO, which is opaque, non-representative and unaccountable.

This new imperialism is based on the monopolisation of knowledge through unequal access to ICTs and the use of WTO instruments such as those relating to the protection of intellectual property rights. In this process of creating a knowledge and information monopoly, the new media multinational corporations that control the news industry globally are heavily involved. These organisations have the power to block or insert news according to their value judgements. Alternative channels are disappearing because they cannot compete, in spite of the possibilities that the Internet presents as a news platform. One case that illustrates this is the assassination of King Birendra of Nepal, in which the only version that was widely disseminated is the one given by CNN. This version's credibility has been questioned, but the challenge has been effectively blocked (Adhikari and Mathe 2001).

Today's ICT sector is dependent on computer software for its functioning. Yet the same proponents of complete liberalisation of trade, who are calling on developing countries to dismantle all barriers to international trade in their countries, are leading the campaign for intellectual property rights protection, which seeks to make access to computer software and newer technologies more difficult for developing countries. Intellectual property rights protection would also transfer control of local indigenous knowledge into the hands of web portal owners through its encoding and establishment of patent rights.

While the WTO's liberalisation of trade recognises the right of manufacturers to move their capital to where labour is very cheap, workers have no such right to move their labour to where it is relatively more costly. North America and the European countries have been installing all sorts of immigration controls against the movement of non-intellectual workers from the developing countries. At the same time, they have been luring Africa's best and most experienced brains to their countries. The resulting brain drain is affecting the capacity of developing countries to engage in research and development. What this means is that African countries supply the factory hands and leave research work to the home countries of the multinational corporations. This way, research into ICTs and other technologies can be conducted there, ever widening the gap between African countries and the industrialised world. The gap in access to the information society expands, with its consequence in the resurgence of imperialism (Ya'u 2000).

Increasingly, the sovereign rights of states to regulate their trading policies and environments have been usurped by the WTO, which is run in the most undemocratic way possible on behalf of the transnational corporations. The leadership of the WTO is answerable only to the business world, yet they make laws with which governments have to comply. Moreover, representation at the WTO is skewed against African and other developing countries. The WTO is now a sort of supranational government composed of and run by unelected people, whose concern is generating profits for firms through international trade. In effect, it is the new imperial power.

This new imperialism is also deepening social exclusion in both developed and developing countries and intensifying the level of worker exploitation. Social exclusion is driven by policies that limit the capacity of the poor to access basic necessities of life such as education. And as Castells (1998) notes, 'the lack of education, and the lack of informational infrastructure, lead most of the world to be dependent on the performance of a few globalised segments of their economies, increasingly vulnerable to the whirlwind of global financial flows'. Exploitation is the result of lowering of labour standards by Northern companies that are shifting production sites to unregulated environments. While there is increasing incidence of poverty in developing countries, there is growing unemployment and inequality in most developed countries. This is as a result of the dismantling of the welfare state, which the new orthodoxy of market ideology engendered in these countries.

For the potential of ICT to be translated into reality, the current paradigm must change. The current asymmetry has to be eliminated. But this can only be done if human beings, rather than the market, are the focus of development. The imperative of this change is that there is a limit to how long the current asymmetry can continue to exist. If the rich continue to get richer and the poor poorer, there will in the end be no market – and without markets, according to the market prophets, there will be no development. The result would be catastrophic for the world. Instead, we need to engineer the hardware core of globalisation to produce an inclusive and human-development-oriented software framework for a truly global world of even opportunities and happiness.

For Africa, the goals of NEPAD are desirable. But as a vehicle to bridge the development gap, and in particular the digital divide, it is deficient in many respects. In the first place, many of its prescriptions are inappropriate. Second, its underlying framework is wedded to the neo-liberal paradigm, which has seen the development gap increasing rather than decreasing. Third, it does not ask, as a serious question, why Africa is underdeveloped in the first place. This is important because, unless you understand the problem, you cannot prescribe an appropriate solution. NEPAD needs to be subjected to democratic input from below in order to make it a vision of what Africans want, and to demonstrate how they could actualise that vision.

REFERENCES

Adhikari, Bipin and S. B. Mathe, 2001, 'Impact of Information Technology on Developing Countries: the Contextual Perspective of the Assassination of King Birendra of Nepal', *The Constitution*, 2, 1 (September).

Aibe, Okoh, 2000, 'Telephony: Subjecting an Essential Commodity to Political Talk', *Vanguard Newspaper* (Lagos), 6 September.

Amoako, K. Y., 1996, 'Africa's Information Society Initiative: an African Framework to Build Africa's Information and Communication Infrastructure', in D. L. Cogburn (ed.), *Information and Communication for Development: Nationalism, Regionalism, and Globalism in Building the Global Information Society*, Washington DC: Center for Strategic and International Studies.

Aperworkin, M. K., 2001, 'The Challenges, Constraints and Opportunities of Telecommunications Reforms in West Africa: a National Service Provider Perspective', paper presented at an ABANTU Workshop on Gender and ICTs Policies in Africa, Accra, Ghana, April.

Bell, Richard, 2002, 'The War Is Only Just Beginning!', in *Computers and Telecommunications in Africa*, London: AITEC.

Benjamin, Peter, 2000, 'Telecentres: the Key to Wider Internet Access?' *News Update*, 36.

Bridges, 2001, 'Spanning the Digital Divide: Understanding and Tackling the Issues', <http://www.bridges.org>.

Castells, Manuel, 1998, 'Information Technology, Globalization and Social Development', paper presented at an UNRISD Conference on Information Technologies and Social Development, Geneva, June.

Cheneau-Loquay, Annie, 2000, 'Africa in Global Communication Networks: from Networks to Concrete Users', *Information Development*, 16, 4 (December).

Cogburn, D. and C. N. Adeya, 1999, 'Globalization and the Information Economy:

Challenges and Opportunities for Africa', paper presented at the African Development Forum (ADF '99), Addis Ababa, October.

de Alcantara, Cynthia, 2001, The Development Divide in a Digital Age: an Issues Paper, Geneva: UNRISD Programme Papers on Technology, Business and Society, August.

Global Knowledge, 2000, 'Report to the Global Knowledge Conference II', Kuala Lumpur, Malaysia, March.

Hamelink, C., 1999, 'ICTs and Social Development: the Global Policy Context', paper presented at an UNRISD Conference on Information Technologies and Social Development, Geneva, June.

Howkins, J. and Robert Valantin, 1997, Development and the Information Age, Ottawa: IDRC.

IPU (International Parliamentary Union), 2002, <http://www.ipu.org>.

ITU, 2001, 2002, 'Telecommunication Statistics', <http://www.itu.org>.

Jensen, Mike, 1999a, 'Policies and Strategies for Accelerating Africa's Information Infrastructure Development', paper presented at the African Development Forum (ADF '99), Addis Ababa, Ethiopia, October.

—— 1999b, 'Africa Goes Online',' in The African Computing and Communications Yearbook, 1999–2000, London: AITEC.

Kirkman, G. S. et al., 2002, Global Information Technology Report, 2001–2002: Readiness for the Network World, New York: Center for International Development and World Economic Forum.

Mansell, R. and Uta Wehn, 1998, Knowledge Societies: Information Technology for Sustainable Development, New York: Oxford University Press.

NEPAD, 2001, 'The New Partnership for Africa's Development (NEPAD)', Midrand: NEPAD Secretariat. Available online at <http://www.dfa.gov.za/events/nepad. pdf>.

NCC (Nigeria Communications Commission), 2000, communiqué issued at the end of Second African Internet Summit (AFRINET 2000), Abuja, Nigeria, October.

Norris, Pippa, 2002, Digital Divide? Civic Engagement, Information Poverty and the Internet in Democratic Societies, Cambridge: Harvard University Press.

OECD, 2001, Understanding the Digital Divide, <http://www.oecd.org/ dsti/sti/prod/ Digital_divide.pdf>.

Rodriguez, F. and Ernest Wilson, 1999, 'Will Poor Countries Be Left Behind?: an Interview', infoDev eXchange, 1 (October–December).

Sy, J. H., 1996, Telecommunication Dependency: the African Saga (1850–1980), Nairobi: Regal Press.

UNECA, 1996, African Information Society Initiative (AISI), Addis Ababa: ECA.

—— 1999, National Information and Communication Infrastructure: Country Profiles, Addis Ababa: United Nations Economic Commission for Africa.

—— 1999b, 'The Way Forward to a People-centred African Information Society', document issued at the end of the African Development Forum (ADF '99), Addis Ababa, October.

USIC (United States Internet Council), 2000, Internet Report for the Year 2000, <http: //www.usic.gov>.

Ya'u, Y. Z., 2000, 'WTO and Access to the Information Society', paper presented at a seminar organised by the Green/EFA Group of the European Parliament and Community Action for Popular Participation, on 'Free Trade: Opening the Market for The Rich?', Abuja, 20 March.

Zell, H. M., 2000, The African Electronic Wormbook, Oxford: African Book Collective.

8 NEPAD in the Twenty-first Century

An Answer to the Educational, Cultural and Scientific Challenges?

Tayeb Chenntouf

Africa is faced with many challenges and these have never been as serious as they are now, at the dawn of the twenty-first century. Challenges in education, culture and science are not amongst the easiest to deal with. If they are not taken up in an adequate way, these challenges could permanently marginalise the continent in relation to world development, as is happening now.

Among the many initiatives which are taken at every level, NEPAD constitutes an African answer to African problems and for the benefit of Africa. The aim of this chapter is to conduct a reading and evaluation of the NEPAD base document adopted in Abuja, Nigeria in October 2001. Is the diagnosis that was put forward still equal to the present situation in education, science and technology? Is priority still given to the chosen objectives? Is the strategy for realising these objectives realistic? In short, the relevance of NEPAD must be assessed as well as its capacity to revive the quantitative and qualitative training of human resources, to give impetus to culture, science and technology in order to fight against poverty and provide concrete encouragement to development.

The context of my approach is the long history of Africa. I am concerned first and foremost with dynamics and processes observable both on the continent and worldwide. Priority is given to transformation and methods of historical change, which are embodied in economic revolutions and development.

Present state of affairs

Education, science and technology are in a state of decline in Africa just when the world is experiencing a third scientific and technical revolution. In this context, Africa is being progressively left behind and its ability to compete in the world economy is more and more under threat.

This decline in education, science and technology is relatively recent; it goes back to the 1980s. Studies and statistics have shown that African countries north and south of the Sahara are experiencing severe problems in this area.

After political independence, energetic policies in the fields of education and training were adopted, with the opening of new universities and research centres, and transfers of technology. This yielded remarkable quantitative advancement. The number of primary-school-going children doubled between 1960 and 1980. Those at secondary level increased fivefold. The annual increase in school attendance at primary level was at 6.5 per cent between 1960 and 1970. Between 1970 and 1980, the level increased by 8.9 per cent. During these decades, tertiary education also developed. The number of institutions increased tenfold in three decades, and in 1997 the total reached 150. In 1972, the Association of African Universities organised a conference in Accra, with an agenda for African universities. The final report recommended a new concept of a university, which should become a developmental university. Africanisation of the curricula and the staff followed suit. In 1997, in the tertiary educational sector, most of the foreign staff were replaced as more local academics and researchers took up positions in the sector; new curricula had been drawn up and the first scientific research communities were created.

During the 1980s, there was a slowing down of progress. These years were marked by a reduction in public spending in many African countries. In practically all countries south of the Sahara, public spending in 1986 fell to the same level as 1975: US$15 per person, per annum, on the average. The highest level had been reached in 1980, with almost US$35 per person (UNESCO 1989). For the first time since independence, a definite decrease in the number of school-going children was noted. The number of children out of school rose to 60 million in 1987. The school-going rate stagnated at just under 80 per cent. That of secondary levels continued to rise but at a slower rate. It only reached 30 per cent at the beginning of the 1990s (World Bank 1988).

Tertiary education was faced with serious problems of quality and training, financing and suitability to the work market. In January 1995, the Association of African Universities organised a conference (in Maseru, Lesotho) on 'African universities in the 1990s and beyond'. The participants attempted to put a stop to the decline of the universities and to reaffirm their role in the development of the continent. This crisis could be seen in all countries. In 1989, Adebayo Adedeji, Under-Secretary-General of the United Nations and Executive Secretary of the Economic Commission for Africa, took note of this situation. It was his considered opinion that 'almost all the advancement in the field of the positive use of human resources since independence, in particular in the fields of education and medical care, were annihilated during the lost decade of the 1980s' (Adedeji 1989). A UNICEF document speaks plainly of 'the decline of education in Africa' (UNICEF 1989).

This decline occurred simultaneously with a new scientific and technical revolution, the third of its kind, that was emerging and taking root in the contemporary world. The first scientific and technical revolution made itself known between 1760 and 1840 and reached its highest point between 1850 and 1914. It originated with the use of coal and steam energy. The second revolution emerged between 1880 and 1930 and blossomed fully between 1950 and 1970. This revolution relied on the use of the combustion engine and organic chemistry. The third revolution began in the 1960s, with the help of biotechnologies, new materials, electronics and information technology. It became widespread between 1980 and 1990 and is still evolving today (Caron 2000).

As with preceding revolutions, the third scientific and technical revolution gave rise to renewed economic activity, as well as causing transformation in the field of work organisation in companies. Owing to automatisation and robotics, this revolution is primarily responsible for a tremendous increase in productivity in countries and economic sectors that participate the most in those activities. In a world where the liberalisation of international exchanges and deregulation have become the general rule, the competitiveness of African economies is severely weakened. Africa has been completely separated from the knowledge revolution. Today, it has the lowest level of human development of all regions of the world.

Since 1995, the total school going rate for the different levels of teaching has remained relatively low. Moreover, Africa is the only continent where the gross average rates of schooling are below 100 per cent. In 2000, only half the number of eligible children were educated. Boys, on average, attend school for less than three years, against only one year for girls. The illiteracy rate of the adult population, at 54 per cent, is the highest in the world.

Development can be neither quick nor sustainable if only a small number of people are trained or acquire skills. The others cannot be integrated into the economy, which becomes even less capable of facing international competition efficiently.

In the world economy of the twenty-first century, education and knowledge are key factors in the economic performance of different countries. International competitiveness relies more and more on mastering information and computer science, the source of telecommunication networks and highly calibrated calculation tools. The third scientific and technical revolution effectively reconstructs the entire skills system.

NEPAD: an African answer

Is NEPAD an answer to all these challenges? One must first specify what it is not and what it is before raising the difficult question of its financing and consequently of its educational, scientific and technical policies and its necessary partnerships.

The document signed in Abuja in October 2001 follows on a series of strategic development programmes for the African continent: the Lagos Plan of Action, the African Alternative Framework to Structural Adjustment Programme (AAF-SAP), the African Economic Community Treaty (also known as the Abuja Treaty), and finally the birth of the African Union. NEPAD is not a substitute for national policy in education, science and technology, even if it determines a consensus and the main orientations. Neither is it a substitute for agreements and relationships which African countries sign with other countries: 70 per cent of developmental aid still comes through bilateral channels.

First and foremost, NEPAD is the sum total of possible partnerships between the African continent and its global partners. On this basis, the writers carry out a diagnosis of education, science and technology in Africa and determine the objectives to be reached by 2015. NEPAD is aware of the global revolution and defines the conditions required to achieve sustainable development: initiatives for peace and security, and good economic and company governance. NEPAD gives preference to sub-regional and regional development approaches by adopting the perspective of liberal globalisation.

The document then targets sectorial priorities, amongst which are human resources, namely education, culture, science, technology, traditional knowledge and ICTs. I will not repeat the diagnosis which has been arrived at, nor the objectives to which African states are committed in the development of human resources.

The financing of NEPAD is extremely problematic, and the Partnership will remain a dead letter if this problem is not solved. The unknown factor is the future financing of education, science and technology. The amount of investment needed is colossal, while development aid is lower than ever. Private African or foreign investments will doubtless be fairly small. In the absence of investment from the African states themselves, education, science and technology will in all probability continue to decline. Development assistance aid has fallen to its lowest level in nearly half a century. The world summit on development financing (held in Monterrey, Mexico, in March 2002) discussed the fight against poverty. Representatives from all developing countries, with the exception of Cuba, reached the so-called Monterrey Consensus, stipulating the new conditions for aid in 73 points. The USA committed itself to increasing its aid, if only from 2004; its aid budget is expected to increase from US$10 billion in 2000 to US$15 billion in 2007. In relative terms, the US effort is far from the United Nations objective of 0.7 per cent of GNP, though it is expected to increase from 0.1 per cent in 2000 to 0.13 per cent in 2007 (World Bank 1988).

The fifteen member countries of the European Union committed themselves to increasing their aid from 0.32 per cent in 2000 to 0.39 per cent in 2006. This aid therefore will increase from US$25 billion to US$35 billion. In total, aid from industrialised countries is expected to reach only US$65 billion in 2007, against US$53 billion in 2000, which is far from the needs of developing countries – a need put at about US$100 billion in 2007 (figures quoted in *Jeune Afrique* 2002).

Private investment cannot make up what is lacking in public financing nor can it be a substitute for this aid. Two recent studies emphasise private investment priorities that are advantageous to neither Africa, education, science nor technology (EIU 2001; Ministère français de l'économie et des finances 2002). Between 2001 and 2005, the necessary funds for development and increase in productivity will be channelled as a priority towards the wealthiest industrialised countries. Africa and the Middle East together represent 2 per cent of the direct foreign investment stock at the end of 2000. The rate will be identical in 2005 according to Economist Intelligence Unit (EIU) forecasts. Investments in African countries are directed essentially to the mining and raw material sectors.

NEPAD's objectives will not be reached if African states do not agree to finance education, culture and science. This effort in financing will be a public one or it will not take place. Investment in education and knowledge cannot be postponed in Africa while waiting for an improvement in the economic conditions and the finances of the various states. This is all the more true since the training of human resources is necessarily a long process which takes place over a period of ten to fifteen years.

Theory and history provide numerous examples of the role of education and knowledge in economic revolutions. The theory of endogenous growth puts the responsibility for long-term economic growth on human resources and the specific institutions favouring technological innovation. The role of education and training in the Industrial Revolution in eighteenth-century England is well known. Closer in time, the contribution of education to economic growth between 1950 and 1962 has been estimated at 12 per cent for the UK, 4 per cent for Belgium and the USA, and 25 per cent for Canada. During the same period, it varied between 12 and 23 per cent in Ghana, Kenya, Nigeria and the Republic of Korea. In 1993, the World Bank (1998) carried out a study in 113 countries, showing that primary education is the factor that contributed by far the most to the growth of the economies of Asia and the East.

Energetic policies in the fields of education, science and technology can only take place as a result of financing from African states. Similarly, it is only in that way that partnerships can be developed.

Priorities

Priorities are numerous simply because everything has to be done from the beginning (UNESCO 1996). However, a strategic approach requires a definition of what is urgent, in order to boost education, science, culture and, indirectly, development in Africa. We will comment on these briefly.

The first priority is definitely the training of teachers at primary and secondary level. Large-scale recruitment took place immediately after political independence. Today, a new generation of teachers is taking up posts in schools and colleges. Training efforts in this field must be carried out consistently. They must necessarily include didactic and psycho-ped-agogical aspects which are often absent or ignored by teachers. The teaching revolution, which is so necessary, will occur more through the quality of the teachers than through curricula and teaching manuals.

The second priority involves teaching programmes and texts in use at all levels of education and training, up to tertiary education. Almost all the programmes were drawn up immediately after independence. In certain countries they were partially reviewed. Teaching programmes are always at the crossroads of three factors: the development and latest results of research; social requirements; and the level and expectation of learners. Today, programmes need to be evaluated to ensure that they are adequate to African and global situations, which are those of the twenty-first century. One must also take into consideration gender issues, citizen-ship and the democratic participation of Africans.

The third priority concerns the universities and, in particular, doctoral training, namely the preparation necessary for future teachers and researchers. The present state of universities and research shows very clearly that their very future is under threat. It is necessary to ensure that universities and research reproduce themselves, and that this reproduction of knowledge as well as teachers and researchers, is consolidated (Witkowski 1991; Gaillard and Waast 1988).

The fourth priority is thinking about Africa and African problems. The dichotomy between pure science and social sciences, between pure research and applied research, is not necessarily relevant in the African context. Matters are most urgent in the fields of social and human sciences. The crisis in post-colonial states, ethnicity and religious funda-mentalism were factors of considerable surprise for researchers and politicians. They were not anticipated by research and caused method-ological and theoretical confusion amongst many researchers. Moreover,

Africa continues to be considered from the outside and by those outside. Its knowledge is still filtered through information, models and paradigms that are not necessarily adequate. Africa is still largely unknown, even by the Africans themselves. It is necessary, in particular, to define the dynamics of African societies in terms of length of time and according to the direction taken by real transformation. It is a question of economic and social dynamics but also of cultural and political dynamics. The relationship, on the one hand, between research and researchers, and on the other hand between research and civil society, should be to explain the significance of recent and present transformation of African societies to civil society.

The fifth priority consists in giving African research more visibility. All existing bibliometrical work is relative to African research in the field of the pure sciences. These studies all come to the conclusion that this research is not known on a world level (La recherche 1989; Waast 1995). This observation is even more obvious in the case of research in the social and human sciences. An impressive mass of theses, studies and research has been carried out in Africa during these past decades. These will remain unknown because of the difficulty of circulating them both in Africa and worldwide. Today, Africa is in a position to put forward an African analysis and points of view on Africa, the world and globalisation. Africa is also in a position to participate in present-day debates on the reviewing of disciplines in the social and human sciences.

The sixth priority is the accelerated training of professional communities. African researchers have little contact with each other within subregions, and even less within Africa as a whole. This situation has improved slightly but, in spite of that, African researchers do not know each other very well and hardly ever work together or in partnership. Paradoxically, they meet more often outside than inside the continent. Many obstacles account for this situation. The training of professional communities enables problems and difficulties in the field of the universities and research to be made known. But, more importantly, it facilitates necessary discussion between researchers, without which there can be no progress in research.

The legal protection of traditional knowledge is the seventh priority. This is not limited to commercial knowledge (traditional medicine and pharmacopoeia). The development of traditional knowledge includes know-how and techniques in agriculture, craft industry, commercial exchanges and social, political and cultural institutions. The material and non-material heritage should also be included. The focus should extend beyond 'closed series': it is also necessary to guarantee the transformation of knowledge, techniques and culture. This development is necessarily dependent on awareness of the past and of the African heritage.

The eighth and final priority is relative to the ICTs (UNESCO 1997). The spectacular failure of technological transfers (handing over of factories and products) means that this question should be approached carefully. These transfers are very costly, require highly qualified staff and, at the same time, pose the difficult problem of languages in Africa. However, ICTs are important in education and research. The challenge to Africa is to be more than a market and a consumer of the new technology and products that are circulated in the world. Africa can itself produce information. In certain fields, it even has a definite advantage over other countries. Databases and programmes can be set up more easily in Africa.

In conclusion, NEPAD could re-launch a more vigorous policy in the fields of education, science and technology. Structural adjustment plans, debt and globalisation have forced these into the background. Schooling for women and the poor, the elimination of illiteracy amongst adults and the energising of the universities and research are still questions for which African answers need to be found. They even constitute a condition for development and for the economic revolution taking place. The priorities mentioned will no doubt act as a booster in this field, at least to begin with. Partnerships can be built to put these into practice. They can be regional and reinforce South–South relations with the help and support of international partners.

REFERENCES

Adedeji, Adebayo, 1989, *Jeune Afrique*, 2114 (4–12 December).
Caron, F., 2000, 'Troisième révolution industrielle et nouvelle économie', *Le Débat*, November–December.
Economist Intelligence Unit, 2001, *Perspectives on Global Investments, 2001–2005*, London: EIU.
Gaillard, J. and R. Waast, 1988, 'La recherche scientifique en Afrique', *Afrique contemporaine*, 148.
Jeune Afrique, 2002, 215 (25–31 March).
La recherche, 1989, 'La science du Tiers-monde est-elle visible?', 210 (May).
Ministère français de l'économie et des finances, 2002, 'Rapport sur les investissements directs dans le monde (1999–2000)', cited in *Jeune Afrique*, 251 (April).
UNESCO, 1989, *Annuaire statistique de l'UNESCO*, New York: Oxford University Press.
—— 1996, *World Science Report*, New York: Oxford University Press.
—— 1997, *World Communications Report: Media and the New Technologies*, New York: Oxford University Press.
UNICEF, 1989, *State of the World's Children 1989*. New York: Oxford University Press.
Waast, R. (ed.), 1995, *Les sciences hors de l'Occident au XXème siècle*, Vol. 6, Paris: ORSTOM.
Witkowski, N., 1991, *L'état des sciences et des techniques*, Paris, La Découverte.
World Bank, 1988, *Human Development Report*, Washington DC: World Bank.
—— 1998, *Human Development Report*, Washington DC: World Bank.

PART 3

Financing Africa's Development

9 NEPAD, Gender and the Poverty Trap

The Challenges of Financing for Development in Africa from a Gender Perspective

Zo Randriamaro

The New Partnership for Africa's Development (NEPAD) is the latest in a long line of policy frameworks intended to place Africa on a path of sustainable growth and development. Currently being celebrated in the international community as a model for international cooperation, this plan is lauded for its vision and African ownership in design and implementation. While the ink is not yet dry on its ratification, researchers, African politicians, G8 leaders and civil society actors are trying to assess NEPAD's implications and how best to ensure its implementation.

This chapter assesses if, and how, NEPAD can address gender equality in Africa. With regards to gender equality considerations, critics have pointed to the gender blindness of NEPAD, despite the fact that one of its long-term objectives is to 'promote the role of women in all activities' (NEPAD 2001: para. 67). The chapter explores its gender blindness as well as how parts of its underlying framework and objectives actually undermine a gender equality agenda. A gender analysis of NEPAD requires consideration first of the design and promotion of NEPAD, which takes place within a particular social and political context, and may thereby explain some of NEPAD's priorities. Second, the main economic policy orientations of the plan are defined by a macro-economic framework that has important gender dimensions.

The social and political context of NEPAD

In order to undertake any gender analysis of NEPAD, the history, rationale and main objectives of this major plan have to be contextualised. In other words, it is critically important to first situate NEPAD within the political and social context of its production. There are some key questions that ought to be asked for a thorough understanding of the plan. How does

Africa's social and political environment determine the NEPAD goals? Who participated in its negotiation? And how was the document finally produced?

An 'irrelevant state'?

It is well known that NEPAD won most of its supporters at the international level because of its emphasis on good governance linked to development, which resonates among the international financial and development institutions and powerful countries in the North. NEPAD responds to a central question in the ongoing debate on the form of the state and its role in Africa by affirming that,

> today, the weak state remains a major constraint on sustainable development in a number of countries. Indeed, one of Africa's major challenges is to strengthen the capacity to govern and to develop long-term policies. At the same time, there is also the urgent need to implement far-reaching reforms and programmes in many African countries. (NEPAD 2001: para. 23)

The goal of these reforms, as articulated in NEPAD, is to 'enhance Africa's rapid integration into the world's economy' (para. 52).

African women have voiced their concerns about economic reforms and the 'marketisation of governance' by which the state is rolled back and reorganised 'in the form of deregulation from public interest to regulation in terms of private interests' (Taylor 2000: 59). In particular, gender equality advocates have underlined that 'current trends indicate that states are being reorganised to serve the interests of market forces and these interests do not coincide with those of the dispossessed'. Moreover, 'the reality for poor women across countries reveals that the reorganising of the state bears little relation to the process of social transformation' (ibid.: 60). These concerns are very relevant to NEPAD, in that it is likely to perpetuate the economic and social exclusion of poor women while further entrenching patriarchal patterns in politics.

NEPAD post-11 September 2001

Of note is the fact that NEPAD has been promoted at the international level at a very interesting time in modern history – right after 11 September 2001, which also has much to do with its overall weaknesses. As NEPAD was being finalised, we witnessed a major shift in US foreign policy with the establishment of the international coalition against terrorism. As such, the discourse has changed. African states are being categorised into 'failed' or 'failing' states that could accommodate terrorists, as opposed to governments that can demonstrate control. As mentioned by some analysts, 'ideas of a "new colonisation" are already emerging – nominally to ensure weak states do not harbour terrorists'.

The idea may 'spread to subaltern states used to police regions' (Coetzee 2001). What this means, as many of these analysts suggest, is that the elements of NEPAD related to security, conflict resolution and governance will take precedence, and are likely to receive special attention from the donor countries, rather than other priority concerns such as poverty eradication. In other words, NEPAD could be the new policy platform to fight international terrorism from Africa, as opposed to tackling the other issues that are critical for women and the poor.

The current trend towards increased militarisation is a cause of major concern from a gender perspective. This trend started at the end of the last decade in regions such as South Asia,[1] where it has contributed to the maintenance of some degree of stability for globalisation. Women and vulnerable groups suffer the most from the horrors of war in affected countries. Despite NEPAD's pledge to promote peace and security, post-September 11 developments and the coalition around the 'Bush doctrine' will most probably have the same effect in Africa. At the same time, the related increase in military spending is likely to lead to the diversion to defence budgets of scarce resources from sectors that are crucial for women and the poor. In addition, civil society and women's struggles for progressive social transformation are threatened by the conflation of protest with terrorist actions and the subsequent intensification of repression by military means.

Furthermore, in global economic governance, the strengthening of the coalition between the international financial and trade institutions and rich countries in support of the Washington Consensus is paralleled and further reinforced by the establishment of the international coalition against terrorism. This tendency was particularly visible during the negotiations in the finalisation of the Monterrey Consensus document which was discussed by heads of states and ministers at the international conference on Financing for Development in Mexico. This development is a major challenge for women's rights and gender equality activists in Africa and beyond, who have fought long and hard against an economic paradigm that is extremely detrimental to women's rights and livelihoods.

Speaking for the people?

The identity of the much-heralded NEPAD's initiators is an important feature that should be critically examined. It is necessary to go beyond the label of 'African leaders' who 'derive their mandate from their people' (NEPAD 2001: para. 47) and examine their respective records in terms of democracy – including economic and political governance – and human rights in their own countries, as a basic criterion for assessing whether they are fit to be the models and leaders of an Africa-wide initiative (Bond 2002). So also should we examine the nature of the preferred alliances of the NEPAD architects.

The records of the major promoters of the NEPAD – the Presidents of South Africa, Algeria, Nigeria and Senegal – include the repression of dissent, bloodshed, mass popular protests and social unrest, and the much-contested position taken by Thabo Mbeki on the issue of anti-retroviral drugs to combat mother-to-child transmission of HIV. Another outstanding feature in the record of the South African President is that 'since taking over from Nelson Mandela in 1999, Mr Mbeki has piloted the South African economy rightwards with unerring skill' (Patel 2002).

Most importantly from a gender perspective, the prevailing notion of democracy in most African countries raises important questions. When it comes to women's rights, what government really represents women's interests? Without considering the huge gender gaps in political participation, which country in Africa can pretend to be truly democratic when the interests of 50 per cent of the population are merely treated with rhetoric and lip-service? These questions are particularly relevant to the stated objective of NEPAD to promote women's participation in the political life of African countries. The lack of democracy and trans-parency in the formulation of this plan is not a good start and sends the wrong signal to African women as to the possibility of a major shift under NEPAD from the prevailing practices of 'democracy'.

Who participated in the formulation of the NEPAD – and therefore, whose perspectives and interests are reflected and addressed in the document – is another important question. The drafting process of NEPAD's main component, the Millennium Africa Recovery Programme from South Africa, involved 'select élites', mainly from the North, including the US President, heads of transnational corporations (TNCs), economists from US universities, the World Bank president, and leaders of the richest countries (Bond 2001). The consultation with other African countries – with the exception of the few that have been singled out to support the promotion of NEPAD – and with civil society and other social forces within the continent had not been considered a priority. Even if this can be interpreted asa strategic option aimed at securing the support of influential players in international cooperation, namely the G8, it also reflects a particular conception of the relations between the state and its citizens which contradicts the claims of NEPAD to demo-cracy, pluralism, transparency, and accountability.

Although consultations with selected members of civil society, including women's groups, political parties, and the media, have been undertaken in some places, these were done mainly after the adoption of the document by the Organisation of African Unity, on a small scale and in a sporadic way. These consultations on a 'done deal' were meant to support the claims of inclusiveness and democratic participation of the NEPAD promoters.

Some civil society and women's organisations have engaged in this consultative process, and believe that they are part of a genuine endeavour to change international power relations, to eradicate poverty in Africa and to achieve its development goals. Many of them have been seduced by the language of NEPAD and have taken its 'pro-poor' and 'people-centred' claims at face value. The strong focus of the plan on the mobilisation of resources and partnership have also raised expectations about possible benefits – both political and material – that would be shared with, or trickle down to, individual organisations involved in this process. However, because NEPAD reinforces the structures, power relations and paradigms that underpin the neo-liberal model and are exclusive of the perspectives and needs of marginalised groups, including women, it would appear that these civil society and women's organisations have been co-opted into a process aimed at managing the exclusion of the large majority of popular social forces, while legitimising the economic framework and macro-economic policies.

Ultimately, the participation of the mass of African peoples is not valued by NEPAD. The alliance with élites, both African and external, has been clearly privileged. The only explicit reference to the participation of the mass of African people is in the implementation of the plan, in line with a patronising concept of participation that has been consistently denounced by women and gender activists. Indeed, it appears that public participation in the conception and formulation of the plan has not been envisioned by its initiators, who consider that they know what is good for the people and that they can therefore speak and decide for them. The ordinary citizens are denied the right to have a voice in decisions that directly affect their lives.

The macro-economic framework of NEPAD

While NEPAD (2001: para. 116) aims 'to ensure that the specific issues faced by poor women are addressed in its poverty reduction strategies', a gender and institutional analysis of its macro-economic framework shows fundamental flaws that will affect negatively the achievement of its stated goals regarding poverty and the role of women in social and economic development. There are also inherent contradictions within NEPAD's main tenets and priorities themselves, as this chapter will show.

SAPs forgotten

Perhaps the most glaring evidence of the gender blindness of NEPAD is the fact that it ignores the devastating impact of the structural adjustment programmes (SAPs) and policies imposed by international financial institutions on women and gender relations, and the major contribution of SAPs to the impoverishment of African countries. In addition to the fact that NEPAD explicitly places the relationships with its Northern partners within the Comprehensive Development Framework of the World Bank, its analysis of SAPs gives a clear indication of the position of its promoters vis-à-vis the macro-economic prescriptions of the International Monetary Fund and World Bank. Indeed, the analysis is limited to one sentence mentioning that SAPs 'promoted reforms that tended to remove serious price distortions, but gave inadequate attention to the provision of social services' (NEPAD 2001: para. 24). It echoes the prevailing analysis of Africa's situation among the Bretton Woods institutions, by repeating that the 'historical impoverishment of Africa [is] due to weak states, dysfunctional economies, which were further aggravated by poor leadership, corruption and bad governance' (para. 22).

NEPAD (2001: para. 115) further demonstrates its willingness to implement the macro-economic prescriptions of the international financial institutions by supporting the Poverty Reduction Strategy Papers (PRSP) approach associated with the Highly Indebted Poor Countries (HIPC) initiative, which includes the same conditionalities as the SAPs. The PRSP processes have raised grave concerns among civil society and women's organisations in many African countries, not only about these conditionalities, but also about the lack of transparency and inclusiveness of these processes. In many cases, there has been little participation of women and the poor themselves. Moreover, a number of gender equality activists believe that the PRSPs enable the global economic system to actually exclude the poor. Gender equality advocates have contended that these programmes 'respond to neo-liberal ideals of self-help, voluntarism, and a reduced dependency/demand on the state' and as such, the 'Poverty Reduction Strategy Paper (PRSP) as envisioned by the World Bank and IMF performs the [same] function of containing protest and providing short-term "relief" or "welfare" to the poor and marginalized groups' (Mbilinyi 2001: 8).

Because NEPAD reproduces the Washington Consensus driven by the Bretton Woods institutions under an African dressing, it does not make mention of the heavy burden Africans still carry as a result of IMF-driven stabilisation measures which have led to cost recovery in basic public services, increased sales taxes, and privatisation of public assets. Neither does it mention the World Bank-led adjustment measures which have brought about steady impoverishment for the majority of African people, a decline in access to credit and productive resources among small farmers and micro and small enterprises as a result of reforms in fiscal policy, cuts in public spending in social services, and a shift in the cost burden to communities, households and individuals, especially women. NEPAD does not mention that these measures have largely contributed to massive capital flight, de-industrialisation and poverty, as well as to the deaths of large numbers among the poorest who have been disconnected from basic utilities and supplies. It is not surprising, therefore, that NEPAD's analysis has missed women, who make up the large majority of the poor and have been disproportionately affected by these measures while bearing the burden of the social costs of SAPs.

The economic framework championed in the plan is likely to keep women in the poverty trap and to reinforce gender inequalities, as it builds on the ideas inherent in South Africa's own neo-liberal macro-economic policy, the Growth, Employment, and Redistribution (GEAR) policy. Analysts from South Africa have criticised GEAR because 'it has yielded no growth, no jobs, and a growing gap between rich and poor'. In addition, 'it mirrors structural adjustment plans to the North' (Coetzee 2001). According to the Gender and Economic Reforms in Africa (GERA) Programme's South Africa project:[2]

> The main thrust of GEAR, since its implementation in 1996, has been to provide a platform for a neo-liberal agenda. As a macro-economic policy, GEAR spells out the role of the state in key areas of fiscal management, trade and investment, social and sectoral policies, and employment and wages. In particular, GEAR has promoted deregulation, which has led to deteriorating conditions of employment, and trade liberalisation, which has placed pressures on companies to either restructure, retrench or go under. This economic restructuring has had a disastrous impact on the two key centres of footwear and leather production in the country (the provinces of the Western Cape and KwaZulu Natal) (Mosoetsa et al, forthcoming).

As the footwear and leather sector is overwhelmingly dominated by women workers, they are the most affected by the disastrous impact of GEAR through economic restructuring. This is only one example among the ample evidence of the deleterious effects of neo-liberal macro-economic policies on women's rights and livelihoods and gender equality in Africa.[3]

This gender blindness of NEPAD confirms the neo-liberal nature of its economic policy options, as such options typically ignore the social content and impact of economic policies, and their implications for social and gender relations. According to some commentators from other African countries, NEPAD is even worse than structural adjustment:

> At least, under adjustment, the World Bank admitted that it was purely an economic programme, and when social costs were felt, made contingencies, however inadequate. In NEPAD, they've made those social

problems part of the plan. They know there are going to be millions of poor people hurt by it, and they're going to do it anyway. Our leaders have betrayed us. (Tandon, quoted in Patel 2002)

Contradictory values

From a gender perspective, the inherent contradictions within the NEPAD priorities are predictable in the light of the introduction, which identifies 'signs of progress and hope' with 'market-oriented economies', and holds the latter as compatible with 'the protection of human rights [and] people-centred development' (NEPAD 2001: para. 7). Given the preferred alliances of the NEPAD initiators and the overwhelming focus of the plan on the private sector, this might be due to a particular conception of human rights. As a South African human rights activist put it: 'when they talk of human rights, the right they want above all is the right of property, the right of capital' (Trevor Ngwane, quoted in Patel 2002). Suffice it to say that most African women are not entitled to these rights.

Moreover, the equation above does not take into account the social relations within the market, in particular those of power that underlie the rules, access to and control over resources and activities in the market. The NEPAD's simplistic conceptual framework does not include the interaction of entrenched social and gender inequalities, along with differences based on race, ethnicity or regional/rural/urban location, which perpetuates the marginalisation of women and other disadvantaged groups in the economy. It is not also clear how women and the large majority of small producers who operate largely outside of mainstream markets can benefit from the 'people-centred development' that NEPAD expects to result from 'market-oriented policies'.

Lack of coherence

With regard to the NEPAD priorities and related actions, 'the generality of the actions under each programme or initiative' has been underlined by a leading economist, along with the absence of 'a framework in which priorities and specifics are assessed' (Kanbur 2001: 4). The fact that one of the two long-term objectives is poverty eradication, which is then listed only as a sub-sectoral priority in the programme of action, is an illustration of this lack of coherence. Another example is the prioritisation of economic and corporate governance as an entire initiative, which is not likely to have a direct effect on poverty in the short term and is already strongly supported by international financial institutions in different countries.

While the democracy and political governance initiative has been positively assessed by the above commentator in terms of poverty reduction, whether the dividends of democracy will effectively accrue to women remains an outstanding issue, given the patriarchal nature of many African states coupled with the male bias in political institutions and practices. Experience shows that men's resistance to perceived challenges to male domination is an important factor that should not be underestimated.

The second long-term objective of NEPAD (2001: para. 67) is 'to promote the role of women in all activities'. This would logically involve mainstreaming gender considerations and women's needs in the different activities of the programme of action. But the actions that will be undertaken to achieve this objective are described as follows: 'promoting the role of women in social and economic development by reinforcing their capacity in the domains of education and training; by developing revenue-generating activities through facilitating access to credit; and by assuring their participation in the political and economic life of African countries' (NEPAD 2001: para. 49)

This demonstrates major limitations in NEPAD's approach to gender equality issues and women's economic empowerment: not only does the analysis of issues stop short of the micro level, but it also has no connection to the macro-economic framework which shapes women's lives. In addition, it is assumed that women's empowerment, which would really require specific actions targeted at the gender-based constraints that are intrinsically linked to women's subordination, will be achieved by addressing instrumental issues related to women's income-generating measures, education, training, and access to credit. In other words, NEPAD argues that gender equality can be achieved by micro, women-specific projects, as opposed to tackling the fundamental structural causes of women's poverty and inequality such as discriminatory laws, cultural norms, male-biased development priorities, land reform, public expenditure, and macro-economic policies, just to name a few.

Moreover, women are perceived as passive, in need of income-generating activities, training, education and credit, with no recognition of their agency and their actual participation in the economic life of their countries through their unpaid and uncounted work in production and reproduction. All this implies that their 'participation in the political and economic life of African countries' is not envisioned as an obligation to ensure the realisation of their basic capabilities and rights, but mainly as a means to improve the overall efficiency of development plans and programmes.

Furthermore, there is no mention of women or gender issues in the initiatives and sectors of the plan that are absolutely critical to addressing women's poverty and promoting their empowerment. A remarkable example of such omission is the section on agriculture. The crucial contribution of women to food security and agricultural production is ignored in the analysis of the issues and, subsequently, in the actions envisaged to address these.

In general, the NEPAD plan is characterised by an instrumental approach to gender issues and a lack of conceptualisation of gender equity and equality. It is fair to say that NEPAD shares this 'add women and stir' characteristic with many other development plans, but it is appalling that an initiative that has the ambition of setting the agenda for Africa's development for the millennium suffers from such critical deficiencies.

Gender implications of the NEPAD initiatives for financing development

Examining the gender implications of NEPAD for financing development requires a critical analysis of the development model that is being promoted by NEPAD. The problems encountered in financing development are multi-dimensional and often rooted in structural causes related to the prevailing development model itself. The issues at stake in financing development are not purely economic and technical, but also have important social and political dimensions that cannot be overlooked.

Which development model?
NEPAD (2001: para. 1) aims 'to extricate ... the continent from the malaise of underdevelopment and exclusion in a globalising world'. The analysis of globalisation by its initiators and what they consider as the major issues to be addressed for Africa to benefit from globalisation are key pointers to the development model that they seek to promote.

The section titled 'Africa and the Global Revolution' in the plan provides insights on NEPAD's definition of globalisation. To begin with, this phenomenon is described as 'an economic revolution'. The document goes on to argues that 'this revolution could provide both the context and the means for Africa's rejuvenation. While globalisation has increased the cost of Africa's ability to compete, we hold that the advantages of an effectively managed integration present the best prospects for future economic prosperity and poverty reduction' (NEPAD 2001: 28). The initiators of NEPAD 'readily admit that globalisation is a product of scientific and technological advances, many of which have been market-driven' (para. 39).

This excessive 'techno-centric' and 'apolitical' character of NEPAD's definition of globalisation has been criticised by some authors (see Bond 2000: 16). Among the criticisms is the fact that NEPAD does not consider that weaker countries will be adversely affected by globalisation and are unable to make threats against the powerful ones. In spite of the extensive analysis of 'the historical impoverishment of the continent' which points to relations of domination between African and developed countries, NEPAD does not incorporate globalisation in the historical processes that have led to the impoverishment and underdevelopment of the continent. Consequently, the solution proposed to Africa's underdevelopment is to put an end to its marginalisation in the process of globalisation. In other words, according to NEPAD's initiators, what Africa needs is simply more globalisation; they do not mention the need for a meaningful change in power relations between Africa and the North, or a significant transfer of resources for financing Africa's development through a fairer redistribution of wealth at the global level.

While the following paragraphs point to many of the fundamental problems facing African countries, such as 'the absence of fair and just global rules' (para. 33), and 'the structural impediments to growth and development in the form of resource outflows and unfavourable terms of trade' (para. 34), NEPAD's analysis never explicitly mentions critical features of globalisation such as the predominant role of firms and private capital, especially transnational corporations (TNCs), whose vision and actions shape the overall process of globalisation, including the creation of new networks of power relations and alliances. Consequently, this analysis also ignores the related changes in class relations that affect millions of working people in Africa and beyond, 'especially the resurgent power of US and EU capital in relation to working classes there and across the world (as reflected in state–corporate 'partnership' and the decline of the social wage during the Reagan, Thatcher and Kohl administrations)' (Bond 2000: 5).

Another important feature of corporate-driven globalisation that has been forcefully denounced by civil society – and confirmed recently by the ENRON disaster – is the fact that it is 'a process that is marked by massive corruption and one that is deeply subversive of democracy' (Bello 2002: 4). In this regard, it is noticeable that NEPAD presents corruption as being mainly an African disease from which the foreign investors that it wants to attract are totally immune.

This bias is also visible in the extensive sections of the plan devoted to political and economic governance, in which African governments are urged to make commitments and undertake institutional reforms for 'meeting basic standards of good governance and democratic behaviour' (para. 82), and to establish 'the necessary policy and regulatory frameworks for private sector-led growth' (para. 85). While it is explicitly stated that high priority will be given to public financial management and capacity building 'to enable all countries to comply with the mutually agreed minimum standards and codes of conduct' (paras

91–2), actions specifically targeted at corporate governance are limited to recommendations from a task force from the Ministries of Finance and Central Banks for possible consideration by the Heads of State Implementation Committee.

Moreover, NEPAD's analysis does not address the critical question of the institutional factors associated with economic reforms under globalisation – financial liberalisation, for instance, which has allowed the largely uncontrolled and exponential growth of speculative finance capital and hindered the capacity of many African countries to mobilise domestic financial resources for development. Not only does such an omission weaken the validity of the analysis, but it also prevents NEPAD from focusing on the role of institutions, which is a key element in strategies for countering the negative effects of globalisation. In this regard, past experience shows that the creation or realignment of mediating institutions is critical to women and vulnerable groups in the globalisation process.

As a result, NEPAD's analysis boils down to the conclusion that Africa mainly suffers from an alleged lack of globalisation – in line with the mantra of the Bretton Woods institutions and the UN senior officials – and overlooks critical factors relating to the crisis of the prevailing economic model itself, in particular the search by footloose capital for new markets, cheaper inputs and labour, along with the switch by big companies of productive reinvestment into financial assets, due to the decline in manufacturing profits during the 1960s; as well as the increased disempowerment of nation-states, paralleled by the increased power of the international financial and trade institutions.

In the absence of a critical analysis of the process of gobalisation and the root causes of Africa's marginalisation in the global economy, the pledge for the creation of 'fair and just conditions in which Africa can participate effectively in the global economy and body politic' (para. 41) appears to be mainly a diplomatic exercise. The outcomes of the international conference on Financing for Development tend to demonstrate that the international community is not ready to respond positively to such a pledge. Indeed, the so-called Monterrey Consensus that emerged at this conference fails to address matters that are critical to the mobilisation of resources for financing development: issues related to debt, aid, trade and investment in developing countries.

With respect to women and gender issues in the context of globalisation, NEPAD does not specifically address the central issue of labour and women's employment. The impact of globalisation on the gender division of labour goes unnoticed in the plan, along with the related issues that ought to be addressed in order to promote African women's economic empowerment in a globalised economy. Thus, the plan does not pay attention to the major trends in the labour market in general. In particular, it seems to ignore that, from 1970 to 1990, women's average share in the labour force increased significantly in all regions except sub-Saharan Africa (UNDP 1995).

It also overlooks the evidence that, in African countries where gains in women's participation in the labour force had been made so far, these are characterised by jobs with low wages, low standards of health and safety, poor workers' rights, low security, and limited career opportunity. The export-processing zones (EPZs), which are among the principal providers of female jobs, have been questioned about their detrimental effects on women's social and reproductive rights, their poor working conditions and the numerous cases of sexual harassment and violence against women (Kerr and Dzodzi 2000).

Of major concern is the fact that job creation – which should logically be the first priority in terms of domestic resource mobilisation – and in particular the creation of decent jobs for women, is not even mentioned in the plan, apart from indirect references through income-generating and poverty reduction activities.

Promoting a post-Washington Consensus in Africa

The position of NEPAD regarding the economic policy prescriptions of the Bretton Woods institutions has been analysed in the previous section, which shows its conformity with the neo-liberal economic framework, also known as the Washington Consensus. By claiming the main requirements of the Washington Consensus – macro-economic stability, liberalisation and privatization – as part of an African initiative, there is no doubt that NEPAD offers a valuable opportunity for further legitimising this economic model and its institutional arrangements, and, by the same token, for justifying the claims of 'national ownership' of policies by the international financial institutions, thus allowing them to get rid of any responsibility for failures.

NEPAD advocates a neo-liberal state whose role is centred on adjusting national economies to the dynamics of a largely unregulated global economy. As such, the main responsibility of the state is to establish an enabling environment for foreign investment as prescribed by the World Bank and IMF and to ensure that the 'internationally agreed' standards for democracy, good governance and the rule of law are met by the country.

Furthermore, it is implied that these principles, as well as peace and respect for human rights, are important in so far as they contribute to creating the 'enabling environment' to attract foreign investment. The values embedded in these principles, which are intrinsically important for any society in their own right, are being instrumentalised and subjected to the pursuit of growth through increased foreign investment:

'their real, material, value to a developing country, above all in economic terms, is as a means to attracting FDIs' (Tandon 2001: 2).

The private sector as an alternative to a developmental state?

The plan clearly endorses an economic framework within which the private sector is the engine of growth. In line with a typical feature of neo-liberal policy making, the private sector plays a pivotal role in the development strategy of NEPAD, based on the assumption that growth will automatically lead to development. No consideration is given to the fact that in this way the plan supports a framework within which the criteria for economic policy making are financial rather than social, and short-term rather than long-term. It appears that in order to 'harness the globalisation process' (NEPAD 2001: para. 34), the initiators of NEPAD have adopted policy options that focus on short-term financial returns at the expense of the long-term investments that are required for sustainable development.

At the same time, there is no clear indication as to the meaning of the 'private sector' in NEPAD. The recurrent references to investment in the plan suggest that the term mainly refers to foreign investors. By contrast, the role of domestic enterprises is barely considered, regardless of the fact that the major part of total waged employment depends on micro and small enterprises (MSEs) for many African countries. Another fundamental issue in African economies that NEPAD fails to address is that most of these MSEs are located in the informal sector (59 per cent in Kenya, 62 per cent in Uganda, 84 per cent in Zambia, 85 per cent in Ghana, and 95 per cent in Sierra Leone) (Mbilinyi 2001: 8). Moreover, these proportions are rising, given the increased informalisation of work in many African countries as a result of economic reforms.

From a gender perspective, it is important to identify who is part of the private sector that is targeted by NEPAD. In this regard, it should be noted that the prevailing definition of the private sector excludes the informal sector in which the major part of women's economic activity is located. In addition, measures to promote the development of the private sector in Africa include mainly policies directed at large-scale industries and ignore the small-scale production in which a majority of women are engaged. For example, in Uganda, a GERA programme study found that the definition used by corporations and the World Bank excludes MSEs, most of which are run by women (Kerr and Dzodzi 2000).

Privatisation *per se* raises a number of issues from both a development and a gender perspective. First, there is no reason to believe that the profit-motivated private sector will act in the interests of the poor and the public at large. This raises the broader issue of the so-called global public goods, as goods – or services – whose benefits accrue to all sectors of society and should therefore be equitably available to all people with equal opportunity. As such, the provision of these global public goods by the state is crucial, and it is very telling that while the target for private investment in infrastructure recommended for developing countries by the World Bank is 70 per cent, many developed countries – including France, Germany and Japan – have very little privatisation in the sector of infrastructure (13 per cent, 9 per cent, and 14 per cent, respectively), and opened areas such as telecommunications to private investment only as late as 1995. The issue of global public goods has important gender dimensions and is particularly relevant to NEPAD, especially in relation to the definition of regional public goods in the operational framework developed by the United Nations Economic Commission for Africa.

Second, many privatisation schemes of public utilities in Africa have resulted in failures in terms of performance and, most importantly, in the disconnection of the poor, including a majority of women, from basic utilities. Water privatisation is a case in point in many countries and has raised a growing popular protest against the denial of the right to meet their basic needs to those who do not have the required purchasing power – the poor, and especially women. By uncritically promoting privatisation, NEPAD contradicts its claimed focus on poverty reduction and people-centred development.

NEPAD, women and the poverty trap

Many readers of NEPAD among civil society have asked: 'Where are the people in this plan?' This is partly because African peoples were not involved in its formulation, so that NEPAD's top-down and neo-liberal approach to development cannot but miss their perspectives, concerns and needs. This silence could also be explained by the fact that its policy options are likely to increase the marginalisation and impoverishment of the majority of African peoples. The question is even more relevant with respect to women as citizens and economic actors, for a number of reasons related to fundamental flaws in the approach of NEPAD to gender and poverty issues.

At the conceptual level, the plan suffers from a narrow understanding of poverty issues that is likely to bring about contradictory outcomes and to increase existing social vulnerabilities and inequalities, including gender inequalities. Thus, in line with the premises of the Washington Consensus, the excessive emphasis on growth as the single most important means for poverty reduction prevents NEPAD from taking into account that 'while growth is critical for sustained poverty reduction, equally critical is the nature of growth generated: to be developmentally beneficial, growth must be socially equitable, pro-poor and environmentally sustainable' (UNDP 1997). The promoters of NEPAD seem to forget that in most

African countries that have experienced some degree of economic growth under SAPs, more often than not it has been a jobless and inequitable growth with high social costs that have been mostly borne by women. Ironically, because of this even the World Bank – one of the architects of the Washington Consensus – has moved towards a broader approach to poverty, including both physical and social deprivation.

With regard to credit – one of the major components of the plan for women's economic empowerment – this narrow understanding of poverty leads the NEPAD initiators and promoters to ignore the interlocking set of disadvantages faced by the poor, especially political issues of community decision making and markets for labour and commodities (Mbilinyi 2001: 61). In this regard, it is critically important for NEPAD to recognise that the capacity of poor women to take independent advantage of credit remains limited as long as the structures of exploitation which made them poor in the first place are not addressed. It is also important to consider that 'credit may not be the most appropriate tool for poverty eradication among the very poor'. In addition, 'Poor people operate in limited segments of highly segmented product and labour markets, and can only engage in forms of production for which the demand is likely to be exhausted quickly. Without complementary access to resources necessary to convert an asset into a profitable enterprise, access to credit cannot form the basis of the longer term movement out of poverty' (ibid.: 62).

Because of its gender blindness, NEPAD does not take into consideration that gender inequalities mediate relationships between macroeconomic policies and poverty reduction strategies, and have an impact on their outcomes and growth performance. While the promoters of NEPAD argue that gender inequalities are addressed at the implementation stage through the planned actions targeted at women, none of these actions addresses key issues of access to resources such as time and property rights. Moreover, poverty is not approached as 'the consequence of intersecting structural inequalities across and within nations such as those based on class, race and gender' (Cagatay 2001: 14). As a result, the plan addresses the symptoms instead of the interlocking structural causes of poverty and its perpetuation.

NEPAD's conceptualisation of the relationship between gender and poverty issues suffers from a misconception that is very common among international development institutions and donor agencies: the conflation of gender issues with poverty issues. The 'feminisation of poverty' has been translated into strategies that identify poverty with gender issues and tend 'to collapse all forms of disadvantage into poverty', including the subordination of women, which ought to be addressed as a gender issue distinct from poverty (Jackson 1998: 59).

Thus, the plan falls short of offering real and sustainable alternatives for reversing the process of impoverishment of the continent. In addition to the analytical biases described above, it merely proposes old solutions to problems linked to new risks and vulnerabilities created by globalisation, under the cover of a new African initiative. Sadly, it is akin to imposing a failed model of development on Africa in the new millennium.

NEPAD's policy options for financing development: a gender analysis

In order to assess the capacity of NEPAD to promote gender equality, there are key questions to be asked with regard to the mobilisation of resources for financing development from a gender perspective. These questions are related to the gender dimensions of specific issues of financing for development such as the mobilisation of domestic financial resources and private capital flows, in relation to NEPAD's strategic options and operational framework as outlined in the Compact for African Recovery (CAR), which elaborates in more detail on these strategic options and proposes the specific actions that would be implemented for the achievement of NEPAD's goals and objectives (ECA 2001).

Domestic resource mobilisation
A basic requirement for mobilising domestic financial resources for development is the reversal of the outflows of resources from African economies in the form of profits repatriation, dividends, debt servicing, transfer and contracts price payments, consultancy fees, etcetera, in order to retain this extracted wealth for reinvestment in African economies. It is appalling that NEPAD does not envision any significant and direct action aimed at such reversal and does not therefore take up a major challenge for financing development.

Of note is NEPAD's position regarding the key issue of debt, namely the absence of any call for full cancellation of the debt of poor countries, and for the removal of the structural adjustment conditionalities attached to debt relief. This is a major concern from a gender perspective, because women carry a disproportionate burden in the debt crisis and reduced public expenditures in the social sectors, as their role as care givers intensifies, thus presenting additional obstacles to income generation. In such a context, the debt relief supported by NEPAD represents only a minimum necessary step to alleviate the pain of the debt crisis. Civil society and women's organisations demand debt cancellation which is the only way to address the causes of the debt crisis.

The focus of CAR on 'closing the savings gap' (ECA 2001: para. 79) has been criticised by some analysts who argue that 'Africa's savings are not only underestimated but also not even recognised as "savings" under a certain accounting convention'. Tandon (2000) goes on to argue that 'there is no "savings gap" in Africa, except that all the savings are externalised and described in the sanitised language of economists as "factor payments abroad"'. This myth that African countries do not have savings has produced another myth with profound economic, social, and political implications: the myth that Africa must rely on foreign capital for its development. CAR clearly states that 'Africa has no alternative except to tap foreign capital in order to raise the productivity levels necessary for sustained increases in living standards' (ECA 2001: para. 204). The fact that this myth is so strongly supported by NEPAD and CAR amounts to putting the seal of approval from African heads of states and major development institutions on increased external dependency of the continent in the new millennium.

In spite of its recognition that 'low and frequently declining levels of real incomes are the chief culprit for low saving levels' (ECA 2001: para. 79), the measures proposed by CAR to increase domestic savings do not include specific actions to address this problem. With regard to incomes, the proposed measures focus on savings mobilisation, not on savings generation, and boil down to 'reforms to increase the returns on domestic investment and reduce risks'. In other words, CAR is more concerned about investors than the ordinary citizens who are assumed to benefit automatically from the 'trickle down' effect of market-oriented and private-sector-led growth, without consideration for inequalities based on class, gender, race, geographical location, and other forms of identity.

In general, the plan does not link the mobilisation of financial domestic resources to other conditions at the global level or in other sectors of its programme of actions. Hence, the planned actions are about matters almost entirely concerned with national policies, while the impact of macro-economic conditionalities and policies on the generation and redistribution of domestic financial resources is not taken into consideration.

With regard to financial systems, the outcomes of financial liberalisation policies in Africa clearly demonstrate that market-based mechanisms, which were imposed by the international financial institutions and supposed to allow a more varied and efficient intermediation between supply and demand, have not been able to address the needs of poor, small producers, especially women (Randriamaro 2001). Research carried out by the GERA programme in Cameroon and other African countries found that financial sector reforms have not improved rural women's access to financial services (Kerr and Dzodzi 2000). These problems are mainly due to critical flaws in the assumptions that underlie financial liberalisation policies. Therefore, 'establishing well-functioning and diverse financial systems' (ECA 2001: para. 78) requires fundamental policy changes that NEPAD is unlikely to undertake, given the nature of its macro-economic framework, policy options and preferred alliances.

Indeed, one of the major changes involves a major shift from financial liberalisation as 'a selective process that has mainly served the interests of foreign capital' (Randriamaro 2001), to financial sector reforms that are explicitly geared to meet the needs of poor, small producers, especially women. This is a matter of equity as well as a matter of efficiency, since MSEs dominate the economic structure in most African countries (ECA 1996). Another change is related to the role of the state, which should 'go beyond withdrawing from its traditional role in finance and development, i.e. removal of controls, privatisation and reduction of budget deficits, and aim at providing an innovative and supportive institutional framework' (Randriamaro 2001). The criteria for the assessment of financial sector reforms should also be changed to include 'their implications for the achievement of development objectives and equity, and not only against such criteria as GDP, exports or budget deficit' (ibid.). Most importantly, the neo-liberal assumption that the private sector and the market will ensure an appropriate allocation of financial resources must be abandoned.

Fiscal policy is another key element of domestic resource mobilisation and allocation that is not explicitly addressed by NEPAD and CAR. One has to assume that fiscal policy reforms fall under the 'public financial management' (NEPAD 2001: para. 91) that should be improved by the economic and corporate governance initiative, in order to create an enabling environment for investment. It appears that fiscal policy reforms are expected to ensure fiscal discipline, as part of such an enabling environment. There is no mention of promoting progressive and redistributive taxation measures required for pro-poor and gender-sensitive fiscal policies, as opposed to the widespread tendency to implement regressive taxation measures, with an overwhelming focus on consumption taxes that particularly affect the poor. Fiscal policy is not used by the NEPAD initiators and promoters as a tool for poverty reduction and sustainable human development.

The potential effect of such a strategic option is that 'the tax and public expenditure economy is being re-subordinated to the profit-seeking commercial economy in conditions in which families and communities are less and less able to absorb the shocks' (Keller-Herzog 1996: 20). This is a cause of major concern from a gender perspective, as it implies that women who already act as the major shock-absorbers under restrictive fiscal policies will be overburdened. This strategic option means that women's so-called 'reproductive tax' – the burden of providing unpaid care to sustain families and communities – will be increased, whereas big corporations will be subsidised by governments through tax breaks and other incentives. The absence of an integrated social protection system in NEPAD and its operational framework makes the prospects even worse.

Special attention should also be paid to the impact of fiscal austerity measures that will continue as part of the macro-economic stabilisation policies that NEPAD intends to implement. These fiscal austerity measures have led to tighter credit conditions with higher interest rates, and have worked to make women's access to formal credit even more difficult and to reinforce the exclusion of poor women.

Another example of the narrow understanding of domestic resource mobilisation in NEPAD is that it does not take account of all the impacts of trade liberalisation, despite the fact that trade is expected to be the major source of domestic resources, along with investment. Thus, it ignores the huge fiscal revenue losses for national budgets that trade liberalisation has entailed. Similarly, it does not make the link between trade issues and their implications for the development of strategic sectors such as agriculture. In particular, it does not consider the role of transnational agri-business and its impact in terms of concentration of market power, market distortion and competition issues. This has important gender implications, as trade liberalisation has proved to have deleterious effects on gender relations and women's rights and livelihoods (Tsikata 2001).

In sum, NEPAD does not address a number of issues that are critical to an effective mobilisation of domestic resources for people-centred, pro-poor, and gender-sensitive development policies. Financial goals are de-linked from and prioritised over social goals. What NEPAD means by domestic resource mobilisation is mainly the establishment of good governance and financial management to attract private capital flows.

Private capital flows

According to CAR, the private sector is 'the major future engine for Africa's economic development'. It goes on to argue that 'it is now beyond dispute that the only source of finance that can provide the long-term finance required for economic growth and poverty reduction is the private sector, both national and international. The Compact recognises that business and markets are the cornerstone of development, and are the essential means of achieving a transition from ODA-dependence to sustainable growth' (ECA 2001: para. 29). With regard to development financing, 'the objective is to make private capital flows provide 70 per cent of external finance in the medium term and 100 per cent in the long term' (para. 204).

Among the implications of this over-reliance on external financing is an increased concentration of power in the hands of TNCs and international financial institutions that exclude the majority of people, especially women, and are not accountable to the public. Indeed, 'decisions about fiscal and monetary policy, about the rules governing financial markets, about corporate accountability, are taken by a small group of officials, politicians, and financiers with little participation of citizens and their elected representatives' (Elson 2001: 4). In this regard, it is remarkable that the measures proposed by CAR for 'Good Corporate Citizenship' do not include specific proposals for the enforcement of the codes of conduct and the accountability of corporations, apart from the development of 'best practices' that are expected to protect African countries from possible 'bad practices' such as the manipulation of transfer price to evade taxation.

The reliance on private capital flows also implies an implicit priority to 'corporate welfare' (Elson 2001: 2) over the welfare of citizens, especially the poor, through contracts including the privatisation of public assets and basic utilities provision of infrastructure, tax breaks, free supply of African countries' natural resources (often non-renewable), full repatriation of profits, etcetera. This bias in favour of corporations contradicts the claims of NEPAD for people-centred development, while endangering the social and economic rights of the poor and disadvantaged groups, including women.

The romanticised conception of the private sector in NEPAD and CAR, and their uncritical support to the promotion of foreign direct investment (FDI) prevent them from taking into account that profit-seeking FDI will not necessarily go into the priority sectors of investment for sustainable and people-centred development. Nor do they mention the possible negative consequences of FDI on employment, balance of payments and income distribution in African countries. CAR points to 'environment disasters and human rights abuses' by 'some multinational companies and their subcontractors', only to call on the good will of corporations to uphold the values and principles of good corporate citizenship, without any meaningful proposal for ensuring compliance and corporate social responsibility and accountability (ECA 2001: para. 223).

Nor does CAR mention in its long apology for the private sector the negative effects that FDI can have when it absorbs local savings, disrupts local industries and leads to excessive capital outflows, or when the jobs it creates are in export enclaves disconnected from the national economy, as happened in several African countries. Moreover, CAR is silent on the recurrent crises that have affected the international financial architecture, thereby failing to address a key issue in global economic governance that has direct implications for the implementation of the plan.

Furthermore, the policy obsession of NEPAD and CAR with foreign investment combined with the primacy given to macro-economic stability is likely to lead to a 'deflationary bias' – an issue which has been underlined by feminist economists and is characterised by an emphasis on austerity measures such as reducing public expenditure and inflation rates, and raising interest rates. It has been suggested that the negative effects of these policies are disproportionately borne by women, and 'that using deflation to deal with problems caused by inappropriate financial liberalization makes the position of poor people, and poor women in particular, worse – as the financial crises in South-East Asia have shown' (Elson and Catagay 2000). Such a scenario is possible at the implementation stage of NEPAD, especially since macro-economic conditionalities are non-negotiable according to the Bretton Woods institutions and are applied without consideration for the peculiar nature of the economic problems experienced by different countries. In particular, the problems posed by financial liberalisation in many African countries, described above, are likely to be overlooked.

Despite the significant emphasis on infrastructure in NEPAD, its development has been left to private sector investment. As infrastructure is an important medium- and long-term developmental concern for women and the poor, by contrast, international development and financial institutions have been advocating that infrastructure should become a more important part of the responsibilities of states. It is predictable that the initiators of NEPAD would argue that African states do not have the resources to fulfil such a responsibility. Because of their support for the neo-liberal agenda, there is less probability that they would point to the fact that, along with social services, public infrastructure has been one of the sectors to experience drastic cuts in public spending as a result of IMF conditionalities. In any case, the entire privatisation of infrastructure investment envisioned by NEPAD and confirmed by the president of Senegal during a meeting with the African Civil Society Caucus at the Monterrey conference on Financing for Development raises questions about the viability of such an option.

Indeed, there is ample evidence from other regions that private investment in infrastructure often occurred as a response to public investment in this sector. Therefore, the withdrawal of public investment is likely to act as a disincentive for private investment. In addition, the experience of South-East Asia, where private capital flows to developing countries have concentrated both in terms of portfolio speculative capital and foreign direct investment, shows that, despite all the incentives provided by governments, the proportion of private capital flows that has gone to infrastructure has been far below expectations (Malhotra 1998).

More generally, the drive of NEPAD and CAR towards the provision of social services by the private sector clearly shows a 'commodification bias' (Elson 2001) that raises grave concerns from a human rights and gender perspective. Thus, according to CAR (2001: para. 210), 'the private sector may also provide a range of social services directly ... most notably in private delivery of water, sewerage, health and education services'. This commodification bias puts the rights of the poor and vulnerable groups to meet their basic needs at the mercy of financial intermediaries. It 'fuels the growth of financial corporations and the corporate welfare state' at the expense of the rights of citizens, especially women.

Indeed, past experience from liberalisation and privatisation policies in Africa and other countries shows that, in this context, not only is the hidden reproductive tax extracted from women increasing, but also 'particularly in poor and middle income families, women are called upon to spend more time and effort in providing non-market substitutes for marketed goods that their families can no longer afford to buy, and providing substitutes for public services that are no longer available'. In addition, 'commodification/privatization bias fuels the growth of financial intermediaries; and the growth of financial intermediaries in search of a high real rate of interest fuels deflationary bias in macro-economic policy, and leads to even more pressure to privatize' (Elson 2001: 11).

Finally, of major concern is the fact that NEPAD seems to adopt an 'open door' policy towards foreign investment. The opening of African economies to competition from foreign companies without any form of protection for domestic industries is a major threat to local enterprises, especially MSEs, where women predominate. While fostering unhealthy competition between African countries to attract foreign investment, this policy is likely to lead to a downwards harmonisation of standards for social and labour rights and for environment protection. In many ways, this proves that this policy is not the outcome of a national consensus between the government, the local private sector, workers, small farmers and producers, including women, and other social and economic actors.

In conclusion, NEPAD and CAR are biased against the interests and needs of the poor and women with respect to the mobilisation and redistribution of resources. Therefore, they are far from upholding the rights of citizens, especially women's rights. They promote a 'new partnership' that concentrates on Northern donors, institutions, TNCs and the wealthy segments of African societies, and excludes the poor and women.

Towards a new partnership for women's economic empowerment

What kind of development should be financed from a gender perspective?
This analysis of the implications of NEPAD from a gender perspective demonstrates that it cannot genuinely represent a pro-poor and gender-sensitive economic framework for poverty eradication and women's empowerment. The fundamental flaws in NEPAD's economic framework and policy orientations also affect its strategic options for the mobilisation of resources and hinder the achievement of its stated objectives and goals. This is compounded by the evidence that these strategic options have not been based on an appropriate reassessment of benefits and costs that result from domestic and international policies from a pro-poor and gender perspective.

Thus, the ample evidence of the regressive gender redistributive effect of social policy constraints imposed by globalisation has not been taken into account. Subsequently, the actions planned in social sectors such as health and education do not specifically address this regressive effect. In particular, NEPAD does not envision the establishment of an integrated system of social protection for women and vulnerable groups, which is required for ensuring the realisation of their fundamental rights as citizens.

With regard to the central issue of women's access to and control over productive resources, strategies and actions should build on the recognition that 'women's advancement in economic activities and their access to (self)-employment and income are influenced by a variety of factors within the political economy of different countries and the general policy environment, as well as by institutional constraints and social relations of power which determine their access to and control over basic resources at household, community and national level' (Rugumamu 1997; Tripp 1997; cited by Mbilinyi 2001).

The actions planned to expand women's access to and control over resources should not be limited to income-generating activities, education, training and credit. First and foremost, these actions should focus on the legal, economic, socio-cultural, and political constraints that perpetuate gender inequalities – constraints that have been thoroughly analysed and documented by a mass of studies undertaken by various stakeholders, including women themselves. In this regard, NEPAD only proposes old recipes that have not worked.

This chapter also points to the relevance of a gendered class analysis for the development of an equitable, people-centred, pro-poor and gender-sensitive economic framework, as well as for addressing the unequal power relationships that characterise current 'partnerships' between Africa and the North. Such analysis is necessary to deconstruct and change the power relations and interlocking structures of oppression that create and perpetuate poverty and gender inequalities, as well as inequities between nations. In particular, this analysis would bring to the fore a critical issue raised by NEPAD: the institutionalisation of a 'male deal' which involves a collaboration between some men at the local, regional and international level and facilitates both the exploitation of the poor's and women's labour and the social management of their exclusion.[4]

For NEPAD really to address the concerns and needs of women and the poor, it must move away from the Washington Consensus and its institutional arrangements, which have been so detrimental to them. To do so, it ought to use a human rights framework for the formulation of alternative policies that can ensure economic and social justice, especially poverty eradication, and gender equality. It must listen to the voices of African women and men from all walks of life – including workers, small producers, communities at the grassroots level and their organisations – and make a clear political choice in favour of the most disadvantaged, including poor women, by prioritising their rights over the interests of foreign capital. It must establish the necessary mechanisms for democratic participation in economic policy and decision making. It must resist the pressures of the forces of globalisation that push governments to sacrifice the rights of their own citizens for an illusory 'new partnership' between unequal partners.

As a first step in this direction, NEPAD and its operational framework should build on the alternative frameworks that have been developed in response to the negative effects of the Washington Consensus, such as the African Alternative Framework to Structural Adjustment Programmes (AAF-SAP) developed by the ECA in 1996. They should also build on women's perspectives and strengths as expressed by the diverse popular and women's organisations in Africa.

With respect to the specific policy recommendations for the development of a genuinely people-centred and gender-sensitive economic framework, NEPAD and CAR should seriously take into consideration the proposals put forward by civil society and women's organisations, namely in relation to the Financing For Development process and the Monterrey Consensus.[5] At the heart of these recommendations is the urgent need for human rights, as they are included in the human rights instruments of the UN and the International Labour Organisation, to be the overarching framework for all development plans and programmes at the national, regional and international levels.

In fact, if all the African states and their Northern supporters acknowledged existing human rights instruments and international commitments that they have signed onto and ratified, considerable progress could be made towards gender equality. To this end, therefore, NEPAD should explicitly be geared to implementing the Convention on the Elimination of All Forms of Discrimination against Women (CEDAW), the Beijing Platform for Action, the Cairo Action Plan, Agenda 21 from the Rio Summit and the UN Millennium Development Goals, all of which give ample and specific programme and policy commitments regarding women's rights and poverty eradication.

A new partnership with women and the poor

To ensure poverty eradication and to promote gender equality, NEPAD's initiators and promoters should envision a major paradigmatic shift from the neo-liberal economic orthodoxy to a development model that builds on a broad-based dialogue – inclusive of women, the poor, and racially and otherwise marginalised groups – between different interests about alternative economic policies and their social content. Of critical importance for NEPAD is the recognition that 'women are being hemmed in by two forces of fundamentalism: the fundamentalism of the market and religious fundamentalism that have brought the world to a dangerous juncture' (Women's Caucus 2002). Therefore, NEPAD's initiators and promoters should listen to the voices of African women, who urge their leaders not to collude with the forces of market fundamentalism that are undermining their rights, livelihoods and the welfare of their families.

NEPAD's initiators and promoters should focus on the establishment of a new social contract based on new alliances with popular forces, in particular women and their organisations, thereby fulfilling the right of excluded groups to participate in decisions about policies that shape their lives, and recognising their unique power to effect change towards people-centred, equitable and sustainable development. They also have to rethink the terms of their 'new partnership' with the North, paying special attention to the demands of their citizens. In this regard, they should echo the voices of African civil society and women's organisations who are demanding political will for:

- transforming Northern policies and multilateral institutions that shape the global economic and political dynamics in order to ensure democratic global governance;
- the urgent implementation of the required reforms in the international financial architecture and trade and investment regimes to redress the imbalances and biases against African countries, including the enforcement of legislative measures to ensure corporate social and environmental responsibility;
- meaningful and concrete commitment to finance the commitments made by the international community in UN development conferences on environment, human rights, population, social development, racism and women.

Ultimately, therefore, African leaders who support NEPAD must pay special attention to women's demand that 'governments of the North must not use aid as a bargaining chip in pursuing their economic, political and military interests'. Moreover, 'Governments of the South must not cave in to pressures to accept aid, trade and investment in exchange for political and military compliance. As women, we will not sacrifice our lives and the lives of our children, our families and our communities for this blood money' (Women's Caucus 2002).

Special mention must be made of Joanna Kerr and Marjorie Mbilinyi for their comments and editorial support.

NOTES

1 Military spending in South Asia has increased in proportion to GNP since 1996, especially in India and Pakistan. See Instituto del Tercer Mundo 1998.
2 The GERA research and advocacy project is studying the effects of globalisation and trade regimes on women working in the leather and footwear industries in South Africa.
3 See among others the findings of the GERA Phase I research on the impact of SAPs in *Demanding Dignity: Women Confronting Economic Reforms in Africa*, NSI/TWN-Africa 2000.
4 On this subject, see among others Turner 1997: 68.
5 See, among others, the Civil Society and the Women's Caucus Statements at the UN International Conference on Financing for Development, Monterrey, March 2002.

REFERENCES

Bello, W., 2002, 'The Twin Debacles of Globalisation', in *Porto Allegre 2002, Focus on the Global South*, Manila: Focus on Global South.
Bond, P., 2000, 'Thabo Mbeki and NEPAD: Breaking or Shining the Chains of Global Apartheid?' Frantz Fanon Memorial Lecture (August), University of Durban-Westville, Durban.
—— 2001, 'Interpreting Thabo Mbeki's Various African Initiatives', Journal, 18 November.
—— 2002, *The New Partnership for Africa's Development: an Annotated Critique*, Cape Town/ Trenton NJ: AIDC/Africa World Press.
Cagatay, N., 2001, *Trade, Gender and Poverty*, New York: UNDP.
Coetzee, D., 2001, 'The New African Initiative', paper presented at the Africa and G8 Civil Society Planning Conference, Ottawa, 21–22 October.
ECA, 1996, *Cadre Africain de Référence pour les Programmes d'Ajustement Structurel en vue du Redressement et de la Transformation Socio-économique*, Addis Ababa: UN Economic Commission for Africa.
—— 2001, *Compact for African Recovery: Operationalising the Millennium Partnership for the African Recovery*, Addis Ababa: UN Economic Commission for Africa.
Elson, D., 2001, 'International Financial Architecture: A View from the Kitchen',

paper presented at the International Studies Association Annual Conference, Chicago, February.

Elson, D. and N. Cagatay. 2000. 'The Social Content of Macroeconomic Policies', *World Development*, 28, 7.

Instituto del Tercer Mundo, 1998, *The World Guide 1997/98: a View from the South*, Oxford: New Internationalist Publications.

Jackson, C., 1998, 'Rescuing Gender From the Poverty Trap', in C. Jackson (ed.), *Feminist Visions of Development: Gender, Analysis and Policy*, London: Routledge.

Kanbur, R., 2001, 'The New Partnership for Africa's Development: an Initial Commentary', unpublished paper, December.

Keller-Herzog, A., 1996, 'Globalisation and Gender: Development Perspectives and Interventions', discussion paper, Canadian International Development Agency (CIDA).

Kerr, Joanna and Dzodzi Tsikata (eds.), 2000, *Demanding Dignity: Women Confronting Economic Reforms in Africa*, Dakar: GERA Programme and NSI/TWN-Africa.

Malhotra, K., 1998, 'Globalisation, Private Capital Flows and the Privatisation of Infrastructure', paper presented at a conference on 'BOOT: in the Public Interest', Australian Centre for Independent Journalism, Sidney.

Mbilinyi, M. (ed.), 2001, *Gender Patterns in Micro and Small Enterprises of Tanzania*, Dar es Salaam: AIDOS.

Mosoetsa, S., M. Sengendo and Z. Randriamaro, forthcoming, *Gender, Trade and Labour in Africa*, GERA Discussion Paper 2.

NEPAD, 2001, 'The New Partnership for Africa's Development (NEPAD)', Midrand: NEPAD Secretariat. Available online at <http://www.dfa.gov.za/events/nepad.pdf>.

Patel, R., 2002, 'Neo-Thatcherite English Premier: an Appalling Diplomat', *Voice of the Turtle*, 9 February, <http://voiceoftheturtle.org>.

Randriamaro, Z., 2001, 'Financing for the Poor and Women: a Policy Critique', in Barry Herman *et al.* (eds.), *Financing for Development: Proposals from Business and Civil Society*, New York: United Nations University Press.

Rugumamu, S. M. 1997. *Lethal Aid: The Illusion of Socialism and Self-Reliance in Tanzania*. Trenton, NJ: Africa World Press.

Tandon, Y., 2000, *SEATINI Bulletin*, 3, 1.

—— 2001, *Fallacies about the Theory of FDIs: Its Ideological and Methodologicals Pitfalls*, Harare: SEATINI.

Taylor, V., 2000, *Marketisation of Governance: Critical Feminist Perspectives from the South*, Suva, Fiji Islands: DAWN.

Tripp, A. M. 1997. *Changing the Rules: The Politics of Liberalization and the Urban Informal Economy in Tanzania*. Berkeley, CA: University of California Press.

Tsikata, D., 2001, 'Trade Liberalisation in Africa: a Gender Analysis', paper presented at the GERA Programme regional workshop on 'Gender, Trade and Development in Africa', Accra, June–July.

Turner, T. E., 1997, 'Oil Workers and Oil Communities in Africa: Nigerian Women and Grassroots Environmentalism', *Labour, Capital and Society*, 30, 1 (April).

UNDP, 1995, *Human Development Report*, New York: Oxford University Press.

UNDP, 1997, *Human Development Report*, New York: Oxford University Press.

Women's Caucus, 2002, 'An Equitable World Is Possible and Necessary', statement at the International Conference on Financing for Development (ICFFD), Monterrey, March.

10 Can African Institutions Finance African Development?

Evidence from the ECOWAS Fund

Chibuike U. Uche

For some time now, international financial institutions have been extensively criticised for the inability of their programmes and schemes to enhance economic development and reduce poverty in Africa. If anything, some have argued that their programmes have further plunged the continent into economic distress. It is often alleged that such programmes, initiated and funded from abroad, have failed to take into consideration the peculiar circumstances of the continent. It is thus not surprising that there is now increased focus on Africa itself for new development institutions and strategies. Along these lines, the New Partnership for Africa's Development (NEPAD) document explicitly states that:

> Across the continent, Africans declare that we will no longer allow ourselves to be conditioned by circumstance. We will determine our own destiny and call on the rest of the world to complement our efforts. There are already signs of progress and hope. Democratic regimes that are committed to the protection of human rights, people-centred development and market-oriented economies are on the increase. African peoples have begun to demonstrate their refusal to accept poor economic and political leadership. These developments are, however, uneven and inadequate and need to be further expedited. (NEPAD 2001: 2)

One possible vehicle for economic development will be the regional development agencies. This chapter examines the problems and prospects of such development agencies using the ECOWAS Fund for Cooperation, Compensation and Development as a case study. The chapter argues that such institutions are unlikely to yield any meaningful results with respect to improving the economic outlook of the sub-region. This is because the problems that have helped entrench underdevelopment in the region have also helped to prevent such institutions from achieving their objectives.

Member countries have, for instance, perpetually lagged behind in contributing their share of the capital for the organisation. There is also a lack of political will on the part of member states to adhere to the rules and regulations of such institutions. It is therefore over-optimistic to expect synergy to arise out of a relationship among poorly managed countries.

The chapter further argues that, although the restructuring of the ECOWAS Fund is a welcome development, it has not gone far enough. So far, the exercise has failed to take into consideration the major factors that inhibited the smooth functioning of the ECOWAS Fund. These factors include the lack of political commitment on the part of member states with respect to implementing ECOWAS decisions and the unending bureaucracy of the ECOWAS institutions. Also important is the fact that the lack of economic and political stability in the region has made long-term investments risky.

Origins of the ECOWAS Fund

The ECOWAS Fund came into being as a consequence of the establishment of the Economic Community of West African States (ECOWAS). The treaty setting up ECOWAS was signed on 28 May 1975 in Lagos, Nigeria.[1] The aim of ECOWAS is to promote cooperation and integration among member states in various fields of economic activity. These include the elimination among member states of customs duties and other charges relating to the import and export of goods; the abolition of quantitative and administrative restrictions on trade among member states; the establishment of a common customs tariff and a common commercial policy towards Third World countries; the abolition among member states of obstacles to the free movement of persons, services and capital; the harmonisation of agricultural policies and the promotion of common projects in the member states, notably in the fields of marketing, research and agro-industrial enterprises; and the implementation of schemes for the joint development of transport, communication, energy and other infrastructure facilities, as well as the evolution of a common policy in these fields (ECOWAS 1975: Article 2).

The ECOWAS Fund was one of the bodies established by ECOWAS to aid it in the achievement of some of its objectives. Specifically, it was established as the development financing institution for ECOWAS. The authorised capital of the fund is US$500 million, of which US$100 million was called up in two equal tranches in 1977 and 1988. The fund was charged with the following functions:

• To provide for the financing of feasibility studies and the execution of development projects in member states;

- To guarantee foreign investments made in member states in respect of enterprises established in pursuance of the provisions of the treaty on the harmonisation of industrial policies;
- To provide appropriate means to facilitate the sustained mobilisation of internal and external financial resources for member states and the community, and to promote development projects in the less developed member states;
- To provide grants for the financing of studies and development activities of national and community interests;
- To provide compensation and other forms of assistance to member states which suffer losses arising from the treaty's liberalisation of trade within the community, or from the creation of community enterprises.

As can be clearly concluded from the above, one of the main objectives for the establishment of the ECOWAS Fund was to institute a compensation mechanism to assist member states that suffer losses because of the implementation of the provisions of the ECOWAS Treaty. On the other hand, the arrangement also provides for member states to contribute to the fund. According to the first Managing Director of the Fund (ECOWAS Fund 1977: 15–16):

> Member States who enjoy revenue gains as a result of the successful operations of Community projects within their territories should be required to pay into the Special Facility Fund a certain proportion of their gains for the benefit of the countries that have suffered losses. For example, if by expanding an aluminum plant in a Member State, or by setting up certain tariff regulations, some Member States gain, while others lose, Member States who gain should be required to pay a certain proportion of their gains into the Special Facility Fund. Additionally, funds in the Special Facility account will be managed or invested in short term, blue chip and readily convertible securities that will accrue income. Member States suffering losses as a result of certain projects undertaken by the Community, within the Community, shall be compensated by the Fund when the nature and extent of their losses are clearly and precisely determined with the aid of the Secretariat.

The second major objective of the ECOWAS Fund is to mobilise funds for the financing of other development projects that are in line with the main objectives of the ECOWAS Treaty. Such projects include infrastructure development, such as roads, water supply, telecommunications and electricity. The importance of such infrastructure in the development process is obvious. In the economies of Japan and the United States, for instance, telecommunications, water, and electricity are used in the production process of nearly every sector. Also, transport is an input for every commodity. Users demand infrastructural services not only for direct consumption but also for raising their productivity. This is done through, for instance, reducing the time and effort needed to secure safe water, to bring crops to market, or to commute to work (World Bank 1994: 14). In a developing country such as Nigeria, however, the situation is different. The dearth of basic infrastructure has unnecessarily added to the production costs of goods and services, thus making the country uncompetitive. According to a 1988 study of Nigerian manufacturers (World Bank 1994: 30):

> 92 per cent of the 179 firms surveyed owned electricity generators. In the face of chronically unreliable public services, many had also acquired radio equipment for communications, vehicles to transport personnel and freight, and boreholes to assure their own private water supply. For firms with fifty or more employees that could practice economies of scale, these extra costs amounted to some 10 per cent of the total machinery and equipment budget. For small firms, the burden could be as high as 25 per cent. Yet because Nigerian regulations prevent firms from selling their excess power capacity, businesses, both large and small, were operating private generators and water systems on average at no more than 25 per cent capacity.

In other words, according to the Economist of 15–21 January 2000:

> Firms wanting to set up in Nigeria are faced with a problem known locally as 'BYOI' (Bring Your Own Infrastructure). Cadbury Nigeria, for instance, in the absence of reliable power or water suppliers, generates 8 megawatts of its own electricity and drills 2,500 feet down to obtain the 70,000 gallons of water an hour it needs for its Lagos food-processing plant …. BYOI adds at least 25 per cent to the operating costs.

Funding infrastructure is therefore central to the success of the ECOWAS Fund. In fact, it is critical if any progress is to be made towards the goal of regional integration and poverty reduction in the subcontinent. The next section will evaluate the operations and performance of the Fund since its establishment, focusing mainly on its project development function.

Operations of the ECOWAS Fund

In general, the management and governance of the ECOWAS Fund comprises the following layers:

*   The Authority of Heads of State, which is the principal governing body of ECOWAS and all its institutions, including the ECOWAS Fund. It is responsible for overseeing the general direction, control and functioning of ECOWAS and all its institutions.

- The Council of Ministers, which is composed of two ministers from each member state. It is responsible for the functioning of the community in general, the approval of the organisational structure of its institutions, and making recommendations to the Authority of Heads of State on policies aimed at the efficient and harmonious development of the community and its institutions.
- The Executive Secretariat, which is made up of the Executive Secretary and two deputies. The Executive Secretary is the principal executive officer of the community, charged with the day-to-day administration of the community and all its institutions, including the ECOWAS Fund.
- The Board of Directors of the ECOWAS Fund, which consists of one minister from each member state, who are also members of the Council of Ministers. It is responsible for overseeing the general direction, control and functioning of the ECOWAS Fund.
- The Managing Director of the ECOWAS Fund and his or her deputy are appointed by the Council of Ministers and are responsible for the day-to-day management of the ECOWAS Fund (DFC 2001).

Based on this operational structure, it is not surprising that the first major problem with the operations of the Fund was its reporting and operational structure. From its inception, the Fund was seen as an institution of ECOWAS, with the implication that the Executive Secretary of ECOWAS has exclusive authority over the Fund (in terms of Article 19 (1) of the revised ECOWAS Treaty). The management of the Fund, however, opposed this, arguing that:

> The Fund as a development financial institution of ECOWAS must be accorded all of the facilities, characteristics, and qualities including autonomy limited only by the Board of Directors and the Authority that will enable it to operate in a purely business-like manner similar to other financial institutions of this nature. The proposal that the Fund should be made into a department within the Executive Secretariat is untenable as it will take away its legal character and give it a form unfamiliar in international capital markets. This would have an adverse effect on the credibility of the Fund. (quoted in Tubman 1982: 4–5)

A former Governor of the Federal Reserve Bank of the USA supported this view. According to him:

> The Fund ought to be in a position paralleling that of similar institutions. If not, it will appear in an unfamiliar form in the international capital markets – an environment in which the unfamiliar is not readily accepted .... In defining and clarifying the status of the ECOWAS Fund within the Community, the latter's leadership should be mindful of the implications of its decisions for the Fund's ability to compete for resources

Table 10.1 Key indicators of development in the West African region

Country	Population density		Gross Domestic Product		HDI ranking (out of 174) 1999	HPI ranking (out of 85) 1999	Life expectancy at birth 1999	Adult illiteracy (%) 1999
	Number (millions) 2000	People per sq. km 2000	Millions of dollars 2000	Per capita income 2000				
Benin	6	57	2,262	380	157	74	53	61
Burkina Faso	11	41	2,406	230	172	84	45	77
Cape Verde	0.441	62	N/A	1,330	105	37	69	26
Côte d'Ivoire	16	50	9,319	660	154	72	46	54
Gambia	1.286	129	N/A	330	161	75	53	64
Ghana	19	84	5,419	350	129	59	58	30
Guinea	7	30	3,120	450	162	N/A	46	–
Guinea-Bissau	1.207	43	N/A	180	169	78	44	62
Liberia	1.13	32	N/A	N/A	N/A	N/A	47	47
Mali	11	9	2,345	240	165	81	43	60
Niger	11	9	1,861	180	173	85	46	85
Nigeria	127	139	41,248	260	151	62	47	37
Senegal	10	49	4,372	500	155	73	52	64
Sierra Leone	5	70	654	130	174	N/A	37	–
Togo	5	86	1,281	300	145	63	49	44

NA = Not Available; HDI = Human Development Index; HPI = Human Poverty Index
Source: World Bank 2002; Ojo 2001; ACP–EU 2000.

in the international capital market. A fundamental factor, which will govern the Fund's access to the market, is the view which investment bankers and other international lenders will form with respect to the Fund's independence from day to day political pressures. (*Ibid.*)

Another initial problem with the operations of the Fund was the near absence of political will, on the part of member states, to meet their commitments. Despite the clear objectives of the ECOWAS Fund, in practice member states failed to meet their responsibilities. Take the issue of payment of the called-up capital of the Fund by member states as an example. Several years after the capital was called, some member states were yet to pay (see Table 10.2). As member states' economies deteriorated in the early 1980s and they came under the spell of various externally monitored structural adjustment programmes, it even became more difficult for them to meet their obligations to the ECOWAS Fund. According to a former Managing Director of the Fund:

> We have an unusual case of a Fund without funds. The paucity of our working capital is well known to the Authority of Heads of State and Government and the Directors gathered here today. And to help improve

Table 10.2 Capital calls in arrears, December 2000

Member state	Arrears
Benin	0
Burkina Faso	0
Cape Verde	99,043
Côte d'Ivoire	1,316,720
Gambia	654,139
Ghana	1,967,205
Guinea	0
Guinea-Bissau	588,614
Liberia	2,979,861
Mali	0
Mauritania	2,423,464
Niger	819,555
Nigeria	0
Senegal	672,160
Sierra Leone	1,574,538
Togo	0
Total	13,095,299

Source: Information Memorandum, EBID, ERIB, ERDF, September 2001.

the situation, on the 6th of August 1994 in Abuja, the Authority decided that Member States should endeavor to pay off the arrears of contributions to the Fund's capital. And the compensation budgets within three years with effect from 1st January 1995 .... The Member States also acknowledge the fact that, within the context of the individual country's Special Adjustment Programmes, it is a daunting task to pay up contributions to the various Community Institutions. This is borne out by the fact that by the end of September 1995 over 27 per cent of the subscriptions to the two tranches of capital remained unpaid. We are talking of a period of 18 years in the case of the first tranche and 8 years for the second tranche. (Apea 1995:1)

The inability of member states to promptly meet their financial obligations to the Fund has undoubtedly had negative effects on the operations of the ECOWAS Fund. Apart from its implications for working capital, it has also negatively impacted on the credit rating of the organisation. This is because international financial institutions are reluctant to deal with any body whose members do not have the discipline to live up to their commitments. In the case of the ECOWAS Fund, this has resulted in a poor institutional credit rating, which has contributed to its poor performance over the years. Along these lines, it has been asserted that:

the ECOWAS Fund has, for a number of years, been struggling hard in order to survive. For that reason, it has regrettably failed to make the expected impact on the economies of the member states of the Community. As a financial institution, the Fund's stock in trade is its operating capital. But as some of us may recall, due mainly to persistent budget deficits since 1989, the institution's operating capital stock has fallen to a precariously low level. This incidentally prompted the Administration and Finance Commission to advise the Board to direct the Fund's Management to discontinue financing new projects with the institution's own resources about two years ago. The implication of this directive was, and still is, that the Fund is expected to depend solely on external donors/lenders for resources to finance its lending operations. If the credit-worthiness rating of the Fund were high enough, there would not be much problem encountered in mobilising the needed funds from the external sources. In spite of this handicap, approaches have been made to several prospective donors, but they have invariably recoiled after scrutinising our administrative structures and our financial statements. I am sorry to say that some have even been forthright in voicing their doubts about the commitment of ECOWAS member states to their own institution. (Apea 1997: 5)

It is therefore not surprising that after over 20 years of existence, the ability of the ECOWAS Fund to raise money from the international capital market has not been impressive. Loans to member states have suffered a similar fate (see Table 10.3).

Table 10.3 ECOWAS Fund: regional distribution of loans (December 2000)

Member state	No. of loans	Committed Unit of Account*	%
Benin	6	14,108,356	17.5
Burkina Faso	3	12,202,267	15.2
Cape Verde	1	3,408,000	4.2
Côte d'Ivoire	3	8,191,192	10.1
Gambia	2	2,993,961	3.7
Ghana	1	660,127	0.8
Guinea	6	7,396,906	9.2
Guinea-Bissau	4	1,421,512	1.8
Liberia	1	967,936	1.2
Mali	2	4,153,278	5.2
Niger	1	384,550	0.5
Nigeria	5	11,603,781	14.4
Senegal	5	12,569,617	15.6
Togo	1	435,459	0.6
Total	41	80,469,942	100.0

Source: Information Memorandum, EBID, ERIB, ERDF, September 2001.
Note: * In 2003 1 UA = US$1.24.

The problem, however, may not just lie with fund mobilisation. There are also problems with the nature of the projects that the ECOWAS Fund is supposed to fund. Essentially, the Fund is supposed to fund development projects, such as infrastructure. Unfortunately, the geography of the region has complicated the problems of funding such development projects. Along these lines, it has been asserted that:

West Africa is highly fragmented as a result of geographic, demographic, political and policy related reasons. The 236 million inhabitants are very unevenly distributed among countries, with Nigeria containing half the total population and several countries having less than a million people. There is no indigenous, widely used language for commerce, such as Swahili in Eastern Africa, but rather three official European languages, still not understood by large segments of the population. The region is roughly one-third desert, one-third Sudano Sahelian, with rather irregular rainfall and one-third humid and rather more favourable for agricultural development. Except in the urbanised areas along the Atlantic coast, population density is low. Nearly half of the area is formed of landlocked countries. Internal distances as well as distances to core markets (about 50 per cent greater than in East Asia) are enormous and transport infrastructure networks are only partially interconnected between countries – since they had been originally conceived to serve the colonial interests rather than the region's, and they are very poorly maintained. Because of natural obstacles, political fragmentation, and inappropriate policies, national markets are tiny and regional markets remain undeveloped. As a result, infrastructure costs are among the highest in the world; electricity costs are on average 4.5 times higher than in the OECD countries and two times higher than in Latin America. The rates for international telephone calls are about 4 times higher than in OECD and 2.5 times higher than in Latin America, also on average. (World Bank 2001: 2)

Even the little infrastructure that is in place has in the main been dictated by the very essence of colonisation. Despite the geographical proximities of the West African countries, colonisation made it difficult for them to relate with their neighbours. This was true among both Francophone and Anglophone states. Essentially, the British and French authorities were only interested in promoting trade between the individual colonies and their respective home countries. This was mainly because what attracted the foreign commercial institutions to the continent was the availability of cheap and abundant raw materials, which could service European factories. There was thus no commercial interest in promoting intra-regional trade. Most of the infrastructure the colonial masters put in place was aimed at evacuating minerals and raw materials from the hinterland to the coastal regions for onward transportation to Europe. This sometimes resulted in the establishment of cross-colony infrastructure, especially in the landlocked countries. Mali, for instance, was linked to Senegal by rail. This ensured that raw materials and minerals from Mali could be exported through the seaport in Dakar. Burkina Faso, another landlocked country, was also linked by rail to Abidjan. This, no doubt, was commercially driven.[2] Telecommunications and air transport arrangements were aimed at servicing inter-continental trade rather than intra-regional trade. Even to date, inter-continental communication, in most cases, is easier and cheaper than communications within the West African region. It is, for instance, usually faster for a courier letter from, say, Nigeria to Senegal, to go through Europe than to go direct (Uche 2001: 27).

Although there is widespread consensus that infrastructure is the key to economic growth and poverty reduction, financing it has proved difficult. This is mainly because such projects are usually long-term and capital-intensive. The problem is that in a poverty-stricken continent, where both the people and government are consumed by solving day-to-day problems, there is little scope for long-term planning.[3] The dynamics of economic and political change in the region also further inhibit long-term planning. Finding viable long-term projects may therefore not be an easy task. This is even worse with respect to private sector projects.

According to a recent ECOWAS Fund annual report:

> The low rates of growth in commitments were due to difficulties often encountered during appraisals, particularly the difficulty of finding guarantees acceptable to the Fund, in the case of private projects, and the long delay in obtaining additional information when such information is required. As regards disbursements, the greatest difficulty encountered during the period after the signing of the loan agreements was how to get the borrowers to satisfy the conditions precedent to the first disbursement. (ECOWAS Fund 2000: 10)[4]

Furthermore, since the adoption of structural adjustment programmes by most of the ECOWAS states, international agencies have not considered these programmes as a priority. Along these lines, it has been argued that:

> Following the debt crisis in 1982, there has been an increasing tendency for virtually all member States of the Community to implement tight economic adjustment and reform programmes with the aid and coordination of the World Bank and IMF, which have been providing substantial financing for this purpose. These programmes place greater emphasis on general policy reform and implementation (exchange rate realignment, reduction in public expenditure, tight controls on new debt, etc.) than on project preparation and financing. Countries which implement these programmes have very little choice in the programme design and execution. One significant aspect of this development has been that a substantial number of projects submitted by member states for the Economic Recovery Programme are either not taken into consideration or are classified as very low priority in the public investment programmes now being implemented in many countries within the framework of structural adjustment. (Fall 1989: 23)

Even when fundable projects are found, the political commitment of some member states sometimes stifles their implementation. For instance, in 1991, eight years after the take-off, the first ECOWAS Priority Telecommunications Programme was reported as experiencing serious difficulties at its completion stage because of the attitude of some member states. Specifically, Mauritania was said to have unilaterally modified the configuration of the Mali–Mauritania microwave link project at the point of its submission to the European Investment Bank (EIB) for financing. After several attempts to safeguard the original arrangement had failed, the EIB decided to cancel the amount of €18.5 million which had been allocated for the financing of this link. This was because the resources were intended for the financing of a specific project and not for a line of credit that the ECOWAS Fund could utilise as it liked. Another example was Mali. The country was granted a loan of €26.4 million by the government of Spain. This was supposed to be for the financing of the Severe–Timbuktu–Gao microwave link. Mali, however, subsequently repudiated this financing (Fall 1991: 19). An internal document of the ECOWAS Fund similarly noted that:

> The mobilisation of resources is a standing directive given to the Fund Management for the financing of programmes in Member States. In some cases, Member States have even written formally to entrust the Fund with the task of negotiating and mobilising resources on their behalf and the Fund has humbly fulfilled this mission. Thus from 1988 to 1989, the Fund mobilised the equivalent of US$100.18 million. This amount does not include the resources mobilised within the context of co-financing of projects from the Fund's own resources. Although Management is pleased to have achieved this result, the rate of utilisation of these resources is a cause for concern. The reasons for this poor performance are as follows: – Refusal of some member states to take the loans for which they themselves had directed the Fund to seek financing. –Withdrawal of the States from the projects for which the funds were mobilised. – Change of the order of priority of projects for which funds were mobilised. –Slow administrative procedures, within the beneficiary States, for the signing and the disbursement of loans. In this respect, no disbursements have been made on some loans approved by the Board in 1988 and 1989. Nor has there been any signing of subsequent loan agreements. – Implementation of Structural Adjustment Programmes. – Application of sanctions in respect of arrears in the repayment of loans. This situation is all the more deplorable as it results sometimes in the payment by the Fund of very high administrative fees and charges in the course of project preparation. (Fall 1991: 11–12)

Another factor that has contributed to the poor financial situation of the ECOWAS Fund is poor management. Between 1991 and 1995, for instance, the annual income generated could not keep up with the Fund's administrative expenses. In the absence of reserves, the resultant shortfalls had to be financed from the capital of the Fund. According to a former Managing Director of the Fund:

> During 1992 and 1993, there were increases in the gaps created by shortfalls in budgetary incomes thus leading to the financing of 43.4 per cent and 46.8 per cent of the excess overheads respectively from capital. However, since 1994, austerity measures have been instituted to curtail expenditures, which are clearly manifested in a declining trend as far as budgetary deficits are concerned. Consequently, in 1994 and 1995, 40.5 per cent and 21.5 per cent respectively of excess overheads were financed from our capital. (Apea 1995: 3)

Such deterioration in the financial situation has led to the diminished credit rating of the organisation. It has also been responsible for the inability of the organisation to access cheap credit, which is vital for long-term development lending (Uche 2001: 26). It is thus hardly surprising that the ECOWAS Fund has been unable to raise additional funding from its member countries. Although the authorised capital of the Fund is US$500 million, only US$100 million has been called up.

Further evidence of poor management can be found in the way the Fund prioritises its objectives. In the past, for instance, it has locked up working capital in the construction of its headquarters. It has, for instance, been asserted that

> part of the Fund's resources have been depleted and locked up in non-revenue earning assets (e.g. its financing of the Secretariat's Headquarters building in Abuja). Possibly as a consequence of these factors, the Fund has had limited success in using its capital base to leverage its borrowings from international financing institutions. (DFC 2001: 22)

Some of its funds have also been lost in bank failures. A substantial amount of deposits placed with the Bank of Credit and Commerce International (BCCI) was lost when the bank collapsed in 1991. An internal report of the ECOWAS Fund noted that:

> You may recall that in November last year, Management informed the Board about the level of risk of the Fund's resources placed with the Lomé and Paris branches of Bank of Credit and Commerce International (BCCI) whose operations were suspended with effect from 5th July 1991. The total amount of resources saved by the Fund with the two branches amounts to US$12.6 million. Efforts are being made ever since to recover these resources. In its lawsuit against BCCI to ensure that its assets are not frozen, the Fund's claim was rejected at the first hearing by the Commercial Court of Paris. The lawyer engaged by the Fund to defend its interests in this matter has made an appeal on his own initiative and at his own expense.... With regard to the Branch in Lomé, the Central Bank of the West African Monetary Union (BCEAO) is currently examining the possibility of restructuring or liquidating the bank. We hope that a final decision will be taken on the issue before the end of the year. The information contained in an unpublished audit report on the assets and liabilities of the two branches indicate that they both have the necessary resources to be able to reimburse the greater portion of the amounts deposited. (Fall 1992: 13)

Unfortunately, not all the expectations of the management of the ECOWAS Fund have been fulfilled. As at the end of 2000, for instance, the Fund still had in its books a provision for loss on its deposits with the BCCI amounting to US$1,528,416 (ECOWAS Fund Annual Report 2000).

Such an unfavourable operating environment subsequently led to a review of the entire organisation. Under the new arrangements, the ECOWAS Fund will be transformed into a holding company and will be renamed the ECOWAS Bank for Investment and Development (EBID). EBID will have two subsidiary companies, the ECOWAS Regional Investment Bank (ERIB) and the ECOWAS Regional Development Fund (ERDF). These new bodies will focus on the private and public sectors, respectively. Such a restructuring exercise also requires the opening up of the constituent organisations to outside capital. The question to ask, however, is how the proposed restructuring will affect the role of the ECOWAS Fund in promoting regional development.

Restructuring the ECOWAS Fund

The need to restructure the Fund was mooted not long after its establishment. With the unending problems that the Fund faced, especially with respect to funding, it was not surprising that the initial idea was to open up the Fund to outside stakeholders. The aim was to give it greater access to the international financial market. Along these lines, it has been suggested that:

> The need to enhance the financial resources of the Fund became apparent following the observation and analysis of the utilisation of the Fund's resources for the period 1985 to 1990. It became apparent that the opening up of the capital of the Fund should make it possible not only to seek new resources but also to enhance the Fund's credibility internationally and to enable it to mobilise resources in the international financial market. It was therefore in the bid to address the Fund's increasing resource requirements that the Council of Ministers decided in 1987 to commission a study on the enhancement of the Fund's financial resources. (ECOWAS Fund n.d.: 1)

On the basis of the study, which was conducted by a Ghanaian consultancy firm, the Authority of the Heads of States and Government agreed in principle to enhance the financial resources of the Fund. A follow-up study was subsequently commissioned. The report of this study, which was submitted in 1991, led to the setting up of an *ad hoc* ministerial committee to oversee the enhancement of the financial resources of the Fund. This project was temporarily suspended in December 1993, because of the precarious financial situation of the Fund at the time. Despite these studies, it was clear that non-member countries were unwilling to invest in such a scheme. This was because it was felt that the member countries lacked both the political will and the economic discipline to adhere to their decisions.

It was therefore not surprising that, in 1994, when the suspension of the enhancement project was lifted, another study was commissioned. This was with a view to enhancing the scope of the project. The study, which was carried out by a London-based consulting firm, was wide-ranging. It was aimed at identifying various ways of making the Fund attractive to non-regional partners. This report was submitted in 1996. Essentially, it recommended that the Fund be transformed into a more commercially oriented institution, without losing sight of its development and integration objectives. This recommendation was approved in 1997 by the Authority of Heads of State and Government. A feasibility study was subsequently commissioned to determine the type of financial institution that the Fund would become.

This review resulted in the establishment of three new institutions to replace the ECOWAS Fund:

- The ECOWAS Bank for Investment and Development;
- The ECOWAS Regional Investment Bank;
- The ECOWAS Regional Development Fund.

Outside investors will be encouraged to invest in the three new institutions. Controlling shares, however, will be maintained by ECOWAS member states and institutions. In the EBID, for instance, out of the paid-up capital of US$225 million, member states are expected to hold 66.6 per cent of the shares. For the ERIB and ERDF, member states are expected to hold 51 per cent and 90 per cent of the US$125 million paid-up share capital for each of the institutions, respectively (see Table 10.4).

Table 10.4 Capital of new institutions (US$ million)

Institution	Main activity	Authorised capital	Paid-up capital		
			Total	Held by ECOWAS and EBID	Sought from investors
EBID	Holding company of ERIB and ERDF	750	225	149.85 66.67%	75.15 33.33%
ERIB	Investment bank	500	125	63.75 51%	61.25 49%
ERDF	Development fund	500	125	112.5 90%	12.5 10%

Source: Information Memorandum, EBID, ERIB, and ERDF, September 2001.

Essentially, EBID will be the holding company and will have controlling shares in both ERIB and ERDF. The objectives of EBID are: (1) to contribute to the realisation of ECOWAS objectives by supporting regional integration infrastructure projects or any other development projects in the public and private sectors; and (2) to further support the development of the community through the financing of special projects through its subsidiaries. Unlike the ECOWAS Fund, EBID will be an autonomous institution with all powers vested in the Board of Directors. The Board of Governors will only serve as a link between EBID and other ECOWAS institutions. The main operational activities of EBID are:

- To acquire majority shareholdings in the equity of ERIB and ERDF;
- To establish any subsidiaries that may be necessary;
- To provide technical assistance and any other services to its subsidiaries;
- To mobilise internal and external resources;
- To guarantee commitments or operations of its subsidiaries.

ERIB, as already mentioned, will be the investment-banking arm of the group. Essentially, it will operate on commercial terms and in competition with other private investment banks. It will be governed by a Board of Directors, which will be its highest executive authority. The managing director of EBID is to be the chairman of the board. In the main, ERIB will focus on the financing of infrastructure. Most of its lending will therefore be for periods of five to twelve years. It is also expected that the bank will offer the following services in order to complement its lending activities:

- Mergers and acquisition advisory services;
- Loan syndication and arranging co-financing;
- Privatisation advisory services;
- Bond issues and fixed income securities;
- Underwriting capital issues by privatised utilities and industrial clients.

The third new institution is ERDF. Like the ECOWAS Fund, it will provide finance on concessional terms to development projects in the ECOWAS region. It is this organisation that will take over the portfolio of the EOCWAS Fund. ERDF will focus mainly on long-term loans, which will be in the range of ten to twenty years, with grace periods on principal of four to seven years. ERDF will focus on the following main products:

- Implementing ECOWAS Special Programmes and Special Funds;
- Resource mobilisation and taking an equity stake in commercial, financial and industrial firms;

- Project financing with a focus on infrastructure, economic and social development sectors;
- Financing of feasibility studies.

ERDF will be governed by a Board of Directors, who will be responsible for policy and financial decisions, while the day-to-day administration will be executed by the management.

In practice, however, it is unlikely that these new structures will change much. Take, for instance, the case of EBID, which is supposed to be the holding company for ERIB and ERDF. Essentially, one cannot but wonder whether you need to establish such a structure just for the purpose of owning and supporting its subsidiaries. The fact that 66 per cent of this institution will be owned by ECOWAS simply means that the targeted foreign investors will be dominated by ECOWAS interests. Furthermore, there is no guarantee that the new structures will eliminate the indiscipline and lack of commitment on the part of member states that have jeopardised the efficient functioning of ECOWAS and its institutions in the past.

The second proposed organisation is ERIB, which will be run on commercial principles. It is supposed to be the investment-banking arm of the group and focus mainly on medium and long-term infrastructure finance. Until now, ECOWAS had no equivalent institution. Unfortunately, the organisational structure provides for control ultimately to lie with ECOWAS countries and its institutions. At least 51 per cent of the shares of ERIB will be owned by them. Based on this condition, it is difficult to see how this new institution will thrive. It is likely that the factors that have ensured the abysmal performance of other ECOWAS-controlled institutions will also affect this new organisation. Admittedly, it can be argued that there are enormous opportunities for such a new organisation.

> The competition in the specialised project finance area in ECOWAS comes from two main sources: private and profit oriented banks and other financial institutions, and official multilateral and bilateral institutions. Overall it is clear that there is competition from both sources but it is not overwhelmingly intense in relation to the overall size of the market.... In all, 58 banks are reported to be licensed in the UEMOA [West African Economic and Monetary Union] region, and about 10 are large. Several of these have international ownership and operate to international standards, for example, Equator Bank, Barclays Bank and Standard Chartered. Others are highly respected and well-established regional banks like EcoBank. There is no doubt that many have considerable strengths, like long established relationships with corporate clients and Governments, and in depth knowledge of local markets and credit conditions. Yet the competition for specialised long term project finance from these banks is only relatively

light. There are several reasons for this, First of all, most of these banks are 'commercial banks' in the traditional sense of the word, with a mix of retail and corporate business and an emphasis on short term funding. Second, the domestic resource mobilisation is limited and mostly short term. Third, there are no bond or long term markets of significance, at least not in volume and liquidity terms. And fourth, few of the existing banks operate in many of the ECOWAS markets i.e. they have only restricted pan regional coverage…. Notwithstanding these limitations, there are new entrants into the project finance area, of which the new EcoBank Development Corporation is the most notable. This is an indication that some local financial institutions have identified the specialist project finance area as a 'market opportunity'. But the number, size and resources of these investment-banking activities within the region does not yet add up to strong competition. To the contrary, given the market needs for project finance, little of that can be satisfied by the established private banks. (DFC 2001: paragraphs 2.2–2.4)

It is thus clear that investors are reluctant to get involved in long-term development activities in the sub-region. This can, at least in part, be explained by the political, economic and social instability that is widespread in the region. The risks associated with medium- and long-term projects are therefore much higher in such regions. It is thus difficult to see how the new ECOWAS institution will take advantage of this opportunity without becoming bogged down in the inherent stability problems in the region. The ECOWAS bureaucracy and lack of commitment on the part of member states will further complicate this. It is also unlikely that investors who have a choice will willingly agree to invest in such an institution when it is clear that control will ultimately lie with a regional body whose members have in the past not shown any political commitment towards regional issues.

As to ERDF, there is very little difference between it and the current ECOWAS Fund. External shareholding is limited to 10 per cent, which makes it even more unattractive to foreign investors. Also, the new structure is unlikely to have much positive impact on the direction of the organisation. As with EBID, ultimate control still rests with ECOWAS countries and there is no institutional fix in the new framework for this problem. Admittedly, there is a large untapped market for the provision of infrastructure finance in the West African sub-region. Along these lines, it has been suggested that:

There is a large market for project finance in the region. With a total population of about 215 million people, the market has a high potential for 'catching up' and a high level of development expenditure. The project finance market is generally large, and the infrastructure sector in particular is important. If this sector is broadly defined to include telecommunications, energy, transport, water and environmental (waste management, etc.) projects, the potential market for annual investments could be estimated at between about US$1.6 to 3.2 billion. The existing multiyear infrastructure programmes defined by ECOWAS already amount to about US$15 billion. However, despite the large market potentials, the actual volumes of investment and project finance have been disappointing in the past (DFC 2001: 4).

Despite this, it is unlikely that the new institution will outperform its predecessor. Ultimate control by ECOWAS member states and the political and economic environment of the region will continue to impede its ability to achieve its main objectives. Prospective investors are bound to be sceptical, as the new structure does not offer them control, which is critical to institutional recovery. Expecting a radical change under the proposed structure is merely wishful thinking.

Conclusion

In general, African institutions have been unable to achieve much success in financing African development. The past performance of the ECOWAS Fund clearly supports this assertion. One of the reasons for this is the lack of commitment on the part of the ECOWAS member states to their sub-regional commitments. Most ECOWAS member states are faced with some form of economic and/or political problems. Most of these countries are most of the time, therefore, engrossed by internal crisis. Unfortunately, most of the stakeholders in the general crisis in the region are not member states of ECOWAS. Commitment of member countries to ECOWAS is therefore secondary to their commitment to the various stakeholders in their domestic crisis. The history of ECOWAS is partly responsible for this problem. Unlike the European Union, where membership is based on applicants meeting certain economic criteria, being located in West Africa automatically guarantees you membership of ECOWAS. There is thus no incentive for members to be politically committed to the organisation or its institutions. This has been one of the main problems of the ECOWAS Fund.

Although the restructuring of the ECOWAS Fund is a welcome development, it has not gone far enough. This is because it has not taken into consideration the main factors that inhibited the functioning of the ECOWAS Fund. These include lack of political commitment on the part of member states with respect to implementing ECOWAS decisions and the unending bureaucracy of ECOWAS institutions. Also important is the fact that the lack of economic and political stability in the region has made long-term investments highly risky. Although there may be enormous opportunities for infrastructure development in the sub-region, the fact remains that the socio-political environment has discouraged any meaningful volume of investment in these areas. Despite these difficulties, infrastructure remains the key to the development of the sub-region. Establishing institutions to help finance infrastructural development without addressing the problems that have made such investments unprofitable or unattractive will, as in the past, yield little result.

NOTES

1 The signatories to the treaty were Benin (formerly Dahomey), Burkina Faso (formerly Upper Volta), Côte d'Ivoire, the Gambia, Ghana, Guinea, Guinea-Bissau, Liberia, Mali, Mauritania, Niger, Nigeria, Senegal, Sierra Leone, and Togo. Cape Verde, the sixteenth state, joined the organisation in 1977 (Kufuor 1994: 60). Mauritania left in 2000.

2 See ECOWAS (2000) for country reports on railway arrangements in the sub-region.

3 One notable exception is Nigeria. It has for instance been suggested that 'Nigeria has received some US$280 billion in oil revenues since the early 1970s. Through foolish investments, graft, and simple theft, this vast fortune has been wholly squandered. In fact, because successive Nigerian Governments borrowed billions against future oil revenues and wasted that money too, it is fair to say that Nigeria blew more than its entire oil windfall. Nigerians are, on average, poorer today than they were in 1974. Despite the recent surge in the oil price, the country is saddled with debts of about US$30 billion. Income per head in 1998 was a wretched US$345, less than a third its volume at the height of the boom in 1980' (Economist, 15–21 January 2000).

4 Perhaps because of these difficulties, ECOWAS has been successful in managing its limited loan portfolio. It has, for instance, been asserted that: 'The portfolio is of reasonable standing, taken into consideration the norms of development finance and the levels of risk in the region. At end-2000, 90 per cent of the portfolio was performing satisfactorily. Amounts in arrears are concentrated in three countries all of which have experienced serious political and economic difficulties in recent years' (DFC 2001: 21).

REFERENCES

ACP-EU. 2000. *Partnership Agreement Between the Members of the African, Caribbean and Pacific Group of States on the One Part, and the European Community and its Member States, of the Other Party (Cotonou Agreement)*. Brussels: African, Caribbean and Pacific Countries–European Union.

Apea, S. K., 1995, 'Attracting Partners in Development', paper presented at the Thirty-fourth Session of the Board of Directors of the ECOWAS Fund, Abuja, December.

—— 1997, 'The ECOWAS Fund: Present Status and Prospects', unpublished report presented at the Thirty-seventh Session of the Board of Directors of the ECOWAS Fund, Abuja, 20–21 August.

DFC, 2001, *Information Memorandum: ECOWAS Bank for Investment and Development (EBID), ECOWAS Regional Investment Bank (ERIB), ECOWAS Regional Development Fund (ERDF),*

Abuja: DFC.

ECOWAS, 1975, Treaty and Communiqué, Lagos: ECOWAS.

—— 2000, Final Report on the Meeting of the ECOWAS Regional Railway Master-Plan, Abuja: ECOWAS.

—— n.d. The Revised ECOWAS Treaty, Lagos: ECOWAS.

ECOWAS Fund, 1977, Statement by the Managing Director of the Fund for Cooperation, Compensation and Development Economic Community of West African States to the First Board of Directors Meeting, Lomé: ECOWAS Fund.

—— 2000, Annual Report, Lagos: ECOWAS Fund.

—— n.d., Draft Terms of Reference on the Transformation of the ECOWAS Fund, Lagos: ECOWAS Fund.

Fall, M. B., 1989, Report of Activities Presented by the Managing Director, Lagos: ECOWAS Fund.

—— 1991, Report of Activities Presented by the Managing Director, Lomé: ECOWAS Fund.

—— 1992, Report of Activities Presented by the Managing Director, Dakar: ECOWAS Fund.

Kufuor, K. O., 1994, 'Democracy and the New ECOWAS Treaty', Oxford International Review, 6, 1.

NEPAD, 2001, Base Document, Midrand: New Partnership for Africa's Development Secretariat.

Ojo, M., 2001, 'The Prospects for Achieving the Objectives of the Second Monetary Zone in the West African Sub Region', West African Journal of Monetary and Economic Integration, 1, 1: 45–67.

Tubman, R. C., 1982, Report of Activities Presented by the Managing Director, Cotonou: ECOWAS Fund.

Uche, C. U., 2001, The Politics of Monetary Sector Cooperation Among the Economic Community of West African States Members, Policy Research Working Paper No. 2647, Washington DC: World Bank.

World Bank, 1994, World Development Report, Washington DC: World Bank.

—— 2001, Memorandum of the President of the International Development Association to the Executive Directors on a Regional Integration Assistance Strategy for West Africa, Washington, DC: World Bank.

—— 2002, World Development Report, Washington DC: World Bank.

11 Financing Africa's Development
Can Aid Dependence Be Avoided?

Kwasi Anyemedu

A central theme of NEPAD is that Africans must take control of their own destiny. In the document, one finds such uplifting declarations as 'Africans must not be the wards of benevolent guardians, rather they must be the architects of their own sustained upliftment' and 'the hopes of Africa's peoples for a better life can no longer rest on the magnanimity of others'. When it comes to the question of mobilisation of resources for development, however, the central NEPAD statement seems, at first sight at least, to be somewhat contrary in spirit to the ringing declarations quoted above. The document states as follows:

> To achieve the 7 per cent per annum growth rate needed to meet the IDGs (International Development Goals) – most importantly, to halve poverty incidence by the year 2015 – Africa needs to fill an annual resource gap of 12 per cent of its GDP, or US$64 billion. This will require increased domestic savings, as well as improvements in the public revenue systems. However, the majority of the needed resources will have to be obtained from outside the continent. The New Partnership for Africa's Development focuses on debt reduction and ODA as complementary external resources required in the short to medium term, and addresses private capital flows as a longer-term concern (para. 144).

This focus on external resource flows and, in particular, aid is to a large extent compelled by the reality of the current African situation. It is generally accepted that, given the low incomes in Africa, there is little scope for increasing significantly domestic savings in the short to medium term. Further – as pointed out in the World Bank's *Can Africa Claim the Twenty-First Century?* – a sharp rise in domestic savings would prevent a rapid increase in consumption and slow the reduction in poverty.

There is, however, another reality. The levels of official development assistance (ODA) required by the programme are unlikely to be attained. Furthermore, aid from both the multilateral and bilateral donors is increasingly accompanied by a growing number and range of policy conditionalities covering both economic and political areas. Already, it is looking as if to 'deserve' the increased amounts of aid that the programme envisages, Africans will have to do as the Western aid donors wish in economic as well as political matters.

Before the Zimbabwe elections, the *Economist* (9–15 March 2002) warned that the refusal of African leaders to criticise Zimbabwe's President Robert Mugabe came 'dangerously close to declaring that African heads of government regard solidarity with doting tyrants as more important than sound economic management, free elections and the rule of law – a grim message to be sending in a year when Africa is trying to present itself as newly serious, responsible and deserving of aid'. In the circumstances, it is not surprising that Nigerian President Olusegun Obasanjo has warned that we must guard against NEPAD being turned against us as a tool for a new conditionality. Wiseman Nkuhlu, Chairman of NEPAD's steering committee and Special Economic Adviser to President Thabo Mbeki, is reported to have rejected a warning by the USA that the African endorsement of Zimbabwe's presidential election could hurt Western support for NEPAD, and declared that, 'For Africans to be dictated to like this is simply irritating' (quoted in Ghana's *Daily Graphic*, 27 March 2002).

The prospect of rather less than the envisaged inflows, and the likelihood of even more pervasive and intrusive conditionalities, requires a response of two kinds. The first is that elaborated by Obasanjo in his statement at the international conference on Financing for Development that 'NEPAD is being drawn up in such a way that, with or without adequate contributions from our development partners, it can be implemented to a significant extent, based on our own visions and our own programmes' (2002).

The second kind of response calls for more attention to be given to domestic savings mobilisation, especially in those areas in which collective or cooperative actions by African states can make an important difference.

It does appear from the NEPAD document that domestic savings mobilisation has not been given as much attention as the other possible sources of finance. It is instructive that, while the NEPAD document stipulates actions which might be taken under the debt, ODA reform, and private capital flows initiatives, no such actions are proposed for domestic savings mobilisation.

The emphasis on aid, and then private capital flows, reflects what might be called the conventional wisdom on the realistic sources of finance for Africa's development. As elaborated, among others, by UNCTAD (2000), the analysis goes like this: the only realistic source of significant finance to initiate a process of rapid growth for Africa is official development assistance. This is because Africa is not yet an attractive destination for private capital, and the current income levels are too low to permit any significant increase in domestic savings. The expectation is that, if African countries are able to achieve rapid growth as a result of the enhanced aid flows, the resultant increase in *per capita* incomes will enhance the capacity of Africa to generate domestic savings. At the same time, if Africa becomes a fast-growing region, it will become more attractive to private investors. The combined effect of these two developments will eventually reduce Africa's dependence on aid.

I acknowledge the realism of the above analysis. Yet the introduction of NEPAD (supposedly to usher in an era in which Africans are more in control of their own destiny), on the one hand, and on the other hand the possibility of even more conditionalities, require that more urgency should be imparted to the task of domestic savings mobilisation. It is also probable that if we devote as much attention and energy to domestic savings mobilisation as we do to the attraction of foreign private capital, we shall find that the scope for domestic savings mobilisation is greater than we think.

As Arthur Lewis (1955) noted several decades ago, 'No nation is so poor that it could not save 12 per cent of its national income if it wanted to; poverty has never prevented nations from launching wars, or from wasting their substance in other ways.' Arthur Lewis wrote at a time when savings of the low-income countries averaged between 4 and 5 per cent of national income, but he thought 12 per cent was feasible.

Domestic savings in sub-Saharan Africa now average 13–14 per cent of GDP, although there are significant differences in individual country performances on this score. Under NEPAD, we should explore ways of increasing this in the shortest possible time so that the transition period from heavy aid dependence to substantially reduced dependence is shortened.

Aid: trends and prospects

Aid or ODA consists of concessional loans and grants to developing countries to promote development in the recipient countries. For loans to qualify for inclusion in ODA figures, they must include a grant element of more than 25 per cent. ODA figures also include technical assistance or cooperation expenditures. It should be noted that the technical cooperation expenditures do not always directly benefit the recipient economy, since they may be for costs incurred outside the country for salaries and benefits of technical experts or for the overheads of firms supplying technical services.

The origins of government-to-government aid can be traced, it is said, to the Renaissance period, when Italian princes used it as a tool of foreign policy. The 1929 British Colonial Development Act, which provided for loans and grants for infrastructural development in the then British colonies, is often regarded as the first example of formal aid. But aid as now conceived, and the machinery for its delivery, can be said to be products of the Second World War. The International Bank for Reconstruction and Development (the World Bank), the leading ODA institution, was established to provide loans for post-war reconstruction, and made its first loan to a developing country, Colombia, in 1950. A major development after the war was the Marshall Plan, initiated by the United States, and which over the period 1948–52 transferred US$17 billion for the rehabilitation of Western Europe. The Marshall Plan is said to have had a grant element of 90 per cent, and the annual flows represented 1.5 per cent of the GNP of the USA.

The Marshall Plan captured the imagination of people, and still today it is evoked when aid is discussed. Katarina Tomasevski (1993) observes that

> The success of the Marshall Plan instigated optimistic visions of what aid can accomplish. A replica of the Marshall Plan was to be tried out in the rest of the world. The idea of a Marshall Plan as a panacea has not withered away. It was advocated by the former UN Secretary-General, Kurt Waldheim, for Africa in 1974; referred to as a solution for the Philippines in 1988; and demanded for Eastern Europe in 1989.

At a recent international conference on Financing for Development in Mexico, the Ghanaian delegation stated rather optimistically that 'It feels as if we stand on the threshold of a new Marshall Plan.'

Trends in aid flows

The trends of ODA flows to developing countries were generally upwards from the 1960s, until it reached a peak in 1992. Since then, aid volumes have declined. Aid received by developing countries (excluding technical cooperation grants) declined by 3.8 per cent in 2000 to US$40.7 billion, and is estimated to have fallen by a further 3.4 per cent in 2001.

A number of reasons have been assigned for this decline in aid flows since the early 1990s. An oft-cited reason is the end of the Cold War. This reduced the competition between the East and the West to offer aid to developing countries as part of an ideological struggle, and at the same time reduced the ability of aid recipients to play off one donor against another. Another important factor has been budgetary difficulties in the donor countries and their consequent squeeze on aid flows. The perception that aid flows have failed to promote development has also reduced support for aid. Another reason cited is the ascendancy of neo-liberal economic ideas, which tend to challenge the need for aid and rather recommend that the developing countries should look principally to private capital flows instead of relying on the public system of aid. The surge in private flows and the relative decline of ODA as a source of finance for developing countries as a whole can be seen in Table 11.1.

Sub-Saharan Africa has not been able to attract as much private flows as the developing regions. This has meant that the shortfall in ODA has not been offset by increased private flows. At the same time, it has meant that, although the total external resource flows into Africa have declined,

Table 11.1 Net disbursements of total official and private flows by type, 1987–97 (%)

	Average share (1987–92)	Average share (1993–7)
Developing countries		
Overseas development assistance (ODA)	61.6	37.2
Other official flows	6.6	4.5
Private flows	26.4	55.1
Grants from NGOs	5.4	3.2
Sub-Saharan African countries		
Overseas development assistance (ODA)	89.5	90.2
Other official flows	11.7	2.4
Private flows	−1.2	7.5
Grants from NGOs	n/a	n/a

Source: OECD, as quoted in Hjertholm and White 2000.

Table 11.2 Main aid recipients ranked by aid *per capita* (1990 and 1999, US$ million)

Ranking, 1990			Ranking, 1999		
1	Israel	295.0	1	Israel	148
2	Jordan	282.5	2	Albania	142
3	Gabon	123.0	3	Nicaragua	137
4	Botswana	118.2	4	Macedonia	135
5	Jamaica	115.7	5	Honduras	129
6	Egypt	107.6	6	Namibia	104
7	Mauritania	107.0	7	Mongolia	92
8	Senegal	99.8	8	Jordan	91
9	Papua New Guinea	96.1	9	Mauritania	84
10	Republic of Congo	92.0	10	Bolivia	70
11	Honduras	87.8	11	Zambia	63
12	Nicaragua	84.0	12	Yugoslavia	60
13	Mauritius	82.9	13	Laos	58
14	Costa Rica	81.0	14	Senegal	58
15	Lesotho	78.0	15	Estonia	57
16	Central African Republic	76.3	16	Armenia	55
17	Bolivia	68.4	17	Kyrgz Republic	55
18	El Salvador	66.5	18	Republic of Congo	49
19	Mozambique	60.2	19	Papua New Guinea	46
20	Côte d'Ivoire	57.9	20	Lebanon	45
21	Togo	57.8	21	Georgia	44
22	Malawi	56.3	22	Latvia	40
23	Mali	56.0	23	Botswana	38
24	Chad	55.5	24	Eritrea	37
25	Benin	55.1	25	Burkina Faso	36
26	Somalia	54.8	26	Lithuania	35
27	Zambia	54.0	27	Benin	34
28	Syria	52.6	28	Haiti	34
29	Guinea	51.0	29	Guinea	33
30	Lebanon	50.0	30	Mali	30

Source: World Bank, 1992, 2002.

the continent's relative dependence on aid has increased. A comparison of figures in the two periods shows that, whereas for developing countries as a whole, the share of ODA as a source of external finance declined in the second period (1993–7), and indeed private flows exceeded ODA in this period, for sub-Saharan Africa the share of ODA in total disbursements of external finance increased.

Africa's heavy dependence on aid can also be seen in other indicators. African countries are among the largest aid recipients, whether measured by aid *per capita* or as a percentage of GNP, as can be seen in Table 11.2. A comparison of the two lists shows the lower *per capita* receipts of individual countries in 1999 as compared to 1990, and also considerable change in the identities of the top thirty aid recipients ranked by *per capita* receipts. In 1990, 19 African countries were numbered among the top thirty, but in 1999, there were only eleven African countries in this group. For Africa as a whole, *per capita* receipts of ODA declined from US$32 billion in 1990 to US$19 billion in 1998. The 1999 list shows the emergence of the Balkan states and other former communist countries as significant recipients of aid.

If we look at what many regard as the criterion for aid dependence, ODA or aid as a percentage of GNP, African countries feature prominently in relation to *per capita* receipts. In 1997, 21 out of the top thirty aid recipients ranked by aid as proportion of GNP were African countries. Rwanda (30.2 per cent) and Mozambique (29.6 per cent) topped the list. Other African countries with ODA equal to 10 per cent or more of their GNP were Madagascar (24.3 per cent), Mauritania (23.9 per cent), Mali (18.1 per cent), Zambia (16.7 per cent), Sierra Leone (16.0 per cent), Burkina Faso (15.6 per cent), Eritrea (14.8 per cent), Chad (14.3 per cent), Tanzania (13.9 per cent), Malawi (13.7 per cent), Uganda (12.8 per cent), Burundi (12.8 per cent), Benin (10.7 per cent), Angola (10.3 per cent), and Guinea (10.1 per cent). African countries in the top thirty but with a ratio of aid to GNP of less than 10 per cent were Central African Republic (9.3 per cent), Togo (8.4 per cent), and Ghana (7.2 per cent).

Although sub-Saharan Africa, as a region, remains the largest recipient of ODA, its share of ODA has been declining, and it has also been experiencing a decline in ODA relative to GNP since 1990. In 1990, sub-Saharan Africa received 37.2 per cent of total ODA inflows as compared to a share of 31.2 per cent in 1999. Over the same period, ODA as a percentage of GNP for the region declined from 5.8 per cent to 4.2 per cent. (Europe and Central Asia increased their share of ODA from 3.5 per cent in 1990 to 14.1 per cent in 1999, and ODA as a proportion of the region's GNP increased from 0.1 per cent to 0.6 per cent over the same period.)

Prospects for aid

Between 1992 and 1997, total ODA from the donor countries declined steadily from 0.33 per cent of their combined GNP to a low of 0.22 per cent. In 1998, there was a slight reversal in this trend, and the proportion of combined GNP given as ODA went up to 0.24 per cent. The situation deteriorated over the period 1998–2000, and aid as a percentage of donors' combined GNP fell back to 0.22 per cent (World Bank 2002).

Even before the UN conference on Financing for Development took place in Mexico in March 2002, some donor countries – notably the UK, which contributed 0.27 per cent of its GNP as aid in 1998 – had pledged to increase their aid budgets. The conference provided a forum for significant pledges of aid. For instance, the USA made an important pledge to build up its spending on aid from 2004 so that by 2006 US ODA would be $5 billion higher than the current $10 billion annual expenditure on aid. Annual US expenditure of $15 billion on aid would be equivalent to 0.16 per cent of US GNP (in 2000); this would not reflect generosity of Marshall Plan proportions, but would still be a very significant increase, and a welcome addition to the resources available for development.

The European Union countries, which provided aid of $25.4 billion in 2000, have also pledged to raise their spending on ODA from the current average of 0.33 per cent to an average of 0.39 per cent of their GNP. This is expected to yield an additional US$7 billion a year by 2006. If these pledges are honoured, there would be at least a temporary reversal in the declining trend of aid flows. The medium-term prospects, however, are uncertain. Two of the four largest donors, Japan and Germany, have fiscal problems that may reduce their capacity to sustain increases in aid, and it is not clear if the US pledge, even if honoured, signals a permanent change in US attitudes to aid. The World Bank (2002) appears to believe that there is little likelihood that a rise in aid will be significant and sustained.

Aid and conditionality

The use of aid to influence broad national development policies is said to go back to the Marshall Plan. The concentration of the World Bank and bilateral donors on project loans throughout the 1960s and 1970s reduced the focus on general policy, although interest in it among lenders was never completely absent. Indeed, in the mid-1960s, USAID officials set out the basic rationale for attaching conditions to development lending:

> In the long run aid's 'influence potential' is much more important than its resource contribution. This is true for two reasons: Total aid from all

sources has probably contributed roughly 20 per cent of total investments in the developing countries in the past few years. The use made of the remaining 80 per cent is clearly much more important in accelerating growth than is the use of aid alone. Furthermore, policies and procedures in import licensing arrangements, investment codes, marketing board pricing policies, power and transportation rate structure, tax provisions, to name only a few, affect economic development at least as powerfully as the presence or absence of adequate infrastructure or technical skills. Successful efforts to influence macroeconomic and sectoral policies are likely to have a greater impact than the added capital and skills financed by aid. (Nelson and Ranis 1966)

Before the early 1980s, however, the International Monetary Fund (IMF) was almost the only major institution substantially involved in policy-based lending. The introduction of the World Bank's structural adjustment programmes in the early 1980s greatly expanded the use of policy conditionality in lending. Since then, the 'influence potential' of aid has been extended beyond the realms of economic policies, and 'good governance', respect for the environment, the observance of human rights, and the holding of free and fair elections have all become matters which can be conditions for the granting or continuance of aid. And it goes without saying that not all the influence that policy conditionality seeks to exercise is directed at growth or development in the recipient countries. Donors use aid to advance their own commercial interests as well as their diplomatic and political objectives.

Sub-Saharan Africa is the region most subject to policy conditionality. This is partly because Africa is the region most dependent on aid, but it is also partly because of the weakness of African states. Tony Killick (1998) has observed that 'the extent to which policies in that region [Africa] are under the direct influence of the IFIs [international financial institutions] and bilateral donors is without historical parallel'. It is clear, therefore, that if NEPAD is truly going to represent an African initiative, then there should be less rather than more conditionality.

It is worth noting that, although many writers in recent times have questioned the effectiveness of conditionality in inducing or extracting the policy changes and reforms desired by the donors, there has been no challenge to the principle of conditionality. Neither has the appropriateness of the content of conditionality been questioned. There has been the tendency, when aid has not produced the desired economic performance, to assume that this is because there has been less than full compliance with the policies stipulated as conditions to aid, or there have been problems with implementation. There has not been a willingness to examine whether the policies enforced on the recipient countries by policy conditionality have been appropriate for the economies concerned. It is rare indeed to find advice such as that given by Dani Rodrik (2000):

> Economic development ultimately derives from a home-grown strategy, not from the world market. Policy makers in developing countries should avoid fads, put globalisation in perspective, and focus on domestic institution building. They should have more confidence in themselves and in domestic institution building, and place less faith in the global economy and the blueprints that emanate from it.

The World Bank, the leading aid organisation and main source of the international development agenda, is convinced that policy conditionality improves economic performance. It is quite clear, therefore, that however 'irritating' African leaders and their officials find the conditionality attached to the aid they receive, the World Bank, the USA and other bilateral donors are not about to abandon the practice of attaching conditions of various sorts to the aid they provide to Africa. Yet dissatisfaction with the current practice of conditionality, even among those who believe that conditionality is appropriate and useful, has been sufficient to elicit several proposals for reform.

Many of the reforms focus on reducing the administrative burden on recipient countries through improved coordination among donors. The World Bank also claims that donors are making greater efforts to 'ensure that policy conditions in adjustment assistance reflect a programme that has the full support of the government and other domestic shareholders'. The most far-sighted of the proposals for reform are based on the ideas of Thorvald Stoltenberg, a former Norwegian Minister of Foreign Affairs. The proposals call for 'development contracts' that will bind aid donors and recipients in a form of reciprocal obligation. The commitments to be made by aid recipients and donors will include a development strategy embodying the priorities of the developing country with respect to the various objectives of development. The trade-off between the short run and the long run, the acceptable changes in income distribution, the minimum goals of human development, and the satisfaction of basic needs and the determination of a minimum set of consumption entitlements for the poor must be based on consensus internal to the developing country itself. Other commitments include:

1   A longer-term perspective, recognising that development may be a matter of decades and that many of the specifics of the policy required cannot be determined or predicated in advance.

2   An emphasis on development, which requires not only stabilisation and adjustment, but also an explicit strategy in which private and public institutions can participate. The structural characteristics,

institutions and traditions of the recipient country will play a significant role in determining the nature of the strategy and the mechanisms of planning which it will apply.

3   Reciprocity in the sense of a guarantee of credits or aid from the donor countries over an extended period, encompassing successive five-year development plans, subject only to limited concepts of conditionality – confined for example to a policy package for enhancing incentives for expanding production, as contrasted with premature efforts to mobilise domestic resources at the beginning of a plan period by curtailing consumption below an irreducible minimum.

4   An assurance that a country's development programme would not be disrupted by external shocks such as export shortfalls by the timely provision of offsetting compensatory or supplementary financing, as long as the country was adhering to a policy framework for enhancing production incentives.

5   The provision of foreign savings support for human development, minimum social security, and environmental protection elements of a country's development programme.

6   The reduction by the developing country of its military expenditure to a defined level, preferably not exceeding 2 per cent of its GNP by the end of its first five-year development plan period.

The NEPAD document states that a critical dimension of Africans taking responsibility for the continent's destiny is the need to negotiate a new relationship with development partners. This new relationship is to involve mutually agreed performance targets and standards for both donors and recipients of aid. It is to be hoped that such a new relationship can be worked out, for old-style conditionality is not likely to be compatible with Africans taking responsibility for their own destiny.

Private capital flows

Private capital inflows come in three broad forms: private debt (mainly commercial banks), foreign direct investment, and portfolio equity flows. In spite of quite vigorous efforts aimed at attracting private capital, not much success has been achieved by Africa. As UNCTAD (2000) points out, long-term bank lending has completely disappeared since the mid-1990s, and, for sub-Saharan Africa, private capital inflows have consisted mainly of foreign direct investment (FDI) and short-term bank lending.

With respect to FDI, the *World Investment Report 2001* (UNCTAD 2002) reveals that total FDI inflows for Africa as a whole declined from US$10.5 billion in 1999 to US$9.1 billion in 2000, while the flows to sub-

**Table 11.3 Shares of regions in global FDI flows
(annual averages in %)**

	1988–90	1998–2000
Developed countries	82.7	76.3
Developing countries	17.1	21.4
Africa	1.8	0.8
Central & Eastern Europe	0.2	2.3

Source: UNCTAD 2002.

Saharan Africa declined from US$8 billion in 1999 to US$6.5 billion in 2000. The total amounts of FDI to Africa declined in 2000 relative to 1999, in spite of the fact that FDI flows for the whole world grew by 18 per cent in 2000, reaching a record of US$1.3 trillion. As a consequence, Africa's share of world FDI flows fell below 1 per cent in 2000.

The top ten African destinations for FDI currently are Angola, Egypt, Nigeria, South Africa, Tunisia, Sudan, Côte d'Ivoire, Mauritius, Uganda, and Lesotho. The bulk of the investment has gone to mineral or petroleum production. Mergers and acquisitions for countries such as South Africa, and the privatisation of state-owned enterprises, have also attracted some FDI.

Among the reasons cited for Africa's inability to attract greater FDI flows are political uncertainty and social unrest; the small size of markets; inadequate and poorly maintained infrastructure; and the shortage of skills. NEPAD seeks to address some of the problems which have inhibited adequate flows of private capital to Africa. The first priority, the NEPAD document declares, is to address the perception of Africa as a 'high risk' continent, especially with regard to insecurity of property rights, regulatory weakness and markets. Accordingly, among the actions proposed under the private capital flows initiative are:

1   the establishment of a task team to carry out audits of investment-related legislation and regulation with a view to risk reduction and harmonisation within Africa;

2   the carrying out of a needs assessment and feasibility study of financial instruments to mitigate the risks associated with doing business in Africa.

As the document points out, initiatives under NEPAD generally relating to the maintenance of peace and security, improvements in political and economic governance, and in infrastructural development, should enhance Africa's prospects in attracting foreign direct investment.

So too should more effective sub-regional or regional integration, which NEPAD may be able to foster. Many studies have singled out large market size as the most potent magnet for the attraction of FDI. A survey by Ernst and Young (1994) found that 'large market potential' was identified as the most important reason for offshore investment by 94 per cent of the 230 global client companies surveyed. The *World Investment Report 2001*, while pointing out that the Southern African Development Community (SADC) maintained its position as the most important sub-region for FDI flows into Africa, observed that while the community's improved attractiveness to FDI may have been principally driven by country-specific factors, at least some of the FDI inflows were motivated by the economic integration of the region.

Domestic savings

Domestic savings may be subdivided into private domestic savings and government domestic savings. Private domestic savings are from two sources: (a) corporate savings or the retained earnings of corporate enterprises, and (b) household savings which represent that part of household income that is not consumed. Government savings are primarily the excess of government revenues over government consumption, defined as all current government expenditures plus capital outlays for military equipment. Important examples of government consumption include the salaries of government employees, government procurement, maintenance expenditures and interest on the national debt. Where they exist, profits from state-owned enterprises can also contribute to government savings. Mainly because of low incomes in sub-Saharan Africa, the region's domestic savings rates are lower than those in other regions. Moreover, within Africa, savings performance varies rather widely.

The figures on domestic savings for individual countries depict a wide diversity in performance across African countries. In 1999, Algeria (30 per cent), Angola (48 per cent), and the Republic of Congo (45 per cent), all no doubt benefiting from petroleum royalties and other revenues, had high domestic savings rates. The only other country which had a domestic savings rate of more than 20 per cent in 1999 was Côte d'Ivoire (25 per cent). At the other extreme, Eritrea and Lesotho had negative savings rates in both 1990 and 1999, and Burundi, Central African Republic, Chad, Mozambique, Sierra Leone and Tanzania had negative savings rates in one of the years. A comparison of performance in the two years shows that the number of countries that improved their savings performance over the period was about the same as those whose savings performance deteriorated.

Table 11.4 Gross domestic investment and savings, 1990 and 1999

Category	Gross domestic investment as % of GDP		Gross domestic savings as % of GDP	
	1990	1999	1990	1999
World	24	22	23	23
High-income countries	21	23	23	22
Middle-income countries	26	24	27	26
Low-income countries	24	20	21	19
Sub-Saharan Africa	15	17	16	14
Middle East and North Africa	24	22	22	19
East Asia and Pacific	35	33	35	37
Latin America and Caribbean	19	21	22	20
South Asia	23	22	19	19

Source: World Bank 2001.

Improving domestic savings performance

The measures usually suggested for enhancing domestic savings include a more effective tax administration, the development of financial intermediaries such as banks, community and postal savings facilities, and the institution of pension and provident funds. There are, however, other crucial areas that are less often mentioned and on which NEPAD can initiate some discussion.

COORDINATION AND HARMONISATION OF CORPORATE TAXES IN AFRICA

Most studies on FDI flows show that tax holidays and other fiscal concessions have little impact on inward investment. Nevertheless, in their anxiety to attract foreign investment, many developing countries institute fiscal concessions that can lead to a considerable loss of revenue. There have been calls for a world-wide harmonisation of taxation on business profits and capital gains, as well as the introduction of obligatory minimum tax rates to mitigate the budgetary revenue losses suffered by developing countries as a result of the use of tax concessions to compete for FDI.

Table 11.5 Structure of demand: selected African countries

Country	Private consumption		Government consumption		Gross domestic investment		Gross domestic savings	
	1990	1999	1990	1999	1990	1999	1990	1999
Algeria	56	59	16	11	29	27	27	30
Angola	36	14	34	38	12	23	30	48
Benin	84	82	11	11	14	18	5	8
Botswana	39	58	24	28	32	20	37	14
Burkina Faso	77	77	15	13	21	27	8	10
Burundi	95	85	11	14	15	10	-5	1
Cameroon	67	71	13	10	18	19	21	19
Central Afr. Rep.	86	81	15	12	12	14	-1	7
Chad	97	89	10	11	7	18	-6	0
Congo	62	45	14	10	16	26	24	45
Côte d'Ivoire	72	65	14	1-	16	26	24	45
DRC	79	83	12	8	9	8	9	9
Egypt	73	7	11	9	29	23	16	14
Eritrea	98	72	33	48	5	45	-31	-20
Ethiopia	74	80	19	15	12	19	7	4
Ghana	85	85	9	11	14	22	5	4
Guinea	70	76	12	7	18	16	18	17
Kenya	67	77	19	16	20	15	14	7
Lesotho	137	115	14	20	53	47	-51	-35
Madagascar	86	88	8	8	17	12	6	5
Malawi	75	80	16	12	20	15	10	7
Mali	80	80	14	12	23	20	6	8
Mauritania	69	73	26	15	20	22	5	12
Mozambique	101	79	12	10	16	35	-12	11
Namibia	51	64	31	26	34	20	18	9
Niger	84	83	15	13	8	10	1	4
Nigeria	56	88	15	12	15	11	29	0
Rwanda	84	89	10	13	15	14	6	-1
Senegal	76	76	15	10	14	21	9	14
Sierra Leone	82	93	10	13	9	5	8	-2
South Africa	63	63	20	19	12	16	18	18
Tanzania	84	72	17	13	23	18	-1	14
Zambia	64	85	19	10	17	17	17	6
Zimbabwe	63	69	19	16	17	18	17	15

Source: World Bank 2001.

Under the auspices of NEPAD, African countries can discuss optimum levels of taxes that take into due account the need for businesses to be competitive as well as minimising avoidable loss of revenue to the state.

RESTRAINING PUBLIC CONSUMPTION EXPENDITURE

The notion that it is difficult to increase domestic savings in poor countries is partly based on the fact that it is difficult to compress private consumption further without worsening poverty. The same reasoning, however, does not apply to some items under public consumption expenditure, which can be reduced with benefits to the poor.

EXPENDITURE ON OFFICIAL VEHICLES

Many African countries spend inordinate amounts of money on official vehicles for their political leaders and top government officials. In Ghana, the former president is reported to have left office with more than a dozen official vehicles still in his possession. Such levels of provision for the comfort of political leaders are excessive by any standards. For African countries running around the globe begging for money, it is unconscionable and indeed obscene for resources to be devoted so lavishly to the comfort of a few.

It is always important to consider the opportunity cost of such expenditures. The cost of a couple of official vehicles could provide blackboards and tables for at least one village school. Under NEPAD, African leaders should encourage each other to be modest so that more of the continent's meagre public revenues can be devoted to poverty alleviation.

FOREIGN TRAVEL AND DIPLOMATIC REPRESENTATION

Foreign travel by African leaders and their officials consumes considerable resources that could be devoted to more productive uses. In recent times this tendency to travel extensively has been justified by the need to attract foreign investment. As already indicated, African countries have not had much success in attracting foreign investment, and where FDI flows have been substantial, this has been due to factors other than the travel of their leaders. In addition, the opportunity cost of these travels can be substantial, and they should be subject to cost–benefit testing. How much FDI flow can we expect from the travels and image enhancement, and after what time lag?

Many African countries have attempted to cut down their diplomatic representation to reduce costs. It is possible that further cuts may be feasible in some cases, and they should be pursued. Under NEPAD, consideration should be given to the pooling or consolidation of African representation at such bodies as the WTO. A beginning can be made on this at the sub-regional level. Such consolidated representation will not only save costs but also encourage African countries to arrive at united and harmonised positions on trade negotiation issues; and if African countries are able to speak with a united voice, this will enhance their capacity to protect their interests more effectively during negotiations.

MILITARY SPENDING

Published figures on military spending would seem to indicate that military expenditures as a percentage of GNP are reasonably low for many African countries. Only Angola, Botswana, Burkina Faso, Burundi, Cameroon, Congo (Brazzaville), the DRC, Eritrea, Kenya, Lesotho, Mozambique, Sierra Leone, South Africa, Zambia and Zimbabwe have military expenditures in excess of 2 per cent of GNP. Given the fact that many countries do not report their military spending accurately, it is possible that many more countries spend more than 2 per cent of their GNP on the military. Any success achieved in reducing military spending translates into an expansion of public domestic savings, and African leaders should explore ways of achieving such reductions.

Many of the countries which in 1997 had large military expenditures such as Angola (21 per cent of GNP), Eritrea (7.7 per cent), and the DRC (5 per cent), were engaged in wars or civil conflicts. Efforts under the NEPAD peace and security initiative to promote peace and security on the continent should eventually have a beneficial impact on domestic savings if they succeed in reducing the need for high military expenditure on the continent.

PUBLIC PROCUREMENT AND CORRUPTION

The government procurement of goods and services is often tainted with corruption, resulting in inflated prices for the country while individual political leaders and officials transfer millions of dollars abroad. Corruption is now widely recognised as a serious obstacle to development. Individual countries in Africa have initiated programmes to combat corruption, with varying degrees of commitment. NEPAD proposes to institute reforms designed to produce 'effective measures to combat corruption and embezzlement'. A very welcome development in this regard has been a decision by African Union ministers to propose for adoption by African heads of state tough new laws aimed at combating corruption in Africa. Under the proposal, African countries will be expected to extradite to their home countries officials who are suspected or have been convicted of corruption. Governments will also have the power to confiscate documents from banks to help win convictions.

There will also be a need for supportive reforms in the advanced countries whose businessmen and suppliers offer bribes and in other ways collude with corrupt developing country officials in their fraudulent activities. Some countries have made bribes no longer tax-deductible as expenses. There have also been calls for an International Convention on Combating Corruption, as well as another convention for the repatriation of misappropriated public funds. These efforts deserve the support of countries so that public funds in Africa and other developing countries are utilised to promote development and the welfare of the citizenry rather than disappearing into individual pockets.

All these areas of public spending not only have the potential for diverting resources away from more development-oriented uses, but also involve expenditures in foreign exchange and therefore have implications for the balance of payments, which is often in deficit or crisis in African countries. Although possible savings in some of the individual items may not be very ample in all cases, the cumulative effect of savings in all these areas can be quite substantial. It is also the case that loans in the region of US$1 million to US$2 million are sometimes contracted by African countries, and the lenders are able to leverage these levels of aid to influence policy in the general economy or major sectors of the economy. No savings are too small to merit attention.

The mobilisation of domestic savings will be facilitated by favourable developments in the international economy. The World Bank's *Can Africa Claim the Twenty-First Century?* has argued that aid dependence cannot be reduced unless Africa recovers its lost share in world trade, and calculates that, since the early 1970s, Africa has lost trade equal to 20 per cent of its GNP. There is no doubt that, if Africa is able to diversify its exports, and the industrialised countries guarantee unrestricted market access for the products of African countries, incomes and government revenues will increase in Africa. Increased incomes and revenues, however, do not automatically translate into higher domestic savings; there is a need to reorient policies and attitudes towards faster accumulation. It is the expectation that, under NEPAD, African countries will recognise the imperative of increasing domestic savings in the shortest possible time, and enhance the chances of Africa pursuing a genuinely home-grown development path.

Conclusion

There is potential tension between the aspirations of NEPAD to ensure that Africa controls its own economic destiny and the major dependence on aid as a source of finance in an era in which aid is subject to heavy policy conditionality. Both African and donor governments have claimed that what is envisaged is a new partnership that will replace old aid and its passive donor–recipient relationship. It remains to be seen how this supposed new relationship will develop. What is clear is that the more Africa relies on its own resources, the greater the likelihood that it will be fully in charge of its own destiny. Africans and their leaders under NEPAD will have to ensure that this goal is achieved sooner rather than later.

REFERENCES

Ernst and Young, 1994, *Investment in Emerging Markets: a Survey of the Strategic Investments of 1000 Global Companies*, New York: Ernst and Young.

Hjertholm, Peter, and Howard White, 2000, 'Foreign Aid in Historical Perspective', in Finn Tarp (ed.), *Foreign Aid and Development*, London: Routledge.

Lewis, W. Arthur, 1955, *Theory of Economic Growth*, New York: George Allen and Unwin.

Killick, Tony, 1998, *Aid and the Political Economy of Policy Change*, London: Routledge.

Nelson, Joan, and Gustav Ranis, 1966, *Measures to Ensure the Effective Use of Aid*, New York: USAID.

Obasanjo, O. 2002. 'Statement at the International Conference on Financing for Development, Monterrey, Mexico', <http://www.nigeriafirst.org/printer_4193.shtml>.

Rodrik, Dani, 2000, 'Development Strategies for the Twenty-first Century', in *Annual World Bank Conference on Development Economics, 2000*, Washington DC: World Bank.

Tomasevski, Katarina, 1993, *Development Aid and Human Rights Revisited*, New York: Pinter Publishers.

UNCTAD, 2000, *Capital Flows and Growth in Africa*, Geneva: UNCTAD.

—— 2002, *World Investment Report, 2001*, Geneva: UNCTAD.

World Bank, 1992, *World Development Report*, Washington DC: World Bank.

—— 2000, *World Development Report*, Washington DC: World Bank.

—— 2000, *Can Africa Claim the Twenty-first Century?*, Washington DC: World Bank.

—— 2001, *World Development Report*, Washington DC: World Bank.

—— 2002, *Global Development Finance*, Washington DC: World Bank.

Appendix
Text of the Accra Conference Declaration

(Adopted at the end of Joint CODESRIA–TWN-AFRICA Conference on Africa's Development Challenges in the Millennium, Accra 23–26 April, 2002)

From the 23 to 26 April, 2002, we, African scholars and activist intellectuals working in academic institutions, civil society organisations and policy institutions from 20 countries in Africa, as well as colleagues and friends from Asia, Europe, North America and South America met at a conference jointly organised by the Council for Development and Social Science Research in Africa (CODESRIA) and the Third World Network-Africa (TWN-Africa) to deliberate on Africa's developmental challenges in the new millennium.

Our deliberations covered such issues as Africa's initiatives for addressing development; Africa and the world trading system; mobilising financing for development in Africa; citizenship, democracy and development; education, health social services and development, and gender equity and equality in development.

Challenges to the space of Africa's own thinking on development
In our deliberations, we recalled the series of initiatives by Africans themselves aimed at addressing the developmental challenges of Africa, in particular the Lagos Plan of Action and the companion African Alternative Framework for Structural Adjustment. Each time, these initiatives were counteracted and ultimately undermined by policy frameworks developed from outside the continent and imposed on African countries. Over the past decades, a false consensus has been generated around the neo-liberal paradigm promoted through the Bretton Woods Institutions and the World Trade Organisation. This stands to crowd out the rich tradition of Africa's own alternative thinking on development. It is in this context that the proclaimed African initiative, the New Partnership for Africa's Development (NEPAD), which was developed in the same period as the United Nations Economic Commission for Africa's *Compact for African Recovery*, as well as the World Bank's *Can Africa Claim the 21ˢᵗ Century?*, were discussed.

The meeting noted the uneven progress of democratisation and in particular of the expansion of space for citizen expression and participation. It also acknowledged the contribution of citizen's struggles and activism to this expansion of the political space, and for putting critical issues of development on the public agenda.

External and internal obstacles to Africa's economic development

The meeting noted that the challenges confronting Africa's development come from two inter-related sources: (a) constraints imposed by the hostile international economic and political order within which our economies operate; and (b) domestic weaknesses deriving from socio-economic and political structures and neo-liberal structural adjustment policies.

The main elements of the hostile global order include, first, the fact that African economies are integrated into the global economy as exporters of primary commodities and importers of manufactured products, leading to terms of trade losses. Reinforcing this, secondly, have been the policies of liberalisation, privatisation and deregulation as well as an unsound package of macro-economic policies imposed through structural adjustment conditionality by the World Bank and the IMF. These have now been institutionalised within the WTO through rules, agreements and procedures, which are biased against our countries. Finally, the just mentioned external and internal policies and structures have combined to generate unsustainable and unjustifiable debt burden which has crippled Africa's economies and undermined the capacity of Africa's ownership of strategies for development .

The external difficulties have exacerbated the internal structural imbalances of our economies, and, together with neo-liberal structural adjustment policies, inequitable socio-economic and political structures, have led the to disintegration of our economies and increased social and gender inequity. In particular, our manufacturing industries have been destroyed; agricultural production (for food and other domestic needs is in crisis; public services have been severely weakened; and the capacity of states and governments in Africa to make and implement policies in support of balanced and equitable national development emasculated. The costs associated with these have fallen disproportionately on marginalized and subordinated groups of our societies, including workers, peasants, small producers. The impact has been excessively severe on women and children.

Indeed, the developments noted above have reversed policies and programmes and have dismantled institutions in place since independence to create and expand integrated production across and between our economies in agriculture, industry, commerce, finance, and social services. These were programmes and institutions which have, in spite of their limitations, sought to address the problems of weak internal markets and fragmented production structures as well as economic imbalances and social inequities within and between nations inherited from colonialism, and to redress the inappropriate integration of our economies in the global order. The associated social and economic gains, generated over this period have been destroyed.

The above informed our reflections on the NEPAD. We concluded that, while many of its stated goals may be well-intentioned, the development vision and economic measures that it canvases for the realisation of these goals are flawed. As a result, NEPAD will not contribute to addressing the developmental problems mentioned above. On the contrary, it will reinforce the hostile external environment and the internal weaknesses that constitute the major obstacles to Africa's development. Indeed, in certain areas like debt, NEPAD steps back from international goals that have been won through global mobilisation and struggle.

The most fundamental flaws of NEPAD, which reproduce the central elements of the World Bank's *Can Africa Claim the 21st Century* and the ECA's *Compact for African Recovery*, include:

(a) the neo-liberal economic policy framework at the heart of the plan, and which repeats the structural adjustment policy packages of the preceding two decades and over-looks the disastrous effects of those policies;

(b) the fact that in spite of its proclaimed recognition of the central role of the African people to the plan, the African people have not played any part in the conception, design and formulation of the NEPAD;

(c) notwithstanding its stated concerns for social and gender equity, it adopts the social and economic measures that have contributed to the marginalisation of women

(d) that in spite of claims of African origins, its main targets are foreign donors, particularly in the G8

(e) its vision of democracy is defined by the needs of creating a functional market;

(f) it under-emphasises the external conditions fundamental to Africa's developmental crisis, and thereby does not promote any meaningful measure to manage and restrict the effects of this environment on Africa development efforts. On the contrary, the engagement that is seeks with institutions and processes like the World Bank, the IMF, the WTO, the United States Africa Growth and Opportunity Act, the Cotonou Agreement, will further lock Africa's economies disadvantageously into this environment;

(g) the means for mobilisation of resources will further the disintegration of African economies that we have witnessed at the hands of structural adjustment and WTO rules;

Call for Action

To address the developmental problems and challenges identified above, we call for action at the national, continental and international levels to implement the measures described below.

In relation to the external environment, action must be taken towards stabilisation of commodity prices; reform of the international financial system (to prevent debt, exchange rate instability and capital flow volatility) as well as of the World Bank and the IMF; an end to IMF/World Bank structural adjustment programmes; and fundamental changes to the existing agreements of the WTO regime, as well as stop the attempts to expand the scope to this regime to new areas including investment, competition and government procurement. Most pressing of all, Africa's debt must be cancelled.

At the local, national and regional levels, development policy must promote agriculture, industry, services including health and public education, and must be protected and supported through appropriate trade, investment and macro-economic policy measures. A strategy for financing must seek to mobilise and build on internal and intra-African resources through imaginative savings measures; reallocation of expenditure away from wasteful items including excessive military expenditure, corruption and mismanagement; creative use of remittances of Africans living abroad; corporate taxation; retention and re-investment of foreign profits; and the prevention of capital flight, and the leakage of resources through practices of tax evasion practised by foreign investors and local elites. Foreign investment while necessary, must be carefully balanced and selected to suit national objectives.

Above all, these measures require the reconstitution of the developmental state: a state for which social equity, social inclusion, national unity and respect for human rights form the basis of economic policy; a state which actively promotes, and nurtures the productive sectors of the economy; actively engages appropriately in the equitable and balanced allocation and distribution of resources among sectors and people; and most importantly a state that is democratic and which integrates people's control over decision making at all levels in the management, equitable use and distribution of social resources.

The Challenge for African scholars and activist intellectuals

Recognising that, by raising anew the question of Africa's development as an Africa-wide concern, NEPAD has brought to the fore the question of Africa's autonomous initiatives for development, we will engage with the issues raised in NEPAD as part of our efforts to contribute to the debate and discussions on African development.

In support of our broader commitment to contribute to addressing Africa's development challenges, we undertake to work both collectively and individually, in line with our capacities, skills and institutional location, to promote a renewed continent-wide engagement on Africa's own development initiatives. To this end, we shall deploy our research, training and advocacy skills and capacities to contribute to the generation and dissemination of knowledge of the issues at stake; engage with and participate in the mobilisation of social groups around their interests and appropriate strategies of development; and engage with governments and policy institutions at local, national, regional and continental levels. We shall continue our collaboration with our colleagues in the global movement.

Furthermore, we call,

(a) for the reassertion of the primacy of the question and paradigm of national and regional development on the agenda of social discourse and intellectual engagement and advocacy;;

(b) on Africa's scholars and activist intellectuals within African and in the Diaspora, to join forces with social groups whose interests and needs are central to the development of Africa;

(c) African scholars and activist intellectuals and organisations to direct their research and advocacy to some of the pressing questions that confront African policy and decision making at international levels (in particular negotiations in the WTO and under the Cotonou agreement), and domestically and regionally;

(d) upon our colleagues in the global movement, to strengthen our common struggles, in solidarity. We ask our colleagues in the North to intervene with their governments on behalf of our struggles, and our colleagues in the South to strengthen South-South co-operation.

We pledge ourselves to carry forward the positions and conclusions of this conference. And we encourage CODESRIA and TWN-Africa to explore, together with other interested parties, mechanisms and processes for follow-up to the deliberations and conclusions of this conference.

Accra, 26 April 2002.

Index